HUMANIZING THE LAWS OF WAR

Over the past 150 years, the International Committee of the Red Cross (ICRC) has been one of the main drivers of progressive development in international humanitarian law, whilst assuming various roles in the humanization of the laws of war. With select contributions from international experts, this book critically assesses the ICRC's unique influence in international norm creation. It provides a detailed analysis of the workings of the International Red Cross, Red Crescent Movement and ICRC by addressing the milestone achievements as well as the failures, shortcomings and controversies over time. Crucially, the contributions highlight the lessons to be learnt for future challenges in the development of international humanitarian law. This book will be of particular interest to scholars and students of international law, but also to practitioners working in the field of international humanitarian law at both governmental and non-governmental organizations.

ROBIN GEIß is a Professor of International Law and Security at the University of Glasgow. He has previously worked as a Legal Advisor to the International Committee of the Red Cross (ICRC) in Geneva.

ANDREAS ZIMMERMANN is a Professor of International and European Law at the University of Potsdam and Director of the Potsdam Centre of Human Rights. Prior to joining Potsdam University, he was director of the Walther-Schücking-Institute of International Law at the University of Kiel.

STEFANIE HAUMER is a Legal Advisor at the Department of International Law of the German Red Cross. Her main research areas include current issues of Humanitarian Law as well Human Rights Law, International Criminal Law and Disaster Laws.

HUMANIZING THE LAWS OF WAR

The Red Cross and the Development of International Humanitarian Law

Edited by

ROBIN GEIß

University of Glasgow

ANDREAS ZIMMERMANN

University of Potsdam

STEFANIE HAUMER

German Red Cross

CAMBRIDGE
UNIVERSITY PRESS

CAMBRIDGE
UNIVERSITY PRESS

University Printing House, Cambridge CB2 8BS, United Kingdom

One Liberty Plaza, 20th Floor, New York, NY 10006, USA

477 Williamstown Road, Port Melbourne, VIC 3207, Australia

4843/24, 2nd Floor, Ansari Road, Daryaganj, Delhi – 110002, India

79 Anson Road, #06–04/06, Singapore 079906

Cambridge University Press is part of the University of Cambridge.

It furthers the University's mission by disseminating knowledge in the pursuit of education, learning, and research at the highest international levels of excellence.

www.cambridge.org
Information on this title: www.cambridge.org/9781107171350

DOI: 10.1017/9781316759967

First published 2017

Printed in United Kingdom by Clays, St Ives plc

A catalog record for this publication is available from the British Library.

Library of Congress Cataloging-in-Publication Data
Names: Geiß, Robin, editor. | Zimmermann, Andreas, editor. | Haumer, Stefanie, 1978- editor.
Title: Humanizing the laws of war : the Red Cross and the development of international humanitarian law / Robin Geiß, University of Glasgow; Andreas Zimmermann, University of Potsdam; Stefanie Haumer, German Red Cross.
Description: Cambridge, United Kingdom ; New York, NY, USA : Cambridge University Press, 2017.
Identifiers: LCCN 2017005166 | ISBN 9781107171350 (hardback)
Subjects: LCSH: International Committee of the Red Cross–Influence. | Humanitarian law.
Classification: LCC KZ6469.I58 H86 2017 | DDC 341.6/7 – dc23
LC record available at https://lccn.loc.gov/2017005166

ISBN 978-1-107-17135-0 Hardback

CONTENTS

CONTRIBUTORS

MICHAEL BOTHE

Michael Bothe is Professor Emeritus of Public Law at Johann Wolfgang Goethe University, Frankfurt am Main. He was Chair, Commission for International Humanitarian Law, German Red Cross, and President of the International Humanitarian Fact-Finding Commission. He also was President of the German Society of International Law and of the European Environmental Law Association and served as counsel in various cases before the International Court of Justice and the German Federal Constitutional Court. He is the author of numerous publications on international law and the use of force, international humanitarian law, international, European and comparative environmental law as well as comparative constitutional law, including 'New Rules for Victims of Armed Conflicts, Commentary on the 1977 Protocols Additional to the Geneva Conventions of 1949', 2nd ed., revised reprint Den Hague/Boston/London 2015 (with K. J. Partsch, W. A. Solf); 'The OSCE in the Maintenance of Peace and Security. Conflict Prevention, Crisis Management and Peaceful Settlements of Disputes', Den Haag et al. 1997 (co-editor with Natalino Ronzitti and Allan Rosas); 'The New Chemical Weapons Convention – Implementation and Prospects', Den Haag et al. 1998 (co-editor with Natalino Ronzitti und Allan Rosas); 'Towards a Better Implementation of International Humanitarian Law', Berlin 2001 (ed.).

ROBERT CRYER

Robert Cryer is Professor of International and Criminal Law at Birmingham Law School. Professor Cryer's expertise is in international and criminal law. He has lectured and spoken widely at both national and international level, primarily on international criminal law and public international law more generally. In addition to writing a number of articles and book chapters, he is also the author of 'Prosecuting International Crimes: Selectivity and the International Criminal Law Regime'

(Cambridge: Cambridge University Press, 2005) and co-author (with Hakan Friman, Darryl Robinson and Elizabeth Wilmshurst) of 'An Introduction to International Criminal Law and Procedure' (Cambridge: Cambridge University Press, 2nd ed., 2010) and (with Neil Boister) of 'The Tokyo International Military Tribunal: A Reappraisal' (Oxford: Oxford University Press, 2008). He is co-editor of the *Journal of Conflict and Security Law* and a member of the editorial board of the *Journal of International Criminal Justice*.

ROBIN GEIß

Robin Geiß is Professor of International Law and Security at the University of Glasgow. Previously he was Professor of International and European Law at the University of Potsdam. Prior to that, he had worked as legal advisor to the International Committee of the Red Cross (ICRC) in Geneva. Professor Geiß studied law in Bielefeld, Edinburgh, Kiel (Ph.D., 2003) and at the New York University (LL.M., 2004), and is a qualified German lawyer (admitted in 2007). Robin Geiß is currently the director of the 'Security Governance in Areas of Limited Statehood' project at the Collaborative Research Centre 700 in Berlin, editor of the *Yearbook of International Humanitarian Law*, and Rapporteur of the International Law Association's (ILA) Study Group on 'The Conduct of Hostilities under International Humanitarian Law – Challenges from 21st-Century Warfare'. He was a member of the international group of experts that, under the auspices of the NATO Cooperative Cyber Defence Centre of Excellence in Tallinn, drafted the 'Tallinn-Manual' on international law applicable to cyberwarfare (Cambridge University Press, 2013). He is the author of 'Failed States' (Duncker & Humblot, 2005) and co-author of 'Piracy and Armed Robbery at Sea' (Oxford University Press, 2011) and has published in a wide range of scholarly journals.

STEFANIE HAUMER

After having specialized in International Criminal Law, including her work at the International Criminal Tribunal for the Former Yugoslavia, Stefanie Haumer turned to the area of International Humanitarian Law. Since 2009 she works as a legal advisor for the department of International Law and International Institutions at the German Red Cross. Her main research areas are current issues of International Humanitarian Law, including specific weapons, as well as various aspects within the fields of Human Rights Law, International Criminal Law and Disaster Laws.

ROBERT HEINSCH

Robert Heinsch, LL.M., is an Associate Professor of Public International Law at the Grotius Centre for International Legal Studies of Leiden University, and the Director of its regular LL.M. Programme in Public International Law. He is also the Programme Director of the newly established Kalshoven-Gieskes Forum on International Humanitarian Law at Leiden University, and has been appointed as Rapporteur of the ILA study group on the 'The Conduct of Hostilities under International Humanitarian Law – Challenges from 21st-Century Warfare'. Furthermore, he held the position of Federal Dissemination Officer for International Humanitarian Law in Germany and was Member of the Presidency of the German Red Cross from 2012 to 2014. Previously, he has worked as a Legal Advisor in the International Humanitarian Law Department of the German Red Cross Headquarters in Berlin and as a Legal Officer in the Presidency of the International Criminal Court in The Hague. In addition, he has worked as a Senior Research Fellow at the Chair for International Law and European Law, Cologne University, and as a Visiting Lecturer at Bochum University, respectively. He is associated with the Institute for International Law of Peace and Armed Conflict (IFHV) at Bochum University; Former Managing Editor of the *Yearbook of International Humanitarian Law* (YIHL); Member of the Editorial Board of the German *Journal of Peace and Armed Conflict* (JILPAC); Former Senior Editor of the *Leiden Journal of International Law* (LJIL); Member of the German Working Group for International Criminal Law; Member of the United Nations Association (UNA); Member of the International Law Association (ILA); and Advisor of the International Criminal Court Case Matrix Network (CMN). He holds a Doctor of Juridical Science (Ph.D. in Law) Degree from the University of Cologne, an LL.M. Degree from University College London, and the First and Second German Legal State Examination.

JEAN-MARIE HENCKAERTS

Jean-Marie Henckaerts is a legal advisor in the ICRC Legal Division since 1996. Since 2011 he heads the ICRC's project to update the commentaries on the Geneva Conventions and their Additional Protocols. The output of this project is published by the ICRC and Cambridge University Press: the updated Commentary on the First Geneva Convention was published in 2016 and on the Second Geneva Convention in 2017. The remaining volumes will be published in subsequent years. Prior to this, he was the head of the project on customary international humanitarian law; he is a co-author of the ICRC study on the subject. He was a member of the ICRC delegation to the Diplomatic Conference on a Second Protocol to the 1954 Hague Convention for the Protection of Cultural Property in the Event of Armed Conflict (The Hague, 1999) and of the Drafting Committee of the 30th International Conference of the Red Cross and Red Crescent (2007). His files in the Legal Division have also covered among others the protection of women, the protection of cultural property and the protection of the natural environment in armed conflict. He holds the degree of Doctor of Juridical Science from The George Washington University Law School (1994) and the degree of Master of Laws from the University of Georgia (1991) both in the United States. He received the degree of Bachelor of Laws from the University of Brussels in 1989. He has published several books and numerous articles on international law, international humanitarian law and human rights law, among others 'Customary International Humanitarian Law', 2 volumes, 'Volume I: Rules', 'Volume II: Practice' (Cambridge University Press, 2005) (with Louise Doswald-Beck) and 'Study on Customary International Humanitarian Law: A Contribution to the Understanding and Respect for the Rule of Law in Armed Conflict', *International Review of the Red Cross*, 87, 857, March 2005.

KATHLEEN LAWAND

Kathleen Lawand is head of the Arms Unit, in the Legal Division of the International Committee of the Red Cross (ICRC). Since joining the ICRC in January 2000, she was posted to India, West Africa, Iraq support, and Afghanistan. From 2008 to 2012, she was head of the Legal Advisors to the ICRC's Operations. Prior to joining the ICRC, she worked for the Organisation for the Prohibition of Chemical Weapons (OPCW), the International Criminal Tribunal for the Former Yugoslavia (ICTY), and the UN High Commissioner for Refugees (UNHCR). She was called to the Québec Bar in 1990, and in 1995 obtained a Master's degree (LL.M.) in public international law from the London School of Economics, with distinction.

ISABEL ROBINSON

Isabel Robinson is a legal advisor to the ICRC's operations in Nigeria. Prior to this, she was working with the ICRC Arms Unit in Geneva. She has been working with the ICRC since 2013 and is the co-author (with Ellen Nohle) of "Proportionality and Precautions in Attack: The Reverberating Effects of Using Explosive Weapons in Populated Areas," *International Review of the Red Cross*, forthcoming (published online by Cambridge University Press on 27 January 2017).

CARSTEN STAHN

Carsten Stahn is Professor of International Criminal Law and Global Justice at Leiden University and Program Director of the Grotius Centre. He has previously served as Legal Officer at the International Criminal Court. He is author of 'The Law and Practice of International Territorial Administration: Versailles to Iraq and Beyond' (Cambridge University Press, 2008/2010). He has published articles on international criminal law and transitional justice in leading international journals (*American Journal of International Law, European Journal of International Law, Journal of International Criminal Justice, Harvard International Law Journal*) and edited several collections of essays in the field ('Peace Diplomacy, Global Justice and International Agency: Rethinking Human Security and Ethics in the Spirit of Dag Hammarskjöld', Cambridge University Press, 2014, 'The International Criminal Court and Complementarity: From Theory to Practice', Cambridge University Press, 2011, 'The Diversification and Fragmentation of International Criminal Law', Martinus Nijhoff, 2012, 'Future Perspectives on International Criminal Justice', T. M. C. Asser Press – Cambridge University Press, 2010). He directs research projects on 'Jus Post Bellum' and 'Post-Conflict Justice and Local Ownership', funded by the Netherlands Organization for Scientific Research (NWO). He is General Editor of the *Leiden Journal of International Law*, Executive Editor of the *Criminal Law Forum*, and Correspondent of the *Netherlands International Law Review*.

ANDREAS ZIMMERMANN

Andreas Zimmermann is Professor at the University of Potsdam and Director of the Potsdam Centre of Human Rights; Doctor of Juridical Science (Heidelberg), LL.M. (Harvard); former Member of the German delegation to the Preparatory Committee and the United Nations Diplomatic Conference on the Establishment of an International Criminal Court; member of the Permanent Court of Arbitration; counsel in various cases before the ICJ; judge ad hoc in various cases before the European Court of Human Rights; arbitrator under the annex to the Vienna Convention on the Law of Treaties; member of the advisory boards on UN issues and on public international law of the German Ministry of Foreign Affairs; member of the advisory committee on international humanitarian law of the German Red Cross, *inter alia* co-editor of 'The Statute of the International Court of Justice – A Commentary' (Oxford University Press, 2006; 2nd ed., 2012) and editor of the 'The 1951 Convention on the Status of Refugees and its 1967 Protocol – A Commentary' (Oxford University Press, 2011).

FOREWORD

It was following the battle of Solferino on 24 June 1859 and upon the initiative of Swiss businessman Henry Dunant that both the International Red Cross and Red Crescent Movement and modern International Humanitarian Law (IHL) came into being. The International Committee of the Red Cross (ICRC), then known as the International Committee for Relief to the Wounded, was founded in Geneva on 17 February 1863. Only a few months later, in December 1863, the 'Württembergische Sanitätsverein' was created in Germany, which became the very first National Red Cross Society as a voluntary aid society auxiliary to the public authorities in the humanitarian field to care for the wounded and sick on the battlefield as envisaged by Henry Dunant.

The year 2013 thus marked the celebration of '150 years of humanitarian action' of both the ICRC and the German Red Cross. Several events were hosted inside and outside Germany to celebrate these important anniversaries while critically reviewing the Red Cross' contribution to certain areas of its operation, such as the development, clarification and implementation of international humanitarian law.

The German Red Cross was honored to partner with the Swiss Embassy in Berlin and the University of Potsdam in organising an expert meeting entitled 'The International Red Cross and Red Crescent Movement at 150: Developing and Clarifying International Humanitarian Law' in Berlin on 24 June 2013. The panelists and commentators were invited to assess the impact of the International Red Cross and Red Crescent Movement on international humanitarian law, both with respect to and beyond the development of treaty regimes, as well as its influence on related areas of international law such as international criminal law.

Given the outstanding quality of contributions, the organisers aspired to make them available to a larger audience and are very pleased to now present this edited book with much gratitude to the various authors involved in the project. Its publication is timely as reflections on the development, clarification and implementation of IHL have continued and progressed in the past years. In particular, the 32nd International Conference of the Red Cross and Red Crescent – bringing together States parties to the Geneva Conventions and the components of the International Red Cross and Red Crescent Movement – has decided to continue a process to strengthen compliance with international humanitarian law in 2015. These efforts serve to demonstrate the endeavour to keep international humanitarian law relevant for today's armed conflicts which are increasingly fought in defiance of its most basic rules amidst a deteriorating regional and global political order.

They also highlight the critical role of the International Red Cross and Red Crescent Movement in the development, clarification and implementation of IHL while illustrating the different, mutually reinforcing mandates, strategies and approaches of the Movement's components with respect to international humanitarian law.

It is in this context that the German Red Cross believes that this publication will contribute to the understanding of how the International Red Cross and Red Crescent Movement has contributed to this process in the past and today. It is my hope and conviction that, despite future challenges, the Movement will continue to make an important contribution to the clarification and development of international humanitarian law, to its adequate application to the realities of modern warfare and, ultimately, to the protection of victims of armed conflict.

Dr. h.c. Rudolf Seiters, President of the German Red Cross

Introduction

The International Red Cross and Red Crescent Movement and the Development of International Humanitarian Law

STEFANIE HAUMER, ROBIN GEIß AND ANDREAS ZIMMERMANN

I. Introduction

When the International Red Cross and Red Crescent Movement[1] came into being more than 150 years ago in Geneva, it could hardly have been foreseen that it would play, and continues to play, a specific and indeed quite significant role with regard to both the clarification of existing international humanitarian law as well as to the further development of international humanitarian law. It is probably safe to state that no other non-State actor has had such a distinguished impact on the (historic) development of a specific area of international law.[2] What is even more surprising is that the International Red Cross and Red Crescent Movement was able to have such an impact, and continues to do so, in an area

[1] See generally on the International Red Cross and Red Crescent Movement and its structure H.-P. Gasser, 'International Committee of the Red Cross (ICRC)', in R. Wolfrum (ed.), *Max Planck Encyclopedia of Public International Law* (Oxford: Oxford University Press, 2012), vol. V, pp. 445–454; H. Wilms, 'International Red Cross and Red Crescent Movement', in R. Wolfrum (ed.), *Max Planck Encyclopedia of Public International Law* (Oxford: Oxford University Press, 2012), vol. VI, pp. 123–125.

[2] See generally on the role of non-State actors, particularly non-governmental organisations, in international law, and their influence on the development of international law S. Charnovitz, 'Nongovernmental Organizations and International Law' (2006) 100 *The American Journal of International Law*, pp. 348–372; S. Hobe, 'Non-Governmental Organizations', in R. Wolfrum (ed.), *Max Planck Encyclopedia of Public International Law* (Oxford: Oxford University Press, 2012), vol. VII, pp. 716–725; J.-P. Lavoyer and L. Maresca 'The Role of the ICRC in the Development of International Humanitarian Law' (1999) *International Negotiation*, pp. 501–525; M. Wagner, 'Non-State Actors', in R. Wolfrum (ed.), *Max Planck Encyclopedia of Public International Law* (Oxford: Oxford University Press, 2012), vol. VII, pp. 741–750.

which is as State-centred, and which touches upon States' fundamental security interests, as is the case with international humanitarian law, i.e. the *ius in bello*, fundamentally connected with the exercise of the core of State sovereignty.[3]

While the main perspective of this book and the various contributions contained therein is on the specific role of the International Committee of the Red Cross (ICRC), its role being specifically mentioned, for instance, in Art. 126 paras 1 and 4 Geneva Convention III,[4] this introduction will focus, albeit briefly, on the role of the other components of the International Red Cross and Red Crescent Movement when it comes to the development of international humanitarian law, namely the respective National Red Cross and Red Crescent Societies, as well as the International Federation of Red Cross and Red Crescent Societies (Federation).

More specifically, this introduction places a particular focus on the relationship between a given State and the respective National Red Cross or Red Crescent Society on its territory, as a further important component of the International Red Cross and Red Crescent Movement in the area of international humanitarian law. The mandate of the respective National Society, while being auxiliary to the public authorities, is also explored, which not only includes the National Society's contribution to the development of international humanitarian law as such, but also analyses its cooperation with the respective government to ensure respect for these rules.[5]

It is almost a mere banality to state that in the realm of international law, States continue to be the core stakeholders – a fact which States have explicitly reiterated in recent years specifically when it comes to the development of international humanitarian law. It is for this very reason that the mandate, which was assigned to the various components of the International Red Cross and Red Crescent Movement with regard to international humanitarian law by States, the cooperation between those components of the universal International Red Cross and Red Crescent Movement and

[3] See also on the role of armed non-State groups: T. Marauhn and Z. Ntoubandi, 'Armed Conflict, Non-International', in R. Wolfrum (ed.), *Max Planck Encyclopedia of Public International Law* (Oxford: Oxford University Press, 2012), vol. I, p. 634 *et seq*.

[4] On the content of Art. 126 of the Geneva Convention III, see J. Pictet et al. (eds.), *The Geneva Conventions of 12 August 1949, III Geneva Convention* (Geneva: ICRC, 1960), pp. 602–613; as well as most recently S. R. Ratner and R. Giladi, 'The Role of the International Committee of the Red Cross', in A. Clapham, P. Gaeta, and M. Sassòli (eds.), *The 1949 Geneva Conventions – A Commentary* (Oxford: Oxford University Press, 2015), p. 525 *et seq*.

[5] See below III.3.

States on the national, as well as on the international level, are of special, even crucial, importance and will hence subsequently be addressed. Indeed, the delegation of the individual mandates from the States to the components of the International Red Cross and Red Crescent Movement creates the very basis for a specific and unique relationship between the States and the components of the International Red Cross and Red Crescent Movement.

II. Historical Development

From the very beginning, the International Red Cross and Red Crescent Movement on the one hand, and international humanitarian law on the other have become closely intertwined. Starting at the roots, it was the founder of the Red Cross and Red Crescent Movement, the Swiss tradesman Henry Dunant, who, in 1862, asked two core questions in his masterpiece *A Memory of Solferino*.[6] His first consideration was, whether it might not 'be possible, in time of peace and quiet, to form relief societies for the purpose of having care given to the wounded in wartime by zealous, devoted and thoroughly qualified volunteers'.[7] Looking back more than 150 years in history, Henry Dunant's groundbreaking idea seems to have been justified. Dunant enumerated several reasons for his considerations, and in particular the idea that a professional and effective supply with medical care could not be guaranteed, if this was to be only organised spontaneously without prior training of staff and logistics *prior* to the outbreak of an armed conflict.

In addition, he pointed out that diplomatic conferences and congresses are convened and conducted to clarify far less important issues than the fundamental questions of humanity and civilisation involved in trying to humanize the laws of war.[8] One might wonder what would be Dunant's reaction, could he see what became of his idea, namely the unique worldwide humanitarian International Red Cross and Red Crescent Movement, encompassing today, as of 2016, 190 National Red Cross and Red Crescent Societies[9] with their umbrella organisation, the Federation, and the ICRC, each component possessing and exercising its own specific mandate to be

[6] See on the historical development also Gasser, 'International Committee of the Red Cross (ICRC)', p. 445 *et seq*.

[7] H. Dunant, *A Memory of Solferino* (Geneva: ICRC, 1862, French ed.), p. 101.

[8] *Ibid*.

[9] See International Federation of Red Cross and Red Crescent Societies (IFRC), 'National Societies', available at: www.ifrc.org/en/who-we-are/the-movement/national-societies.

addressed hereinafter. What is more is that, as of today, the International Red Cross and Red Crescent Movement consists of approximately 15 million volunteers, with operations in more than 80 countries and thousands of delegates in the field,[10] which certainly is to be considered a truly stunning development.

The second question Henry Dunant raised constituted the very starting point for the development of what became first the 1864 Geneva Convention for the Amelioration of the Condition of the Wounded and Sick in Armed Forces in the Field, in 1906 quite significantly revised and replaced by the 1906,[11] and then the 1929 Geneva Conventions,[12] and finally later the 1949 Geneva Conventions and its 1977 Additional Protocols, with the latter instruments still, more than 150 years later, considered to constitute the very core of international humanitarian law. Dunant asked whether '[it] would [. . .] be desirable that they [i.e. the States representatives] [. . .] formulate some international principle, sanctioned by a Convention inviolate in character, which, once agreed upon and ratified, might constitute the basis for societies for the relief of the wounded in the different European countries?'[13] This second idea, namely the development of international legal rules and the continuous adaptation of those rules to an ever-changing reality, while being well advanced, has not been entirely completed to date – and probably never will be. What Henry Dunant proposed already in 1862 was to take advantage of a time of relative calm and quiet to investigate and try to solve a question of enormous and worldwide importance, i.e. the question of how to best address the impacts of war and to mitigate the suffering of its victims. He noted that (already in his days) new and terrible methods of destruction were invented daily and welcomed, or indeed even encouraged, in most – if not all – of the great European States, which already then were engaged in an armament race.[14] It is submitted that over the years Dunant's statement has lost none of its timeliness and urgency. As a matter of fact, until today the human race is most creative in

[10] See www.rcrcmeetings.org/wp-content/uploads/2013/11/EN_Bkg_RCRCMovement_FINAL.pdf.

[11] Convention for the Amelioration of the Condition of the Wounded and Sick in Armies in the Field, Geneva, 6 July 1906, available at: www.icrc.org/ihl/INTRO/180?OpenDocument.

[12] Geneva Convention for the Amelioration of the Condition of the Wounded and Sick in Armies in the Field, Geneva, 27 July 1929, available at: www.icrc.org/ihl.nsf/52d68d14de6160e0c12563da005fdb1b/9fb461bd48bb4efac125641e004025e0; Convention relative to the Treatment of Prisoners of War, Geneva, 27 July 1929, available at: www.icrc.org/ihl.nsf/52d68d14de6160e0c12563da005fdb1b/eb1571b00daec90ec125641e00402aa6.

[13] H. Dunant, *A Memory of Solferino*, p. 111.

[14] H. Dunant, *A Memory of Solferino*, p. 101.

inventing ever new means to damage each other. However, it has already for a long time been recognised as forming part and parcel of customary law that persons who do not (or no longer) directly participate in hostilities must be spared from the impact of these hostilities.[15] Hence, the parties to the conflict must at all times distinguish between those who do not participate in hostilities and the actual fighters. Accordingly, their attacks must not be directed against the former.[16] Besides, it is also beyond doubt that any use of means of warfare by the parties to an armed conflict must be in line with this principle of distinction.[17] Moreover, ever since and until today, the use of means of warfare which are of a nature or meant to cause superfluous injury or unnecessary suffering is similarly prohibited.[18]

III. Current Role of the International Red Cross and Red Crescent Movement in the Development of International Humanitarian Law

1. *General Questions*

Still as of today, two of the main tasks of the International Red Cross and Red Crescent Movement are, on the one hand, to ensure respect for existing legal rules and, on the other, to contribute to the further development of rules applicable in times of armed conflict.[19] This is what the States

[15] See generally on the principle of distinction, Y. Dinstein, 'Warfare, Methods and Means', in R. Wolfrum (ed.), *Max Planck Encyclopedia of Public International Law* (Oxford: Oxford University Press, 2012), vol. X, pp. 771–777; H. Krieger, 'Protected Persons' in R. Wolfrum (ed.), *Max Planck Encyclopedia of Public International Law* (Oxford: Oxford University Press, 2012), vol. VIII, p. 543 *et seq.* (para. 20); G. D. Solis, *The Law of Armed Conflict: International Humanitarian Law in War* (Cambridge: Cambridge University Press, 2010), p. 250 *et. seq.*

[16] See Art. 48 of the Protocol Additional to the Geneva Conventions of 12 August 1949, and Concerning the Protection of Victims of International Armed Conflicts, adopted on 8 June 1977 (Additional Protocol I); see generally on this provision H.-P. Gasser and K. Dörmann, 'Protection of the Civilian Population' in D. Fleck (ed.), *The Handbook of International Humanitarian Law* (3rd ed., Oxford: Oxford University Press, 2013), pp. 232–234.

[17] C. Bell and J. Pfeiffer, 'Indiscriminate Attack' in R. Wolfrum (ed.), *Max Planck Encyclopedia of Public International Law* (Oxford: Oxford University Press, 2012), vol. V, p. 140 *et seq.*; W. Boothby, 'Weapons, Prohibited' in R. Wolfrum (ed.), *Max Planck Encyclopedia of Public International Law* (Oxford: Oxford University Press, 2012), vol. X, p. 841; Y. Dinstein, '*Warfare, Methods and Means*', p. 771 *et seq.*; S. Oeter, 'Methods and Means of Combat' in D. Fleck (ed.), *The Handbook of International Humanitarian Law* (3rd ed., Oxford: Oxford University Press, 2013), p. 121 *et seq.* (190 *et seq*).

[18] Boothby, 'Weapons, Prohibited', p. 841; Solis, *The Law of Armed Conflict*, p. 269 *et. seq.*

[19] See Arts. 3 para. 2, 5 para. 2 lit. c) and g), para. 4) lit. a) Statutes. The text of the Statutes of the International Red Cross and Red Crescent Movement is available at: www.icrc.org/eng/resources/documents/misc/statutes-movement-220506.htm.

parties to the Geneva Conventions, together with the components of the Red Cross and Red Crescent Movement, assigned the various components of the Movement to do when they adopted the Statutes of the International Red Cross and Red Crescent Movement at the International Conference of the Red Cross and Red Crescent in 1986. More specifically, the International Red Cross and Red Crescent Movement was assigned the mission 'to prevent and alleviate human suffering wherever it may be found, to protect life and health and ensure respect for the human being, in particular in times of armed conflict and other emergencies'.[20] This mission is reflected and developed in more detail in the mandates of the individual Movement components. Hence, it is the States parties to the Geneva Conventions themselves that have established the International Red Cross and Red Crescent Movement, as well as each of its components, with their individual and specific mandates when it comes to the development of international humanitarian law.[21]

2. *Role of the International Committee of the Red Cross*

Taking a look at the various individual components of the International Red Cross and Red Crescent Movement, the role of the ICRC under the Statutes is, in particular, to work for a faithful application of international humanitarian law, to take cognizance of any complaints based on alleged breaches of that law and to prepare any development thereof.[22] Not the least, the ICRC has often been tasked by the international community to provide initial drafts for major codification projects, such as e.g. the 1949 Geneva Conventions and their 1977 Additional Protocols.[23] This book will address these various projects in the chapters to come in significantly more detail.[24] In addition, and as international law is obviously not only composed of treaty law, the role of the ICRC with regard to the codification and development of customary law will also be scrutinized.[25]

[20] Preambular para. 1 Statutes. [21] See Arts. 3, 5 and 6 Statutes.

[22] See Art. 5 para. 2 lit. c) and g) Statutes which foresee that the ICRC maintains relations with governmental authorities while recognising the primary role of States in the development of international humanitarian law. See also Art. 5 para. 6 Statutes, as well as operative paragraph 6 of Resolution 'Strengthening legal protection for victims of armed conflicts', 31IC/11/R1.

[23] Gasser, 'International Committee of the Red Cross (ICRC)', p. 449 (para. 14).

[24] For further details, see below IV.3.

[25] *Ibid.*; for the contribution of J.-M. Henckaerts, 'The International Committee of the Red Cross and the Clarification of Customary International Humanitarian Law', see Chapter 3 of this volume.

3. *Role of National Red Cross and Red Crescent Societies*

National Red Cross and Red Crescent Societies have been mandated by the international community to themselves disseminate, but also to assist their respective governments in disseminating, international humanitarian law.[26] Furthermore, they also cooperate with the governments of their respective State to ensure respect for international humanitarian law, as well as to protect the distinctive emblems recognised by the Geneva Conventions and their Additional Protocols.[27]

When it comes to the respective national level, it is predominantly the contribution of National Red Cross and Red Crescent Societies, and the range of options which exist for States and the respective National Societies to cooperate in regards to the development, implementation and enforcement of international humanitarian law which should not be underestimated. Not the least, one very important tool consists in the cooperation within the National Committee on International Humanitarian Law where such a committee exists in a given State party to the Geneva Conventions.[28] To date, 108 countries have established such a National Committee on International Humanitarian Law,[29] which generally at least includes representatives of the relevant national ministries such as defence, foreign affairs, internal affairs, justice and education, aiming at the better fulfilment of the State's obligations under the Geneva Conventions, including in the field of dissemination.[30] Although neither the Geneva Conventions nor any other international humanitarian law treaty contains a legal obligation to set up such bodies, their number is growing and they are recognised as an important step in ensuring the effective

[26] See generally on the question who disseminates the Conventions, E. Mikos-Skuza, 'Dissemination of the Conventions, Including in Time of Armed Conflict' in A. Clapham, P. Gaeta and M. Sassòli (eds.), *The 1949 Geneva Conventions – A Commentary* (Oxford: Oxford University Press, 2015), p. 600 *et seq*.

[27] See Art. 3 para. 2 Statutes.

[28] See generally on the role and impact of National Committees for the implementation of international humanitarian law, ICRC Advisory Service on International Humanitarian Law/A.-M. La Rosa, 'Preventing and Repressing International Crimes: Towards an 'Integrated' Approach Based in Domestic Practice – Report of the Third Universal Meeting of National Committees for the Implementation of International Humanitarian Law', vol. I, pp. 67–74, available at: www.icrc.org/eng/resources/documents/publication/p4138.htm.

[29] See Table of National Committees and other national bodies on international humanitarian law, 30 September 2015, available at: www.icrc.org/en/document/table-national-committees-and-other-national-bodies-international-humanitarian-law.

[30] Mikos-Skuza, 'Dissemination of the Conventions, Including in Time of Armed Conflict', p. 601.

application of international humanitarian law.[31] The respective National Red Cross or Red Crescent Society often plays a key role. It may already be instrumental in the formation of a National Committee where no such committee previously existed. In many cases, it may also provide a (executive) secretariat for the respective committee and contribute its expertise through membership, advice and specific knowledge on international humanitarian law. Besides, it also has a specific role to play because of its function as an auxiliary to the state's authorities in the humanitarian field on the basis of its mandate in the field of international humanitarian law.[32]

In many countries, senior members of the judiciary and of the armed forces are also members of the respective National Committee on International Humanitarian Law, as are leading academic specialists, representatives of humanitarian organisations, and the media. The aim of such a committee usually is to evaluate national legislation in the light of obligations contained in a range of international humanitarian law instruments.[33] The committee should monitor the application of international humanitarian law by the respective State party, be able to propose new legislation or amendments to existing laws, so as to bring the domestic laws of the respective State party in line with its obligations under international humanitarian law, as well as provide guidance on the interpretation of relevant rules of international humanitarian law. In addition, such National Committees on International Humanitarian Law should also play an important part in promoting a wider understanding of international humanitarian law. Last but not least, and depending on its respective composition, such a National Committee on International Humanitarian Law may also provide a forum for consultation and coordination between the National Red Cross or Red Crescent Society and the various departments and institutions of the government. Current issues and upcoming challenges of international humanitarian law are discussed and views and positions are exchanged and possibly reconciled. Hence, National Committees on International Humanitarian Law bring together State representatives and representatives of the respective National Red Cross or Red

[31] Mikos-Skuza, 'Dissemination of the Conventions, Including in Time of Armed Conflict', p. 601; A. R. Ziegler and S. Wehrenberg, 'Domestic Implementation' in A. Clapham, P. Gaeta and M. Sassòli (eds.), *The 1949 Geneva Conventions – A Commentary* (Oxford: Oxford University Press, 2015), p. 652 *et seq.*

[32] See ICRC, National Committees – Overview, 1 May 2012, available at: www.icrc.org/eng/war-and-law/ihl-domestic-law/national-committees/overview-national-committees.htm.

[33] *Ibid.*

Crescent Society if these are members of the Committee on the national level.

Furthermore, National Red Cross or Red Crescent Societies also quite often work closely together with relevant domestic authorities on a bi- or multilateral level when it comes to the application, implementation and enforcement of international humanitarian law. This encompasses, amongst others, the exchange of experts' views on relevant issues of international humanitarian law, joint publications[34] and the organisation and realisation of thematic symposia as well as public events.

As the mandate of National Red Cross or Red Crescent Societies is not restricted to the national level but encompasses the international level as well, a well-coordinated close preparation for international conferences, in particular for the biannual International Conference of the Red Cross and Red Crescent, constitutes a necessary requirement for a trustful cooperation during the Conference. This is especially important for crucial international humanitarian law issues to be addressed by the International Conference concerning questions of implementation and enforcement of international humanitarian law, such as the issue of a better compliance with existing rules of international humanitarian law, an issue that will be discussed in more detail later.[35]

In addition, National Red Cross or Red Crescent Societies, in fulfilling their obligation to disseminate international humanitarian law, often closely cooperate with the respective State's armed forces in the training and education of soldiers,[36] as well as in national and international military exercises. Various courses and seminars on international humanitarian law are offered and addressed to lawyers, trainee lawyers, diplomats and students.[37] Publications[38] in relevant military and legal journals on

[34] To provide but one example, one might *inter alia* refer to the collection of '*Documents on International Humanitarian Law*', edited by the (German) Federal Foreign Office, the German Red Cross, and the (German) Federal Ministry of Defence (2nd ed., 2012).

[35] See below III. 6. b).

[36] To provide one example, one might point to the annual conference of the German Ministry of Defence, the German Red Cross and the Institute for International Law of Peace and Armed Conflict of the Ruhr University Bochum on international humanitarian law, which aims at strengthening the dialogue between the legal advisors of the German armed forces and those of the German Red Cross.

[37] One example of a widely recognised course on international humanitarian law is the J. Pictet Competition, which is annually sponsored, amongst others, by a number of National Red Cross Societies. For more information, see www.concourspictet.org/index_en.htm.

[38] A prominent example of a publication activity by a National Society is the *Journal of International Law of Peace and Armed Conflict* (*Humanitäres Völkerrecht – Informationsschriften*, HuV-I), which is published quarterly by the German Red Cross Headquarters

specific issues of international humanitarian law and providing experts' contributions to military manuals complement the overall picture of the work of National Red Cross or Red Crescent Societies when it comes to international humanitarian law and its dissemination.

4. *Role of the International Federation of Red Cross and Red Crescent Societies*[39]

The Federation constitutes the third independent component of the International Red Cross and Red Crescent Movement.[40] According to Art. 6 para. 4 lit. j) of the Statutes of the International Red Cross and Red Crescent Movement, the functions of the Federation in the field of international humanitarian law in turn are rather restricted to 'assist the International Committee [of the Red Cross] in the promotion and development of international humanitarian law and collaborate with it in the dissemination of this law and of the Fundamental Principles of the Movement among the National Societies'.

At the same time, however, the Federation – as the 'peacetime branch' of the Movement – is of immeasurable value for the coordination of efforts in disaster relief and humanitarian aid in emergency situations.[41] Consequently, it also addresses related fields of law as, in particular, the area of international disaster response laws. It is in this specific field that the Federation plays an active role in the codification and continuous development of applicable rules of international law. This is particularly important because a comprehensive legal regime alike to the Geneva Conventions does not yet exist, while the work of the International Law Commission on the matter is still ongoing.[42] Accordingly, one might state that

and the Institute for International Law of Peace and Armed Conflict of the Ruhr University Bochum. For more information, see www.ifhv.de/index.php/publications/jilpac-huv-i.

[39] See generally on the legal status of the International Federation of Red Cross and Red Crescent Societies under international law S. Peterke, *Der völkerrechtliche Sonderstatus der Internationalen Föderation der Rotkreuz- und Rothalbmondgesellschaften* (Berlin: BWV Berliner Wissenschafts-Verlag, 2006), *passim.*; S. Mehring, 'International Federation of Red Cross and Red Crescent Societies', in R. Wolfrum (ed.), *Max Planck Encyclopedia of Public International Law* (Oxford: Oxford University Press, 2012), vol. V, p. 791.

[40] Mehring, 'International Federation of Red Cross and Red Crescent Societies', p. 790.

[41] Mehring, 'International Federation of Red Cross and Red Crescent Societies', p. 792.

[42] See ILC, Draft Articles on the 'Protection of persons in the event of disasters' adopted by the ILC's drafting committee in 2014, Annual Report to the UN 6th Committee, A/69/10 2014, chapter 5.

relevant rules and regulations applicable in situations of natural or man-made disasters are scattered all over international and national legislation. It is therefore even more important that on 30 November 2007 at the 30th International Red Cross and Red Crescent Conference, the States parties to the Geneva Conventions and the International Red Cross and Red Crescent Movement unanimously adopted the 'Guidelines for the domestic facilitation and regulation of international disaster relief and initial recovery assistance'[43] (also known as the 'IDRL Guidelines'), which was followed up in 2008 by the United Nations General Assembly encouraging States to make use of them.[44]

5. *Interplay Between the Various Components of the International Red Cross and Red Crescent Movement in the Development of International Humanitarian Law*

As previously mentioned, each of the components of the Red Cross and Red Crescent Movement fulfils its very own role with a view to further foster, develop and enhance the status of international humanitarian law. These roles in part complement each other. Given this structure and, in particular, the universality of the International Red Cross and Red Crescent Movement, the impact deriving from this complementarity may be said to be quite impressive. The complementarity of the respective mandates of the various components of the International Red Cross and Red Crescent Movement guarantees that these components are able to achieve their respective mandates universally throughout the world on both the national as well as the international level. This universality of the International Red Cross and Red Crescent Movement, i.e. that all Societies have equal status and share equal responsibilities and duties in helping each other as part of the International Red Cross and Red Crescent Movement which is of a worldwide character, constitutes one of its seven fundamental principles enshrined in the Statutes of the International Red Cross and Red Crescent Movement,[45] and, at the same time, also constitutes a major strength of the overall Movement. As of today, 190 recognised National

[43] 30th International Conference of the Red Cross and Red Crescent, Resolution 4, available at: www.ifrc.org/PageFiles/102485/Resolution%204.pdf.

[44] See UN General Assembly Res. 63/139, 63/141, and 63/137.

[45] See preambular para. 2 Statutes, which lists and defines the seven fundamental principles of the Movement.

Societies exist in nearly every country of the world.[46] Hence, it is mainly these National Red Cross or Red Crescent Societies which guarantee that the principle of universality became, in fact, a reality.

6. *Interplay Between the International Red Cross and Red Crescent Movement and Individual States*

a) General Issues

To enable the components of the International Red Cross and Red Crescent Movement to effectively fulfil their mandates, States have agreed to support their work whenever possible.[47] The current 196[48] States parties to the Geneva Conventions cooperate with the components of the International Red Cross and Red Crescent Movement in accordance with the Geneva Conventions.[49] With a view to international humanitarian law, the cooperation on the international level concerns to a great extent the cooperation between States as well as regional organisations on the one hand, and the ICRC on the other. However, National Red Cross or Red Crescent Societies play a considerable role as well. As mentioned earlier,[50] they closely cooperate and consult with their respective government before relevant international conferences, or participate themselves in such events.

Every four years, the International Conference of the Red Cross and Red Crescent assembles representatives of all the various components of the International Red Cross and Red Crescent Movement alongside delegates from all the States parties to the Geneva Conventions.[51] This Conference, which is the supreme deliberative body of the International Red Cross and Red Crescent Movement, constitutes one of the paramount fora for the development of international humanitarian law.[52] Together, States and the various components of the Movement identify gaps and weaknesses in the law governing armed conflicts, and aim to strengthen international humanitarian law to adapt it to current challenges.

However, it is generally acknowledged that the most urgent issue currently facing international humanitarian law is not to be seen in the first

[46] See IFRC list of all National Societies available at: www.ifrc.org/en/what-we-do/where-we-work/.

[47] Art. 2 para. 3 Statutes.

[48] See ICRC database at: www.icrc.org/applic/ihl/ihl.nsf/.

[49] Art. 2 para. 1 Statutes.

[50] See above III.3.

[51] Gasser, 'International Committee of the Red Cross (ICRC)', p. 447 (para. 6).

[52] Art. 8 Statutes.

instance in the lack of rules, but rather in the lack of compliance with existing rules. Accordingly, the 31st International Conference of the Red Cross and Red Crescent in 2011 adopted a resolution inviting Switzerland and the ICRC to jointly initiate a States' consultation process in order to develop solutions to strengthen compliance with international humanitarian law.[53] Four years later, the outcome of this process was presented to the 32nd International Conference of the Red Cross and Red Crescent in 2015. At this Conference, an agreement on a resolution which would have established a system of regular meetings of States parties to the Geneva Conventions, as well as a decontextualised reporting system on the individual States' compliance with international humanitarian law could however not be reached. Instead, a continuation of the process until the next International Conference in 2019 was agreed upon.[54] As part of this overall and still ongoing negotiation process, individual National Red Cross or Red Crescent Societies cooperated with each other and supported their respective governments within this process.

At the International Conference, National Red Cross or Red Crescent Societies may also try to provide specific directions and add a particular focus to the Conference when it comes to an envisaged development of international humanitarian law. They may do so through thematic initiatives and pledges, which they sustain in cooperation with each other or together with their respective governments. By supporting thematic initiatives of the ICRC and the Federation, National Red Cross or Red Crescent Societies can add weight to specific issues and promote these issues on the domestic level, for instance, through cooperation with their respective government on a specific item or issue. Pledges made at the International Conference on joint projects concerning publications, events or legal initiatives within the overall Movement and with external partners,

[53] For more information on the process see ICRC, 'Strengthening Compliance with International Humanitarian Law (IHL): The Work of the ICRC and the Swiss Government', 21 April 2015, at: www.icrc.org/eng/what-we-do/other-activities/development-ihl/strengthening-legal-protection-compliance.htm; Swiss Federal Department of Foreign Affairs (FDFA), Joint Initiative by Switzerland and the ICRC on Strengthening Compliance with International Humanitarian Law, at: www.eda.admin.ch/eda/en/fdfa/foreign-policy/international-law/international-humanitarian-law/icrc-initiative.html; Draft Resolution 'Strengthening Compliance with International Humanitarian Law', 32IC/15/19.2, at: http://rcrcconference.org/wp-content/uploads/sites/3/2015/10/32IC-DR-and-concluding-report-on-Strengthening-Compliance-with-IHL_EN.pdf.

[54] ICRC, 'No Agreement by States on Mechanism to Strengthen Compliance with Rules of War', press release, 10 December 2015, at: www.icrc.org/en/document/no-agreement-states-mechanism-strengthen-compliance-rules-war.

in particular governments, contribute to the worldwide dissemination and implementation of international humanitarian law.

The cooperation, internationally and nationally alike, between States and the respective National Red Cross or Red Crescent Society, agreed upon in the Statutes of the Movement, also flows from the auxiliary role National Societies play in relation to the public authorities in the humanitarian field.[55] Despite this role, National Red Cross or Red Crescent Societies are nevertheless independent from their respective State. They maintain a 'specific and distinctive relationship'[56] with the government. However, the development and enforcement, as well as the dissemination of international humanitarian law benefit from a close and trusting cooperation between a government and the National Red Cross or Red Crescent Society active on its territory.[57] Not the least, the contribution of National Red Cross or Red Crescent Societies, in particular as far as the development and the enforcement of international humanitarian law is concerned, is worthy of a closer look.

b) Development of International Humanitarian Law

As far as the development of international humanitarian law is concerned, National Red Cross or Red Crescent Societies can not only exchange experts' views with their governments; rather a coordinated approach can double the weight of a country's voice in fora such as the International Red Cross and Red Crescent Conference. Furthermore, a close cooperation between a National Red Cross or Red Crescent Society and the respective State through continuous experts' dialogue and humanitarian diplomacy

[55] Art. 3 para. 1 Statutes. The concept of National Red Cross and Red Crescent Societies being auxiliaries to the public authorities in the humanitarian field dates back to the origin of the International Red Cross and Red Crescent Movement. When describing his *Memory of Solferino*, Henry Dunant suggested the creation in peacetime, of 'relief societies for the purpose of having care given to the wounded in wartime by zealous, devoted and thoroughly qualified volunteers'. See above, II. See also Resolution 2, 30th International Conference (2007), in which States recognised the importance of the independent and auxiliary role of National Societies; Resolution 4, 31st International Conference (2011), furthering the auxiliary role: Partnership for stronger National Societies and volunteering development.

[56] In 2007, the International Conference of the Red Cross and Red Crescent defined the relationship between public authorities and National Societies as a 'specific and distinctive partnership', see Resolution 2, 30th International Conference (2007), recalled in Resolution 4, 31st International Conference (2011).

[57] The development of, the respect for and the dissemination of international humanitarian law are matters of common concern for the National Societies and the ICRC, Art. 5 para. 4 lit. a) Statutes.

can constitute a strong factor in order to influence the State practice of a given State and its *opinio iuris* when it comes to its obligations under international humanitarian law. This in turn will then flow into the confirmation and possible further development of rules of customary law. Another impact of National Red Cross or Red Crescent Societies on the international law-making processes, in particular concerning the development of treaty law and (its transformation into) domestic legislation, derives from the fact that delegates of National Red Cross or Red Crescent Societies are regularly consulted during the drafting of domestic legislation in the field of international humanitarian law, for instance, in expert commissions, by the relevant ministries, at round tables or via the National Committee on International Humanitarian Law.[58]

c) Enforcement of International Humanitarian Law

As regards to the enforcement of international humanitarian law, National Red Cross or Red Crescent Societies similarly contribute in cooperation with the State. A National Red Cross or Red Crescent Society, which under the principles of the International Red Cross and Red Crescent Movement is independent from the respective State party, might have a better starting position than a State when approaching a non-State armed group to enhance compliance with international humanitarian law, when such non-State armed group itself is a party to an armed conflict with that respective State authority.

A further strong advantage of a National Red Cross or Red Crescent Society is based on the fact that the employees and volunteers of the National Society are familiar with the prevailing local circumstances, such as structures, language, culture and customs as they themselves form part of the local society as is e.g. the case with the staff of the Syrian Arab Red Crescent or the Yemen Red Crescent Society that are actively contributing to the humanitarian and dissemination activities in their respective conflict-torn countries. No foreign organisation could act likewise successful as the one being itself located in a country. Acting according to the fundamental principles of neutrality and impartiality makes the staff and volunteers of such National Red Cross or Red Crescent Societies even more credible in the eyes of the members of a non-State actor. It might be said that staff and volunteers of National Red Cross or Red Crescent

[58] See above III.3.

Societies in general seek to live up to those principles. In any of its activities, at all times and under all circumstances, the respective National Red Cross or Red Crescent Society has to strictly adhere to these principles and must, in particular, refrain from engaging in any kind of controversies of a political, racial, religious or ideological nature, and must also be seen not to take sides in hostilities and to provide relief guided solely by the needs of a person in order to maintain the confidence of all parties to the conflict.[59] As a matter of fact, States agreed, at all times, to respect the adherence by all the components of the Movement to the Fundamental Principles.[60]

Situations where it is difficult to adhere to these principles might nevertheless arise. One example may be seen in the situation of the South African Red Cross during the time of the apartheid regime, when it wished to do humanitarian work in the townships in order to provide help to those injured in riots, although its members, employees and volunteers were then still exclusively of the white race.[61] To address this kind of problem, some National Societies have modified their recruitment procedures and their structures in order to maintain a balanced representation of the communities.[62] In South Africa, e.g., all vacant posts are now widely advertised in all regions of the country and the selection of candidates is no longer decided according to ethnic criteria or qualifications already obtained but on the basis of their training potential.[63]

A further option concerning the enforcement of international humanitarian law for a National Red Cross or Red Crescent Society is to critically accompany and monitor a State's processes when it comes to the implementation of international humanitarian law, reminding the State in a confidential dialogue of its obligations arising under international humanitarian law if necessary, e.g. in case economic or other interests threaten to outweigh legal obligations. With 190 National Red Cross or Red Crescent Societies existing around the globe, this constitutes a powerful tool of enforcement.

[59] See preambular para. 2 Statutes, fundamental principles of impartiality and neutrality; ICRC, 'Principles in action: How do neutrality and independence contribute to humanitarian effectiveness?', 7 June 2015, at: www.icrc.org/en/document/principles-action-how-do-neutrality-and-independence-contribute-humanitarian-effectiveness.

[60] Art. 2 para. 4 Statutes.

[61] J.-L. Chopard, 'Dissemination of the humanitarian rules and cooperation with National Red Cross and Red Crescent Societies for the purpose of prevention' in (1995) No. 306 *International Review of the Red Cross*, passim.

[62] *Ibid.* [63] *Ibid.*

7. Which Role for the Various Components of the International Red Cross and Red Crescent Movement?

As stated in the Statutes of the Movement, National Red Cross and Red Crescent Societies form the basic units and constitute a vital force of the overall International Red Cross and Red Crescent Movement – they cooperate closely with the ICRC in the fields of the development, the implementation and the enforcement of international humanitarian law.[64] It stands to reason that the closer such cooperation is, the more influential the overall Movement as a whole can be in this field.

As said at the outset, the Red Cross and Red Crescent Movement and international humanitarian law continue to be closely intertwined. Although this volume's primary focus is on the achievements or possible shortcomings of one particular component of the International Red Cross and Red Crescent Movement, namely the ICRC, in the field of international humanitarian law, the ICRC's contribution must always be assessed against the background of it being embedded in the overall Movement. It is only through the activities of all of its components that the International Red Cross and Red Crescent Movement can be as active worldwide as it is today. The influence and contribution of the National Red Cross and Red Crescent Societies and with it the impact of the Movement as a whole must not be underestimated, and should accordingly be kept in mind when reading the following chapters with their main focus on the role of the ICRC.

IV. Background, Purpose and Structure of the Book

1. Background

The development of international humanitarian law, deriving from Dunant's ideas, and the particular contribution of the ICRC to this development will be addressed in the various contributions contained in this volume. It compiles revised contributions that were made to an international experts meeting ('The International Red Cross and Red Crescent

[64] The ICRC 'shall maintain close contact' with the National Societies. 'In agreement with them, it shall cooperate in matters of common concern', such as the respect for and development and ratification of the Geneva Conventions and the dissemination of international humanitarian law, Art. 5 para 4 lit. a Statutes. This is what the international community envisaged when the International Conference adopted the Statutes of the Movement in 1965.

Movement at 150: Developing and Clarifying International Humanitarian Law') held on 24 June 2013 in Berlin on the occasion of the 150th anniversary of the International Red Cross and Red Crescent Movement. Celebrating '150 years of humanitarian action', the German Red Cross, together with its partners the Swiss Embassy in Berlin and the University of Potsdam, seized the occasion of this meeting to critically take stock of the Red Cross' contribution within certain fields of its operations, namely the development and clarification of international humanitarian law. Experiences from the past were considered, followed by a stock-taking of the *status quo* of international humanitarian law and an assessment of future challenges.

2. *Purpose*

Over the past 150 years, the ICRC has assumed various roles in the progressive development and humanization of the laws of war, ranging from a 'gentle moderniser' to a 'decisive promoter' of (rapid) normative development. This book offers a look behind the scenes of the numerous facets of the creation, development and clarification of international humanitarian law, and the various ways in which the International Red Cross and Red Crescent Movement, and especially the ICRC, has contributed to it.

It compiles a critical analysis on how the International Committee of the Red Cross has played its role, and particularly of the different approaches, strategies, modes of interaction, and methods the various components of the Red Cross and Red Crescent Movement have adopted at different times and with regard to different projects. Milestone achievements as well as failures and shortcomings of the Movement's influence will be highlighted.

3. *Structure*

Firstly, the book addresses the ICRC's efforts and impact on the conceptualization and substantive content of the Geneva Conventions of 1949, which started way before the actual negotiations on the drafting of these treaties.[65] Robert Heinsch offers a panoramic view from initial experts' meetings that commenced in late 1945 up until the conclusion of the

[65] R. Heinsch, 'Role and Impact of the ICRC in the Development of Core International Humanitarian Law Treaties: The International Committee of the Red Cross and the Geneva Conventions of 1949', Chapter 1 in this volume.

diplomatic conference in 1949 and the subsequent ICRC's commentaries thereon, which are currently in the process of being updated.[66]

Following this, a contemporary witness, i.e. Michael Bothe, presents an inside perspective on the creation process of the first two Additional Protocols of 1977.[67] This chapter highlights tensions and challenges at the time, and points out what role the ICRC played in alerting States to persistent regulatory insufficiencies and protective gaps. Concerns were shared by many States and National Red Cross and Red Crescent Societies alike. And still today, these amendments of the law through the first two Additional Protocols determine the daily work not only of the ICRC, but of all components of the International Red Cross and Red Crescent Movement. This refers, in particular, to the previously mentioned dissemination work, especially that of the National Red Cross or Red Crescent Societies, and is a matter in the legal dialogue with stakeholders such as the relevant domestic ministries, national parliaments and non-governmental organisations working in the field of international humanitarian law. In addition, in Germany, the preparation for the ratification of the first two Additional Protocols by the German Parliament constituted the main reason for the establishment of the previously mentioned National German Committee on International Humanitarian Law.

Although the legal gaps regarding the protection of persons who do not directly participate in the hostilities were rather obvious at the time, many initial ideas and suggestions of the International Red Cross and Red Crescent Movement were overthrown by diplomatic compromises during the negotiations on the texts of the Additional Protocols. The dimension of this is still visible today, in particular with regard to treaty-based rules regarding non-international armed conflicts. Still, situations of non-international armed conflicts do not take place within a legal vacuum. Many rules of international humanitarian law applicable in situations of

[66] See on this process J.-M. Henckaerts, 'Bringing the Commentaries on the Geneva Conventions and Their Additional Protocols into the Twenty-First Century' (2012) 94 No. 888 *International Review of the Red Cross*, pp. 1551–1555; see also most recently A. Clapham, P. Gaeta and M. Sassòli (eds.), *The 1949 Geneva Conventions – A Commentary* (Oxford: Oxford University Press, 2015).

[67] M. Bothe, 'The International Committee of the Red Cross and the Additional Protocols of 1977', Chapter 2 in this volume; as to the content of the two Additional Protocols see also ICRC, *Commentary on the Additional Protocols of 8 June 1977 to the Geneva Conventions of 12 August 1949* (Dordrecht: Martinus Njihoff Publishers, 1987), *passim*, as well as M. Bothe, K. J. Partsch and W. A. Solf, *New Rules for Victims of Armed Conflicts – Commentary on the Two 1977 Protocols Additional to the Geneva Conventions of 1949* (The Hague/Boston/London: Martinus Njihoff Publishers, 2nd ed., 2013).

international armed conflict apply *mutatis mutandis* in non-international armed conflicts as well, due to relevant State practice and the respective *opinio iuris* of States by way of having become part of customary law.[68]

Referring to customary law, Chapter 3 written by Jean-Marie Henckaerts illustrates that the role of the ICRC is by no means restricted to the preparation of drafts for the codification of treaty law.[69] Rather the impact of bi- or multilateral consultations is also reflected in the development and clarification of customary international law. The author of this chapter accordingly analyses the ICRC's various contributions ever since the adoption of the Geneva Conventions in 1949. At the same time, he also assesses the ICRC's continuous work in the area of customary international law. In the end, it may even be that over time the ICRC has been most influential not when it embarked on institutionalised codification or clarification processes, but rather by providing legal advice on a bi- or multilateral level as part of its daily work and thereby providing the initial impetus and guidance for State practice and *opinio iuris* to develop.

While pointing out the impact of the ICRC's Customary Law Study,[70] the relevance of the criticism which the Study received when it was first published in 2005 is, however, also addressed in this chapter. That is to say, albeit mandated by the 26th International Conference of the Red Cross and Red Crescent, the ICRC's Customary Law Study sparked substantial criticism. One of the issues scholars questioned was its far-reaching assimilation of the rules applicable in international and non-international armed conflicts. Reactions to the Study[71] are scrutinized in this chapter

[68] Marauhn and Ntoubandi, 'Armed Conflict, Non-International', p. 632 (para. 28); D. Thürer, *International Humanitarian Law: Theory, Practice, Context* (The Hague: The Hague Academy of International Law, 2011), p. 51 *et. seq.*

[69] J.-M. Henckaerts, 'The International Committee of the Red Cross and the Clarification of Customary International Humanitarian Law', Chapter 3 in this volume.

[70] J.-M. Henckaerts and L. Doswald-Beck (eds.), *Customary International Humanitarian Law*, 2 vols. (Cambridge: Cambridge University Press, 2005), Volume I. Rules, Volume II. Practice.

[71] See e.g. J. B. Bellinger and W. J. Haynes, 'A US Government Response to the International Committee of the Red Cross Study', *Customary International Humanitarian Law* (2007) 89 No. 866 *International Review of the Red Cross*, pp. 443–471; M. Bothe, 'Customary International Humanitarian Law: Some Reflections on the ICRC Study' (2005) 8 *Yearbook of International Humanitarian Law*, pp. 143–178; Y. Dinstein, 'The ICRC Customary International Humanitarian Law Study' (2006) 36 *Israel Yearbook on Human Rights*, pp. 1–15; D. Turns, 'Weapons in the ICRC Study on Customary International Humanitarian Law' (2006) 11(2) *Journal of Conflict and Security Law*, pp. 201–237; E. Wilmshurst and S. Breau (eds.), *Perspectives on the ICRC Study on Customary International Humanitarian Law* (Cambridge: Cambridge University Press, 2011).

and have been an item of intensive discussion, amongst other fora, within the various National Committees on International Humanitarian Law.

As armed conflicts have changed over time, caused in particular by changes in the manner of warfare and developments in the field of military technology, international humanitarian law has had to be constantly reviewed, clarified and, at times, adapted in order to still suit the arising challenges. When taking a progressive approach in such a development and clarification of international humanitarian law, the ICRC raised significant controversy. The ICRC's Interpretive Guidance on the Notion of Direct Participation in Hostilities[72] constitutes the most recent and conspicuous example in point. Hence, in Chapter 4, Robert Cryer concentrates in particular on how the ICRC has shaped and conceptualised the experts' process that eventually led to the publication of the ICRC's Interpretive Guidance and how the ICRC changed and adapted its approach to the dynamics of this process overtime.[73] Despite the continuing controversy over some of its content, the Interpretative Guidance has already significantly influenced international norm development, the contemporary debate, and has been referred to by international[74] as well as national[75] courts and tribunals. On the initiative of National Red Cross and Red Crescent Societies, the Interpretative Guidance was translated and disseminated to the relevant stakeholders on the national level, especially to the judiciary.[76]

The influence of the International Red Cross and Red Crescent Movement has not always been as controversial as these examples might suggest at first glance. On various other occasions the impact of activities of

[72] N. Melzer, 'Interpretive Guidance on the Notion of Direct Participation in Hostilities under International Humanitarian Law' (Geneva: ICRC, 2009) [hereinafter Guidance], reprinted in *International Review of the Red Cross*, 90 (2008), pp. 991–1047.

[73] R. Cryer, 'The International Committee of the Red Cross' 'Interpretive Guidance on the Notion of Direct Participation in Hostilities: See a Little Light', Chapter 4 in this volume.

[74] See e.g. *The Prosecutor v. Thomas Lubanga Dyilo*, Closing submissions of the Defence, ICC-01/04-01/06, 15 July 2011, p. 12.

[75] See e.g. the termination decision by the German Federal Public Prosecutor concerning the killing of the German national Bünyamin E. in Mir Ali (Northern Pakistan) by a drone of 20 June 2013, AZ: 3 BJs 7/12-4, available at: www.generalbundesanwalt.de/docs/drohneneinsatz_vom_04oktober2010_mir_ali_pakistan.pdf

[76] French, Spanish, Japanese and Chinese versions are available at: www.icrc.org/eng/resources/documents/publication/p0990.htm; The Guidance was also translated into German by the German Red Cross: N. Melzer, *Unmittelbare Teilnahme an Feindseligkeiten – Anleitung des IKRK zur Interpretation des Begriffs nach dem humanitären Völkerrecht. Synoptische Gegenüberstellung des Textes in englischer und deutscher Sprache* (Berlin: Deutsches Rotes Kreuz, 2012).

the International Red Cross and Red Crescent Movement and the ICRC in particular has been much more subtle and indirect. For instance, in the realm of arms control, the International Red Cross and Red Crescent Movement frequently opted for more cautious and nuanced tactics as it did, e.g., with regard to the banning of anti-personnel mines and cluster munitions. To learn more about the different approaches that the International Red Cross and Red Crescent Movement has assumed with respect to weapons over the years, Chapter 5 in this volume, authored by Kathleen Lawand and Isabel Robinson, who have been privy to many of those developments and hence provide unique insight, focuses on the treaty regimes prohibiting or limiting the use of certain weapons.[77] Amongst the tools the ICRC applied were medical and technical expertise on the humanitarian impact of certain weapons, as well as legal analyses of their compliance with the rules of international humanitarian law. However, neither the ICRC nor National Red Cross and Red Crescent Societies limited themselves to bilateral talks, but rather lobbied for the prohibition and abandonment of certain weapons in various international and national fora. Chapter 5 also takes into consideration contemporary and future challenges stemming from revolutionary technological advancements in the area of cyberwarfare and autonomous weapons systems.

As every legal rule is only as strong as its enforcement, the efficiency of international humanitarian law, and in particular its regime of grave breaches, highly depends on the penalization through the legal regime of international and national criminal law and the effective enforcement of this law; be it the preventive function of deterrence of the criminal legal regime or the repressive one of actual investigation and prosecution. As the ICRC is mandated by the international community 'to work for the faithful application of international humanitarian law'[78] and 'to take cognizance of any complaints based on alleged breaches of that law,'[79] a natural relationship between the ICRC and those institutions enforcing international humanitarian law, especially international criminal courts and tribunals, exists. Due to the different roles, this relationship varies from constructive engagement and normative support via a strategic engagement to a critical distance deriving from an institutional restraint

[77] K. Lawand and I. Robinson, 'Development of Treaties Limiting or Prohibiting the Use of Certain Weapons: The Role of the International Committee of the Red Cross', Chapter 5 in this volume.

[78] Art. 5 para. 2 lit. c) Statutes.

[79] *Ibid.*

to preserve a structural independence.[80] However, cases before the International Criminal Court are only admissible provided the State, which has jurisdiction, is unwilling or unable genuinely to carry out the investigation or prosecution.[81] Primarily, it is, thus, stakeholders on the national level who have to address questions of international criminal law and the grave breaches regime in particular.

As part of their dissemination work, National Red Cross and Red Crescent Societies offer specific training in international humanitarian law and certain aspects of international criminal law for prosecutors, judges and trainee lawyers. An exchange of experts' views in this area also takes place within the ratification process and the implementation into national law of the international criminal law treaties, including any amendments to these. It is against this background that Carsten Stahn explores the relationship of the ICRC to international criminal law in Chapter 6 of this book.

After the previously mentioned chapters, the book will be rounded off in Chapter 7 by the editors Robin Geiß and Andreas Zimmermann with a comprehensive critical assessment of the role of the International Committee of the Red Cross when it comes to international norm creation and the progressive development of international humanitarian law. Achievements, failures and shortcomings are highlighted. This chapter provides explanations with regard to the versatility in the ICRC's approach and considers how the ICRC's specific role differs from that of other non-State actors such as non-governmental organizations, which somewhat similarly attempt to influence the development of international law in certain related areas such as human rights. Finally, the concluding chapter provides an outlook on how the International Red Cross and Red Crescent Movement's role in humanitarian norm creation and development is likely to evolve with respect to contemporary and future challenges, e.g. the issue of violence against civilians and other protected persons as well as the continuous and in some areas such as the armed conflict in Syria almost pervasive lack of compliance with fundamental humanitarian law rules.

[80] C. Stahn, 'Between 'Constructive Engagement', 'Collusion' and 'Critical Distance': The International Committee of the Red Cross and the Development of International Criminal Law', Chapter 6 in this volume.

[81] Art. 17 para.1 lit. 1) Rome Statute.

In sum, this volume compiles and compares the various ways in which the various components of the International Red Cross and Red Crescent Movement, namely and in particular the International Committee of the Red Cross, have inspired, conceptualised and influenced humanitarian norm creation processes in terms of both substance and procedure. It identifies the different (strategic) approaches that have been adopted in this regard and provides explanations as to why the ICRC has assumed rather different roles at different times. Critical assessments make failures and shortcomings visible and point to lessons to be learnt for the future engagement of the International Red Cross and Red Crescent Movement when engaging in the development of international humanitarian law with the aim to humanize the laws of war.

PART I

The International Committee of the Red Cross' Influence on the Development of Core International Humanitarian Law Treaties

1

The International Committee of the Red Cross and the Geneva Conventions of 1949

ROBERT HEINSCH

I. Introduction[1]

From its inception on 9 February 1863, the International Committee of the Red Cross (ICRC or the Committee)[2] has played a pivotal role with regard to the creation and development of International Humanitarian Law (IHL). It is probably not exaggerated to say that there is no other field of international law in which a non-State entity has had such an impact on the norm-development process as well as on the dynamic interpretation of the respective rules. This includes many of the norms of Geneva Convention IV for the substantial protection of civilians as well as the grave breaches regime in all four Geneva Conventions. At the same time it bears mentioning that not all of the ICRC's numerous attempts to influence the development of the humanitarian legal framework have always been successful. Indeed, there are a number of examples – also with respect to the Geneva Conventions – where the Committee did not manage to come through with the initiatives they originally had in mind. One striking example is that in 1945 the ICRC wanted to have the entirety of the provisions of the Geneva Conventions be applied also to non-international armed conflicts, which obviously did not materialise in the end.[3]

[1] The author would like to thank his former Research Assistant Ms. Thyla Fontein, LL.M., for her invaluable assistance with regard to the gathering of documents and material supporting the research on the topic of this chapter.

[2] The ICRC was originally a draft committee established by the Geneva Public Welfare Society, and consisted of five committee members; it was therefore also referred to as the 'Committee of Five', F. Bugnion, 'Birth of an Idea: The Founding of the International Committee of the Red Cross and of the International Red Cross and Red Crescent Movement: From Solferino to the Original Geneva Convention (1859–1864)', *International Review of the Red Cross*, 94 (2012), 1299, at 1309.

[3] See in this regard later the elaborations on Common Article 3, Section III.3.

Obviously, one of the reasons for the impact of the ICRC lies in the way the First Geneva Convention came into being, as a result of Henry Dunant's idea. He stated that '[o]n certain special occasions, as, for example, when princes of the military art belonging to different nationalities meet at Cologne or Châlons, would it not be desirable that they should take advantage of this sort of congress to formulate some international principle, sanctioned by a Convention inviolate in character, which, once agreed upon and ratified, might constitute the basis for societies for the relief of the wounded in the different European countries?'[4] So, in many ways, the ICRC was created as a first step which then stimulated the drafting and signing of the First Geneva Convention for the Protection of the Wounded in the Field in 1864 which paved the way for the ICRC playing a crucial role in influencing the wording and development of the Geneva Conventions. This was of course a long process that required several stages until the most important step in 1949, when the Four Geneva Conventions as we know them today were accepted by the States participating in the Diplomatic Conference in Geneva. This chapter will mainly focus on the impact the ICRC had on the drafting and creation of the 1949 Geneva Conventions, but it will also briefly deal with the historical development leading up to this important moment in the history of international law. It will also show how after the ratification of the 1949 Geneva Conventions the ICRC continued to contribute to the interpretation and progressive development of the Geneva law.

As mentioned already, the fact that in 1863 and 1864 the ICRC (which at that time was still called the 'Permanent International Committee for the Relief of Wounded Soldiers'[5]) was the decisive entity which was responsible for initiating the ambitious project of setting up rules for the protection of wounded soldiers in the field, gave this organisation an advantage which it seems to have used for everyone's benefit until today. From the beginning, the ICRC was always involved and usually 'at the table' when States discussed the necessity of a new convention. In 1863, this meant that the representatives of the newly founded International Committee approached the leaders of the major powers in Europe and tried to persuade them of the necessity and the advantage of having such a

[4] H. Dunant, 'Memories of Solferino', as quoted by F. Bugnion, 'From Solferino to the birth of contemporary international humanitarian law', available at: www.icrc.org/eng/resources/documents/article/other/solferino-article-bugnion-240409.htm.

[5] See Bugnion, 'Birth of an Idea', 1299, at 1311; see also D.-E. Khan, *Das Rote Kreuz: Geschichte einer humanitären Weltbewegung* (München: C. H. Beck, 2013), 23. For coherency purposes, the term ICRC is used throughout the text independent of the time period.

convention. In the event, one can distinguish three different roles the ICRC took over with regard to the First Geneva Convention:[6] First, the ICRC initiated the idea of developing such a Convention and tried to seek as much backing as possible from governments, especially that of Switzerland.[7] The latter government's interest in the project resulted in the fact that the respective Diplomatic Conference eventually took place in Geneva. The ICRC also was one of the driving forces that successfully tried to gain the support of Napoleon III for this project.[8] Second, the ICRC was the entity which early in the process formulated a draft convention that would become the foundation of the treaty text discussed during the Diplomatic Conference.[9] Finally, although the ICRC was not taking part in its official capacity, i.e. was not accredited as an independent entity during the deliberations in Geneva, but was according to Article 3 of the Provisional Rules of Procedure of the Diplomatic Conference taking part in the capacity of an 'expert'.[10] Two of its members, General Dufour and Gustave Moynier played a central role as representatives of the Swiss Delegation during the conference. Gustave Moynier is usually seen as 'the main architect of the Convention'.[11] In addition, all the five delegates of the ICRC present during the Diplomatic Conference participated as experts in the various drafting committees, and played a role in coming to the results, which made it into the final version of the text.

But let us go first back to the historical evolution of the Geneva Conventions: After the turn of the century, when it became obvious that the rules which had been agreed upon for the protection of the wounded and sick in the field would also be needed to protect the respective persons – as well as the shipwrecked – at sea, this led to the drafting and signature of the Second Geneva Convention for the Amelioration of the Condition of Wounded, Sick and Shipwrecked Members of Armed Forces at Sea in 1906.[12] During the conference leading to the adoption of the

[6] F. Bugnion, 'The International Committee of the Red Cross and the Development of International Humanitarian Law', *Chicago Journal of International Law*, 5 (2004), pp. 191–215, 193.

[7] *Ibid.* [8] *Ibid.* [9] *Ibid.*

[10] Final Record of the Diplomatic Conference of Geneva of 1949, Volume II, Section B, Federal Political Department, Berne, p. 15.

[11] *Ibid.*

[12] At the same time, the regulations concerning the conduct of hostilities at sea led to the 1907 Hague Convention applying the respective rules to maritime warfare in order to 'accord with the revision of the Geneva Convention in 1906 and became known as the Tenth Hague Convention', see J. A. C. Gutteridge, 'The Geneva Convention of 1949', *British Yearbook of International Law*, 26 (1949), pp. 294–326, 296. However, in this process it is important to

Second Geneva Convention of 1906, the ICRC assumed a similar position in initiating the process and drafting of the first version of the text of the convention. The next step towards enhancing the 'Geneva regime' that followed after World War I was the project to set up an international treaty which provided for a better protection of the prisoners of war. In the end, the ICRC and the Red Cross as such came out of the 'Great War' with a growth in their reputation.[13] A lot of people had experienced first-hand the work of the Red Cross and had seen the need for maintaining the fundamental principles of humanity. Consequently, the ICRC had a good starting point after WWI to initiate and support a process which cumulated with the signing and ratification ofthe Third Geneva Convention for the Protection of the Prisoners of War, which was signed in 1929, in order to expand the rather short provisions for the treatment of prisoners of war contained in the Annex to Hague Convention IV, the Regulations Respecting the Laws and Customs of War on Land ('the Hague Regulations').[14] While the Hague Regulations only contained 17 articles dealing with the definition and the protection of prisoners of wars, the 1929 Geneva Convention III Relative to the Treatment of Prisoners of War expanded the protective regime to a total of 97 articles and was negotiated by 47 States,[15] and later ratified by 53 States.[16] This convention not only reversed the 'general participation clause', the clause which governed the conduct of hostilities in the 1899 and 1907 Hague Conventions and had the effect that a convention 'would apply in war only if all the belligerents were party to that treaty',[17] and which had been

note that the ICRC did not take part in either the 1899 or the 1907 Peace Conferences in The Hague.

[13] G. Best, *War and Law since 1945* (Oxford: Clarendon Press, 1994), p. 52.

[14] *Ibid.*

[15] See for details, S. Krähenmann, 'Protection of Prisoners in Armed Conflict', in. D. Fleck (ed.), *The Handbook of International Humanitarian Law*, (3rd ed., Oxford: Oxford University Press, 2013), p. 361.

[16] Source: ICRC, Treaty database, available at: www.icrc.org/ihl/INTRO/305?OpenDocument; the States which ratified the Third Convention were the following: Argentina, Australia, Austria, Belgium, Bolivia, Brazil, Bulgaria, Canada, Chile, China, Colombia, Czechoslovakia, Denmark, Egypt, El Salvador, Estonia, Fiji, France, Germany, Greece, Hungary, India, Indonesia, Iraq, Israel, Italy, Jordan, Latvia, Liechtenstein, Lithuania, Mexico, Monaco, Myanmar, Netherlands, New Zealand, Norway, Pakistan, Papua New Guinea, Philippines, Poland, Portugal, Romania, Serbia, Slovakia, South Africa, Spain, Sweden, Switzerland, Thailand, Turkey, United Kingdom of Great Britain and Northern Ireland, the United States and Venezuela.

[17] M. E. O'Connell, 'Historical Development and Legal Basis', in D. Fleck (ed.), *The Handbook of International Humanitarian Law* (3rd ed., Oxford: Oxford University Press, 2013), p. 13.

incorporated in earlier law of war treaties.[18] The Third Convention was also responsible for protecting and safeguarding millions of prisoners of war in the period between 1939 and 1945, and even after the war.[19] In this regard, this can easily be seen as one of the major successes of the work of the ICRC between the two World Wars.[20]

What was still missing at that time, and which was already obvious after WWI, was an international treaty for the additional protection for civilians affected by armed conflict. The ICRC was aware of this gap and tried to fill it by preparing a draft convention for the protection of civilians in armed conflict (the so-called 'Tokyo draft' named after its original presentation at the International Conference of the Red Cross in Tokyo in 1934),[21] which was designed to add to the rather limited protection of the 1907 Hague Regulations which only included three articles pertaining to the protection of the physical integrity of civilians.[22] However, the outbreak of World War II destroyed all hopes of reaching agreement on this new Convention, and in this regard the ICRC draft was only to be seen as the first step on which the drafters could build after another World War had passed.

This chapter will look more closely at how the ICRC helped to prepare the drafts for the 1949 Diplomatic Conference, how it influenced the negotiations during the Conference, and how it continued to have an impact on the interpretations of the Conventions long after their adoption and indeed up until today. Since the four Geneva Conventions, the *travaux préparatoires* and the minutes from the Conference as such cover hundreds and probably even thousands of pages, this contribution focuses on certain crucial legal provisions and innovations which stood out from the results of the 1949 Diplomatic conference or which highlight especially the important role the ICRC played. The following areas will be addressed:

[18] T. Meron, 'The Geneva Conventions and Public International Law', *International Review of the Red Cross*, 91 (2009), pp. 619–625, 621; see also P. Spoerri, 'The Geneva Conventions of 1949: Origins and Current Significance', Statement, 12 August 2009, available at: www.icrc.org/eng/resources/documents/statement/geneva-conventions-statement-120809.htm.

[19] J. S. Pictet, 'The New Geneva Conventions for the Protection of War Victims', *American Journal of International Law*, 45 (1951), pp. 462–475, 463 with reference to the Report of the International Committee of the Red Cross on its Activities during the Second World War, 1 September 1939 – 30 June 1947, 3 Vols., Geneva, 1948, pp. 736, 320, 539 in English, French and Spanish.

[20] *Ibid.*

[21] Meron, 'The Geneva Conventions and Public International Law', 620; see also Gutteridge, 'The Geneva Convention of 1949', 295.

[22] *Ibid.*

(II.) the process as such in which the ICRC was involved and which led to the diplomatic negotiations in Geneva as, (III.) well as selected examples on how the ICRC influenced material provisions of the Conventions, including (1) Common Article 2, and (2) Common Article 3. We will also deal briefly with some major achievements with regard to (3) Geneva Convention IV, and (4) with respect to the ICRC's influence concerning the inclusion of the grave breaches regime in the Geneva Conventions. In a last step, the analysis will critically consider the role of the ICRC after the signing and ratification of the Conventions concerning their interpretation, further development and implementation (IV.) and come to a general conclusion on the ICRC's involvement and influence regarding this core project in the domain of humanitarian law development (V.) at the end.

II. The ICRC's Influence on the 1949 Geneva Conventions: The Process Leading to the 1949 Diplomatic Conference in Geneva

The starting point for the revision of the Geneva Conventions and the respective support role of the ICRC after World War II was different compared to the situation after World War I. Some commentators observed that the role of the Red Cross between 1939 and 1945 was not seen as completely uncontroversial.[23] This had at least partly something to do with the fact that as one of the prime principles of the Red Cross movement, the principle of neutrality is not always seen as a positive characteristic in a war against a regime of terror like the Nazi regime in the Third Reich. However, World War II clearly demonstrated again that there was a need for revision of the Geneva Conventions, and with millions of civilians being affected, it was also clear that the project of adding a Fourth Geneva Convention should be back on the table.

Interestingly enough the ICRC started the process at a time when the war was still going on, and some observers might have wondered whether 'there was still a place for humanitarian rules in an era of total warfare'.[24] On 15 February 1945, the then president of the ICRC, Max Huber, sent a memorandum to governments and national Red Cross and Red Crescent societies, including a provisional programme for the diplomatic conference and an invitation to gather information about the topics to be

[23] Best, *War and Law since 1945*, p. 52.

[24] Spoerri, 'The Geneva Conventions of 1949: Origins and Current Significance'.

discussed.[25] The process gained more momentum on 5 September 1945 when Max Huber sent another letter to the 'Big Five' (the United States, USSR, United Kingdom, France and China) suggesting to hold a conference of governmental experts as soon as possible.[26] And while the USSR immediately signaled that they were hesitant to participate, the other four only reluctantly agreed, and in the end it was not before April 1947 that the 'Conference of Government Experts for the Study of the Conventions for the Protection of War Victims' would finally be organised.[27]

However, the initial reluctance of some powerful States did not stop the ICRC from attempts to accelerate the process. In October 1945, the ICRC hosted an informal meeting of neutral members of the so-called 'Mixed Medical Commission',[28] i.e. the Commission according to Article 69 (1) of the 1929 Geneva Convention III that had been dealing with the examination of sick and wounded prisoners of war and had been responsible for deciding whether they were eligible for repatriation.[29] The following three years then reflect the special way in which the ICRC and the Red Cross/Red Crescent Movement at large, including the national Red Cross and Red Crescent Societies, interacted in order to bring forward an elaborate draft for the diplomatic discussions of States.[30] After an initial meeting of the Board of Governors of the 'League of Red Cross Societies' (the predecessor of the International Federation of Red Cross and Red Crescent Societies)[31] in Oxford in July 1946, the ICRC presented

[25] 'Mémorandum adressé par le Comité international de la Croix-Rouge aux Gouvernements des Etats parties à la Convention de Genève et aux Sociétés nationales de la Croix-Rouge', *International Review of the Red Cross*, 27 (1945), 85; see also Pictet, 'The New Geneva Conventions for the Protection of War Victims', 464.

[26] Best, *War and Law since 1945*, p. 81.

[27] Pictet, 'The New Geneva Conventions for the Protection of War Victims', 466.

[28] Article 69 (1) of the 1929 Geneva Convention III provided that 'On the opening of hostilities, belligerents shall come to an understanding as to the appointment of mixed medical commissions. These commissions shall consist of three members, two of whom shall belong to a neutral country and one appointed by the detaining Power; one of the medical officers of the neutral country shall preside. These mixed medical commissions shall proceed to the examination of sick or wounded prisoners and shall make all appropriate decisions with regard to them'. The ICRC often helped with appointing neutral members to the Commission during WWII, see Pictet, Vol III of the 1960 Commentary to the 1949 Geneva Conventions, p. 526.

[29] Bugnion, 'The International Committee of the Red Cross', 194.

[30] See also for this procedure Pictet, 'The New Geneva Conventions for the Protection of War Victims', pp. 464–467.

[31] The League of the Red Cross Societies was founded in 1919 in order to strengthen and unite, for health activities, already-existing Red Cross Societies and to promote the creation of new Societies; see www.ifrc.org/en/who-we-are/history/. The origin of the League was

its first drafts and suggestions to a conference of National Red Cross and Red Crescent Societies that took place in Geneva in August 1946.[32] This included 145 delegates from 45 National Societies, in addition to delegates from the ICRC and the League of Red Cross Societies.[33] The Conference of Government Experts which was then finally convened in 1947 had its primary purpose in gathering ideas for the revision of the existing three Geneva Conventions of 1906 and 1929, but focused mainly on laying the ground for a new, fourth Convention on the condition and protection of civilians in times of war.[34] The conference had primarily been initiated by the ICRC and included 70 experts designated by the governments of 15 States.[35]

Taking into account the results of the two conferences of 1946 and 1947 and of additional, bilateral consultations with governments, the experts of the ICRC prepared four draft conventions covering the three existing fields plus the protection of civilians. In the end, the ICRC finished the draft of the four Conventions at the beginning of 1948 and circulated the approximately 250 pages to all governments and national Red Cross Societies in May of that year ('the Stockholm Draft Conventions').[36] These drafts were then presented to the participants of the 17th International Red Cross Conference which was convened in Stockholm[37] and took place from 20 to 30 August 1948.[38] The Legal Commission of the Conference checked the drafts in detail and approved them with only a few changes.[39] After the Stockholm Conference the ICRC again took on the

an international medical conference initiated by the president of the American Red Cross, Henry Davison, which resulted in the birth of the League of Red Cross Societies, 'which was renamed in October 1983 to the League of Red Cross and Red Crescent Societies, and then in November 1991 to become the International Federation of Red Cross and Red Crescent Societies'. See www.ifrc.org/en/who-we-are/history/#sthash.XJAzN2za.dpuf.

32 Although delegates from Red Crescent National Societies like the Egyptian Red Crescent took part in the conference, the official title of the conference was 'Preliminary Conference of National Red Cross Societies for the Study of the Conventions and of Various Problems Relative to the Red Cross', Report on the Work of the Preliminary Conference of National Red Cross Societies for the Study of the Conventions and of Various Problems Relative to the Red Cross' (Geneva, 26 July– 3 August 1946) (1947), available at: www.loc.gov/rr/frd/Military_Law/pdf/RC_report-1946.pdf.

33 Bugnion, 'The International Committee of the Red Cross', 195.

34 Spoerri, 'The Geneva Conventions of 1949: Origins and Current Significance'.

35 Bugnion, 'The International Committee of the Red Cross', 195.

36 Pictet, 'The New Geneva Conventions for the Protection of War Victims', 466.

37 Bugnion, 'The International Committee of the Red Cross', 195.

38 Pictet, 'The New Geneva Conventions for the Protection of War Victims', 467.

39 Seventeenth International Red Cross Conference (Stockholm, August 1948), Report, (Swedish Red Cross, 1948); 17th International Conference of the Red Cross, Sténogramme

task to redraft the Conventions and came up with four new common articles to meet the Stockholm objective to 'repress violations of the Humanitarian Conventions'. Some commentators have remarked that during this phase the ICRC did not always consult with respective governments, but tried to press for their own ideas.[40] However, one should be aware that the ICRC and then President Max Huber knew how to balance the incorporation of States' concerns, and at the same time to promote the concerns of humanity in a way that it deemed necessary after two World Wars. And this in particular is a good demonstration of the very special role the ICRC still has, and which lies rooted in the original inception of the Geneva Conventions as described at the beginning of the chapter. But it has also much to do with the special and careful approach towards the States, which the ICRC has used over the years. At this point, it seems to be important to recall what the exact role of the ICRC is in this context. When the Committee was created in 1863, it had been given a special function with respect to IHL.[41] The 1949 Geneva Conventions and their 1977 Additional Protocols, as well as the Statutes of the International Red Cross and Red Crescent Movement, foresee the ICRC as the 'guardian' and 'promoter' of international humanitarian law.[42] This particular role includes a number of different aspects, like e.g. endorsing international humanitarian law treaties, monitoring the respect of international humanitarian law by the parties to armed conflicts, the dissemination of international humanitarian law, as well as supporting and developing new rules of international humanitarian law. The latter is especially relevant for the current issue of its impact on the Geneva Conventions. However, the important aspect is that the ICRC is an independent body which has *not* been created by States, and therefore also enjoys a certain independence from these main actors of international law. This obviously is an advantage when it comes to the 'guardian' function of the ICRC, but also when trying to push for new developments in order to expand the scope and protective regime of international humanitarian law and to ensure that the principles

des séances de la Commission juridique and Résume des débats des sous-commissions de la Commission juridique (Aug. 1948).

[40] Best, *War and Law since 1945*, p. 93.

[41] Cf. F. Bugnion, *The International Committee of the Red Cross and the Protection of War Victims*, 2003; D. P. Forsythe, *The Humanitarians: The International Committee of the Red Cross*, 2005.

[42] See for a description of the role of the ICRC Article 5 of the Statutes of the International Red Cross and Red Crescent Movement, adopted by the 25th International Conference of the Red Cross at Geneva in 1986, amended in 1995.

of humanity are sufficiently respected. At the same time, the ICRC always needs to take into account that new treaties can only be created, need to be ratified, and have to be applied and respected by the States. In this regard, it is crucial that any demands for new developments are reflecting a certain realistic approach and also take into account the possible interests of States.

What the ICRC did in order to achieve this delicate balancing of interests in the preparation for the new Geneva Conventions was to convene a small committee of experts in Geneva in 1948. The committee consisted of Professor Hersch Lauterpacht, at the time, probably the UK's most distinguished international law professor; Jean Graven, one of Switzerland's most distinguished academics; Captain Martinus Mouton of the Netherland's navy and a judge in its supreme court of appeal; and finally, the respected British lawyer Colonel Henry Philimore, bringing fresh insights from dealing with violations of the law of armed conflict and the newly developing war crimes prosecution, since he had been involved in the Prosecution team at the International Military Tribunal in Nuremberg.[43] Most importantly was that ICRC President Max Huber chaired this expert commission, himself being a very distinguished international scholar, and former judge of the Permanent Court of International Justice. This expert commission in the end came up with the draft articles which would become the grave breaches articles common to the Geneva Conventions. The inclusion of these provisions, which form a core component of the Conventions' implementation and enforcement scheme, can rightly be designated as one of the most important revolutionary changes of the Geneva Conventions in 1949. At the same time this illustrates the special diplomatic approach that the ICRC has often chosen. While the ICRC has always been in close contact with the government representatives of the Member States of the Geneva Conventions, especially during and in preparation for the International Conference,[44] which takes place every four years, and enables the Committee to directly liaise with States on

[43] Best, *War and Law since 1945*, p. 94.

[44] On the role of the International Conference of the Red Cross and Red Crescent, see F. Bugnion, 'The International Conference of the Red Cross and Red Crescent: Challenges, Key Issues and Achievements', *International Review of the Red Cross*, 91 (2009), pp. 675–712; and M. Meyer, 'The Importance of the International Conference of the Red Cross and Red Crescent to National Societies: Fundamental in Theory and in Practice', *International Review of the Red Cross*, 91 (2009), pp. 713–733; see also D. Casalin and C. Lamb, 'Participation of States in the International Conference of the Red Cross and Red Crescent and Assemblies of Other International Organization', *International Review of the Red Cross*, 91 (2009), pp. 733–758.

certain controversial issues, it used the influence of personalities like ICRC President Max Huber in order to prepare the ground for new developments in IHL.[45] The approach followed by Max Huber, relying on a 'spirit of complete impartiality and independence' is reflected in one of the statements he made during the Diplomatic Conference: 'Institutions must live, subsist and enter into history by virtue of their fidelity to moral values, in spite of the changes imposed upon them by time and their own desire to adapt themselves to changing conditions'.[46] Another example of the ICRC's special approach is the appointment of academics for the preparation committee who were not official members of the ICRC, and therefore might have had more persuasive force towards the government representatives, especially when they came from the country which was pessimistic towards a special issue. The composition of the expert group deliberately included Sir Hersch Lauterpacht in order to appease the United Kingdom, which did not communicate with the British Red Cross at the time, and had a rather difficult relationship with the ICRC. The ICRC anticipated that if the most important international law scholar of the United Kingdom (and maybe of the world) would be among the authors of the grave breaches provisions, the United Kingdom would have a hard time arguing against this.[47]

Overall, the time period after World War II and the preparatory process leading to the 1949 Diplomatic Conference in Geneva demonstrates in an illustrative manner the special role of the ICRC with regard to the revision of the Geneva Conventions: the ICRC started the first initiatives for a revision of the Geneva Conventions during the final phase of the war by suggesting a diplomatic conference to States. This initiative gained more force after the end of the war when the ICRC contacted the 'Big Five' in August 1945 which resulted in a constant flow of contacts and cooperation with governments and national Red Cross and Red Crescent Societies, expert meetings and circulation of drafts. In the end one could speak about a 'three-step preparatory approach': (1) in 1946, the initial board meeting of the League of Red Cross Societies took place in Oxford and the first drafts were presented by the ICRC to the national Red Cross and Crescent Societies at a conference in Geneva; (2) in 1947, a conference of government experts initiated by the ICRC was convened in order

[45] For a detailed overview of the role of Max Huber in this context, please refer to Y. Sandoz, 'Max Huber and the Red Cross', *European Journal of International Law*, 18 (2007), pp. 171–197.

[46] Final Record of the Diplomatic Conference of Geneva 1949, Volume II, Section A, Federal Political Department Berne, p. 12

[47] Best, *War and Law since 1945*, p. 161.

to hear the views of the States on questions regarding the revision of the Geneva Conventions; and (3) finally, the 1948 International Conference was organised in Stockholm and the ICRC presented drafts of the four Geneva Conventions taking into account the information gathered during the previous three years. Even after this conference, the ICRC continued to work on the draft conventions, especially with regard to the provisions dealing with the 'grave breaches', which then became the basis for the 1949 Diplomatic Conference in Geneva.

III. Examples of the ICRC's Influence on Core Substantive Provisions of the Geneva Conventions of 1949

The first part of this chapter has shown what kind of influence and impact the ICRC already had during the preparatory stages which led to the 1949 'Diplomatic Conference for the Establishment of International Conventions for the Protection of Victims of War', convened by the Swiss Federal Council, and which took place in Geneva from 21 April to 12 August 1949.[48] At the Conference, 63 States were represented, of which 59 acted with full voting powers, while four were attending just as observers.[49] Although this was a conference of government officials, the ICRC had been invited to work together with the different commissions, between which the drafting of the four Conventions had been split.[50] While the confirmation that the ICRC delegates could participate only came through only shortly before the opening ceremony,[51] they became an important part of the drafting of the final versions of the Conventions. As it was formulated at the beginning of the Conference: 'The Heads of Delegations are unanimously of the opinion that our work will be greatly facilitated if the International Committee takes part in it in the capacity of expert'.[52] These included five delegates who participated in the various working committees during the conference, namely Paul Carry, Jean Pictet, Claude Pilloud, Frederic Siordet and Rene Wilhelm.[53] As one of the government delegates formulated it later in the conference: 'We are also most grateful to the International Committee for having placed their

[48] Pictet, 'The New Geneva Conventions for the Protection of War Victims', 467.

[49] *Ibid.* [50] *Ibid.*

[51] See Bugnion, 'The International Committee of the Red Cross', 197 with reference to the fact that the Soviet Union was hesitant to participate in the ICRC; cf. also C. Rey-Schyrr, 'Les Conventions de Genève de 1949: une percée décisive', *International Review of the Red Cross*, 81 (1999), pp. 209–239, at 232, 234.

[52] *Travaux préparatoires*, Volume IIA, p. 15. [53] *Ibid.*

representatives at the disposal of the Conference. By their expert knowledge of the matter, they have greatly facilitated our work'.[54] How much influence these experts exercised becomes obvious when one browses through the hundreds of pages from the *travaux préparatoires* and sees how often the ICRC delegates contributed to the discussion.[55] In the following section, we will look more closely at some important examples of innovations in the Geneva Conventions and what the role of the ICRC was in reaching the final results.[56]

1. *Common Article 2: 'Armed Conflict'*

One of the new achievements of the 1949 Geneva Conventions is a certain number of common provisions which are valid for all four treaties. The inclusion of these 'common articles' was at least partly due to the influence of the ICRC and is reflected in the Final Record of the Diplomatic Conference of Geneva of 1949.[57] Here we will first look at Common Article 2.[58]

From the outset, one cannot deny that the introduction of Common Article 2 represented a very important step in the development of

[54] Final Record of the Diplomatic Conference of Geneva 1949, Volume II, Section B, Federal Political Department Berne, pp. 515–516.

[55] For an overview on the *travaux préparatoires*, see *e.g.*: F. Bugnion, 'The Geneva Conventions of 12 August 1949: From the 1949 Diplomatic Conference to the Dawn of the New Millennium', *International Affairs*, 76 (2000), pp. 41–50, with reference, amongst others, to: G. I. A. D. Draper, *The Red Cross Conventions* (London: Stevens and Sons, 1958); Gutteridge, 'The Geneva Convention of 1949', pp. 294–326; Pictet, 'The New Geneva Conventions for the Protection of War Victims', pp. 462–475.

[56] For a general summary of the main new achievements in the Geneva Conventions at the time refer to Gutteridge, 'The Geneva Convention of 1949', pp. 294–326; Pictet, 'The New Geneva Conventions for the Protection of War Victims', pp. 462–475; R. T. Yingling and R. W. Ginnane, 'The Geneva Convention of 1949', *American Journal of International Law*, 46 (1952), pp. 393–427.

[57] See e.g. with regard to its influence on Common Article 2, Final Record of the Diplomatic Conference of Geneva 1949, Volume II, Section B, Federal Political Department Berne, pp. 79, 84, 95, and especially 108.

[58] The exact wording of this newly introduced article is 'Article 2. In addition to the provisions which shall be implemented in peacetime, the present Convention shall apply to all cases of declared war or of any other armed conflict which may arise between two or more of the High Contracting Parties, even if the state of war is not recognized by one of them. The Convention shall also apply to all cases of partial or total occupation of the territory of a High Contracting Party, even if the said occupation meets with no armed resistance. Although one of the Powers in conflict may not be a party to the present Convention, the Powers who are parties thereto shall remain bound by it in their mutual relations. They shall furthermore be bound by the Convention in relation to the said Power, if the latter accepts and applies the provisions thereof.'

International Humanitarian Law. It was the moment when Paragraph 1 of Common Article 2 first complemented, and on the long run, replaced the concept of 'war' by the factual concept of 'armed conflict' as the decisive condition in order to trigger the application of the Geneva Conventions and International Humanitarian Law in general: 'In addition to the provisions which shall be implemented in peacetime, the present Convention shall apply to all cases of declared war or of any other armed conflict which may arise between two or more of the High Contracting Parties, even if the state of war is not recognized by one of them.' The ICRC had tried to support this development since before the war.[59] Although nobody at this time knew the terminology 'armed conflict', we should be aware of the fact that especially nowadays – with armed conflicts having reached characteristics which the drafters of the Geneva Conventions probably never thought of – the inclusion of the concept of armed conflict has been decisive in order to make the Geneva Conventions applicable to the conflicts of the twenty-first century.[60]

Equally important was the addition of the second paragraph which clarified that the field of application had been broadened further still by the sentence '(2) The Convention shall also apply to all cases of partial or total occupation of the territory of a High Contracting Party, even if the said occupation meets with no armed resistance.' As a result, States could now no longer deny the state of occupation just because a big State's invasion of a smaller State's territory encountered no armed opposition.[61]

And finally, the third paragraph rejected the spirit of the 'general participation clause' (*si omnes* clause) which one still encountered in the 1907 Hague Conventions and other treaties predating 1929. According to this clause a State party to an armed conflict was no longer bound by a certain IHL provision if another State, that had not committed to be bound by the respective treaty, joined as a party to the armed conflict. This clause had already been explicitly rejected by the 1929 Prisoner of War Convention and the Wounded and Sick Convention of 1906, which stated in Article 82 that '[i]n time of war if one of the belligerents is not a party to the Convention, its provisions shall, nevertheless, remain binding as

[59] Best, *War and Law since 1945*, passim.

[60] For the discussions in the Drafting Committee and the role of the ICRC delegate Pilloud refer to the *travaux préparatoires*, Volume IIB, 9–11, 42–43, and 47–49: 'The Chairman drew attention to the important role which the ICRC would be called upon to play as an expert in the work of the Committee. He asked Mr. Pilloud to be at the disposal of the Committee for any clarification which might be required' (p. 9).

[61] Best, *War and Law since 1945*, p. 143.

between the belligerents who are parties thereto'.[62] The influence of the ICRC becomes apparent here from the *travaux préparatoires* as reflected in the Final Record of the Diplomatic Conference. The ICRC had suggested adding to the third paragraph the following two sentences: 'In the event of an international conflict between one of the High Contracting Parties and a Power which is not bound by the present Convention, the Contracting Party shall apply the provisions thereof. This obligation shall stand unless, after a reasonable lapse of time, the Power not bound by the present Convention states its refusal to apply it, or in fact fails to apply it'.[63] This proposal, which was submitted by the ICRC, was taken up by the Delegation of Norway, with, however, the deletion of the words 'after a reasonable lapse of time',[64] which in the end was the role model for the final version of Paragraph 3. With the introduction of Paragraph 3 of Common Article 2, this applied now to all four Geneva Conventions and even went a step further: 'Although one of the Powers in conflict may not be a party to the present Convention, the Powers who are parties thereto shall remain bound by it in their mutual relations. They shall furthermore be bound by the Convention in relation to the said Power, if the latter accepts and applies the provisions thereof.' The idea underlying this paragraph, namely that 'even if one belligerent is not a Party to the Convention, but accepts it for the specific conflict only, the parties shall be bound by the Convention in relation to it',[65] had already been proposed in the context of the 1929 Convention, but at that time did not succeed in making it in the actual text.[66] In this regard, the main ideas which the ICRC had planned to incorporate in Common Article 2 were quite successfully accepted by States.

However, with regard to the final version of Common Article 2, one has to admit that not all aspirations which the ICRC tried to push forward during the negotiations were successful. Since the Spanish Civil War it had been a priority on the agenda of the ICRC to also cover non-international armed conflicts by international humanitarian law. Therefore, the Red Cross Movement placed part of their focus on the extension of the Geneva Convention's scope of application to civil wars.[67] The ICRC put this special emphasis into action, and included the matter on the

[62] Meron, 'The Geneva Conventions and Public International Law', 621.

[63] Final Record of the Diplomatic Conference of Geneva 1949, Volume II, Section B, Federal Political Department Berne, p. 108.

[64] *Ibid.* [65] Meron, 'The Geneva Conventions and Public International Law', 623.

[66] *Ibid.* [67] Best, *War and Law since 1945*, p. 169.

agenda of the meeting of governmental experts in 1947. Interestingly, in the beginning the issue of civil wars did not draw as much attention from the States as one might have expected. This may have been due to the form of presentation.[68] In Geneva in 1947 and at the Stockholm conference in 1948, the inclusion of non-international armed conflicts was referenced to as part of the first two common articles regarding the new Conventions' scope of application.[69] At this stage, the Geneva Conventions were intended to apply equally 'to all cases of declared war' between High Contracting Parties and to 'all cases of partial or total occupation' and 'in all cases of armed conflict not of an international character'.[70] One would have expected that the introduction of the applicability of the Geneva Conventions in *toto* also to armed conflicts of a non-international armed conflict at the beginning of the Conventions would have triggered strong reactions from government representatives. However, almost the contrary was the case. It seems as if States first wanted to wait and see the substantive content of the norms that had henceforth to be applied before discussing to what kind of situations these provisions should be applied.[71] Later it became obvious that States were not willing to agree to anything which would lead to the consequence that the Geneva Conventions would be applicable to non-international armed conflicts in their entirety. In particular, the United States, France and their followers were very doubtful towards expanding the Geneva Conventions to non-international armed conflict; the United Kingdom was in stark opposition.[72] The consequence in the end was that the ICRC's attempt to include also 'non-international armed conflicts' in Common Article 2 was unsuccessful. Nevertheless, as the *travaux préparatoires* show, ICRC delegates participated actively during the Diplomatic Conference,[73] even though they did not come through with their approach as highlighted by ICRC Delegate Carry who said that 'the International Committee of the Red Cross was in favor of the text which they themselves submitted to the Stockholm Conference and which provided for the full application of the Conventions in the event of conflicts not of an international nature'.[74] The reason for this also becomes clear from the following statement of said ICRC delegate: 'In a diplomatic conference, however, realistic and practical views must be taken, and the Committee was aware from the outset of the work that the original text,

[68] *Ibid.* [69] *Ibid.* [70] *Ibid.* [71] *Ibid.*

[72] Best, *War and Law since 1945*, pp. 170–175.

[73] See, e.g., Final Record of the Diplomatic Conference of Geneva 1949, Volume II, Section B, Federal Political Department Berne, pp. 79, 90, 94, 95, and 108.

[74] ICRC delegate Carry, Final Record of the Diplomatic Conference of Geneva 1949, Volume II, Section B, Federal Political Department Berne, pp. 336–337.

even in the Stockholm wording, had no chance whatever of being adopted by the Governments and that compromise solution should accordingly be sought'.[75]

2. *Common Article 3: The Minimum Standards Applicable in Non-International Armed Conflict*

Although the ambitious attempt to apply the entirety of provisions of the Geneva Conventions to non-international armed conflicts was unsuccessful in the end, the energy which was put into this endeavour by the ICRC helped to ultimately secure the adoption of Common Article 3 providing at least for some minimum guarantees in the context of non-international armed conflict. Nevertheless, the main reason why Common Article 3 finally made its way into the Geneva Conventions was because of the proposal submitted by France. The French proposal mainly concentrated on basic human rights protections as already laid down in the Universal Declaration of Human Rights (UDHR) adopted by the United Nations General Assembly in its resolution 217 A on 10 December 1948,[76] and which were probably seen as being applicable in any case. When the ICRC presented its ideas on the extension of the scope of application at the Stockholm Conference, it might have not completely taken into account all the political and practical aspects which were then occupying various subcommittees in 1949.[77]

What made the French proposal such a decisive step towards the achievement of international humanitarian law for the first time being applicable in non-international armed conflicts, was that it successfully eliminated all possible reasons for objections related to politically sensitive issues like States' rights and subjects' duties.[78] At the same time, the French proposal managed to do this by relying on very strong human rights elements in the actual wording, more than in any other provision of the Geneva Conventions. In combination with the phrase that 'an impartial humanitarian body, such as the International Committee of the Red Cross, may offer its services to the Parties to the conflict', Common Article 3 went on to become 'the most striking and useful of all their humanitarian provisions.'[79] Although the final wording of Common Article 3 in the

[75] *Ibid.*
[76] Universal Declaration of Human Rights, General Assembly Resolution 217 A, 10 December 1948, available at: www.ohchr.org/EN/UDHR/Documents/UDHR_Translations/eng.pdf.
[77] Best, *War and Law since 1945*, p. 174. [78] *Ibid.* [79] *Ibid.*

end did not come from the ICRC itself, it is clear that without the original proposal of the ICRC to extend the scope of the Geneva Conventions to non-international armed conflicts, the French proposal would not had been successful. As one can often observe with regard to the drafting of international treaty provisions, sometimes pushing for the maximum goal will ultimately result in at least a minimum achievement.

It is also interesting to observe that no one really knew at the time what 'armed conflict not of an international character' was supposed to mean. Sufficient to know that most people seemed to agree it should not cover 'exploits of bandits or riots of any kind', while it definitely was encompassing civil wars and probably colonial rebellion. In the end, the example of Common Article 3 shows that although the ICRC usually tries to follow a realistic approach towards the development of international humanitarian law, sometimes it can also be beneficial to go beyond and pursue a more utopian approach to achieve a 'small revolution' at least.

3. *Geneva Convention IV: The Protection of Civilians in Armed Conflicts*

The setting up of the Fourth Geneva Convention and its more elaborate provisions for the protection of civilians has been one of the crucial and pivotal achievements of the 1949 Diplomatic Conference. Enhancing the protection of the civilian population in times of war had been on the ICRC's agenda for a long time, even prior to World War II. Obviously, the glaring gap in the legal protection of civilians became strikingly apparent in the time between 1939 and 1945. Above all, World War II had shown the urgent need to regulate the treatment of civilians both in occupied territory and in the territory of the belligerent, and the humanitarian actors made it clear that civilians must be protected as far as the necessities of modern warfare would allow.[80] During World War II, it became obvious that one could distinguish three groups of civilians who were especially affected, namely: (1) so-called 'enemy aliens', i.e. civilians living or moving in a foreign country during the period when their home State would become an official enemy of the State they were travelling in; (2) civilians coming from a country which was under military occupation; and (3) civilians who would be affected by the attacks of enemy States, while being the direct target of that attack or being hit by coincidence.[81]

[80] Best, *War and Law since 1945*, p. 115. [81] *Ibid.*

In the end, the latter category – and with it the clear regulation of the principle of distinction as a rule of the conduct of hostilities – had to wait until later to be regulated. It was to be seen more as part of the 'Hague Law' aspect of International Humanitarian Law, and would only be picked up during the drafting of the Additional Protocols in 1977. And although the ICRC had made it crystal clear during World War II that indiscriminate bombing against civilians, and using the bombing as a means to terrorize the civilian population, was violating the basic principles of international humanitarian law,[82] the Red Cross had to admit that putting this issue on the agenda in Geneva probably would have made things much more difficult during the diplomatic negotiations – not only because there could have been a good argument made for the rule belonging rather to the area of Hague Law, and not Geneva Law.[83]

Nevertheless, the mere fact that a convention for the protection of civilians came into existence owes much gratitude to the work of the ICRC. The emphasis on the protection of civilians already dominated the ICRC's work after World War I. However, the Draft Convention for the Protection of Civilians, which the Committee had prepared in 1934, had not been signed or ratified when World War II broke out in 1939.[84] According to the 1934 draft, the envisaged convention was supposed to cover two categories of civilians: (a) enemy civilians on the territory of a belligerent and (b) civilians in the power of the enemy in occupied territories. The protection of this category of 'enemy civilians' reflected a completely new idea: The provisions on the protection of civilians in occupied territories had the objective to complete and specify the regulations already set forth in Articles 42–56 of the 1907 Hague Regulations.[85] The 1934 Draft Convention prepared by the Commission was adopted at the 15th International Conference of the Red Cross in Tokyo in 1934 and contained four distinct subjects: (1) the status of enemy civilians, (2) enemy civilians on the territory of a belligerent, (3) enemy civilians on the territory occupied by a belligerent, and (4) implementation of the Convention. The draft was to be discussed at the Diplomatic Conference convened by the Swiss government at the beginning of 1940 but the outbreak of World War II prevented

[82] Best, *War and Law since 1945*, p. 106. [83] *Ibid.*

[84] Pictet, 'The New Geneva Conventions for the Protection of War Victims', p. 473.

[85] See Draft International Convention on the Condition and Protection of Civilians of Enemy Nationality who are on Territory Belonging to or Occupied by a Belligerent. Tokyo, 1934; as summarised in the ICRC treaty database, available at: www.icrc.org/applic/ihl/ihl.nsf/Treaty.xsp?action=openDocument&documentId=85EE9A58C871B072C12563CD002D6A15.

the conference from taking place.[86] Governments were not willing to commit to international legal obligations at that time, so the ICRC ultimately – and much to its dismay – had to refrain from announcing a Diplomatic Conference, which had originally been scheduled for early 1940.[87] The consequence was that States were only willing to treat civilians living in enemy territory similar to Prisoners of War, but did not apply the same rules to the protection of civilians in occupied territories.[88] However, the proposals contained in the Tokyo Draft were reconsidered in 1949. They were an important basis for the drafts that eventually led to the adoption of the 1949 Geneva Convention IV (GV IV), which represented a new Convention for the Protection of Civilians, as detailed as that for the Prisoners of War.

Part I of GV IV offers regulations dealing with the general protection of the civilian population against the effects in armed conflict, and this includes one of the most important insertions in the GC IV: the possibility to 'establish hospital and safety zones and localities so organized as to protect from the effects of war, wounded, sick and aged persons, children under fifteen, expectant mothers and mothers of children under seven'. This had been on the ICRC's agenda for quite a while after the bad experiences during World War II, and realizing that these safety zones should be established if possible already 'at times of peace' but also after the 'outbreak of hostilities'.[89] The ICRC had tried in Stockholm in 1948 to introduce a formulation, which was more mandatory with regard to the establishment of these zones ('shall endeavor to set up').[90] Although the final text only included the permissive mode with regard to the establishment of safety zones, even this version has to be seen as a success of the ICRC's influence since at least the possible existence of these zones was acknowledged and made possible. Since the experience of 'total war' between 1939 and 1945, it had been the ICRC's vision to enable the creation of such zones which would be excluded from combat, and which should be established well in advance of the conflicts in which they were supposed to protect especially the civilian population.[91]

The new regulations which were agreed upon in GV IV included general rules for the protection of individuals in both belligerent and occupied

[86] *Ibid.*

[87] Gutteridge, 'The Geneva Convention of 1949', p. 295; New Zealand Red Cross, 'The Red Cross and the Geneva Conventions – 60 Years On', *Victoria University of Wellington Law Review*, 41 (2010), p. 113.

[88] Pictet, 'The new Geneva Conventions for the Protection of War Victims', p. 473.

[89] Best, *War and Law since 1945*, p. 116. [90] *Ibid.*

[91] Best, *War and Law since 1945*, p. 104.

countries (Section II), the protection of 'enemy' civilians in belligerent countries (Section III), and regulations for occupied territories (Section IV).[92] In order to illustrate how the ICRC tried to influence the discussions and enhance the protection of the civilian population, Article 59 GC IV dealing with the Occupying Powers' duties with regard to relief schemes is a good example. As the Rumanian delegate, Dr. Dimitriu, pointed, it had been the ICRC that had highlighted the importance of including a provision like this into Geneva Convention IV:

> The very lengthy debates which took place in Committee III were a proof of the extreme importance of Article 59. While the [version] adopted by the Committee appears more restrictive than that of Stockholm, it is nevertheless the outcome of a compromise solution based on the desire to provide protection for the civilian population. In the course of these debates the Representative of the International Committee of the Red Cross asked us to give the matter our careful attention, and not to leave an Occupying Power complete freedom to send a very large number of civilian persons to their death, perhaps on the strength of some such accusation as attempted homicide.[93]

Another example of the way the ICRC would try to influence the wording of specific provisions can be seen in the context of the article dealing with the beginning and end of hostilities (Draft Article 4), where the ICRC expert pointed out the rationale behind the suggested wording, which in a slightly amended form would find its way into Article 6 GC IV:

> Mr. Pilloud (International Committee of the Red Cross) reminded the Committee that the Conference of Experts, which had drawn up in part the text submitted to the Stockholm Conference, had taken as a basis the provisions of the Prisoners of War Convention. For example, internment should end, in the case of civilians, at the same time as captivity in the case of prisoners of war, viz. at the cessation of hostilities, since hostilities alone justified such measures. [. . .] [He] explained that the clause had been condensed. A distinction must be made between the application of the Convention in national territory and in occupied territory. In national territory the Convention would cease to be applicable at the end of hostilities, whereas in occupied territory it would cease at the end of the occupation.[94]

[92] See also the respective discussions in the drafting committee, cf. Travaux préparatoires, Volume IIA, pp. 812–821; with once again a reference to 'the collaboration of Mr. Claude Pilloud, Expert from the International Red Cross, [which] has been extremely valuable' (p. 812).

[93] Final Record of the Diplomatic Conference of Geneva 1949, Volume II, Section B, Federal Political Department Berne, p. 430.

[94] Final Record of the Diplomatic Conference of Geneva 1949, Volume II, Section B, Federal Political Department Berne, p. 624.

It is unfortunately not possible to trace back the influence of the ICRC on every single provision that was included in the Geneva Conventions, because part of the ICRC's strategy was in the end to leave the final word to the States, since it was the States' sole competence to conclude the final version of the treaty. In that regard, a lot of the decisive work of the ICRC had been done before the conference as described in the first section of this chapter, although the ICRC delegates participated as experts in the Diplomatic Conference. As the ICRC delegate Carry stated at the end of the conference with regard to the voting on Geneva Convention IV, the ICRC's role, and especially concerning Article 5 GC IV:

> The vote which took place just now on the Civilians Convention is the reward of several years of arduous work on the preparation and framing of texts, the urgent necessity of which had long been realized by the International Committee of the Red Cross. Remembering its painful experiences in the past when, in default of formal treaty provisions, its efforts on behalf of civilians in enemy hands were often invalidated, the International Committee of the Red Cross can congratulate itself today on the adoption of a Convention which should have concrete results.
>
> The texts which have been drawn up should serve to remedy a grave deficiency. They include fundamental provisions of great importance. Some of the Articles, however, particularly Article 3A, now Article 5 in the final text, embody restrictions dictated by reasons of national security. The International Committee of the Red Cross after assisting as an expert in the work of the Committees considered that it *was not within its competence to take part in the discussion of the Articles themselves, as these were within the exclusive competence of the Governments.*
>
> But you can scarcely be surprised that the I.C.R.C., which is and should remain exclusively concerned with humanitarian questions, cannot forget the tragic occasions when thousands of human beings were imprisoned and cut off from the world, simply because they were regarded as constituting a danger to the security of the State, and were therefore denied the right of being visited by the Committee. [...] The International Committee of the Red Cross therefore expresses the sincere hope that the High Contracting Parties will interpret this text and also all those which involve any restrictions to the application of the conventions in as wide and humanitarian a spirit as possible, in order to realize to the fullest extent the ideal which has throughout inspired the work of this Conference and which is the fundamental ideal of the Red Cross, namely the elimination from war of all suffering, that is to say all unnecessary suffering.[95]

95 Final Record of the Diplomatic Conference of Geneva 1949, Volume II, Section B, Federal Political Department Berne, p. 526 [italics by author].

Also an interesting new aspect at that time was the provision for a central information agency for civilians, which was supposed to be organized by the ICRC and have the same mandate as the one for Prisoners of War.[96] In general, it can be stated that the ICRC delegates were very active during the drafting process of the Diplomatic conference, and the States seemed willing and happy to rely on the experience of the Committee from its work during World War II.[97]

4. *The Grave Breaches Regime*

Finally, another important area in which the ICRC's involvement both as a driving force as well as in terms of substantive construction was crucial was the innovative 'grave breaches regime' of the 1949 Geneva Conventions. The grave breaches regime introduced the provisions which provided for criminal prosecution of the most serious violations of international humanitarian law. This was in the spirit of the International Military Tribunal's famous statement that 'Crimes against International Law are committed by men, not by abstract entities, and only by punishing individuals who commit such crimes can the provisions of International Law be enforced'.[98] As a consequence, there were voices which advocated for a repression and prosecution of 'war crimes' of certain actions representing violations of the Conventions.[99] As mentioned before, the inclusion of the grave breaches regime had been due to an initiative of the ICRC long before the Diplomatic Conference took place in 1949. Probably the most important step to enable this new aspect of International Humanitarian Law was the establishment by the ICRC of a small group of 'war crimes experts', including Lauterpacht, Mouton, Phillimore, Jean Graven and Max Huber. After the Stockholm Conference, the States had asked the ICRC to initiate further examinations dealing with the repressions of breaches of the Geneva Conventions.

[96] See Pictet, 'The New Geneva Conventions for the Protection of War Victims', 473; see also Gutteridge, 'The Geneva Convention of 1949', pp. 318–325.

[97] For examples of the ICRC delegates' contributions, see Travaux préparatoires, Volume IIB, 138, 139, 140, 468, 526; Volume III, 100, 111.

[98] Judgment of the International Military Tribunal, in The Trial of German Major War Criminals: Proceedings of the International Military Tribunal sitting at Nuremberg, Germany, Part 22, London, 1950, p. 447.

[99] See Gutteridge, 'The Geneva Conventions of 1949', 304; with reference to Report on the Work of the Preliminary Conference of National Red Cross Societies for the study of the Conventions, p. 93 in footnote 2.

The establishment of this little group of experts has to be seen as decisive in order to facilitate consensus on a matter, which had been of great controversy when being discussed among States in the preparation for the Diplomatic Conference in Geneva. The discussion whether to use the term 'war crimes' in the Geneva Conventions had caused much controversy, because one wanted to avoid the impression that any violations not listed as war crimes were excluded from being seen as war crimes. In particular, the United Kingdom objected to any mentioning of the term 'war crimes'.[100] They justified this with the parallel work of the International Law Commission to put the results of the Nuremberg Trial into a General Assembly Resolution.[101] This led to the attitude of the United Kingdom that the term 'war crimes' should not be mentioned at all.[102] The draft articles which came out of the group of experts' discussion solved this problem through the invention of the concept of 'grave breaches' which avoided the war crimes terminology, although everyone knew what these breaches were supposed to mean, especially because they were coined as 'crimes against the law of nations' and there was an obligation to 'undertake to extradite for trial elsewhere if they would not bring to trial themselves'.[103] They even included a reference with regard to the rule that it was supposed to exclude the 'superior orders defence' and at the same time establish 'full responsibility [...] to the person giving the order'.[104] While the first version of the common articles on grave breaches was too progressive for most of the States, and it was necessary to cut down the wording, including the reference to the crimes against the law of nations or the superior order provisions,[105] the grave breaches regime as such survived the Diplomatic Conference and is seen as one of the major achievements of the 'new' Geneva Conventions, establishing the obligation of the High Contracting parties 'to enact any legislation necessary to provide effective penal sanctions for persons committing, or ordering to be committed, any of the grave breaches of the (respective) Convention defined in the following article'.[106] The influence of the ICRC's work on the grave breaches regime can be seen in the Fourth Report drawn up by the Special Committee of the Joint Committee which illustrated that States would use the articles proposed by the ICRC as their own amendment:

[100] Gutteridge, 'The Geneva Conventions of 1949', 305.

[101] *Ibid.*, with reference to General Assembly Resolution 177 (11), adopted at the 123rd Plenary Meeting on 21 November 1947.

[102] Summary of the contents of FO 369/3966 K. 2487, registered on 16 February 1948.

[103] Best, *War and Law since 1945*, p. 161.

[104] *Ibid.*

[105] Best, *War and Law since 1945*, p. 163.

[106] Common Articles 49, 50, 130, 147 GC I–IV.

> The Joint Committee itself dealt, in its Sixth Meeting of 4 May, with the question of whether the Stockholm text of the Articles 39–40/43–44/119/130 or the corresponding articles in 'Remarks and Proposals' of the Red Cross should serve as a basis for discussion. The Netherlands Delegation *had tabled the International Committee of the Red Cross' Articles as their own amendment*. This amendment has been replaced by the joint amendment submitted by the Netherlands, Australia, Belgium, Brazil, the United States of America, France, Italy, Norway, the United Kingdom and Switzerland [. . .] The basic document was the Stockholm text containing corrections as indicated in the rectifying note submitted by the I.C.R.C.[107]

However, in the end it became also clear that the States would not go as far as suggested by the ICRC's draft insofar as the article on grave breaches was included in the Geneva Conventions, while the reference to an international jurisdiction was omitted:

> [T]he Stockholm Conference had, in Resolution XXIII, expressed the wish that the International Committee of the Red Cross should continue its work on the repression of abuses and infractions of the humanitarian Conventions and should submit a proposal on the subject to a subsequent Conference. For this reason the International Committee of the Red Cross convened a Committee of Experts in December 1948, which prepared new texts; these appear in the 'Remarks and Proposals' of the International Committee of the Red Cross [. . .]. This Draft contained comparatively far-reaching innovations, which impinged on the domain of international penal law.
>
> The Special Committee of the Joint Committee considered it advisable to proceed more cautiously; it followed the lead of the Experts Committee in devoting a special article to "grave" violations, but without any reference to an international jurisdiction.[108]

Overall, it was stated during the Diplomatic Conference that 'the proposals made by the International Committee of the Red Cross were gratefully used'.[109] As a consequence, the member States have since then been obliged to either prosecute or extradite persons 'alleged to have committed, or to have ordered to be committed, such grave breaches'. As is well-known, the practical relevance of the grave breaches regime has not been as important as the drafters probably envisaged it to be, mainly because the High Contracting Parties were rather reluctant to initiate war crimes proceedings against both their own nationals or citizens of third States.

[107] Final Record of the Diplomatic Conference of Geneva 1949, Volume II, Section B, Federal Political Department Berne, p. 114 [italics by author].

[108] *Ibid*., p. 134. [109] *Ibid*., p. 114.

Nevertheless, one needs to take into account that without the grave breaches regime as initiated by the ICRC and passed by the States in 1949, the establishment of the ICTY in 1993, the ICTR in 1994, and the ICC in 1998/2002 would have been much harder to achieve. This already becomes obvious by the fact that all of the previously mentioned courts and tribunals with a jurisdiction covering international armed conflicts have incorporated the grave breaches regime into their Statutes, usually as the first and undisputed part of the war crimes provision(s). For example, according to Article 2 of the ICTY Statute '[t]he International Tribunal shall have the power to prosecute persons committing or ordering to be committed grave breaches of the Geneva Conventions of 12 August 1949'. Furthermore, under Article 8(1) and (2)(a) of the ICC Statute, '[T]he Court shall have jurisdiction in respect of war crimes [. . .]. For the purpose of this Statute, "war crimes" means: (a) Grave breaches of the Geneva Conventions of 12 August 1949 [. . .].' The drafters of the ICTY/ICTR Statutes, the Judges of the said Tribunals, as well as the member States of the Rome Statute, have frequently referred to the grave breaches regime, and in most Statutes of International Criminal Courts and Tribunals, they are part of the material jurisdiction of the respective institutions.[110]

IV. The ICRC's Influence on the Geneva Conventions After 1949

The previous sections of this chapter have highlighted the role of the ICRC especially with regard to the preparation and drafting of the Four Geneva Conventions, showing that the ICRC has not only acted as the guardian of existing international humanitarian law rules, but that it also takes on the responsibility to support new treaty texts and to engage in the diplomatic discussion with States. However, this is not the only function which the ICRC has exercised with regard to the Geneva Conventions. While the treaty text as such obviously takes pride of place, there are other aspects which should not be forgotten.

First of all, one of the most important tools for the application of the Geneva Conventions in practice as well as in academia is the official ICRC

[110] For an instructive overview of the role of the grave breaches regime in international criminal law, refer to C. Byron, '*War Crimes and Crimes Against Humanity in the Rome Statute of the International Criminal Court*', (Manchester: Manchester University Press 2009), Chapter 2: War Crimes (I): grave breaches; see also R. Cryer et al., *An Introduction to International Criminal Law and Procedure*, (3rd ed., Cambridge: Cambridge University Press 2014), Chapter 12.1.5 The Relationship between War Crimes and IHL, pp. 268–269, and Chapter 12.1.6 A Brief History of the Law of War Crimes, pp. 269–271.

Commentary which was published between 1952 and 1959 in four volumes, and until today remains one of the main sources for the interpretation of the provisions of the Geneva Conventions. The commentary was written and published under the general editorship of Jean S. Pictet, then Director for General Affairs of the ICRC, and also one of the ICRC delegates taking part in the 1949 Diplomatic Conference. Under his leadership, the authors went through article by article, Convention by Convention, and offered helpful information about the drafting and meaning of every provision, and also offering examples of how certain issues had been dealt with in the past. For example, while the Geneva Conventions remain rather vague about the meaning of the term 'armed conflict', the commentary goes into more detail when stating that '[a]ny difference arising between two States and leading to the intervention of members of the armed forces [. . .] even if one of the parties denies the existence of a state of war.'[111]

However, it is obvious that a series of commentaries, which were published between 1952 and 1959, are limited to the negotiating history and the view of legal experts at the time. This is the reason why now the ICRC under the leadership of Jean-Marie Henckaerts is in the process of updating the Commentaries on the 1949 Geneva Conventions as well as on the 1977 Additional Protocols.[112] In this regard, the ICRC is again taking on the responsibility to enable practitioners and academics to apply the law of 1949 to current situations appearing in the twenty-first century, taking also into account the change in the type of conflicts, and a new understanding of certain concepts from the side of States. Areas which obviously are in need of an update are, for example, Common Article 1 with its obligation for Member States to 'undertake and ensure respect for the (respective) Convention in all circumstances'. The scope of this obligation has 'significantly expanded since the 1950s'.[113] Other examples encompass the understanding of the rights and obligations surrounding humanitarian activities and the abilities of 'any other impartial humanitarian organization' as well as the very important field of occupation law.[114] In updating the commentaries, the ICRC is able not only to draw on their long-existing experience in the area of the law of armed conflict, but will

[111] J. S. Pictet, *Commentary to the Geneva Conventions*, 1952, vol. I, Common Article 2, p. 31.

[112] J.-M. Henckaerts, 'Bringing the Commentaries on the Geneva Conventions and Their Additional Protocols to the Twenty-First Century', Interview, available at: www.icrc.org/eng/resources/documents/interview/2012/geneva-conventions-commentaries-interview-2012-07-12.htm.

[113] *Ibid.* [114] *Ibid.*

also take into account the expertise of outside experts which will be able to contribute through a series of expert meetings.[115] With the first Commentary on the First Geneva Convention having been published in 2016, the international community can of course once again hope that the ICRC is fulfilling its mandate as the guardian of the Geneva Conventions.

In 2005, the ICRC created another milestone with regard to the understanding and developing of the law laid down in the 1949 Geneva Convention: the two-volume 'Customary International Humanitarian Law' Study, edited by Louise Doswald-Beck and Jean-Marie Henckaerts. As a result of a ten-year expert process, the Customary Law Study showed which rules of international humanitarian law are to be seen as customary law, and are applicable either in international armed conflicts, in non-international armed conflicts, or in both. Although this study is of course in no way binding, the mere fact that the Study offers two big volumes of State Practice and many references to international and national jurisprudence, makes it very authoritative. Although some member States, like the United States and Israel, have published letters in which they reflect doubts about the methodology of the Study, and expressly contradict some of the results which were found by it, in general the Study has contributed to a better understanding of the law governing armed conflict. And most importantly for our topic of interest, the ICRC's influence on the Geneva Conventions, it has made clear that the most important rules of the four Conventions are deemed to be seen as customary law.[116]

V. Conclusion

Although for lawyers acting in the field of international humanitarian law, it is almost natural to accept the special role that the ICRC has played for now more than 150 years since the creation of the First Geneva Convention, it should not be taken for granted. Although international law has come a long way since 1864, it is still an area of law which is very much dominated by sovereign States which have certain interests, and are rarely willing to give up any power, making clear who the real creators of international law are. In this regard, it is even more important to highlight that the ICRC was able before, during, and after the creation of the 1949 Geneva

[115] *Ibid.*

[116] For an extensive discussion and overview of the Customary Law Study, *cf.*, e.g., E. Wilmshurst and S. Breau, *Perspectives on the ICRC Study on Customary International Humanitarian Law* (Cambridge: Cambridge University Press, 2011).

Conventions to stress, emphasise and put forward the humanitarian concerns which need to be taken into account during times of armed conflict. It is also crucial to reiterate that the ICRC must be seen as probably the first non-State actor to influence the legislative process of an international convention. More than 150 years ago when international affairs were still very much State-dominated, this was almost a revolution. Until now there is nothing that compares to this, even though we now can refer to other drafting processes where NGOs more and more play an important role. One might think of the fact that during the drafting of the Rome Statute in 1998 more than 200 NGOs participated in the deliberations. In contrast to NGO actors, the ICRC of course has a special role with regard to the Geneva Conventions because of the original inception of the Geneva Conventions, but it has also much to do with the special and careful approach towards the States, which the ICRC has used over the years. Even if the ICRC had the advantage of 'being there from the start', there are many ways one could think of how the Committee might have lost this position. And there were obviously moments in history where this could have happened. After World War II, there were voices which indicated that the ICRC should be dissolved and their functions handed over to the National Red Cross Societies.[117] However, through the work of the ICRC's independent experts and its skilled guidance through the whole process, the new Conventions 'recognized its special status as a neutral intermediary and entrusted it with new tasks for the protection of war victims'.[118] Therefore, the ICRC's role has over and again been affirmed by the States, which finally are deciding on the way in which international law should develop.

In conclusion, it is important to stress the crucial role of the ICRC in the setting up, drafting and further development of the law of the Geneva Conventions. The ICRC was the main actor that initiated the process of reviewing the three already-existing Geneva Conventions and drafting a new Fourth Geneva Convention dealing with the protection of civilians. In cooperation with the League of Red Cross National Societies, the individual national Red Cross and Red Crescent Societies, government representatives as well as international law experts, this led to the drafts which were the basis for the 1949 Diplomatic Conference during which States'

[117] The Soviet Union was of the opinion that the ICRC had failed in protecting Soviet prisoners of war who were in the hands of German troops, and therefore did for some time not see the ICRC as keeping this important role with regard to the Geneva Conventions, cf. Bugnion, 'The Geneva Conventions of 12 August 1949: From the 1949 Diplomatic Conference to the Dawn of the New Millennium', 43.

[118] *Ibid.*

representatives agreed on the current version of the four Geneva Conventions. As has been elaborated earlier, this included important changes to the then-existing regime of international humanitarian law, like (1) the further refinement of the scope of application of IHL with regard to 'armed conflicts', (2) introducing for the first time IHL rules for 'non-international' armed conflict, (3) setting up detailed provisions for the protection of civilians, especially in occupied territories, and finally (4) codifying that certain 'grave breaches' of the Geneva Conventions would lead to penal consequences. In an area of law which is dominated by a constant search for the balance between military necessity and the principles of humanity, it is indispensable to have an actor who ensures that the latter is upheld and not sacrificed to motives which might make sense from a perspective of a military commander, but might forget the interests of the weak and unprotected. Although they are not given legislative power in this context, the ICRC's role together with the other components of the Red Cross and Red Crescent movement can therefore not be underestimated. From a general Public International Law perspective, the influence of the ICRC with regard to the drafting and signing of the Geneva Conventions might also have paved the way for a still ongoing process of a change of the legislative process in international law, giving non-State actors a more important role and influence in this procedure. In this regard, the ICRC might be at the forefront of a development which has not yet reached its climax.

2

The International Committee of the Red Cross and the Additional Protocols of 1977

MICHAEL BOTHE

I. The History of the Additional Protocols of 1977

It is the traditional role of the International Committee of the Red Cross (ICRC) to prepare draft treaties for the purpose of developing international humanitarian law (IHL), in particular by filling regulatory loopholes.[1] In doing so, it tried in particular to address regulatory insufficiencies which had become apparent in recent conflicts. In this spirit, the four Geneva Conventions of 1949 (GC)[2] were a reaction to the experiences of World War II and conflicts which had happened before that war, in particular the Spanish Civil War. But the four Conventions left aside one crucial area of the law of armed conflict which had been violated during the war – to an extent that one could think it had become obsolete – namely the law relating to the conduct of hostilities[3] and the protection of the civilian population against the harmful effects of hostilities.[4] The

[1] J. Pictet, 'General Introduction' in Y. Sandoz, C. Swinarski and B. Zimmermann (eds.), *ICRC Commentary on the Additional Protocols of 8 June 1977 to the Geneva Conventions of 12 August 1949* (Geneva: Martinus Nijhoff Publishers, 1987), pp. xxix–xxxv, p. xxix; M. Bothe and K. J. Partsch, 'General Introduction and Guide to Documentation' in M. Bothe, K. J. Partsch and W. A. Solf, *New Rules for Victims of Armed Conflicts, Commentary on the Two 1977 Protocols Additional to the Geneva Conventions of 1949* 2nd ed., reprint revised by M. Bothe (The Hague/Boston/London: Martinus Njihoff Publishers, 2015), pp. 1–16, pp. 1 *et seq*.

[2] The four Geneva Conventions of 12 August 1949 for the Protection of War Victims, Geneva, 12 August 1949, in force 21 October 1950, 75 UNTS.

[3] Pictet, 'General Introduction', note 1, p. xxix.

[4] ICRC, Foreword to the Final Act of the Diplomatic Conference of Geneva of 1974–1977, www.icrc.org/applic/ihl/ihl.nsf/Treaty.xsp?documentId=D7D9F26C38F99332C12563CD002D6CB8&action=openDocument; E. Crawford, 'Geneva Conventions Additional Protocol I (1977)' in R. Wolfrum (ed.), *The Max Planck Encyclopedia of Public International Law* (Oxford: Oxford University Press, May 2011), www.mpepil.com, MN 3.

ICRC was well aware of this and its efforts did not cease with the end of the 1949 Conference.

At the XIXth International Red Cross Conference held in New Delhi in 1957, the ICRC submitted the *Draft Rules for the Limitation of the Dangers incurred by the Civilian Population in Time of War*, the so-called Delhi Rules.[5] At the Conference, they became the object of major controversies, in particular regarding the (il)legality of nuclear weapons.[6] The Delhi Rules *inter alia* encompassed provisions, protecting the civilian population from the destructive force of newly developed weapons, accounting for the rapid technological advance.[7] Article 14 (1) of the Delhi Rules was seen as a reprobation of nuclear weapons, on which agreement at the time was not possible.[8] The conference ultimately did not adopt the Rules, but only took note of them and requested the ICRC to submit them, together with the amendments which had been proposed, to governments. The ICRC did as requested but did not receive a response. Nevertheless, the Delhi Rules had an impact on the ensuing development. Many provisions finally adopted in the 1977 Protocols additional to the Geneva Conventions resemble the corresponding provisions of the Delhi Rules.[9]

The ICRC continued its effort in adopting new resolutions at the XXth and XXIst International Conferences of the Red Cross, held in Vienna in 1965 and Istanbul in 1969. In 1965, Resolution XXVIII was adopted, which contained four principles relating to the 'Protection of the Civilian

[5] ICRC, Draft Rules for the Limitation of the Dangers incurred by the Civilian Population in Time of War (Geneva, September 1956), www.icrc.org/ihl/INTRO/420.

[6] Bothe and Partsch, 'General Introduction and Guide to Documentation', note 1, p. 2; Pictet, 'General Introduction', note 1, p. xxix; J. Pokstefl and M. Bothe, 'Bericht über Entwicklungen und Tendenzen des Kriegsrechts seit den Nachkriegskodifikationen', *Zeitschrift für ausländisches öffentliches Recht und Völkerrecht*, 35 (1975), pp. 574–640, p. 575.

[7] ICRC, Foreword to the Draft Rules for the Limitation of the Dangers incurred by the Civilian Population in Time of War (Geneva, September 1956), www.icrc.org/ihl/INTRO/420.

[8] 'Without prejudice to the present or future prohibition of certain specific weapons, the use is prohibited of weapons whose harmful effects – resulting in particular from the dissemination of incendiary, chemical, bacteriological, radioactive or other agents – could spread to an unforeseen degree or escape, either in space or in time, from the control of those who employ them, thus endangering the civilian population'; C. Pilloud and J. Pictet, 'Protocol I – Part IV, Section 1' in Y. Sandoz, C. Swinarski and B. Zimmermann (eds.), *ICRC Commentary on the Additional Protocols of 8 June 1977 to the Geneva Conventions of 12 August 1949* (Geneva: Martinus Nijhoff Publishers, 1987), pp. 585–804, p. 590.

[9] M. Bothe, K. Ipsen and K. J. Partsch, 'Die Genfer Konferenz über humanitäres Völkerrecht', *Zeitschrift für ausländisches und öffentliches Recht und Völkerrecht*, 38 (1978), pp. 1–159, p. 40.

Populations Against the Dangers of Indiscriminate Warfare' and which urged 'the ICRC to pursue the development of International Humanitarian Law'.[10]

In addition, a number of events made the development of IHL more urgent. It appeared to be especially important to strengthen the protection of victims of non-international armed conflicts (NIAC) beyond the scope of Common Article 3 GC.[11] Coinciding with the rapidly rising number of NIAC was a proportional increase of the civilian participation therein.[12] Moreover, the techniques of these new participants were unconventional, as they utilized guerrilla tactics.[13] Furthermore, the interest in the law of armed conflicts was reinvigorated in the mid-1960s by a number of armed conflicts which split world opinion,[14] such as the conflicts in Vietnam,[15] the Middle East[16] and the struggles against colonial and alien domination and racist regimes, the so-called wars of national liberation.[17] All this provided an impetus for further development of IHL.

An additional driving force came from the concern for human rights.[18] The UN International Conference on Human Rights, convened 1968 in Teheran, marked an important starting point, since it lead to the adoption of Resolution 2444 (1969) by the General Assembly, affirming the need for basic human rights to be applied in all armed conflicts.[19] In the

[10] Bothe and Partsch, 'General Introduction and Guide to Documentation', note 1, p. 2; Pictet, 'General Introduction', p. xxx; ICRC, Final Act of the Diplomatic Conference of Geneva of 1974–1977, www.icrc.org/applic/ihl/ihl.nsf/Treaty.xsp?documentId=D7D9F26C38F99332C12563CD002D6CB8&action=openDocument.

[11] ICRC, Foreword to Additional Protocol (II) to the Geneva Conventions (1977), www.icrc.org/applic/ihl/ihl.nsf/Treaty.xsp?documentId=AA0C5BCBAB5C4A85C12563CD002D6D09&action=openDocument (ICRC, Foreword AP II).

[12] According to the ICRC about 80 per cent of the victims of armed conflicts since 1945 have been victims of NIAC and NIAC are often fought more cruelly than international conflicts; ICRC, Foreword AP II.

[13] Crawford, 'Geneva Conventions Additional Protocol I (1977)', note 4, MN 3.

[14] *Ibid.*; Bothe and Partsch, 'General Introduction and Guide to Documentation', note 1, p. 2.

[15] The Vietnam Conflict raised in particular questions regarding the rules concerning the conduct of hostilities and the status of 'irregular' fighters.

[16] Especially the problem of human rights in occupied territories, e.g. the occupied Palestinian territories, Bothe and Partsch, 'General Introduction and Guide to Documentation', note 1, pp. 2 *et seq.*

[17] D. W. Glazier, 'Wars of National Liberation' in MPEPIL, note 4, MN 1.

[18] Crawford, 'Geneva Conventions Additional Protocol II (1977)', note 4, MN 5; S. Junod, 'General Introduction to the Commentary on Protocol II' in MPEPIL, note 4, *ICRC Commentary*, note 1, pp. 1319–1336, pp. 1326 *et seq.*

[19] *Ibid.*

following years, a competition developed between the Red Cross (ICRC and Red Cross Movement) and the UN, relating to leadership in the process of developing the relevant legal rules.[20] The problems of specific political situations mainly sought their forum in the UN. But the ICRC, submitting a wealth of thoughtful material to the international community, with the support of Switzerland as depositary of the Geneva Conventions, managed to retain its leadership role. The ICRC, so to say, had the better ideas. An essential step was the submission of eight volumes of material submitted to the Red Cross Conference 1969 in Istanbul.[21]

II. The Diplomatic Conference on the Reaffirmation and Development of International Humanitarian Law Applicable in Armed Conflicts in Geneva from 1974 to 1977: Preparation and Main Results

Similar to the procedure before the 1949 conference, the ICRC convened and serviced two *Conferences of Government Experts on the Reaffirmation and Development of International Humanitarian Law Applicable in Armed Conflicts* in Geneva from 24 May to 12 June 1971 and from 3 May to 3 June 1972 to which it presented its proposals and ideas.[22] About forty government delegations attended the first conference.[23] The ICRC did not present a draft to the experts, but a list of the most important problems of humanitarian law.[24] The second session comprised more than 400 experts sent by 77 governments, most of them from Western Countries.[25] The main issues submitted to the Conference were for example methods and means of warfare, especially new forms of warfare like guerrilla

[20] R. R. Baxter, 'Humanitarian Law or Humanitarian Politics? The 1974 Diplomatic Conference on Humanitarian Law', *Harvard International Law Journal* 16 (1975), pp. 1–26, 5 *et seq*.

[21] XXIe Conférence internationale de la Croix-Rouge, ICRC 'In the Red Cross worldwide', *International Review of the Red Cross*, 51 (1969), 589; Bothe and Partsch, 'General Introduction and Guide to Documentation', p. 3.

[22] Bothe and Partsch, 'General Introduction and Guide to Documentation', note 1, p. 3; Pictet, 'General Introduction', note 1, p. xxxi.

[23] ICRC, *Draft Protocols additional to the Geneva Conventions of 12 August 1949, Commentary* (Geneva: ICRC, 1973), p. 1.

[24] Junod, 'General Introduction to the Commentary on Protocol II', in ICRC Commentary, note 1, p. 1327.

[25] Bothe and Partsch, 'General Introduction and Guide to Documentation', note 1, p. 3; Pictet, 'General Introduction', p. xxxi; H. Frick, 'Ein neues Kapitel im humanitären Kriegsvölkerrecht? Zwei Zusatzprotokolle zu den Vier Genfer Rotkreuzkonventionen kurz vor der Verabschiedung', *Vereinte Nationen*, 24 (1976), pp. 178–184, p. 180.

warfare and the protection of the civilian population against the dangers of hostilities as well as a better protection of the victims of NIAC.[26] Subsequently, in 1973 the ICRC published two draft Protocols additional to the Geneva Conventions, one relating to international, the other to NIAC and sent them to all governments, accompanied by a commentary.[27] Thus, the ICRC handed the texts over to the States and their decision-making power.[28]

The two draft Protocols constituted the basic working documents for the *Diplomatic Conference on the Reaffirmation and Development of International Humanitarian Law Applicable in Armed Conflicts* (CDDH) from 1974 to 1977 in Geneva.[29] The CDDH was convened and organized by the Swiss government and all States which were parties to the Geneva Conventions or members of the United Nations were invited.[30] All in all 155 nations attended, 11 national liberation movements and 51 intergovernmental or non-governmental organizations participated as observers, so that the total number of delegates ranged around 700.[31] The Conference held four sessions from 1974 to 1977.[32] The first meeting was from 20 February to 29 March 1974, the second from 3 February to 18 April 1975, the third from 21 April to 11 June 1976 and the fourth from 17 March to 10 June 1977.[33] The number of the participating States varied from 107 to 124 in the various sessions.[34] The Conference was subdivided into three *Main Committees*, one *Ad hoc Committee* on 'conventional weapons',[35] all four committees of the whole. In addition, there were a Credentials Committee, a Drafting Committee, and a General Committee as well as numerous working groups.[36]

[26] Bothe and Partsch, 'General Introduction and Guide to Documentation', note 1, pp. 3 *et seq.*

[27] ICRC, *Draft Protocols additional to the Geneva Conventions of 12 August 1949, Commentary*; Bothe and Partsch, 'General Introduction and Guide to Documentation', note 1, p. 4; Pictet, 'General Introduction', note 1, p. xxxi.

[28] Pictet, 'General Introduction', note 1, p. xxxii.

[29] Bothe and Partsch, 'General Introduction and Guide to Documentation', p. 4.

[30] Pictet, 'General Introduction', note 1, pp. xxxii *et seq.* [31] *Ibid.*, p. xxxiii.

[32] Bothe and Partsch, 'General Introduction and Guide to Documentation', note 1, p. 4; Pictet, 'General Introduction', note 1, p. xxxii.

[33] *Ibid.* [34] *Ibid.*, p. xxxiii.

[35] The special designation as 'Ad hoc Committee' reflects the unwillingness of a great number of States to negotiate at the Conference the prohibition of specific weapons. The report adopted by that Committee later was an important basis for the UN Conference on Conventional Weapons in 1980.

[36] Bothe and Partsch, 'General Introduction and Guide to Documentation', note 1, pp. 4 *et seq.*

Although the preparatory conferences just mentioned provided a broad input from all parts of the world, the conceptual work of the ICRC was the decisive foundation for the elaboration of these two treaties. A major conceptual and political point was that the conference was only tasked with the development and confirmation. There could not be any revision or retrogression. The text of the Conventions had to be left intact.[37] This sometimes resulted in difficult drafting problems and makes several elements of the text difficult to read and understand. The two Protocols were finally adopted by consensus on 8 June 1977.[38] The representatives of 102 States and of 3 National Liberation Movements signed the Final Act on 10 June 1977.[39]

III. ICRC Leadership: The Procedures of the CDDH

The Conference was convened by the Swiss Federal Council.[40] The Head of the Political Department (as it then was) was the President of Conference. Nevertheless, the day-to-day impact of the team of the ICRC was essential. ICRC representatives were involved in the work of the conference as experts and called upon to participate continuously, particularly in presenting orally the articles of the draft Protocols.[41] A representative of the ICRC was on the podium of each of the Conference Commissions and of the plenary.[42] He or she spoke when necessary and participated in the negotiations, also in the informal negotiations. The impact of this participation varied depending on the issues and persons involved. The head of

[37] Bothe and Partsch, 'General Introduction and Guide to Documentation', note 1, p. 6 *et seq.*

[38] *Official Records of the Diplomatic Conference on the Reaffirmation and Development of International Humanitarian Law Applicable in Armed Conflicts, Geneva, 1974–1977*, vols. I–XVII (Bern: Federal Political Department, 1978), vol. VII, CDDH/SR. 56, paras 4 and 62 (*Official Records*). Protocol Additional to the Geneva Conventions of 12 August 1949, and relating to the Protection of Victims of International Armed Conflicts (Protocol I), Geneva, 8 June 1977, in force 7 December 1978, 1125 UNTS; Protocol Additional to the Geneva Conventions of 12 August 1949, and relating to the Protection of Victims of Non-International Armed Conflicts (Protocol II), adopted 8 June 1977, in force 7 December 1978, 1125 UNTS; Bothe and Partsch, 'General Introduction and Guide to Documentation', p. 5; Pictet, 'General Introduction', pp. xxxiii *et seq.*

[39] Text reproduced in D. Schindler and J. Toman (eds.), *The Laws of Armed Conflicts*, 4th ed. (Leiden/Boston: Nijhoff, 2004), p. 699. Israel did not sign the Final Act.

[40] Bothe and Partsch, 'General Introduction and Guide to Documentation', note 1, p. 4; Pictet, 'General Introduction', note 1, p. xxxii.

[41] Pictet, 'General Introduction', note 1, p. xxxiii.

[42] Bothe and Partsch, 'General Introduction and Guide to Documentation', pp. 10 *et seq.*

the ICRC delegation was Jean Pictet, then vice-president of the ICRC, the great champion of international humanitarian law, and respected coordinator of the work on the ICRC Commentaries to the four Geneva Conventions. His knowledge and devotion certainly had an impact. Just one example of his personal input: When in the debate there appeared a real threat that the protection of air crews descending in distress might be watered down (now Article 42 AP I) by an attempt to exclude that protection when they were drifting to areas controlled by the party to which they belonged[43], he launched a fervent appeal to uphold the fundamental principle of international humanitarian law: attacks against persons who are *hors de combat* are prohibited.[44] That view prevailed in the end.[45]

IV. Comparison of the 1973 Draft and the Final Text of 1977

The drafts submitted in 1973 took into consideration most of the views given by the experts of the Government Experts Conference.[46] But the ICRC did not include all proposals made at these conferences, as the ICRC could not agree to a number of them or because the proposals brought forward were contradictory.[47]

1. *Protocol I: Protection of Victims of International Armed Conflicts*

The proposals of the ICRC concerning Protocol I were largely accepted by the Conference.[48] Several controversial issues had already been abandoned as a result of the previous resistance encountered at the Government Experts Conference. For example, a special distinctive sign for doctors who were not 'medical personnel' in the sense of the Protocol or the general provision on reprisals was abandoned.[49] Most provisions of the 1973 Protocol I draft were adopted without diminishing the protective content. Only in a few cases, the ICRC proposals were seriously

[43] *Official Records*, vol. VI, pp. 104–110, CDDH/SR. 39.

[44] *Official Records*, vol. VI, pp. 106–107, CDDH/SR. 39, para. 88 *et seq.*

[45] *Cf.* W. A. Solf, 'Article 42 – Occupants of aircraft', *New Rules*, note 1, pp. 258–264, pp. 256 *et seq.*; J. de Preux, 'Article 42 – Occupants of aircraft' in *ICRC Commentary*, note 1, pp. 493–503, p. 495.

[46] Pictet, 'General Introduction', note 1, p. xxxi.

[47] *Ibid.*

[48] Bothe, 'introduction', in New Rules, note 1, p. 17; Pictet, 'General Introduction', note 1, p. xxxiv.

[49] Bothe, note 48, p. 17.

modified, for example the provisions on objects indispensable to the survival of the civilian population, works and installations containing dangerous forces, extradition and superior orders.[50] Some rules were significantly developed, for example Article 11 ('Protection of persons'), Article 29 ('Notifications and agreements concerning medical aircrafts') as well as Article 75 ('Fundamental guarantees').[51] Furthermore, a few new elements were added to the ICRC proposals, in particular the provisions on mercenaries, journalists, missing and dead persons and the International Fact-Finding Commission.[52]

2. *Protocol II: Protection of Victims of Non-International Armed Conflicts*

One of the main aims of the Conference of Government Experts in 1971 and 1972 was to offer better protection for the victims of NIAC.[53] In the consultations preceding the Diplomatic Conference, it had even been suggested to adopt a uniform protocol relating to the protection of civilian populations in all armed conflicts, but on the basis of the expert discussions the ICRC decided to draft a separate Additional Protocol containing rules for non-international conflicts.[54]

The 1973 draft contained 47 articles, divided into eight parts and had four main concepts:[55] Firstly, that it should apply to all conflicts which do not take place between States, including wars of national liberation. Secondly, that the definition of the field of application should be similar to that in Common Article 3 of the Geneva Conventions.[56] Thirdly, that a

[50] See the synoptic table in Bothe and Partsch, New Rules, note 1, p. 19 *et seq.*

[51] Further examples: Articles 22, 23, 28, 36, 51, 61–63 AP I; Bothe and Partsch, 'Introduction', note 1, p. 18.

[52] *Ibid.*

[53] M. Bothe and K. J. Partsch, 'Introduction to Protocol II' in M. Bothe, K. J. Partsch and W. Solf, (eds.), *New Rules for Victims of Armed Conflicts, Commentary on the Two 1977 Protocols Additional to the Geneva Conventions of 1949* (The Hague/Boston/London: Martinus Njihoff Publishers, 1982), pp. 604–618, p. 604.

[54] Crawford, 'Geneva Conventions Additional Protocol I (1977)', note 4, MN 14; Bothe and Partsch, 'Introduction', p. 693; Junod, 'General Introduction to the Commentary on Protocol II', in ICRC Commentary, note 1, p. 1333. Norway still maintained the proposal of a single Protocol during the Diplomatic Conference.

[55] Junod, 'General Introduction to the Commentary on Protocol II', ibid., p. 1333; *Official Records*, vol. I, Part Three, pp. 33 *et seq.*

[56] Common Article 3 of the GC and AP II coexist. This is a fundamental change in comparison with the 1972 draft. The ICRC accepted the point of view expressed by numerous experts, that it is desirable that Common Article 3 and Protocol II should coexist autonomously: In fact, to link the Protocol to Common Article 3 would have resulted in

relatively high standard of protection should be guaranteed to the civilian population, persons in the power of another Party to the conflict and also to the members of armed forces or of comparable units on the insurgent side, by limiting the use of methods and means of combat. And finally, that these guarantees should be granted to both sides of the conflicts on the basis of complete equality.[57] In general, the original draft of Protocol II and the version adopted during the Committee phase of the Conference were far more comprehensive in scope and detail, similar to AP I, as both were discussed at the same time, than the document that was finally adopted.[58] The reluctance of a number of delegates, which will be discussed in greater detail in the next chapter, lead to a simplified version, containing only the essential rules. A comparison of the Committee draft with the simplified draft shows that in the latter, Part VI on means and methods of combat,[59] Part VI on relief[60] and Part VIII on the execution of the Protocol as well as the terms 'parties to the conflict', the 'adverse Party' or even 'adversary' were deleted.[61] Not everyone was satisfied with the result, but finally the AP II was adopted by consensus too.[62] Those who had favoured a protocol containing a higher level of protection had to concede that it was better to have 'half an egg instead of only an empty shell'.[63]

3. *Evaluation*

Despite all the difficulties, especially the inevitable political nature of many debates,[64] it must be emphasised that the result of the conference *grosso modo* corresponds to the ICRC draft as far as AP I is concerned. As to AP II, at least essential elements of the ICRC draft were maintained. It is also

restricting the latter's scope of application. Junod, 'General Introduction to the Commentary on Protocol II', in ICRC Commentary, note 1, p. 1328.

[57] Bothe and Partsch, 'Introduction', in New Rules, note 1, p. 693.

[58] Crawford, 'Geneva Conventions Additional Protocol I (1977)', MN 14; Junod, 'General Introduction to the Commentary on Protocol II', p. 1334; Bothe and Partsch, 'Introduction', p. 606.

[59] Its basic principles are enshrined in Article 4 AP II ('Fundamental guarantees'), ICRC, Foreword AP II.

[60] The provisions concerning impartial humanitarian organizations were adopted in a less binding form than originally foreseen, Articles 33–35 of the ICRC draft, now only Article 18 AP II; ICRC, Foreword AP II.

[61] Bothe and Partsch, 'Introduction', in New Rules, note 1, p. 695; Junod, 'General Introduction to the Commentary on Protocol II', ICRC Commentary, note 1, p. 1335.

[62] *Ibid.*, p. 1336.

[63] Expression used by Bloembergen, Netherlands; see Bothe and Partsch, 'Introduction', p. 607.

[64] Pictet, 'General Introduction', note 1, p. xxxiv.

noteworthy that almost all of the provisions were adopted by consensus. Indeed, of the 150 articles of the two Protocols, only 14 required a formal vote. Several draft articles and proposals were not put to a vote.[65] Countries from all regions of the world participated in the codification.[66] AP I currently has 174 State Parties and AP II 168 State Parties.[67]

V. Underestimated Problems and Loopholes

While recognizing the overall decisive and positive impact of the ICRC, there is no denying the fact that it underestimated certain difficulties and left a few loopholes. The Conference encountered difficulties of various kinds: some were legal-technical, some concerned military interests and some were based on political considerations.[68] Four problems where the ICRC's initial approach could be questioned will be highlighted.

1. *Wars of National Liberation*

The 1973 ICRC draft did not address the issue of wars of national liberation, apparently assuming that this was covered well enough by the Protocol on NIAC (AP II) and attempting to avoid the problem of qualifying special conflicts.[69] The draft was based on the strict distinction between international and non-international conflicts. Only in cases where conflicts crossed national boundaries did the conflict become international.[70] Wars against colonial and racist regimes were covered by Draft Protocol II.[71] Therefore, the Draft Protocol I limited its scope of application to situations referred to in Common Article 2.[72] The ICRC was aware of the desire of numerous States to include wars of national liberation in

[65] *Ibid.* [66] *Ibid.*

[67] List of State Parties: www.icrc.org/ihl/%28SPF%29/party_main_treaties/$File/IHL_and_other_related_Treaties.pdf (October 2015).

[68] Bothe and Partsch, 'General Introduction and Guide to Documentation', in New Rules, note 1, p. 7.

[69] B. Zimmermann, 'Article 1 – General principles and scope of application' in *ICRC Commentary*, note 1, pp. 33–57, p. 49.

[70] D. P. Forsythe, 'The 1974 Diplomatic Conference on Humanitarian Law: Some Observations', *The American Journal of International Law*, 69 (1993), pp. 77–91, p. 80 uses the term 'geomilitary scale'.

[71] K. J. Partsch, 'Article 1 – General principles and scope of application' in *New Rules*, note 1, pp. 35–51, p. 38.

[72] This provision is contained in Article 1 (3) of the Final Act.

Protocol I.[73] Yet, in its 1973 Commentary, it indicated that the majority of experts involved in drafting the Protocol did not consider those wars as international.[74]

The first problem the conference had to solve regarding wars of national liberation was the participation of liberation movements. This procedural issue blocked the first session of the Conference for a number of weeks. It was only after four weeks of difficult negotiations that the decision was taken to allow liberation movements recognized by regional organizations to participate with a right to speak and to make proposals, but without the right to vote.[75]

Concerning the substance of the controversy, immediately after the opening of the Conference, amendments were presented with the aim of recognizing the international character of wars of national liberation, which led to a highly controversial debate. The amendments' supporters mainly argued that there already existed a legal conviction and international practice recognizing wars of national liberation as international conflicts.[76] The opponents on the other hand considered the expansion of the protocol's scope as an introduction of *jus ad bellum* into *jus in bello*. Furthermore, they argued that the rules contained in Protocol I and the 1949 Convention were unsuitable for situations of wars of national liberation.[77] The main opponents in the debate were, on the one hand, most Western delegations and, on the other, the East European, Asian and African groups. Against the hard-core Western position not to

[73] The majority of experts considered wars of national liberation as being not of an international character, Zimmermann, 'Article 1 – General principles and scope of application', in ICRC Commentary, p. 47.

[74] ICRC, *Draft Protocols additional to the Geneva Conventions of 12 August 1949, Commentary*, p. 6; Zimmermann, 'Article 1 – General principles and scope of application', ibid., p. 49; F. Kalshoven, 'Reaffirmation and Development of International Humanitarian Law Applicable in Armed Conflicts: The First Session of the Diplomatic Conference, Geneva, 20 February – 29 March 1974', *Netherlands Yearbook of International Law*, 5 (1974), pp. 2–34, p. 6.

[75] Bothe and Partsch, 'General Introduction and Guide to Documentation', note 1, p. 8.

[76] G. Abi-Saab, 'Wars of National Liberation in the Geneva Conventions and Protocols' *Académie de Droit International de la Haye (ed.), Recueil des Cours*, 165 (1979), pp. 353–445, 376 *et seq.*; Partsch, 'Article 1 – General principles and scope of application', note 71, p. 40; Baxter, note 20, pp. 13 *et seq.*

[77] Abi-Saab, 'Wars of National Liberation in the Geneva Conventions and Protocols', pp. 380 *et seq.*; W. T. Mallison and S. V. Mallison, 'The Juridical Status of Privileged Combatants under the Geneva Protocol of 1977 Concerning International Conflicts', *Law and Contemporary Problems*, 42: 2 (1978), 4–35, 12; Forsythe, note 70, p. 81.

mention wars of national liberation at all, there were different variations of the contrary position, namely to choose as decisive the exercise of the right to self-determination, or the fight against colonial domination, alien occupation and racist regimes or a combination of both. To resolve the controversies, the delegations of Canada and New Zealand suggested the establishment of an inter-sessional Working Group (CDDH/I/78).[78] But the proposal combining the said criteria was put to a vote and the following text was adopted in a roll call vote by a majority of 70 votes to 21 with 13 abstentions:

1. The present Protocol which supplements the Geneva Conventions of 12 August 1949 for the Protection of War Victims, shall apply in the situations referred to in Article 2 common to these Conventions.
2. The situations referred to in the preceding paragraph include armed conflicts in which peoples are fighting against colonial domination and alien occupation and racist regimes in the exercise of their right of self-determination, as enshrined in the Charter of the United Nations and the Declaration on Principles of International Law concerning Friendly Relations and Cooperation among States in accordance with the Charter of the United Nations.

Between the first and the second session, the United States announced that it was willing to live with the new provision equating wars of national liberation to international armed conflicts (now Article 1 (4) AP I).[79] This solved the diplomatic deadlock in which the conference had been stuck. Political developments which occurred soon after the Conference have made that problem largely obsolescent. Nevertheless, the controversy during the first session gave the impression that the ICRC and the Western States were not well prepared to respond to the needs of the developing countries.[80]

2. *The Protection of the Victims of Non-International Armed Conflicts*

Incorporating wars of liberation into the regulatory scope of AP I was a necessary concession to the developing countries, which dramatically

[78] Partsch, 'Article 1 – General principles and scope of application', note 71, p. 42; *Official Records*, vol. VIII, p. 97.
[79] Bothe and Partsch, 'General Introduction and Guide to Documentation', note 1, p. 8.
[80] Baxter, note 20, 17.

reduced their support of AP II. AP II was no longer necessary to give better protection and legal status to liberation movements and their members fighting against colonial powers. Therefore, another interest perceived as primordial by many developing countries gained importance, namely their concern about possible restrictions imposed on their newly gained sovereignty which might result from the high level of protection provided by the new AP II. They were thus against such a protocol, or at least insisted on a lower level of protection.[81] The ICRC and many of the Western and East European delegations had underestimated the resistance which many developing countries would offer against the high level of protection for victims of NIAC.[82] Furthermore, some articles seemed to be too detailed to be realistic or to be applied in internal conflicts.[83] This opposition finally prevailed during the heated final plenary session of the conference,[84] leading to a severe reduction of the content of AP II. A new draft, for which the delegate of Pakistan was the major spokesman,[85], only provided 28 Articles in comparison to the 47 Articles contained in the version adopted during the Committee phase of the Conference. Certain sections (e.g. the rules on methods and means of combat) were almost entirely deleted.[86] Already during the second session, Article 1, which determines the material field of the application of AP II, was significantly reduced in comparison to the ICRC draft by introducing a higher threshold for its application. The ICRC draft had been based on Common Article 3 of the Geneva Convention. It defined the NIAC negatively in two respects, namely excluding, on the one hand, situations that were covered by Common Article 2 of the Conventions, and on the other hand,

[81] C. Lysaght, 'The Scope of Protocol II and its Relation to Common Article 3 of the Geneva Conventions of 1949 and other Human Rights Instruments', *The American University Law Review*, 33 (1983), pp. 9–27, p. 10; C. L. Cantrell, 'Humanitarian Law in Armed Conflict: The Third Diplomatic Conference', *Marquette Law Review*, 61 (1977), pp. 253–278, p. 277.

[82] Cf. Junod, 'General Introduction to the Commentary on Protocol II', ICRC Commentary, note 1, pp. 1334 *et seq.*

[83] *Ibid.*, p. 1335. [84] *Official Records*, Vol. VII, CDDH/ SR. 49, pp. 59 *et seq.*

[85] CDDH/427 and Corr. 1. The head of the delegation of Pakistan, Judge Mushtaq Hussain, took an initiative to save the Protocol; *Official Records*, Vol. IV, pp. 13 *et seq*; Junod, 'General Introduction to the Commentary on Protocol II', note 82, p. 1335; Crawford, 'Geneva Conventions Additional Protocol I (1977)', note 4, MN 14 and 15, Bothe and Partsch, note 53, pp. 695 *et seq.*

[86] Cantrell, 'Humanitarian Law in Armed Conflict: The Third Diplomatic Conference', p. 273; See also W. A. Solf, 'Part IV Civilian Population, Introduction' in *New Rules*, note 1, pp. 769–776, 775 (the comparative table).

internal disturbances and tensions as well as isolated and sporadic acts of violence (Art. 1, paragraph 2 of the ICRC draft).[87] In contrast, the provision adopted by the Conference requires that the insurgent groups are under a responsible command and that they control a part of a territory that enables them to implement AP II, which considerably raises the threshold of application.[88]

Related to the question of the definition of the NIAC is the problem of the relation of Article 1 AP II to Common Article 3 of the Geneva Convention[89] and whether the existence of a NIAC shall be determined subjectively, by the concerned State, or objectively.[90] The proposals of those opposing the objective determination of a NIAC were rejected. Although a compromise (CDDH/I/GT 56)[91] was adopted unanimously by Committee I[92], the developing countries, under the leadership of the

[87] Article 1 of the ICRC Draft 'Material field of application':

1. The present Protocol shall apply to all armed conflicts not covered by Article 2 common to the Geneva Conventions of August 12, 1949, taking place between armed forces or other organized armed groups under responsible command.
2. The present Protocol shall not apply to situations of internal disturbances and tensions, *inter alia* riots, isolated and sporadic acts of violence and other acts of a similar nature.
3. The foregoing provisions do not modify the conditions governing the application of Article 3 common to the Geneva Conventions of August 12, 1949.

[88] Article 1 of AP II. Material field of application:

1. This Protocol, which develops and supplements Article 3 common to the Geneva Conventions of 12 August 1949 without modifying its existing conditions of application, shall apply to all armed conflicts which are not covered by Article 1 of the Protocol Additional to the Geneva Conventions of 12 August 1949, and relating to the Protection of Victims of International Armed Conflicts (Protocol I) and which take place in the territory of a High Contracting Party between its armed forces and dissident armed forces or other organized armed groups which, under responsible command, exercise such control over a part of its territory as to enable them to carry out sustained and concerted military operations and to implement this Protocol.
2. This Protocol shall not apply to situations of internal disturbances and tensions, such as riots, isolated and sporadic acts of violence and other acts of a similar nature, as not being armed conflicts.

[89] *Official Records*, vol. VIII, CDDH/I/SR. 24, pp. 229 *et seq.*

[90] *Official Records*, vol. VIII, CDDH/I/SR. 24, pp. 233 *et seq.*; See as well the Amendment to Article 1 by Romania (CDDH/I/30) in *Official Records*, Vol. IV, p. 7.

[91] *Official Records*, vol. X, CDDH/I/238/Rev./1, pp. 93 *et seq.* Only two minor changes have been made: The compromise begins with 'The present Protocol' instead of 'This Protocol' and it refers to 'Protocol I' instead of 'the Protocol Additional to the Geneva Conventions of 12 August 1949, and relating to the Protection of the Victims of International Armed Conflicts (Protocol I)'.

[92] *Official Records*, vol. VIII, CDDH/I/SR. 29, p. 287.

Columbian representative, attempted to reopen the discussion during the final adoption phase by an oral amendment. After an appeal by the representative of the ICRC, the Columbian representative withdrew this amendment.[93] However, this was only a small success. Seen as a whole, AP II as adopted was considered unsatisfactory by the ICRC and many States. The final version reduced the number of articles to 28 as compared to the original 47 Articles of the ICRC draft and the Committee version. However, it was recognized that this was the only viable compromise.[94]

In light of the fierce debates, which took place during the final weeks of the conference,[95] it is amazing to notice the subsequent development of relevant customary international law towards providing a level of protection which could not be achieved during the conference. The law relating to NIAC has to a large extent been approximated to that of international armed conflicts (IAC). In particular, the ICTY and the ICTR played a decisive role in this development. In 1995 the ICTY stated that:

> [...]in the area of armed conflict the distinction between interstate wars and civil wars is losing its value as far as human beings are concerned. Why protect civilians from belligerent violence, or ban rape, torture or the wanton destruction of hospitals, churches, museums or private property, as well as proscribe weapons causing unnecessary suffering when two sovereign States are engaged in war, and yet refrain from enacting the same bans or providing the same protection when armed violence has erupted 'only' within the territory of a sovereign State? If international law, while of course duly safeguarding the legitimate interests of States, must gradually turn to the protection of human beings, it is only natural that the aforementioned dichotomy should gradually lose its weight.[96]

By the beginning of the twenty-first century, that concept had passed into the realm of positive law, as the ICRC observed in its customary law study[97] which convincingly shows the approximation of the rules governing the NIAC to those of the IAC. Thus, thirty years later, the 1973 concept of the ICRC finally prevailed.

93 *Official Records*, vol. VII, CDDH/SR. 49, pp. 66, 68.

94 *Official Records*, vol. VII, CDDH/SR. 49, p. 60.

95 *Official Records*, vol. VII, CDDH/SR. 49, pp. 59 *et seq.*

96 ICTY, *Prosecutor v. Dusko Tadić*, Appeals Chamber Decision on the Defence Motion for Interlocutory Appeal on Jurisdiction, 2 October 1995, para. 97.

97 *Cf.* J.-M. Henckaerts and L. Doswald-Beck, *Customary International Humanitarian Law*, 2 vols. (Cambridge: Cambridge University Press, 2004), vol. I, p. XXIX.

3. *Nuclear Weapons*

The ICRC was well aware of the fact that including the controversial issue of nuclear weapons had led to the failure of its Delhi Rules,[98] as Article 14 (1) of the Delhi Rules was seen by several governments as a condemnation of nuclear weapons.[99] Therefore, a need to avoid the issue was felt. In the beginning, the ICRC addressed the issue in a declaration, which does not stand out for its clarity. The ICRC further stated in its introduction to the 1973 draft Protocols that '[p]roblems relating to atomic, bacteriological and chemical warfare are subjects of international agreements or negotiations by governments, and in submitting these draft Protocols the ICRC does not intend to broach these problems. It should be borne in mind that the Red Cross as a whole clearly made known its condemnation of weapons of mass destruction at several International Red Cross Conferences and urged governments to reach agreements banning their use'.[100] The ICRC explained its position once more in the introduction to the commentary of the draft articles:

> It should be recalled that, apart from some provisions of a general nature, the ICRC has not included in its drafts any rules governing atomic, bacteriological and chemical weapons. These weapons have either been the subject of international agreements such as the Geneva Protocol of 1925 or of discussions within intergovernmental organizations. This, however, does not imply that the ICRC or the Red Cross as a whole is not interested in a problem whose humanitarian aspects are of a paramount importance. Also the so-called conventional weapons . . . are still not covered by these protocols. Yet they are also a matter of concern for the ICRC . . . [101].

The declaration is mostly understood as an indication of the existence of a 'nuclear consensus', a general understanding between the ICRC and the participating States to exclude further discussions on nuclear weapons from the negotiations.[102] During the general debate, some governments

[98] C. Pilloud, 'Les Conventions de Genève de 1949 pour la protection des victimes de la guerre, les Protocols additionnels de 1977 et les armes nucléaires', *German Yearbook of International Law*, 21 (1979), pp. 169–179, 171 *et seq.*; W. A. Solf, 'Methods and Means of Warfare Introduction' in *New Rules*, note 1, pp. 217–221, p. 218; Pilloud and Pictet, 'Protocol I – Part IV, Section 1', note 8, p. 590.

[99] Pilloud and Pictet, 'Protocol I – Part IV, Section 1', note 8, p. 590.

[100] *Official Records*, vol. I, Part 3, p. 2.

[101] ICRC, *Draft Protocols additional to the Geneva Conventions of 12 August 1949, Commentary*, p. 2; Pilloud and Pictet, 'Protocol I – Part IV, Section 1', p. 590.

[102] S. Oeter, 'II. Means of Combat' in D. Fleck (ed.), *The Handbook of International Humanitarian Law*, 3rd ed. (Oxford: Oxford University Press, 2013), p. 153 *et seq.*; H. Meyrowitz,

were opposed to the Conference dealing with specific weapons at all,[103] especially the nuclear powers which were apparently determined not to address the issue.[104] Early in the diplomatic conference the delegation of the United Kingdom explained that

> they were not intended to broach problems concerned with atomic, bacteriological or chemical warfare, which were the subject of existing international agreements and current delicate negotiations by Governments elsewhere. It was on the assumption that the draft Protocols would not affect those problems that the United Kingdom Government had worked and would continue to work towards final agreement on the Protocols.[105]

A similar statement was made by the United States.[106] Furthermore, immediately prior to the adoption of draft additional Protocol I, France stressed that in its view the rules of the Protocol did not apply to the use of nuclear weapons.[107]

It is notable that these views were not disputed by other governments, although several delegations had openly attempted to extend the scope of Protocol I to nuclear weapons and had urged to prohibit them.[108] When the Conference defined the mandate that was given to the Ad Hoc Committee to study certain conventional weapons which cause superfluous injury and unnecessary suffering the delegations of Romania[109] and China[110] proposed to delete the word 'conventional', which would have extended the Committee's mandate to nuclear, bacteriological and chemical weapons.[111] The Conference approved the mandate including the word 'conventional' by 68 votes to none, with 10 abstentions.[112]

'Le statut des armes nucléaires en droit international – 1er part', *German Yearbook of International Law*, 21 (1982), pp. 219–251, 229 *et seq.*

103 *Official Records*, vol. V, CDDH/SR. 9, para. 28 (France); CDDH/SR. 11, para. 64 (Ukrainian Soviet Socialist Republics); CDDH/SR. 11; para. 73 (Hungary); CDDH/SR. 12, para. 24 (Union of Soviet Socialist Republics); CDDH/SR.17, para. 36 (Argentina).

104 Solf, 'Methods and Means of Warfare Introduction', in New Rules, note 1, p. 219.

105 *Official Records*, vol. V, CDDH/SR. 13, para. 36.

106 *Official Records*, vol. VII, CDDH SR. 58, para. 82, Vol. XIV, CDDH/III/SR. 40, para. 123.

107 *Official Records*, vol. VII, CDDH/SR. 56, p. 193.

108 *Official Records*, vol. V, CDDH/SR.10, para. 36 (Ghana); CDDH/SR.11, para. 13 (Romania); vol. V, CDDH/SR.12, para. 18 (China); vol. V, CDDH/SR.12, para. 32, (Iraq); vol. IX, CDDH/I/SR.60, para. 23, (Philippines); vol. XIV, CDDH/III/SR.8 para. 87, (Albania); Oeter, note 102, pp. 153 *et seq.*

109 *Official Records*, vol. V, CDDH/SR. 9, para. 31.

110 *Official Records*, vol. V, CDDH/SR. 9, para. 40.

111 Pilloud and Pictet, 'Protocol I – Part IV, Section 1', note 8, p. 592.

112 *Official Records*, vol. V, CDDH/SR. 9, para. 50.

China especially criticized the 'super powers', accusing them of a mass production of lethal weapons, particularly nuclear weapons, and urged the conference to prohibit the use of nuclear weapons.[113] Nevertheless, no amendments dealing with the subject were proposed for inclusion in Protocol I during the whole conferences.[114] Later in the Conference, the Western Powers addressed the question by declarations interpreting AP I as not applying to weapons of mass destruction.[115] After the consensus adoption of the Protocols, the United States,[116] the United Kingdom[117] and France[118] confirmed their positions interpreting Protocol I: They expressed the understanding that the rules developed in the course of the conferences had been designed with a view to conventional weapons only and that these rules had not been intended to have any effect on and did not regulate or prohibit the use of nuclear weapons.

At the time of signature the United States and Great Britain made declarations similar to their previous statements and confirmed their view interpreting Protocol I as not applying to weapons of mass destruction.[119] On the occasion of ratification several other States affirmed this position.[120] Some commentators say that the declarations of the United Kingdom and the United States were reservations.[121] Others have expressed the opinion that they form a part of the context of Protocol I relevant for its interpretation in accordance with Article 31 (I) Vienna Convention on the Law of Treaties.[122]

The position of the ICRC remained somewhat ambiguous. On the one hand, it found itself constrained to exclude nuclear weapons from the scope of application of the Protocol to facilitate the participation of the

113 *Official Records*, vol. V, CDDH/SR.12, para. 18 (China).

114 Solf, 'Methods and Means of Warfare Introduction', note 104, p. 219.

115 *Official Records*, vol. VII, CDDH/SR. 58, para. 82; vol. VII, CCDH/SR. 58, para. 119 and CDDH/SR. 56, para. 3.

116 *Official Records*, vol. VII, CDDH/SR. 58, para. 82.

117 *Official Records*, vol. VII, CCDH/SR. 58, para. 119.

118 *Official Records*, vol. VII, CDDH/SR. 56, para. 3.

119 Printed in: Solf, 'Methods and Means of Warfare Introduction', pp. 219 *et seq.* (United States) and pp. 822 *et seq.* (United Kingdom).

120 Belgium, Canada, France, Germany, Ireland, Italy, the Netherlands and Spain, R. R. Baxter, 'The Evolving Laws of Armed Conflicts', *Military Law Review*, 60 (1973), pp. 99–11, p. 109.

121 Bothe, Ipsen and Partsch, note 9, pp. 43 *et seq.* (individual opinion of Professor Knut Ipsen).

122 Solf, 'Methods and Means of Warfare Introduction', note 104, p. 220; Oeter, note 102, p. 159.

Western nuclear powers at the conferences and to ensure the eventual ratification by those powers. On the other hand, it indicated in its introduction to the draft articles commentary that nuclear weapons were at least incorporated in some general provisions.[123] According to the ICRC commentary, 'those are the general rules that already existed in a codified form or as customary law and which were confirmed in the Protocol, namely the provisions of Article 33 of the Draft, the present paragraphs 1 and 2 of Article 35 AP I and the customary rule confirmed by Article 43 of the Draft (present Article 48 AP I)'.[124] Thus, the ICRC repeated its view that the Protocol was without prejudice to the already existing general rules although it declared that it had not included any rules governing atomic weapons in its 1973 drafts. The general rules remain completely valid and continue to apply to nuclear weapons.[125]

India affirmed this view by explaining in an understanding concerning Article 33 that the basic rule contained in Article 35 applied to all categories of weapons, namely nuclear, bacteriological, chemical or conventional weapons.[126] When ratifying the Protocol in 1999, Ireland made a similar statement in its declaration concerning Article 35, stating 'that nuclear weapons, even if not directly governed by Additional Protocol I, remain subject to existing rules of international law as confirmed in 1996 by the International Court of Justice in its Advisory Opinion on the Legality of the Threat or Use of Nuclear Weapons'.[127]

The controversy about nuclear weapons was one of the reasons for the considerable slowdown of the ratification process in Western Europe. In a way, the question was laid to rest by the 1996 Advisory Opinion of the ICJ on nuclear weapons.[128] The Court considered the controversy as immaterial because customary law rules of the same content as those of AP I applied to nuclear weapons.[129] These rules would, as a matter of principle, rule out the legality of the use of nuclear weapons. But the Court left a

[123] ICRC, *Draft Protocols additional to the Geneva Conventions of 12 August 1949, Commentary*, p. 2.

[124] Pilloud and Pictet, 'Protocol I – Part IV, Section 1', note 8, p. 590.

[125] Pilloud and Pictet, 'Protocol I – Part IV, Section 1', p. 593; Solf, 'Methods and Means of Warfare Introduction', note 104, p. 220; Oeter, 'II. Means of Combat', note 102, p. 157.

[126] *Official Records*, vol. VI, CDDH/SR. 39, p. 115 (India).

[127] ICRC, 'Ratification of the Protocols Additional to the Geneva Conventions of 12 August 1949 by Ireland', *International Review of the Red Cross*, 81 (1999), pp. 418–422, p. 420.

[128] ICJ, *Legality of the threat or use of nuclear weapons*, Advisory Opinion of 8 July 1996.

[129] ICJ, *Legality of the threat or use of nuclear weapons*, Advisory Opinion of 8 July 1996, para. 64 *et seq*.

possible exception for extreme situations in the form of a *non liquet*: The Court was unable to say whether there were such extreme situations where the use of nuclear weapons would be lawful.[130] The official position of the nuclear powers seems to have comfortably settled in the niche thus left by the Court, if necessary by misinterpreting the Court a little. Thus, the situation is where the first declaration of the ICRC in 1973 put it. It is still ambiguous.

4. *Protection of the Natural Environment*

In its draft Additional Protocols, the ICRC made no reference to the protection of the natural environment against the harmful effects of warfare. But this was the decade when the development of international environmental law started with vigour. The first UN Conference on environmental protection was held in 1972.[131] Other fora dealing with military questions addressed the issue of environmental protection while the Diplomatic Conference in Geneva was going on. The United States and the Soviet Union engaged in bilateral negotiations, addressing the 'dangers of the use of environmental modifications for military purposes'[132] in 1974 and the UN General Assembly adopted the *Convention on the Prohibition of Military or any Other Hostile Use of Environmental Modification Techniques* in 1976.[133]

The ICRC was already confronted with respective proposals of delegations at the Second Conference of Government Experts,[134] yet refrained

[130] ICJ, *Legality of the threat or use of nuclear weapons*, Advisory Opinion of 8 July 1996, para. 105.

[131] *See* Report of the UN Conference on the Human Environment, www.unep.org/Documents.Multilingual/Default.asp?DocumentID=97.

[132] Summit meeting between President Nixon and General Secretary Brezhnev, July 1974, www.state.gov/www/global/arms/treaties/environ1.html; *see also* W. A. Solf, 'Article 55 – Protection of the Natural Environment', *New Rules*, note 1, pp. 385–390, p. 386.

[133] The Convention was drafted by the UN Conference of the Committee on Disarmament and adopted by the UN General Assembly in December, 1976. Its Art. 1 prohibits '*military or any other hostile use of environmental modification techniques having widespread, long-lasting or severe effects as the means of destruction, damage or injury to any other State Party*', *see* United Nations, General Assembly, UN Doc. A/Res/31/72, www.un-documents.net/a31r72.htm.

[134] ICRC, *Report on the Conference of Government Experts on the Use of Certain Conventional Weapons* (Geneva, 1975), p. 76, www.loc.gov/rr/frd/Military_Law/pdf/RC-conf-experts-1974.pdf.

from including them in its draft Protocols.[135] Thus, pleas for environmental protection were reiterated at the Diplomatic Conference.[136] In September 1974 the Delegation of the German Democratic Republic sought a revision of the means and methods of combat, proposing to replace draft Articles 33 and 34 with a text, which *inter alia* prohibited 'means and methods which destroy natural human environmental conditions'.[137] Several months thereafter, the Arab Republic of Egypt, Australia, Czechoslovakia, Finland, the German Democratic Republic (GDR), Hungary, Ireland, Norway, Sudan and Yugoslavia proposed to add a paragraph to Article 33, forbidding the 'use methods and means which disturb or alter the ecological balance of the human environment'.[138] A similar amendment to Article 33 was suggested by the Democratic Republic of Vietnam and Uganda.[139] Environmental protection was then the subject of a new proposal, introduced by Australia, to prohibit both the destruction of the natural environment as a warfare technique and reprisal attacks against the environment.[140] Hungary, Czechoslovakia and the GDR advocated a similar prohibition, emphasizing the importance of a stable environment for the survival of mankind.[141] Eventually, the informal task force '*Group Biotope*' was formed in Committee III and reached the conclusion that the normative approach should be twofold, given that environmental protection is both an end in itself and a means to the end of the survival of mankind.[142] This dual approach reflected the variety of the aforementioned proposals and was ultimately implemented in Article 35 AP I (the amended draft Art. 33) and in the new Article 55 AP I.[143] Article 35 (3) AP I elevated the protection of the environment to one of the 'basic rules' of the Protocol and prohibits 'methods or means of warfare which are intended, or may be expected, to cause widespread, long-term and severe damage to the natural environment'. Containing the same prohibition, the new Art. 55 AP I paragraph 1 additionally emphasises the purpose of preventing adverse effects on 'the health or survival of the population'.

135 *Cf.* Draft Additional Protocols, *Official Records*, vol. I, Part 3.
136 *Cf.* Solf, 'Article 55 – Protection of the Natural Environment', note 132, p. 386.
137 *Official Records*, vol. III, CDDH/III/108, p. 155.
138 *Official Records*, vol. III, CDDH/III/222, p. 156.
139 *Official Records*, vol. III, CDDH/III/238, p. 157.
140 *Official Records*, vol. III, CDDH/III/60, p. 220.
141 *Official Records*, vol. III, CDDH/III/64, p. 221.
142 *Cf. Official Records*, vol. XV, CDDH/III/275, p. 358.
143 *Cf.* Solf, 'Article 55 – Protection of the Natural Environment', note 132, p. 387.

Moreover, Article 55 (2) specifically forbids 'attacks against the environment by way of reprisals'.

However, due to the restrictive nature of the three (cumulative!) requirements which define the prohibited damage, the articles are virtually useless. The debate on the legal protection of the environment in times of armed conflict continued.[144] Finally, some 30 years after the adoption of the said articles, the ICRC accurately criticized their inefficacy in a 2011 report, in which it identified the protection of the natural environment as one of the four areas in which humanitarian law had to be strengthened:[145] '[. . .] each of the three criteria ("widespread, long-term and severe") establishes a high, yet imprecise, threshold [. . .] Secondly, these criteria apply cumulatively, implying that the norm in question only protects the environment against exceptionally catastrophic events – what may be called "ecocide"'.[146] On the other hand, the ICRC also affirmed that customary international law 'contains some obligations for [the] protection of the environment', in particular the 'due regard' principle, yet insisted that 'their exact extent and implications would certainly need further clarification or development'.[147]

During the decades following the adoption of the Protocols, armed conflicts have inflicted great harm upon the environment and affected populations. Examples, highlighted by the ICRC in the aforementioned report, include the 'deliberate destruction of more than 600 oil wells in Kuwait'[148] during the 1991 Gulf War and the bombing of 'the Jiyeh power station [which] led to the release of approximately 10,000 to 15,000 tons of fuel into the Mediterranean Sea'[149] in Lebanon in 2006. In the light of the atrocious effects of such incidents, the ICRC's recent efforts are indeed meritorious.

Yet States did not share the ICRC's concerns and views as to the priority of environmental protection in armed conflict. As the president of ICRC,

[144] On the development of this discussion, see M. Bothe, 'Military Activities and the Protection of the Environment', *Environmental Policy and Law*, 37 (2007), pp. 232–238.

[145] ICRC, Report for the 31st International Conference of the ICRC, Strengthening Legal Protection for Victims of Armed Conflicts (Geneva, October 2011), Doc. 31IC/11/5.1.1, p. 5, www.icrc.org/eng/assets/files/red-cross-crescent-movement/31st-international-conference/31-int-conference-strengthening-legal-protection-11-5-1-1-en.pdf.

[146] *Ibid.*, p. 15.

[147] *Ibid.*, p. 5; Henckaerts and Doswald-Beck, note 97, Rule 43, pp. 143–146, p. 143.

[148] ICRC, Report for the 31st International Conference of the ICRC, Strengthening Legal Protection for Victims of Armed Conflicts, p. 15.

[149] *Ibid.*, p. 14.

Dr Jakob Kellenberger, put it: 'With regard to [. . .] the protection of the natural environment [. . .] further consultation and research with a view to strengthening the law is not considered a priority by a number of States at this stage'.[150] Nevertheless, the ICRC is not alone: In 2011, the International Law Commission (ILC) included the 'protection of the environment in relation to armed conflicts' in its long-term program of work.[151] In May 2013, the ILC incorporated the topic in its program of work and appointed Ms. Marie G. Jacobsson as the responsible Special Rapporteur, who has delivered three reports which have led to the provisional adoption of a number of principles.[152] Overcoming its initially passive stance, the ICRC has turned into an advocate of environmental protection against the harmful effects of warfare. Its endeavour has gained considerable momentum, yet it remains to be seen whether or not this will translate into actual legal progress.

VI. Conclusion

Taken as a whole and despite certain problems which have been described, the preparation and negotiation of the two Additional Protocols of 1977 once more demonstrated the crucial role of the ICRC in the sphere of humanitarian law. The impact of the ICRC was both substantive and procedural. The final outcome largely corresponded to the proposals and concerns of the ICRC and meant a major improvement for the protection of civilians in international and non-international conflicts.[153] The content of the Protocols cannot be thought of without the conceptual work of the ICRC. The procedural approach used by the ICRC, its central role in the elaboration of the relevant texts was decisive and seemed to be generally accepted at the time.

Recently, certain States have shown some resistance against the leading role of the ICRC in the development of international humanitarian law,

[150] Statement addressed to the permanent missions in Geneva by Dr Jakob Kellenberger, President of the ICRC, 5 December 2011, www.icrc.org/eng/resources/documents/statement/ihl-development-statement-2011–05–12.htm.

[151] M. Bothe, 'Protection of the Environment in Relation to Armed Conflicts', in J. Crawford, A.G. Koroma, A. Pellet, S. Mahmoudi (eds.), *The International Legal Order: Current Needs and Possible Responses*. Liber Amicorum Djamchid Momtaz (Leiden: Nijhoff Publishers 2017), pp. 641–659.

[152] *Cf.* Sixty-fifth session of the ILC (6 May – 7 June and 8 July – 9 August 2013), UN Doc. A/68/10, p. 105f.

[153] Pictet, 'General Introduction', note 1, p. xxxiv.

claiming an exclusive (or next to exclusive) role for the 'States', meaning State bureaucracies, in this domain, a kind of '*chasse gardée*' for national ministries. In a polite form, this is reflected in the relevant resolution of the 31st Red Cross/Red Crescent Conference.[154] Yet this short survey of the salutary leading role played by the ICRC in the 1970s has shown, it is submitted, that all those concerned with the suffering of the victims of armed conflicts are well advised to listen to the visions of the ICRC.

[154] 31st International Red Cross and Red Crescent Conference, Resolution 1, Strengthening legal protection for victims of armed conflicts, OP 6 ('recognizing the primary role of States in the development of international humanitarian law').

PART II

The International Committee of the Red Cross and the Development of International Humanitarian Law Beyond Treaty Regimes

3

The International Committee of the Red Cross and Customary International Humanitarian Law

JEAN-MARIE HENCKAERTS

Introduction

The role of the ICRC as a guardian and promoter of international humanitarian law (IHL) is well known.[1] For the major part of its 150-year existence it is best known for its efforts in preparing for the development of new treaty law. Henry Dunant and the initial committee members were successful in having the first multilateral treaty for the protection of war victims adopted in 1864. As is well known, updates and additions to this treaty were prepared by the ICRC and adopted in 1906, 1929, 1949, 1977 and 2005.

Hence, the ICRC has come to be identified with the Geneva Conventions and their Additional Protocols. But the role of guardian and promoter of IHL is not limited to treaty law. It concerns all IHL and thus also includes customary law. The ICRC also relies on both treaty and customary IHL in its activities to promote respect for and knowledge of IHL. In December 1995, the ICRC was specifically mandated by the international community to undertake a comprehensive assessment of customary international humanitarian law (see later discussion).

In February 2005, after nearly ten years of extensive research and wide consultation involving more than 100 governmental and academic experts, the ICRC published this assessment comprised of two

[1] This role is recognized in the Statutes of the Red Cross and Red Crescent Movement, adopted by the International Conference of the Red Cross and Red Crescent, Geneva, October 1986, Article 5. For a general discussion of this concept, see Y. Sandoz, 'Le Comité international de la Croix-Rouge gardien du droit international humanitaire', *Jugoslovenska revija za međunarodno pravo [Yugoslav Review of International Law]* 43 (1996), pp. 357–389, available in English at www.icrc.org/eng/resources/documents/misc/about-the-icrc-311298.htm.

volumes.[2] The first volume sets out in a transparent manner the methodology followed and lists a total of 161 rules which were assessed to be of customary nature based on this methodology.[3] The second volume transparently lays out the practice on which the assessment of custom was based. This part continues to be updated by the ICRC, in partnership with the British Red Cross Society, in the ICRC's freely accessible, online Customary IHL Database.[4] It now contains practice of more than 190 States, collected through a network of ICRC delegations, national rapporteurs and a number of National Red Cross Societies.[5] The ICRC study on customary international humanitarian law was not intended to be and cannot be expected to be exhaustive, both in terms of areas covered and the number of rules identified, as well as in terms of the practice collected.

Part I of this chapter looks at some of the historical background to the ICRC's reliance on customary international humanitarian law. Part II explains the specific mandate given to the ICRC to carry out a comprehensive assessment of customary humanitarian law. Part III discusses the main functions custom can play and gives some examples of the contemporary relevance of customary humanitarian law. Part IV addresses the impact of the ICRC study on recent references to customary humanitarian law. Finally, Part V focuses on reactions to the methodology used by the study.

I. Historical Background

It can be argued that, for too long, the ICRC limited its consideration of humanitarian law to codified treaty law, in particular the Geneva Conventions and their Additional Protocols, at the exclusion of customary law. This attitude has been criticised, e.g. in relation to the ICRC's approach to violations of the immunity of the civilian population against attacks in the

[2] J.-M. Henckaerts and L. Doswald-Beck (eds.), *Customary International Humanitarian Law*, 2 vols. (Cambridge: Cambridge University Press & ICRC, 2005 reprinted with corrections 2009), Vol. I: Rules, Vol. II: Practice (2 Parts). For more information, see www.icrc.org/eng/customary-law.

[3] This volume has been translated in the official UN languages and several additional languages: Arabic (Cairo: ICRC, 2007), Chinese (Beijing: China Law Press, 2007), Farsi (Tehran: Majd Publishers, 2008), French (Brussels: Editions Bruylant, 2006), Russian (Moscow: ICRC 2006), Serbian (Belgrade: ICRC 2005), Spanish (Buenos Aires: ICRC 2007) and Turkish (Istanbul: Galatasary University, 2011). A Portuguese translation is forthcoming. In addition, the rules have been translated into nearly 50 languages available at: www.icrc.org/eng/resources/documents/misc/customary-law-translations.htm.

[4] For more information, see www.icrc.org/customary-ihl/eng/docs/home.

[5] See www.icrc.org/customary-ihl/eng/docs/credit.

Vietnam War. Bugnion notes, 'In this matter as in others, the International Committee tended to attach such undue importance to written law that it identified humanitarian law with the Conventions. The inevitable conclusion that a matter not regulated by the Conventions is not the subject of any rule is legally unsound . . . '.[6]

Since the Vietnam War, however, the ICRC has increasingly relied on customary IHL in its appeals to warring parties, e.g. the customary rule of civilian immunity against attacks and prohibition of indiscriminate attacks.[7] The reason for this was usually the non-applicability of treaty law absent ratification by one or more of the parties to the conflict. For example, in an appeal issued in 1979 with respect to the conflict in Rhodesia/Zimbabwe, the ICRC stated: 'Fundamental humanitarian rules accepted by all nations – such as the obligation to distinguish between combatants and civilians, and to refrain from violence against the latter – have been largely ignored.'[8] The reference to 'fundamental humanitarian rules accepted by all nations' can be understood as an indirect reference to customary IHL.

The appeals in the context of the Iran–Iraq War in 1983, referred to the 'indiscriminate bombardment of towns and villages'.[9] The prohibition of indiscriminate attacks was codified in Article 51(4)–(5) of Additional Protocol I, but neither Iran nor Iraq were party to the Protocol at the time. Hence, the ICRC's appeal must have relied on the consideration that this prohibition was part of customary international law. Later in the same context, the ICRC referred to the 'laws and customs of war' when it stated that civilian zones continued to be bombed '[i]n violation of the laws and customs of war, and in particular of the essential principle that military targets must be distinguished from civilian persons and objects'.[10] Finally, in 1987, the ICRC referred explicitly to customary law. It made a solemn appeal to the Iranian and Iraqi governments 'once again strongly urging them to put an end to the bombing and attacks on civilians'. This was described as 'the latest in a series of attempts by the ICRC to remind Iran and Iraq that the bombing and attacks on civilians constitute a grave

[6] See F. Bugnion, *The International Committee of the Red Cross and the Protection of War Victims*, (Oxford: ICRC/Macmillan, 2003), p. 735.

[7] See *ibid.*, p. 736.

[8] ICRC, Conflict in Southern Africa: ICRC appeal, 19 March 1979, § 2, *International Review of the Red Cross*, No. 209 (1979), p. 87.

[9] Conflict between Iraq and Iran, ICRC appeal, *International Review of the Red Cross*, No. 235 (1983), p. 221.

[10] ICRC, Press Release No. 1480, Conflict Between Iran and Iraq and Breaches of International Humanitarian Law: A Renewed ICRC Appeal, 15 February 1984, *International Review of the Red Cross*, No. 239 (1984), pp. 113–115.

violation of international humanitarian law and of customary law, which totally prohibit such practices'.[11]

Reliance on customary IHL occurred again during the first Gulf War. On 14 December 1990 after the UN Security Council adopted Resolution 678 (1990) but before the outbreak of major hostilities against Iraq, the ICRC sent a memorandum to all States party to the Geneva Conventions. In the memorandum, the ICRC referred to the rule of distinction, the prohibition to attack civilians and civilian objects, the prohibition of indiscriminate attacks, the prohibition of excessive incidental civilian loss and damage and the obligation to take all feasible precautions.[12] These rules had been codified in Additional Protocol I,[13] but several addressees of the Memorandum directly concerned with the situation were not party to the Protocol I at the time. An outline of legal aspects of the Gulf War referred explicitly to the parties to the conflict being bound by the treaties they had ratified, as well as by customary international law. With respect to the binding character of Protocol I, the outline stated:

Iraq, the United States, the United Kingdom and France have not ratified Additional Protocol I to the Geneva Conventions of 12 August 1949; its provisions are therefore not binding unless they codify customary rules.[14]

> The ICRC continued to rely on customary international law in later appeals, in particular when one or more parties to the conflict had not ratified Additional Protocol I, for example in the conflicts in Lebanon,[15] NATO's air operations over Kosovo,[16] between Armenia and Azerbaidjan,[17] and Turkey's military operations in northern Iraq.[18]

In the 1990s the same started to happen in the context of non-international armed conflicts. In 1992, for example, the ICRC called on the parties to the

[11] ICRC, Press Release No. 1532, Iran–Iraq Conflict: The ICRC Solemnly Appeals, 13 February 1987.

[12] Memorandum on the Applicability of International Humanitarian Law, 14 December 1990, *International Review of the Red Cross*, No. 280 (1991), pp. 24–26.

[13] See in particular Additional Protocol I, Articles 48, pp. 51–52, and 57.

[14] Outline of legal aspects of the conflict in the Middle East, 21 January 1991, *International Review of the Red Cross*, No. 280 (1991), p. 29.

[15] ICRC, Communication to the Press No. 89/8, ICRC appeal against shelling in Lebanon, 28 July 1989.

[16] Statement by the ICRC, 26 April 1999, *International Review of the Red Cross*, 81 (1999) No. 834, pp. 409–411.

[17] ICRC, Communication to the Press No. 93/25, Nagorno-Karabakh conflict: 60,000 civilians flee fighting in southwestern Azerbaijan, 19 August 1993.

[18] ICRC, Press Release No. 1797, ICRC calls for compliance with international humanitarian law in Turkey and Northern Iraq, 22 March 1995.

conflict in Afghanistan not to target civilians and facilities used only by the civilian population and to spare civilian persons and objects.[19] This call relied on customary international law as Afghanistan was not party to Additional Protocol II at the time; it ratified the Protocol in 2009, and some rules invoked were not covered by AP II.

Then in 1993, the ICRC enjoined the parties to the conflict in Somalia not to 'attack civilians or facilities used by the civilian population' and 'not to launch military operations that may cause incidental civilian casualties or damage to civilian objects disproportionate to the direct military advantage anticipated'.[20] This appeal relied implicitly on customary international law as Somalia is not a party to Additional Protocol II and, in addition, the principle of proportionality to which reference was made is not set out in Protocol II.

A 1994 Memorandum on Respect for International Humanitarian Law in Angola referred specifically to Common Article 3 and customary international law as Angola is not a party to Additional Protocol II. Moreover, the Memorandum contained many rules on the conduct of hostilities which were implicitly based on customary international law.[21]

At the time, guidance on customary rules applicable to the conduct of hostilities in non-international armed conflicts could be found in a document issued by the International Institute of Humanitarian Law.[22] But this document was limited to the conduct of hostilities and was not based on any extensive research into practice. It was based on the conclusions of the 14th San Remo Round Table on IHL on 13 and 14 September 1989.

II. Mandate for the Study

The need for a more thorough analysis of customary international humanitarian law became apparent in 1994 during the armed conflicts in the former Yugoslavia and Rwanda. These conflicts undermined the credibility of international humanitarian law. The world witnessed the unfolding

[19] ICRC, Press Release No. 1712, Afghanistan: ICRC appeal for compliance with humanitarian rules, 5 May 1992; Press Release No. 1724, Kabul: ICRC urges respect for civilians as medical facilities struggle to cope, 20 July 1992; Press Release No. 1726, Afghanistan: New ICRC appeal for compliance with humanitarian rules, 14 August 1992.

[20] ICRC, Communication to the Press No. 93/17, Somalia: ICRC appeals for compliance with international humanitarian law, 17 June 1993.

[21] ICRC, Memorandum on Respect for International Humanitarian Law in Angola, 8 June 1994, § II, reprinted in *International Review of the Red Cross*, No. 320 (1997), pp. 503–504.

[22] Rules of international humanitarian law governing the conduct of hostilities in non-international armed conflicts, reprinted in *International Review of the Red Cross*, No. 278 (1990), pp. 383–408.

horrors but was unable to stop them and to enforce the law. One of the cardinal principles of humanitarian law – the distinction between civilians and combatants and between civilian objects and military objectives – was repeatedly and wilfully violated in these conflicts with apparent impunity. To address such problems an Intergovernmental Group of Experts for the Protection of War Victims met in Geneva in January 1995 and adopted a series of recommendations aimed at enhancing respect for humanitarian law, in particular by means of preventive measures that would ensure better knowledge and more effective implementation of the law. The recommendations included several measures, which have been realized in the meantime such as the setting up of an ICRC Advisory Service for International Humanitarian Law,[23] and of national IHL Committees.[24]

With regard to customary law, the intergovernmental group of experts proposed that:

> the ICRC be invited to prepare, with the assistance of experts in IHL [international humanitarian law] representing various geographical regions and different legal systems, and in consultation with experts from governments and international organizations, a report on customary rules of IHL applicable in international and non-international armed conflicts, and to circulate the report to States and competent international bodies.[25]

In December 1995, the 26th International Conference of the Red Cross and Red Crescent endorsed the recommendations from the intergovernmental group of experts. Thus, the Conference officially mandated the ICRC to prepare a report on customary rules of international humanitarian law applicable in international and non-international armed conflicts.[26]

This assignment fits the role entrusted to the ICRC pursuant to the 1986 Statutes of the International Red Cross and Red Crescent Movement 'to

[23] Meeting of the Intergovernmental Group of Experts for the Protection of War Victims, 23–27 January 1995, Recommendation III, *International Review of the Red Cross*, No. 310 (1996), p. 84. On the Advisory Service on IHL, see www.icrc.org/eng/what-we-do/building-respect-ihl/advisory-service.

[24] *Ibid.* Recommendation V, at 85. As of November 2013, there are more than 100 such committees. For an overview, see www.icrc.org/eng/resources/documents/misc/table-national-committees.htm.

[25] *Ibid.* Recommendation II, at 84.

[26] 26th International Conference of the Red Cross and Red Crescent, 3–7 December 1995, Resolution 1, International humanitarian law: From law to action. Report on the follow-up to the International Conference for the Protection of War Victims, published in *International Review of the Red Cross*, No. 310 (1996), pp. 58–60.

carry out mandates entrusted to it by the International Conference'.[27] The assignment also fits the ICRC's role as guardian and promoter of international humanitarian law. This role is equally recognized in the Statutes of the Movement, in particular the ICRC's role 'to work for the understanding and dissemination of knowledge of international humanitarian law applicable in armed conflicts'.[28] But it also fits within its role 'to work for the faithful application of international humanitarian law applicable in armed conflicts'.[29] The formulation 'faithful application of international humanitarian law' refers to the application of both treaty law and customary international law. As a result, the ICRC cannot properly fulfil this task without having an insight into the content of customary international law.

The Conference gave this mandate to the ICRC, in light of the uneven ratification record of humanitarian law treaties and the rudimentary nature of treaty law governing non-international armed conflicts. Both Yugoslavia and Rwanda had ratified Additional Protocol II when their armed conflicts broke out but, as explained later, the Protocol does not cover many of the issues that arise in non-international armed conflicts. Therefore, it became more urgent than ever to know to what extent such gaps in treaty law were filled by customary international law.

III. Functions of Customary International Law

1. *Unifying Function*

Customary international law can provide a common set of rules applicable to all States regardless of their ratification of specific treaties. While the Geneva Conventions have today been universally adhered to,[30] the same cannot be said of other treaties of humanitarian law.

For example, Additional Protocols I and II to the Geneva Conventions have been ratified by more than 170 and 160 States, respectively. This is

[27] Statutes of the Red Cross and Red Crescent Movement, adopted by the International Conference of the Red Cross and Red Crescent, Geneva, October 1986, Article 5(2)(l).

[28] Statutes of the Red Cross and Red Crescent Movement (1986), Article 5(2)(g). On the ICRC's role in the interpretation of international humanitarian law see also Bugnion, *The International Committee of the Red Cross*, pp. 914–922.

[29] Statutes of the Red Cross and Red Crescent Movement (1986), Article 5(2)(c).

[30] Palestine was the most recent State to adhere to the Geneva Conventions on 2 April 2014. As a result, the Conventions are binding on all States as a matter of treaty law, regardless of whether they are also part of customary international law.

an impressive ratification record by any measure. However, an important number of States still remain outside the framework of this treaty regime. The same is true for other treaties, such as the 1954 Hague Convention on the Protection of Cultural Property in Time of Armed Conflicts and its Protocols, as well as the 1980 Convention on Certain Conventional Weapons and its Protocols. This situation implies that in different conflicts, different treaty regimes apply, which is not satisfactory from the perspective of the legal protection of war victims.[31] Customary rules of IHL apply equally to all armed conflicts, regardless of the ratification record of the parties to the conflict.

For example, during the armed conflict between Ethiopia and Eritrea from May 1998 until June 2000, Eritrea was not yet a party to the Geneva Conventions and Additional Protocol I. Hence, these treaties were formally inapplicable to the conflict. The Ethiopia-Eritrea Claims Commission had to grapple with this issue when it examined claims emerging from the conflict.[32] The Commission decided that it would work on the assumption that the Geneva Conventions, as well as Additional Protocol I, represented customary international law. However, if either party to the arbitration proceedings wished to challenge this assumption that party would have the burden of proof with respect to the Geneva Conventions, whereas the Commission would have the burden of proof with respect to Additional Protocol I.[33]

[31] For the list of States parties to the IHL treaties, see www.icrc.org/ihl.

[32] This Commission was set up after the end of the armed conflict between Ethiopia and Eritrea in 2000 in order to: 'decide through binding arbitration all claims for loss, damage or injury by one Government against the other, and by nationals (including both natural and juridical persons) of one party against the Government of the other party or entities owned or controlled by the other party that are (a) related to the conflict that was the subject of the Framework Agreement, the Modalities for its Implementation and the Cessation of Hostilities Agreement, and (b) result from violations of international humanitarian law, including the 1949 Geneva Conventions, or other violations of international law'. Agreement between the Governments of the State of Eritrea and the Federal Democratic Republic of Ethiopia, Algiers, 12 December 2000, Article 5(1). For an extensive analysis of the work of the Commission, see S. D. Murphy, W. Kidane and T. R. Snider, *Litigating War. Mass Civil Injury and the Eritrea-Ethiopia Claims Commission*, (Oxford: Oxford University Press, 2013).

[33] See Eritrea Ethiopia Claims Commission (*The State of Eritrea* v. *The Federal Democratic Republic of Ethiopia*), Partial Award, *Prisoners of War, Eritrea's Claim 17*, 1 July 2003, § 41 and Partial Award, *Prisoners of War, Ethiopia's Claim* 4, § 32 (concerning the Geneva Conventions); Eritrea Ethiopia Claims Commission, Partial Award, *Central Front, Eritrea's Claims 2, 4, 6, 7, 8 & 22*, 28 April 2004, § 23 and Partial Award, *Central Front, Ethiopia's Claim 2*, § 17 (concerning Additional Protocol I).

Hence, in a Partial Award of 19 December 2005 relating to issues on the conduct of hostilities, the Commission confirmed the customary status of a number of provisions of Additional Protocol I.[34] For example, with respect to the legality of an aerial bombardment of Eritrea's Harsile water reservoir by the Ethiopian air force, Ethiopia maintained that Article 54(2) of Additional Protocol I (concerning attacks against objects indispensable for the survival of the civilian population) did not apply because it was 'a new development in 1977 that had not become a part of customary international humanitarian law by the 1998–2000 war'.[35] The Commission rebutted Ethiopia's claim and concluded that Article 54(2) had become part of customary international law by the time of the attacks and Ethiopia was found in violation of the customary rule. However, because there had been no damage to the water reservoir the Commission held that the finding of the violation itself constituted satisfaction for Eritrea.[36]

The fact that different treaties have different levels of ratification also impacts coalition warfare when different coalition partners have not subscribed to the same treaties. In such cases, only customary humanitarian law provides a common set of rules that is applicable to all coalition partners. Therefore, even if a State is a party to a particular treaty, it may still be relevant to know to what extent that treaty reflects customary law and is, as such, binding on coalition partners which have not ratified it. This was the case, e.g. during the First Gulf War, NATO's air operations over Kosovo and more recently Libya.[37]

The unifying role of custom with respect to non-international armed conflicts is exemplified by the work of the International Commission of

[34] Eritrea Ethiopia Claims Commission, Partial Award, *Western Front, Aerial Bombardment and Related Claims*, 19 December 2005, § 95 (finding Articles 48, 51(2), 51(4)–(5), 52, 57 and 58 of Additional Protocol I to be customary).

[35] Eritrea Ethiopia Claims Commission, Partial Award, *Western Front, Aerial Bombardment and Related Claims*, 19 December 2005, § 103.

[36] *Ibid.*, §§ 104–5. Compare Henckaerts and Doswald-Beck (eds.), *Customary International Humanitarian Law*, Vol. I: Rules, Rule 54 and commentary.

[37] See e.g. Report of the International Commission of Inquiry to investigate all alleged violations of international human rights law in the Libyan Arab Jamahiriya, UN Doc. A/HRC/17/44, 1 June 2011, para. 76: 'In relation to the international armed conflict, the full provisions of the four Geneva Conventions, as well as customary international humanitarian norms relating to international armed conflict apply to engagements. Libya and most of the States involved in the military intervention [except Turkey and the United States] have also ratified Additional Protocol I to the Geneva Conventions Relating to the Protection of Victims of International Armed Conflict'.

Inquiry on Darfur in 2004–2005.[38] As the Commission reviewed facts related to the conflict in Darfur (Sudan) at a time when Sudan was not yet a party to Additional Protocol II, customary international humanitarian law applicable in non-international armed conflicts was of particular relevance for the work of the Commission. The Commission deemed it sufficient to mention 'only those customary rules on internal armed conflict which are relevant and applicable to the current armed conflict in Darfur' and listed 24 such rules.[39]

2. *Adapting Function*

The second function of customary international law lies in adapting international law to new realities. The formation of customary international law can be a more flexible process than the adoption of new treaties. The adoption, ratification and entry into force of treaties is regulated by strict formal procedures which makes the treaty process at times lengthy and cumbersome, including the process to amend treaties. Treaties tend therefore to be more static than custom, which is by nature based on a dynamic process.[40]

Thus, e.g. treaty law was able to adapt only partially to the increasing prevalence of non-international armed conflicts and the need for regulation of this type of armed conflict. Customary law on the other hand has been more dynamic and has evolved over time as State practice has changed.

Humanitarian treaty law offers only a rudimentary framework for the regulation of non-international armed conflicts, in particular with respect to the conduct of hostilities. Common Article 3 of the Geneva Conventions, the only provision of the Geneva Conventions that is formally applicable to non-international armed conflicts, does not as such deal with the conduct of hostilities. In addition, AP II does not deal with the conduct of hostilities and a number of other issues in sufficient detail either. For

[38] See Report of the International Commission of Inquiry on Darfur to the United Nations Secretary-General, pursuant to Security Council Resolution 1564 of 18 September 2004, 25 January 2005, available at www.unrol.org/files/com_inq_darfur.pdf.

[39] *Ibid.*, para. 166.

[40] On the other hand, treaties can, at times, regulate new issues faster or provide a more detailed regulation beyond what the customary process can produce. See e.g. Convention on Cluster Munitions, Dublin, 30 May 2008 (development of a clear prohibition through treaty law long before any specific custom on the subject could develop) and Arms Trade Treaty, New York, 2 April 2013 (development of a detailed regulatory framework far beyond a level of detail that can be achieved through the customary process).

example, unlike AP I, AP II does not provide for the obligation to distinguish between military objectives and civilian objects. As a result, it does not contain any protection for civilian objects in general, nor does it define civilian objects and military objectives. This is problematic in practice because even in non-international armed conflicts, armed forces (both State armed forces and non-State armed groups) are required to limit their military operations to military objectives. AP II lacks other key provisions on the conduct of hostilities, such as the prohibition and definition of indiscriminate attacks and the obligation to take precautions in attack and against the effects of attack.

Detailed provisions on the conduct of hostilities can be found in AP I but not in AP II, even though the draft of the protocol did contain them. In fact, the original drafts of both protocols submitted to the diplomatic conference that led to the adoption of the Additional Protocols were very similar.[41] Even during the diplomatic conference Committee III which worked on the draft of Protocol II accepted a substantial number of the draft provisions submitted by the ICRC, often with consensus, although sometimes with minor changes. But in the last weeks of a 4-year long negotiation, many parts of draft Protocol II were simply deleted. The main reason for this was that it transpired during the diplomatic conference that consensus could only be reached on a much-simplified text, not on the version elaborated by Committee III on the basis of the ICRC draft. This simplification process consisted, in particular, of removing or revising all articles that referred to the 'parties to the conflict'. A good example of this diplomatic manoeuvre is the provision on dissemination in the Additional Protocols. Whereas AP I imposes an obligation on all 'High Contracting Parties' to disseminate the Conventions and the Protocol as widely as possible,[42] AP II summarily requires that '[t]his Protocol shall be disseminated as widely as possible' without specifying to whom this obligation is addressed.[43] At the time, a number of States could not accept that armed groups as 'parties to the conflict' would have specific rights and obligations

[41] ICRC, Draft Additional Protocols to the Geneva Conventions of August 12, 1949, Geneva, June 1973, published in *Official Records of the Diplomatic Conference on the Reaffirmation and Development of International Humanitarian Law Applicable in Armed Conflicts*, Geneva, 1974–1977, Vol. I, Part III.

[42] Article 83(1) of the Protocol Additional to the Geneva Conventions of 12 August 1949 and Relating to the Protection of Victims of International Armed Conflict of 8 June 1977 (hereinafter AP I).

[43] See Article 19 of the Protocol Additional to the Geneva Conventions of 12 August 1949 and Relating to the Protection of Victims of Non-International Armed Conflicts, Geneva of 8 June 1977 (hereinafter AP II).

under international law, e.g. the obligation to disseminate humanitarian law.

This reticence was based on the reasoning of the then-newly independent States that recognizing such rights and obligations and, in general, a detailed regulation of non-international armed conflicts would encourage rebellion and secession, threatening their frail sovereignty. However, this reasoning was misleading as recognition of rights and obligations of non-State armed groups under international law predated AP II by at least 30 years. Indeed, Common Article 3 of the Geneva Conventions already imposed obligations on 'each Party to the conflict' not of an international character and even encouraged the parties to 'further endeavour to bring into force, by means of special agreements, all or part of the other provisions of the present Convention' and so went further than AP II. Common Article 3 specifies, on the other hand, that its application 'shall not affect the legal status of the Parties to the conflict', a provision that is repeated in some later treaties applicable to non-international armed conflict.[44]

The simplification process of AP II has, unfortunately, left the Protocol with an awkward structure. The basic rules on the distinction between military objectives, civilian objects and their subsequent definitions are missing, though the Protocol retained mention of detailed rules on specific objects, namely objects indispensable to the survival of the civilian population, works and installations containing dangerous forces and cultural objects and places of worship.[45] While these shortcomings in treaty law have somewhat been rectified in subsequent treaties applicable to non-international armed conflicts, it is through the parallel development of customary law that they have been rectified the most.

The ICRC's assessment of customary international law indicates that the main rules on the conduct of hostilities, the use of means and methods of warfare and the treatment of persons in the hands of a party to the conflict are customary, not only in international but also in non-international armed conflict. As a result, it can be said that the divide between the law on international and non-international armed conflicts has been significantly

[44] See e.g. Convention for the Protection of Cultural Property in the Event of Armed Conflict, The Hague, 14 May 1954, Article 19(4); Protocol on Prohibitions or Restrictions on the Use of Mines, Booby-Traps and Other Devices, as Amended, Geneva, 3 May 1996, Article 1(6).

[45] See Article 14 AP II (objects indispensable to the survival of the civilian population); Article 15 AP II (works and installations containing dangerous forces); Article 16 AP II (cultural objects and places of worship).

narrowed down. This has reversed some of the effects of the simplification process of Additional Protocol II that took place in 1977.

This is not to say that the law on international and non-international armed conflicts is now exactly the same. In *Tadić*, the ICTY Appeals Chamber famously noted that 'only a number of rules and principles governing international armed conflicts have gradually been extended to apply to internal conflicts; and this extension has not taken place in the form of a full and mechanical transplant of those rules to internal conflicts; rather, the general essence of those rules, and not the detailed regulation they may contain, has become applicable to internal conflicts.'[46] Later in the *Hadzihasanović* appeal on command responsibility the Appeals Chamber stated that 'the rules applicable to international armed conflicts do not automatically apply to an internal armed conflict and what may constitute a war crime in the context of an international armed conflict does not necessarily constitute a war crime if committed in an internal conflict'.[47]

Similarly, the ICRC study shows that a difference continues to exist between the regulation of international and non-international armed conflicts. Of the 161 rules the study has identified, 12 apply to international armed conflicts only. These relate to what continues to be considered the 'reserved domain' of international armed conflicts which are the definition of combatants and armed forces, conditions for POW status, the regulation of occupied territory, and the regulation of belligerent reprisals.[48] On the other hand, two rules were found to apply to non-international armed conflicts only. These relate to the prohibition of belligerent reprisals

[46] ICTY, *Prosecutor* v. *Tadić*, Decision on the Defence Motion for Interlocutory Appeal on Jurisdiction, Appeals Chamber, 2 October 1995, Case No. IT-94-1-AR72, para. 126.

[47] ICTY, *Prosecutor* v. *Hadžihasanović and Kubura*, Decision on Command Responsibility, IT-01-47-AR72, 16 July 2003, para. 12.

[48] These are Henckaerts and Doswald-Beck (eds.), *Customary International Humanitarian Law*, Vol. I: Rules, Rules 3 (definition of combatants), 4 (definition of armed forces), 41 (export and return of cultural property in occupied territory), 49 (war booty), 51 (public and private property in occupied territory), 106–8 (conditions for POW-status, spies, mercenaries), 130 (transfer of own civilian population in occupied territory), and 145–7 (reprisals). For an analysis of whether even these areas could be merged, see E. Crawford, 'Blurring the Lines Between International and Non-international Armed Conflicts: The Evolution of Customary International Law Applicable in Internal Armed Conflicts', *Australian International Law Journal*, 15 (2008), pp. 29–54; E. Crawford, *The Treatment of Combatants and Insurgents under the Law of Armed Conflict*, (Oxford: Oxford University Press, 2010) and E. Debuf, *Captured in War: Lawful Internment in Armed Conflict*, (West Sussex: Pédone/Hart, 2013), pp. 110–111.

and the granting of amnesty at the end of active hostilities.[49] With respect to the remaining 146 rules applicable in both international and non-international armed conflicts, three important nuances exist. First, several rules were found to be only 'arguably' customary in non-international armed conflicts, recognizing that practice was not as dense in certain areas.[50] Secondly, the wording of some rules of customary humanitarian law is different for international and non-international armed conflicts.[51] Finally, some rules of customary international humanitarian applicable in non-international armed could only be identified as applicable to States.[52] Hence, important differences in substance and scope continue to exist.

IV. Impact of the ICRC Study

Because of its origin – a mandate from the international community – the Study was intended as a working tool for practitioners involved with humanitarian law, not a handbook of theoretical considerations. Given the time and resources needed to collect and assess practice and *opinio iuris* for the purpose of identifying rules of customary IHL, the Study has proven its usefulness in practice.

Since its publication, the ICRC study has been used as a legal reference in international and non-international armed conflicts. With respect

[49] These are Henckaerts and Doswald-Beck (eds.), *Customary International Humanitarian Law*, Vol. I: Rules, Rules 148 (reprisals in non-international armed conflicts) and 159 (amnesty).

[50] The following rules were considered only 'arguably' customary in non-international armed conflicts: Henckaerts and Doswald-Beck (eds.), *Customary International Humanitarian Law*, Vol. I: Rules, Rules 21 (target selection), 23–4 (specific precautions against the effects of attack), 44–5 (specific rules on the natural environment), 62–3 (improper use of flags, military or military emblems, insignia or uniforms), and 82 (recording of the placement of landmines). For Rule 114 (return of the remains and personal effects of the dead), the study argues that the rule should apply equally in both international and non-international armed conflicts (*ibid.* at 412).

[51] The following rules have different formulations for international and non-international armed conflicts: Henckaerts and Doswald-Beck (eds.), *Customary International Humanitarian Law*, Vol. I: Rules, Rules 124 (ICRC access to persons deprived of their liberty), 126 (visits to persons deprived of their liberty), 128 (release and return of persons deprived of their liberty), and 129 (displacement).

[52] The following rules were found to be customary applicable to States only: Henckaerts and Doswald-Beck (eds.), *Customary International Humanitarian Law*, Vol. I: Rules, Rules 141 (legal advisors for armed forces), 143 (dissemination among the civilian population), 144 (ensuring respect *erga omnes*), 149–150 (responsibility and reparation), 157–8 (jurisdiction over and prosecution of war crimes), and 161 (international cooperation in criminal proceedings).

to international armed conflicts, this has been the case mainly in relation to States not party to Additional Protocol I (e.g. Afghanistan, Iraq, Israel or the United States). In international armed conflicts where all States involved are party to Additional Protocol I, such as the 2008 conflict between Georgia and Russia, customary humanitarian law and the study have been used to a lesser extent.

In non-international armed conflict, customary humanitarian law is relevant regardless of whether or not a State is party to Additional Protocol II. In States not party to Additional Protocol II, such as Sri Lanka and Syria, Common Article 3 of the Geneva Conventions is the main humanitarian treaty provision in force. Customary humanitarian law is therefore an important source of applicable humanitarian law rules. As a result, in its report of 2011, the Secretary-General's Panel of Experts on Accountability in Sri Lanka relied extensively on rules of customary international humanitarian law, including several identified by the ICRC study.[53] The same is true for the 2013 report of the independent international commission of inquiry on the Syrian Arab Republic.[54]

In States party to Additional Protocol II, such as Colombia or Libya, customary humanitarian law usefully complements the legal framework of Additional Protocol II.[55] Thus, for example, Colombia's operational law handbook refers to several rules of customary humanitarian law identified by the ICRC study.[56] There is also significant case law from the

[53] Report of the Secretary-General's Panel of Experts on Accountability in Sri Lanka, 31 March 2011, para. 183 ('In order to determine the content and meaning of customary international law, the Panel relies upon various sources, including the ICRC's study, *Customary International Humanitarian Law* (2005), which comprehensively analyses state practice and attitudes . . . '). For specific references to the study see *ibid.*, paras 194 (referring to Rule 1), 196 (Rules 7 and 35), 200 (Rule 2), 201 (Rules 11–13), 203 (Rule 14), 204 (Rules 15–20), 207 (Rules 25, 28, 30–2), 211 (Rules 53 and 55), 215 (Rule 98), 216 (Rule 118), 217 (Rules 112–13 and 115–17), 218 (Rule 115), 237 (Rule 97), 239 (Rules 23–4), 240 (Rule 136), and 241 (Rule 95).

[54] Report of the independent international commission of inquiry on the Syrian Arab Republic, A/HRC/22/59, 5 February 2013, pp. 15, 19, 23, 58, 66, 89–90, 110, 113, 116, 120 and 124.

[55] See Henckaerts and Doswald-Beck (eds.), *Customary International Humanitarian Law*, Vol. I: Rules, e.g. Rules 7–24 on the conduct of hostilities; Rules 31–2 on humanitarian relief personnel and objects; Rule 34 on journalists; Rules 43–5 on the environment; Rules 115–16 on the dead; Rule 117 on the missing; Rule 123 on persons deprived of their liberty, which are additional to the treaty rules in Additional Protocol II.

[56] Colombia, *Manual de Derecho Operacional, Comando General de la Fuerzas Armadas*, Manual FF.MM 3-41 Público, Primera Edición, 2009, referring to Rules 1 and 21 (page 37), Rules 14 and 87 (page 38), Rule 140 (pages 38–9), Rule 9 (page 40), Rule 25 (pages 42–3 and 45), Rule 28 (page 43), Rule 27 (pages 44–5), Rule 31 (pages 45–6), Rule 34 (page 46, 47), Rules 15, 16, and 18 (page 52), Rules 19, 20, 21, 22, 129 b, and 70 (page 53), Rules

Colombian constitutional court referring to customary humanitarian law and the study.[57] With respect to Libya, the International Commission of Inquiry analysed the facts under both treaty law binding upon Libya, including Additional Protocol II, as well as customary humanitarian law.[58]

In addition, UN special Rapporteurs have regularly relied on customary humanitarian law, e.g. the report by several special Rapporteurs of the UN Human Rights Council and the Representative of the Secretary-General on Internally Displaced Persons on their mission to Lebanon and Israel in the wake of the 2006 conflict.[59] Another example is the 2009 combined report of several mandate-holders of the UN Human Rights Council Special Procedures and the Special Representative of the Secretary-General for Children and Armed Conflict which referred to several rules in the study as being part of customary humanitarian law.[60]

72, 73, 74, 77, 78, 79, 80, 86 (page 54), Rules 46, 47, 48, 50, 52, 54, 65, 53 (page 55) and Rule 8 (page 56).

57 See, e.g., Colombia, Constitutional Court, Sentencia C-291/07, 25 April 2007, with numerous references throughout.

58 Report of the International Commission of Inquiry to investigate all alleged violations of international human rights law in the Libyan Arab Jamahiriya, UN Doc. A/HRC/17/44, 1 June 2011, paras. 103 (referring to ICRC Customary IHL Study, Henckaerts and Doswald-Beck (eds.), *Customary International Humanitarian Law*, Vol. I: Rules, (Rules 98–9, 117, 123, and 125–6), 141 (Rule 34), 156 (Rules 1, 11, and 14), 157 (Rules 15–21), 158 (Rules 31–2, 53, and 55), 182 (Rule 70), 183 (Rules 77 and 81) and 186 (Rule 81).

59 Report of the Special Rapporteur on extrajudicial, summary or arbitrary executions, Philip Alston; the Special Rapporteur on the right of everyone to the enjoyment of the highest attainable standard of physical and mental health, Paul Hunt; the Representative of the Secretary-General on human rights of internally displaced persons, Walter Kälin; and the Special Rapporteur on adequate housing as a component of the right to an adequate standard of living, Miloon Kothari, Mission to Lebanon and Israel (7–14 September 2006), UN Doc. A/HRC/2/7, 2 October 2006, para. 22 and following.

60 Human Rights Situation in Palestine and Other Occupied Arab Territories, Combined Report of the Special Rapporteur on the right of everyone to the enjoyment of the highest attainable standard of physical and mental health, the Special Representative of the Secretary-General for Children and Armed Conflict, the Special Rapporteur on violence against women, its causes and consequences, the Representative of the Secretary-General on the human rights of internally displaced persons, the Special Rapporteur on adequate housing as a component of the right to an adequate standard of living, and on the right to non-discrimination in this context, the Special Rapporteur on the right to food, the Special Rapporteur on extrajudicial, arbitrary or summary executions, the Special Rapporteur on the right to education, and the Independent Expert on the question of human rights and extreme poverty, UN Doc. A/HRC/10/22, 20 March 2009, paras. 11 (principles of distinction, proportionality and precaution, referring to Rules 6–9, 11–13, 15–24 and 97), 46 (prohibition of attacking, destroying, removing or rendering useless objects indispensable to the survival of the civilian population, referring to Rule 54), 66 (protection of medical personnel and facilities, referring to Rules 25 and 28–9), 66 (prohibition of attacks against

The study has also found its way into national and international case law. In Israel, for example, customary international law can be invoked directly before national courts and tribunals. As a result, the Supreme Court has on several occasions pronounced itself on the customary nature of rules of humanitarian law.[61] In recent years, it has done so with increasing reference to the ICRC study. For example, in a judgement of December 2005 on the so-called neighbour procedure used by the Israel Defence Forces (IDF) to capture persons, the Israeli Supreme Court referred with approval to the study's findings on the customary nature of the precautions to give effective, advance warning (Rule 20) and to remove civilians from the vicinity of military objectives (Rule 24) as well as the prohibition of human shields (Rule 97).[62] In its judgement of December 2006 on the policy of targeted killing, the Israeli Supreme Court referred with approval to the study's conclusions concerning the principle of distinction between civilians and combatants and between civilian objects and military objectives (Rules 1 and 7), the principle that civilians are protected against attack, unless and for such time as they take a direct part in hostilities (Rule 6), the prohibition of indiscriminate attacks (Rule 11) and the prohibition to cause excessive incidental loss of civilian life, injury to civilians, damage to civilian objects, or a combination thereof (Rule 14).[63] Subsequently, in a judgement of January 2008 concerning the reduction of fuel and electricity supply from Israel to Gaza, the Court referred to customary international humanitarian law and the ICRC study stating that 'each party to a conflict is obliged to refrain from disrupting the passage of basic humanitarian relief to populations needing it in areas under its control' but found that Israel had not violated this obligation.[64] The US Supreme Court cited the study in its *Hamdan* decision relating to the US

schools, referring to Rule 38), and 83 (prohibition of arbitrary displacement of civilians, referring to Rules 24 and 129–31).

[61] See, e.g., Israel, The Supreme Court sitting as the High Court of Justice, *Affo and others* v. *Commander of the IDF in the West Bank*, 10 December 1988, HCJ 785/87, HCJ 845/87, HCJ 27/88, *International Legal Materials*, 29 (1990), p. 139 (concerning the customary nature of Article 49 of the Fourth Geneva Convention).

[62] Israel, The Supreme Court sitting as the High Court of Justice, *Adalah and others* v. *GOC Central Command, IDF and others*, 23 June 2005, HCJ 3799/02, paras. 20–21 and 24.

[63] Israel, The Supreme Court sitting as the High Court of Justice, *The Public Committee against Torture in Israel and others* v. *The Government of Israel and others*, 13 December 2006, HCJ 769/02, paras. 23, 29–30 and 41–42; see also references to the commentary of the study in paras. 33–4, 40 and 46.

[64] Israel, The Supreme Court sitting as the High Court of Justice, *Jaber Al-Bassiouni Ahmed and others* v. *The Prime Minister and Minister of Defence*, 30 January 2008, HCJ 9132/07, paras. 14ff.

military commissions, where it stated that 'one of the Red Cross' own treatises defines 'regularly constituted court' as used in Common Article 3 to mean 'established and organized in accordance with the laws and procedures in force in a country'.'[65]

At the international level, the International Criminal Tribunal for the former Yugoslavia (ICTY) often operates on the basis of Article 3 of its Statute which gives the Tribunal jurisdiction over 'violations of the laws or customs of war'. The report of the UN Secretary-General submitted pursuant to the Security Council decision to establish the International Criminal Tribunal for the former Yugoslavia stated that 'the application of the principle *nullum crimen sine lege* requires that the international tribunal [International Criminal Tribunal for the former Yugoslavia] should apply rules of international humanitarian law which are beyond any doubt part of customary law so that the problem of adherence of some but not all States to specific conventions does not arise.'[66] As a result, in order to satisfy the principle of legality (*nullum crimen, nulla poena sine lege previa*), any conviction based on Article 3 of the Statute requires proof that the crime in question was part of customary international law at the time the alleged crime was committed.[67] For example, in *Prosecutor* v. *Hadžihasanović and Kubura*, the appeals chamber of the Tribunal concluded that the prohibition of wanton destruction of cities, plunder of public or private property, attacks against cultural property, and, more broadly, of attacks on civilian objects were customary norms whose violation, including in non-international armed conflict, entails individual criminal responsibility under customary international law. In doing so, it cited practice recorded in Volume II of the ICRC study on customary humanitarian law, rather than the rules in Volume I of the study.[68] Earlier in the same case, the appeals chamber had to determine whether it could apply the principles of command responsibility to war crimes committed in a non-international conflict. Since Additional Protocol II is silent on the matter of command responsibility, the appeals chamber

[65] US Supreme Court, *Hamdan* v. *Rumsfeld, Secretary of Defense, et al.*, Case No. 05–184, 29 June 2006, p. 69.

[66] UN Secretary-General, Report submitted pursuant to paragraph 2 of Security Council Resolution 808 (1993), U.N. Doc. S/25704, 3 May 1993, para. 34.

[67] See T. Meron, 'The Revival of Customary Humanitarian Law', *American Journal of International Law*, 99 (2005), p. 817.

[68] ICTY, Appeals Chamber, *Prosecutor* v. *Hadžihasanović and Kubura*, Decision on Joint Defence Interlocutory Appeal of Trial Chamber Decision on Rule 98 *bis* Motions for Acquittal, IT-01-47-AR73.3, 11 March 2005, paras. 29–30, 38 and 45–6.

examined whether command responsibility applied in non-international armed conflict on the basis of customary international law and concluded that it did.[69] This conclusion confirms a similar finding in the ICRC study on customary international humanitarian law.[70] A more recent example is the trial judgement in *Prosecutor* v. *Gotovina et al.* where the trial chamber cited the customary nature of Rule 50 of the ICRC's Customary IHL Study on seizure of property with approval.[71]

Since its publication, the ICRC itself has also relied on the study in many contexts. As stated in President Kellenberger's foreword, '[t]he ICRC believes that the study does indeed present an accurate assessment of the current state of customary international humanitarian law. It will therefore duly take the outcome of this study into account in its daily work, while being aware that the formation of customary international law is an ongoing process.'[72] Examples of such reliance can be found in the reports of the ICRC on its operations in Colombia.[73] This does not mean of course that the ICRC does not continue to rely on treaties and work for their faithful application where they are applicable. Thus in Colombia, both Common Article 3 and Additional Protocol II, as well as customary international humanitarian law are used as frameworks.[74]

Finally, there are also many examples of use of customary international humanitarian law and the study in reports by non-governmental

[69] ICTY, Appeals Chamber, *Prosecutor* v. *Hadžihasanović and Kubura*, Decision on Command Responsibility, IT-01-47-AR72, 16 July 2003, para. 31.

[70] See Henckaerts and Doswald-Beck (eds.), *Customary International Humanitarian Law*, Vol. I: Rules, Rule 153.

[71] ICTY, Trial Chamber I, *Prosecutor* v. *Gotovina, Čermak and Markač*, Judgment, IT-06-90-T, 15 April 2011, para. 1779.

[72] Henckaerts and Doswald-Beck (eds.), *Customary International Humanitarian Law*, Vol. I: Rules, p. xvii.

[73] See e.g. *Situación Humanitaria. Informe de Actividades Colombia 2012 [Humanitarian Situation. Report on Activities in Colombia 2012]*, ICRC Bogotá, March 2013, available in Spanish at www.icrc.org/spa/assets/files/2013/colombia-report-2012.pdf, referring to Rules 1 and 2 (at 15), Rule 117 (at 19), Rules 131–2 (at 27), Rule 93 (at 37), Rules 135–7 (at 41), Rules 10 and 22 (at 45), Rule 70 (at 49), Rule 124B (at 69), and Rule 118 (at 75). For previous reports, see *Situación Humanitaria. Informe de Actividades Colombia 2011 [Humanitarian Situation. Report on Activities in Colombia 2011]*, ICRC Bogotá, March 2012, available in Spanish at www.icrc.org/spa/assets/files/2012/informe-colombia-2011.pdf; *Informe 2010 Colombia [Report 2010 Colombia]*, ICRC Bogotá, March 2010, available in Spanish at www.icrc.org/spa/assets/files/other/icrc_003_t20102104.pdf; *Report 2009 Colombia*, ICRC Bogotá, April 2010, available in English at www.icrc.org/eng/assets/files/other/annual-report-2009-colombia-icrc.pdf.

[74] *Situación Humanitaria. Informe de Actividades Colombia 2012[Humanitarian Situation. Report on Activities in Colombia 2012]*, at 10.

organizations, particularly in relation to countries not party to the Additional Protocols.[75]

V. Reactions to the Study

The study's methodology is explained in its introduction and has been summarized in an article that first appeared in the *International Review of the Red Cross*.[76] In essence, the methodology followed sought to apply the test of 'general practice accepted as law' as set out in the Statute of the International Court of Justice.[77] The study therefore looked inductively at the practice collected. It did not start from preconceived ideas about what could or should be customary in a particular treaty, in particular the Additional Protocols. That is why the study does not follow the structure of the Protocols. Although several rules are formulated similar or identical to rules in the Protocol, other rules have no specific equivalent in treaty law.[78] The identification of such rules is evidence that the analysis of

[75] See, e.g. Amnesty International, *The Conflict in Gaza: A Briefing on Applicable Law, Investigations, and Accountability*, (London, 2009), pp. 15 and 30 (references to Rule 156 on the definition of war crimes and to Rule 150 on reparation); Human Rights Watch, *War on the Displaced: Sri Lankan Army and LTTE Abuses against Civilians in the Vanni*, (New York, 2009), pp. 21 and 26 (references to Rule 158 on investigation and prosecution of war crimes; Rule 55 on access for humanitarian relief and to Rule 56 on freedom of movement of humanitarian relief personnel); Human Rights Watch, *Precisely Wrong: Gaza Civilians Killed by Israeli Drone-Launched Missiles*, (New York, 2009), pp. 30–32 (reference to Rule 158 on investigation and prosecution of war crimes); Human Rights Watch, *Rain of Fire: Israel's Unlawful Use of White Phosphorus in Gaza*, (New York, 2009), pp. 60–66 (references to Rule 85 on incendiary weapons and to Rule 156 on the definition of war crimes); Human Rights Watch, *The Human Cost: The Consequences of Insurgent Attacks in Afghanistan*, (New York, 2007), pp. 83–89 (references to Rule 1 and 7 on distinction; Rule 2 on acts or threats of terror; Rule 4 on the definition of armed forces; Rule 8 on military objectives; Rule 12 on indiscriminate attacks; Rule 14 on proportionality; Rules 15–18 on precautions in attack and to Rule 65 on perfidy); Karen Human Rights Group, *Development by Decree. The politics of poverty and control in Karen State*, (KHRG, April 2007), pp. 118–119 (references to Rule 54 on attacking objects indispensable for civilian survival; to Rule 55 on access for humanitarian relief and to Rule 131 on measures to be taken in case of displacement); National Lawyers Guild, *Onslaught: Israel's Attack on Gaza and The Rule of Law*, (New York, 2009), pp. 21–25 (references to Rule 71 on indiscriminate weapons; to Rule 84 on incendiary weapons and to Rule 109 on wounded and sick).

[76] J.-M. Henckaerts, 'Study on Customary International Humanitarian Law: A Contribution to the Understanding and Respect for the Rule of Law in Armed Conflict', *International Review of the Red Cross*, 87 (2005) No. 857, pp. 175–212.

[77] Statute of the International Court of Justice, Article 38(1)(b).

[78] See in particular Rule 44 on due regard for the natural environment, Rule 64 on suspension of combat as a method of deception, Rule 66 on non-hostile contacts between commanders,

custom was driven by the collection of practice and not by existing treaty frameworks.

The reactions and critique generally did not question the ICRC's authority in issuing the study but discussed the methodology of the study and asked whether the study had actually followed its own methodology. In addition to the reaction by the US government,[79] there have been numerous reactions from scholars.[80] In addition, the British Institute of International and Comparative Law, together with Chatham House, have organized a series of Discussion Group meetings that culminated in the

Rule 76 on the use of herbicides, Rule 81 on landmines, Rules 84–85 on the use of incendiary weapons, Rule 105 on the protection of family life, Rule 140 on reciprocity, Rule 148 on reprisals in non-international armed conflicts, Rule 157 on universal jurisdiction and Rule 158 on the obligation to investigate war crimes.

[79] J. B. Bellinger and W. J. Haynes, 'A US government response to the International Committee of the Red Cross Study *Customary International Humanitarian Law*', *International Review of the Red Cross*, 89 (2007) No. 866, p. 443.

[80] See, in particular, M. Bothe, 'Customary International Humanitarian Law: Some Reflections on the ICRC Study', *Yearbook of International Humanitarian Law*, 8 (2005), 143; M. Cowling, 'International Lawmaking in Action – The 2005 Customary International Humanitarian Law Study and Non-International Armed Conflicts', *African Yearbook on International Humanitarian Law*, I (2006), p. 65; R. Cryer, 'Of Custom, Treaties, Scholars and the Gavel: The Influence of the International Criminal Tribunals on the ICRC Customary Law Study', *Journal for Conflict and Security Law*, 11 (2006), p. 239; Y. Dinstein, 'The ICRC Customary International Humanitarian Law Study', *Israel Yearbook of Human Rights*, 36, 2006, 1; C. Emanuelli, 'L'étude dur CICR sur le droit humanitaire coutumier: La coutume en question', *Revue Générale de Droit International Public*, 110 (2006) No. 2, p. 435; D. Fleck, 'International Accountability for Violations of the *Ius in Bello*: The Impact of the ICRC Study on Customary International Humanitarian Law', *Journal for Conflict and Security Law*, 11 (2006), p. 179; J. L. Greer, 'A Critique of the ICRC's Customary Rules Concerning Displaced Persons: General Accuracy, Conflation, and a Missed Opportunity', *Military Law Review*, 192 (Summer 2007), p. 116; J. J. Marsh, 'Lex Lata or Lex Ferenda? Rule 45 of the ICRC Study on Customary International Humanitarian Law', *Military Law Review*, 198 (Winter 2008), p. 116; J. J. Marsh, 'Rule 99 of the Customary International Humanitarian law Study and the Relationship Between the Law of Armed Conflict and International Human Rights Law', *The Army Lawyer*, May 2009, p. 18; H. Krieger, 'A Conflict of Norms: The Relationship between Humanitarian Law and Human Rights Law in the ICRC Customary Law Study', *Journal for Conflict and Security Law*, 11 (2006), p. 265; M. MacLaren and F. Schwendimann, 'An Exercise in the Development of International Law: The New ICRC Study on Customary International Humanitarian Law', *German Law Journal*, 6 (2005) No. 9, p. 1217; L. M. Nicholls, 'The Humanitarian Monarchy Legislates: The International Committee of the Red Cross and Its 161 Rules of Customary International Humanitarian Law', *Duke Journal of Comparative & International Law*, 17 (2006), p. 223; P. Rowe, 'The Effect on National Law of the Customary International Humanitarian Law Study', *Journal for Conflict and Security Law*, 11 (2006), p. 165; and D. Turns, 'Weapons in the ICRC Study on Customary International Humanitarian Law', *Journal for Conflict and Security Law*, 11 (2006), p. 201.

publication of a book of commentary on the study.[81] This author has responded to some of these comments.[82]

Several methodological issues discussed in the ICRC's study have also been raised, and are the subject of debate, in the International Law Commission as part of its current work on the identification of customary international law.[83] The ICRC study is a concrete example of how the theory on customary international law plays out in practice, in particular in the area of IHL. It is noteworthy that the ICRC study followed the two-elements approach (requiring both practice and *opinio juris*) which the ILC has also endorsed.[84] The ICRC's study shows that this approach is workable.

The following is a summary of the essence of the discussion on the methodology of the study.

1. *The Relevance of Physical and Verbal Acts of States*

It has not been contested that both physical and verbal acts of States constitute practice that contributes to the creation of customary international law.[85] Physical acts include, for example, battlefield behaviour, the use of certain weapons and the treatment afforded to different categories of persons. Verbal acts include military manuals, national legislation, national case law, instructions to armed and security forces, military communiqués during war, diplomatic protests, executive decisions and regulations, pleadings before international tribunals, statements in international *fora*, and government positions on resolutions adopted by

[81] E. Wilmshurst and S. Breau (eds.), *Perspectives on the ICRC Study on Customary International Humanitarian Law* (Cambridge: Cambridge University Press, 2007).

[82] See, e.g., J.-M. Henckaerts, 'Customary International Humanitarian Law – A Rejoinder to Judge Aldrich', *British Yearbook of International Law*, 76 (2006), p. 525; J.-M. Henckaerts, 'The ICRC Customary International Humanitarian Law Study – A Rejoinder to Professor Dinstein', *Israel Yearbook on Human Rights*, 37 (2007), p. 259; and J.-M. Henckaerts, 'Customary International Humanitarian Law – A Response to US Comments', *International Review of the Red Cross*, 89 (2007) No. 866, p. 473.

[83] For more information on the International Law Commission's work on this topic, see in particular First, Second and Third report on formation and evidence of customary international law, by Michael Wood, Special Rapporteur, UN Doc. A/CN.4/663 of 17 May 2013, A/CN.4/672 of 22 May 2014 and A/CN.4/682 of 27 March 2015.

[84] See ILC, Identification of customary international law, Text of the draft conclusions provisionally adopted by the Drafting Committee, Draft conclusion 2. Two constituent elements: 'To determine the existence and content of a rule of customary international law, it is necessary to ascertain whether there is a general practice that is accepted as law (*opinio juris*).', UN Doc. A/CN.4/L.869, 14 July 2015.

[85] See *ibid.* Draft conclusion 6. Forms of practice.

international organizations. This list shows that the practice of the executive, legislative and judicial organs of a State can contribute to the formation of customary international law.

A study on customary international law, therefore, has to look at the combined effect of what States say (verbal acts) and what they actually do (physical acts). An examination of operational practice (physical acts) alone would not be enough. In order to arrive at an accurate assessment of customary international law, one has to look beyond a mere description of actual military operations and examine the legal assessment of such operations. This requires an analysis of official positions taken by the parties involved, as well as by other States. This is in line with the two-element approach endorsed by the ILC in its current work on the formation of customary international law.[86] The ICRC followed this approach in its study and found it to be a workable approach.

When a given operational practice is generally accepted – e.g. the targeting of military installations – this supports the proposition underlying that practice, namely that military installations constitute lawful military targets. But when an operational practice is generally considered to be a violation of existing rules – e.g. the targeting of civilian structures – that is all it is, a violation, not of a nature to modify existing rules.[87] This explains why acts such as attacks against civilians, pillage and sexual violence remain prohibited notwithstanding numerous reports of their commission. The conclusion that these acts are considered to be violations of existing rules can be derived only from the way they are received by States and relevant international bodies through verbal acts, such as military manuals, national legislation, national and international case law, resolutions of international organizations and official statements. These verbal acts provide the lens through which to look at operational practice.

As a result of the previous considerations, the study also had to take into account resolutions adopted by States in the framework of international organizations, in particular the United Nations and regional

[86] See ILC, Draft conclusions, Identification of customary international law.

[87] According to the ICJ '[i]f a State acts in a way *prima facie* incompatible with a recognized rule, but defends its conduct by appealing to exceptions or justifications contained within the rule itself, then whether or not the State's conduct is in fact justifiable on that basis, the significance of that attitude is to confirm rather than to weaken the rule'. See ICJ, *Case concerning Military and Paramilitary Activities in and against Nicaragua (Nicaragua* v. *United States), Merits, Judgment*, 27 June 1986, *ICJ Reports 1986*, p. 98, para. 186.

organizations.[88] However, the study is premised on the recognition that, with a few exceptions, 'resolutions are normally not binding in themselves and therefore the value accorded to any particular resolution depends on its content, its degree of acceptance and the consistency of State practice outside it'.[89]

2. *The Distinction Between Practice of Contracting and of Non-Contracting States*

The study did not assume that a rule is customary merely because it is contained in a widely ratified treaty. Widespread ratification was considered an indication only and was assessed in relation to other elements of practice, in particular the practice of States not party to the treaty in question. Consistent practice of States not party was considered as important positive evidence. Contrary practice of States not party was considered as important negative evidence.

As a result, the distinction between contracting parties and non-contracting parties was taken into consideration in the assessment of each rule. To this effect, so-called 'negative lists' were used – lists of countries that are not party to relevant treaties – to identify practice of non-party States. It is interesting to note how these lists can differ considerably from one treaty regime to the other. For example, the list of States party to Additional Protocol I differs considerably from the list of States party to the 1954 Hague Convention on the Protection of Cultural Property.[90] This also means that to the extent that different treaties contain the same or similar rules, a State's practice and ratification record have to be matched up with respect to all relevant treaties. Although the United States is not

[88] The study looked at resolutions adopted by the UN Security Council, General Assembly, ECOSOC and Commission on Human Rights, as well as by *inter alia* the African Union (AU), Council of Europe, European Union (EU), Gulf Cooperation Council (GCC), League of Arab States (LAS), Organization of American States (OAS), Organization of the Islamic Conference (OCI) and the Organization for Security and Cooperation in Europe (OSCE).

[89] Henckaerts and Doswald-Beck (eds.), *Customary International Humanitarian Law*, Vol. I: Rules, pp. xxxv–xxxvi. See also ILC, Draft conclusions, Identification of customary international law, Draft conclusion 12.

[90] Azerbaijan, Eritrea, India, Indonesia, Iran, Israel, Malaysia, Myanmar, Pakistan, Sri Lanka, Thailand, Turkey and the United States of America are not party to Additional Protocol I but are party to the 1954 Hague Convention on the Protection of Cultural Property (at January 2014). The same was true, until 2010, for Iraq prior to its ratification of Additional Protocol I on 1 April 2010 and, until 2011, for Morocco which ratified the Protocol on 3 June 2011.

a party to Additional Protocol I, for example, it is a party to Protocol II and Amended Protocol II to the Convention on Certain Conventional Weapons (CCW), which contain a number of rules that are identical to those in Additional Protocol I. Thus, while the United States has not formally accepted the rules of distinction and proportionality and the prohibition of indiscriminate attacks through ratification of Additional Protocol I, it has formally accepted these rules, at least with respect to mines, booby traps and other devices, through ratification of Amended Protocol II to the CCW, which applies in both international and non-international armed conflicts.[91]

As a result of the weight accorded to negative practice of non-contracting parties, a number of provisions in Additional Protocol I, for example, were not found to be customary (e.g. the prohibition of reprisal attacks against civilians as contained in Additional Protocol I).

The study did not, however, limit itself to the practice of States not party to the relevant treaties of international humanitarian law. To limit the study to a consideration of the practice of only the 30-odd States that have not ratified the Additional Protocols, for example, would not comply with the requirement that customary international law be based on widespread and representative practice. Therefore, the assessment of the existence of customary law took into account the fact that, at the time of writing, Additional Protocol I had been ratified by 162 States and Additional Protocol II by 158 States (as of 1 September 2015, 174 and 168, respectively). Similarly, the assessment of customary law took into account the fact that, at the time of writing, the Geneva Conventions had been ratified by 192 States (now 195 States). Although ratification does not *ipso facto* mean that a State party regards the ratified treaty rules as customary, such ratification does constitute an element to be taken into account in the overall assessment of practice.

3. *The Contribution of Specially Affected States*

The study duly noted the contribution of States that have had a greater extent and depth of experience in the field of the law of armed conflict and have typically contributed a significantly greater quantity and quality of practice than other States. A perusal of the study reveals the significant contribution to practice made by such States. Because of its experience

[91] See Protocol on Prohibitions or Restrictions on the Use of Mines, Booby Traps and Other Devices, Articles 2–3.

with armed conflict, the United States, for example, has contributed a significant amount of practice to the formation of customary humanitarian law. It also has taken positions on many points of interpretation of the law and these are often noted in the commentaries.

Hence, there are States that have contributed more practice than others because they have been involved more often in armed conflict and their position on the law is thus easy to identify. Whether such practice counts more than the limited practice of other States in terms of satisfying the requirement of 'widespread and representative' practice is a separate question. The statement of the International Court of Justice in respect to the need for the practice of 'specially affected' States to be included was made in the specific context of the law of the sea – and, in particular, in order to determine whether, after the passage of only a short period of time, a rule in a (not widely ratified) treaty had become part of customary international law.[92]

Furthermore, the law of the sea governs situations which are based on inherent, geographic facts that objectively make certain States specially affected – e.g. because they have a coastline, because they have a bay, because they are archipelagic or because they are landlocked. It is questionable whether the same considerations can apply to humanitarian law because humanitarian law governs situations of armed conflict which can potentially affect any State, i.e. no State is inherently free from armed conflict. Therefore, all States have a legitimate and equal interest in the development of humanitarian law and, as a result, it can be argued that there is no place for a rule on 'specially affected' States in international humanitarian law.

4. *The Required Density of Practice*

While it is agreed that practice has to be 'extensive and virtually uniform' in order to establish a rule of customary international law,[93] there is no specific mathematical threshold for how extensive practice has to be. This is because the density of practice depends primarily on the subject matter. Some issues arise more often than others and generate more practice. One only has to compare, for example, the practice with regard to targeting and

[92] ICJ, *North Sea Continental Shelf cases, Judgment*, 20 February 1969, *ICJ Reports* 1969, p. 43, para. 74.

[93] *Ibid.* See also ILC, Draft conclusions, Identification of customary international law, Draft conclusion 8. The practice must be general.

the practice with regard to the white flag of truce. Questions of targeting – e.g. the distinction between civilians and combatants and between civilian objects and military objectives – are discussed every day in connection with various armed conflicts, are addressed in nearly every military manual, analysed in international *fora*, in judgements, and so forth. Practice on the protection of the white flag of truce, on the other hand, is rather sparse. In general, the topic is rarely discussed, as there are relatively few concrete cases. Nevertheless, whatever practice there is on the protection of the white flag of truce is uniform and confirms the continued validity of the rule, regardless of limited concrete practice. Such a differentiated approach is inevitable in any area of international law.[94]

Furthermore, in order to correctly quantify the density of practice it is necessary to determine the correct value of each element of practice. While some elements of practice may constitute single precedents, other elements may reflect numerous precedents. This is particularly the case of military orders, instructions and manuals, as they reflect what armed forces are trained and instructed to do and what they end up doing most of the time. Hence, a single military manual may represent numerous precedents and thus a substantial quantum of practice.[95]

In addition, the nature of the rule has to be taken into account – whether it is prohibitive, obligatory or permissive. Prohibitive rules, for example, of which there are many in humanitarian law, are supported not only by statements recalling the prohibition in question but also by abstention from the prohibited act.[96] The prohibition to use certain weapons, e.g. biological weapons, is supported by the continued abstention from using such weapons, every day in every conflict. Such abstention alone is

[94] Thus, in the *'Wimbledon'* case, the Permanent Court of International Justice relied on two precedents only, those of the Panama and Suez Canals, to find that the passage of contraband of war through international canals was not a violation of the neutrality of the riparian State. Permanent Court of International Justice, The *'Wimbledon'* case, (1923), PCIJ Series A, No. 1, pp. 1, 28. Obviously the Court could not cite more examples, as the number of international canals is limited. See also C. H. M. Waldock, 'General course on public international law', *Recueil des cours*, 106 (1962), 1, at 44, who observes that 'on a question concerning international canals, of which there are very few in the world, the quantum of practice must necessarily be small'.

[95] This may be compared to the facts in the *'Wimbledon'* case, *ibid.*, in which the Permanent Court of International Justice relied on two precedents only. But those two precedents represented a significant amount of practice, as many vessels, from all over the world, passed through the Panama and Suez Canals. So a reference to just two precedents represented a wider body of practice than a first impression might suggest.

[96] See ILC, Draft conclusions, Identification of customary international law, Draft conclusion 6. Forms of practice ('Practice … may, under certain circumstances, include inaction.')

obviously not enough; evidence is required that this is done out of a sense of legal obligation (see next).

5. *The Assessment of* Opinio Juris

After collecting and weighing the extent of the practice, a separate analysis had to be conducted in order to determine whether the practice attested to the existence of a rule of law or was inspired merely by non-legal considerations of convenience, comity or policy. The conclusion that practice reflects belief in the existence of a rule of law and not merely a policy was never based on any single instance or type of practice but was the result of consideration of all the relevant practice. For example, it may be difficult to determine whether a State votes in favour of a resolution condemning attacks on cultural property in armed conflict because it believes this prohibition to reflect a rule of (customary) law or whether it does so following a policy decision; and the vote could be based on both considerations at the same time. However, the totality of the practice on the subject of attacks on cultural property indicates that this prohibition is a rule of law, not merely a matter of policy.

In the same vein, military manuals may put forward propositions that are based on law, but may also contain instructions based on policy or military considerations that go beyond the law although, of course, they should never fall *below* the requirements of the law. This distinction was always kept in mind when assessing the collected practice. Rules that were supported by military manuals were, taking into account the totality of practice, supported by practice of such a nature that it was clear that a rule of law was involved and not merely a policy consideration or a consideration of military or political expediency that can change from one conflict to the next. For example, the fact that the United States decided, as a matter of policy rather than law, that it will apply the rules in its military manuals regardless of whether the conflict is characterized as international or non-international was recognized as a policy decision in the study. Hence, US military manuals were never cited as supporting evidence for rules applicable in non-international armed conflicts.

6. *The Persistent Objector Rule*

The study may have caused some confusion by stating in the introduction that it took no view as to whether it is legally possible to be a 'persistent objector' in relation to customary rules of international humanitarian law. Although persistent objection may not be possible in the case of rules of *jus cogens*, presumably not all rules of customary international humanitarian law are *jus cogens* and therefore persistent objection would be possible. The study actually recognizes this; with respect to Rule 45 on widespread, long-term and severe damage to the natural environment, the study noted that France, the United Kingdom and the United States have persistently objected to the rule being applicable to nuclear weapons and that the United States may be considered a persistent objector with respect to Rule 45 in general, including for conventional weapons. It is required, however, that the State concerned must have objected to the emergence of a new norm during its formation and continue to object afterwards; it is not possible to be a 'subsequent objector'.[97] That there are no other examples of persistent objection in the study should not come as a surprise. The 160 remaining rules in the study reflect basic rules of international humanitarian law against which no State has felt the need to persistently object. These are rules that have been tried and tested in practice and make sense from a military and humanitarian point of view.

Furthermore, it is important to distinguish persistent objection, which only frees individual States from being bound by an existing customary rule, from situations in which the practice and *opinio juris* of many States is contrary to a potential rule which, as a result, does not become part of customary international law. As a result, for example, the prohibition of reprisals against civilians in general, as contained in Additional Protocol I, was not found to be customary by the study.

Conclusion

Whereas the founding of the ICRC is closely linked to the emergence of humanitarian treaty law, the ICRC's work on and with customary IHL only came to full speed some 130 years later. As the ICRC celebrated its 150th anniversary in 2013 the organisation has finally come full circle and published a thorough assessment of customary international humanitarian law. This area of law is now well integrated into the ICRC's work and the practice underlying norms of customary IHL is being updated regularly.

The ICRC was mandated by States to undertake this assessment in order to contribute to the clarification of the content of customary humanitarian law, by definition a body of unwritten rules. The ICRC took this mandate very seriously and invested a considerable amount of time and resources to

[97] ILC, Draft conclusions, Identification of customary international law, Draft conclusion 15. Persistent objector. See also M. H. Mendelson, 'The Formation of Customary International Law', *Recueil des Cours* 159 (1998) p. 244.

conduct this exercise in a scientific manner. The organisation spent eight years on research and expert consultations in order to produce a credible study. The study seeks to provide a snapshot of custom today that is as accurate as possible. The result is the most comprehensive and thorough study of its kind to date. As Judge Meron noted with respect to the study:

> Such an effort has never been undertaken before. No restatement of international law has even tried to amass such a rich collection of empirical data.[98]

The resulting 161 rules are gleaned from the collected practice which can be found in Volume II. The rules were all distilled from the collected practice and drafted on that basis. That the study erred on the side of caution when it came to identifying custom is exemplified by a number of conclusions:

First, several rules codified in widely ratified treaties could not be determined to be customary. This is the case for example of the rule of doubt in Article 50(1) of Additional Protocol I and the prohibition of reprisals against civilians in Article 51(6) of the Protocol even though the ICTY concluded that this prohibition was customary.[99]

Second, several rules were only found to be 'arguably' customary in non-international armed conflicts.[100] This meant that practice generally pointed in that direction but was less extensive.

Although the ICRC study has become the starting point of any discussion on customary humanitarian law, it should not be seen as the final word because, per definition, it cannot be exhaustive and the formation of customary law is an ongoing process. As mentioned, the ICRC, in partnership with the British Red Cross Society, continues to update the practice contained in Volume II of the study,[101] allowing the ICRC and others to continue to evaluate and assess the scope and content of customary IHL on a broad range of topics.

[98] T. Meron, 'Revival of Customary Humanitarian Law', *American Journal of International Law*, Vol. 99, No. 4, October 2005, p. 833.

[99] Henckaerts and Doswald-Beck (eds.), *Customary International Humanitarian Law*, Vol. I: Rules, pp. 520–523.

[100] *Ibid.* Rules 21, 23–24, 44–45, 62–63 and 82.

[101] See www.icrc.org/customary-ihl/eng/docs/v2.

4

The International Committee of the Red Cross' 'Interpretive Guidance on the Notion of Direct Participation in Hostilities': See a Little Light

ROBERT CRYER

I. Introduction

In some ways, the topics the International Committee of the Red Cross (ICRC) has engaged in over the last, say, twenty years, have been sufficiently complex and controversial that they could perhaps be best explained by what on the playground would be called 'dares'. After all, surely few angels would dare to tread on the hazardous ground that amounted to the customary law of international and non-international armed conflict. Yet that is precisely what the ICRC did with its monumental *Customary Humanitarian Law* Study in 2005.[1] Admittedly, at the other end of the spectrum in terms of success was the SIrUS project, which attempted to create objective measures for superfluous injury and unnecessary suffering, but floundered on the basis of State (at best) ambivalence a few years before.[2] Somewhere in between, seemingly, is the most recent contribution of the ICRC to the debate on International Humanitarian Law (IHL). This is their interpretative guidance on direct participation in hostilities (DPH).[3]

This is an area of law in which there has been a great deal of debate, by which is meant deep controversy, and that difficulty has only increased in the last ten or so years, with the advent of 'targeted killings' and the use of drone strikes by Western powers (even though the latter do not, as it

[1] J.-M. Henckaerts and L. Doswald-Beck, *Customary International Humanitarian Law*, 2 vols. (Cambridge: Cambridge University Press, 2005).

[2] ICRC, *The SIrUS Project: Towards a Determination of Which Weapons Cause Superfluous Injury or Unnecessary Suffering* (Geneva: ICRC, 1997).

[3] N. Melzer, *Interpretative Guidance on the Notion of Direct Participation in Hostilities Under International Humanitarian Law* (Geneva: ICRC 2009) [hereinafter *Guidance*] reprinted in *International Review of the Red Cross*, 90 (2008), pp. 991–1047.

stands, necessarily raise any particular IHL issues that other weapons do not).[4] As a result, the simple fact of the attempt to grapple with such a vexed, albeit central, issue of IHL is a cause for at least two cheers. That said, the guidance has come in for considerable criticism, it is part of the purpose of this chapter to investigate, and appraise some of those critiques, and link them to broader debates about IHL.

II. Background to the Guidance

Prior to the ICRC guidance it must be said, there was little detailed commentary on DPH that could be prayed in aid. The treaty law on point was (and is) to say the least, fragmentary. The first provision on point is the Delphic reference in Common Article 3 of the 1949 Geneva Conventions to 'Persons taking no active part in hostilities, including members of armed forces who have laid down their arms and those placed *hors de combat*. . .'. Even the most detailed of the Red Cross Commentaries, that to the Fourth Convention merely says that 'this applies first and foremost to civilians – that is to people who do not bear arms'.[5] The only other two treaty provisions that are directly on point are Article 51(3) of Additional Protocol I (API, for international armed conflicts), which reads 'Civilians shall enjoy the protection afforded by this Section, unless and for such time as they take a direct part in hostilities'. Similarly, Article 13(3) of Additional Protocol II (APII, for non-international armed conflicts) states 'Civilians shall enjoy the protection afforded by this Part, unless and for such time as they take a direct part in hostilities'.

The authoritative ICRC Commentary to API does provide some help here.[6] So, for example, it asserts that hostile acts 'should be understood to be acts which by their nature and purpose are intended to cause actual harm to the personnel and equipment of the armed forces.'[7] In addition 'It seems that the word 'hostilities' covers not only the time that the civilian actually makes use of a weapon, but also, for example, the time that he is

[4] Amongst the voluminous literature see, e.g. N. Melzer, *Targeted Killings* (Oxford: Oxford University Press, 2008); C. Finkelstein, J. D. Ohlin and A. Altman (eds.), *Targeted Killings: Law and Morality in an Asymmetrical World* (Oxford: Oxford University Press, 2012). Admittedly, autonomous weapons systems raise novel issues, even though they are still subject to the traditional law.

[5] J. Pictet (ed.), *Commentary to the IV Geneva Convention Relative to the Protection of Civilian Persons in Time of War* (Geneva: ICRC, 1958), p. 40.

[6] Y. Sandoz, C. Swiniarski and B. Zimmermann (eds.), *Commentary on the Additional Protocols to the Geneva Conventions of 12 August 1949* (Geneva: ICRC/Nijhoff, 1987).

[7] *Ibid.*, p. 618.

carrying it, as well as situations in which he undertakes hostile acts without using a weapon.'[8] Finally, 'direct participation means acts of war which by their nature or purpose are likely to cause actual harm to the personnel and equipment of the enemy armed forces. It is only during such participation that a civilian loses his immunity and becomes a legitimate target', and this is to be differentiated from participation in the war effort in general.[9] The commentary on Article 13(3) of APII adds that 'direct' implies that 'there is a sufficient causal relationship between the act of participation and its immediate consequences'.[10] Unfortunately, there was little further clarification.[11]

Although the issue of direct participation in hostilities is far from a new one, being traceable at least back to the Lieber code,[12] the changing character of war led many to think that the time was ripe for a reappraisal of the concept.[13] Therefore, in 2003, the ICRC set up a set of five meetings

[8] *Ibid.*, pp. 618–619.

[9] *Ibid.*, p. 619. See also M. Bothe, K. J. Partsch and W. A. Solf, *New Rules for Victims of Armed Conflicts: Commentary to the Two 1977 Protocols Additional to the Geneva Conventions of 1949* (The Hague: Nijhoff, 1982), pp. 301–304.

[10] *Ibid.*, p. 1453.

[11] For example, the usually very useful UK *Manual of the Law of Armed Conflict* (Oxford: Oxford University Press, 2004) contains very little on point. See also D. Turns, 'Targeting' in N. D. White and C. Henderson (eds.), *Research Handbook on Conflict and Security Law* (Celtenham: Edward Elgar, 2013), pp. 342–374, p. 358.

[12] C. Garraway, 'The Changing Character of the Participants in War: Civilianization of Warfighting and the Concept of "Direct Participation in Hostilities"' in R. A. Pedrozo and D. P. Wollschlaeger (eds.), *International Law and the Changing Character of War* (Newport RI: US Naval War College, 2011), pp. 177–205, p. 177. For a useful further history back to Grotius, see E. Camins, 'The Past as Prologue: The Development of "Direct Participation" Exception to Civilian Immunity', *International Review of the Red Cross*, 90 (2008), pp. 853–881.

[13] Garraway, *ibid.*, p.178; J. Williamson, 'Challenges of Twenty-First-Century Conflicts: A Look at Direct Participation in Hostilities', *Duke Journal of Comparative and International Law*, 20 (2009–2010), pp. 457–472, 459–460. There is some brief discussion on the issue scattered in the *Customary Study*, but this hardly exhausted the issue, and was not the focus of that endeavour. See A. P. V. Rogers, 'Combatant Status' in E. Wilmshurst and S. Breau (eds.), *Perspectives on the ICRC Study on Customary International Humanitarian Law* (Cambridge: Cambridge University Press 2007), pp. 101–127, p. 107–108. During the gestation of the *Guidance*, considerable discussion of participation in hostilities took place in *Public Committee Against Torture in Israel* v *Government of Israel* (2006) HCJ 769/02. On the case see e.g. R. S. Schondorf, 'The *Targeted Killings* Judgment: A Preliminary Assessment', *Journal of International Criminal Justice*, 5 (2007), pp. 301–309; W. J. Fenrick, 'The *Targeted Killings* Judgment and the Scope of Direct Participation in Hostilities', *Journal of International Criminal Justice*, 5 (2007), pp. 332–338; A. Cassese, 'On Some Merits of the Israeli Judgment on Targeted Killings', *Journal of International Criminal Justice*, 5 (2007), pp. 339–345. However, although it seems that the Court was influenced by the preparatory

of (about 50) experts on IHL coming from the military, academic, and governmental spheres to attempt to get clarity on point.[14] The discussion centred around three questions: (1) Who is a civilian for the purposes of the principle of distinction? (2) What conduct amounts to direct participation in hostilities? and (3) What modalities govern the loss of protection against direct attack?[15]

Unfortunately, the discussions with experts became fractious, and in the end the experts did not sign on to the document,[16] a matter which clearly caused considerable bitterness amongst the participants.[17] Instead of drafting by consensus, therefore the *Guidance* was written by Nils Melzer for the ICRC. Rather than lament this, though, it is better to see it as the dissensus backdrop to which the ICRC guidance attempts to bring some clarity. As such, we ought not to be too quick to condemn the guidance unless a better way of interpreting and applying this area of law can be found. As our mothers probably told us all, if we have nothing positive to say, say nothing. As an aside, whether the ICRC should have kept silent on point is another issue. My view is that, if nothing else, the guidance has started a debate that needs to be had, and previously, had been left to the

material for the *Guidance* that was available at the time (Fenrick, *ibid.*, p. 333), the judgment relied as much on human rights as on humanitarian law, see A. P. V. Rogers, 'Direct Participation in Hostilities: Some Personal Reflections', *Military Law and Law of War Review*, 48 (2009), pp. 143–164, 159 [hereinafter 'Direct Participation']; and was hardly the last word on point.

14 As such the ICRC *Guidance* cannot simply be seen as the musings of a group, sitting in their ivory towers, issuing the edicts of *weltfremd* scholars or pacifists who have no time, experience, or sympathy for the realities of conflict and the fact that IHL is intended to be a law that is at first instance intended to be used in practice, thus applied, thus operationalizable rather than academically pure, although see Rogers, 'Direct Participation', 160. For a sympathetically critical attempt to apply it in a specific conflict see D. van der Toorn, 'Direct Participation in Hostilities': A Legal and Practical Road Test of the International Committee of the Red Cross's Guidance through Afghanistan', *Australian International Law Journal*, 17 (2010), pp. 7–28.

15 Melzer, *Guidance*, p. 13. For discussion of the process see ICRC, *Overview of the ICRC's Expert Process (2003–2008)*, available at: www.icrc.org.

16 N. Melzer, 'The ICRC's Clarification Process on the Notion of Direct Participation in Hostilities under International Humanitarian Law', *Proceedings of the American Society of International Law*, 103 (2009), pp. 299–307.

17 See W. Hays Parks, 'Part IX of the ICRC "Direct Participation in Hostilities" Study, No Mandate, No Expertise, and Legally Incorrect', *New York University Journal of International Law and Politics*, 42 (2009–2010), pp. 769–830, 783–785 [hereinafter 'Part IX']; *contra* N. Melzer, 'Keeping the Balance Between Military Necessity and Humanity: A Response to Four Critiques of the ICRC's Interpretive Guidance on the Notion of Direct Participation in Hostilities', *New York University Journal of International Law and Politics*, 42 (2009–10), pp. 831–916, 895.

individual judgment of States,[18] more often than not in a non-transparent and essentially unreviewable way. Almost any light in the shadows is better than leaving things in the dark.

The Guidance itself is relatively brief. Unlike the *Customary Humanitarian Law* study, which ran to three volumes, one of pure prose, and two wrist-aching volumes of practice, the guidance on DPH, although accompanied by a commentary, runs, in all, to about 90 fairly well-spaced pages. After discussing aspects of the guidance,[19] we will return to some more general comments about the authors and interpreters of IHL.

III. The Guidance and Its Critics

Before engaging directly with the *Guidance* itself, it is worth entering two caveats. The first is a limitation that the ICRC was right to impose upon itself. This was to limit the *Guidance* to the concept of DPH from the point of view of targeting, not detention,[20] or, for example, use of child soldiers and the like.[21] As experience has shown, the ICRC already had bitten off a huge chunk of IHL to chew with targeting. On detention, the Copenhagen Process had proved difficult enough, and that was only one other issue that arose.[22] So, again, when appraising the guidance, its limited scope needs to be remembered. It is not intended, for example, as an interpretation of the war crime of using child soldiers in the Rome Statute.[23]

[18] See e.g. Hays Parks, *ibid.*, 796 (who is happy with this, and criticises the ICRC for going against it), Rogers, 'Direct Participation', pp. 158–159.

[19] For a very useful early overview see D. Akande, 'Clearing the Fog of War: The ICRC's Interpretative Guidance on Direct Participation in Hostilities', *International & Comparative Law Quarterly*, 59 (2010), pp. 180–192. For critical reviews see W. H. Boothby, 'Direct Participation in Hostilities – A Discussion of the ICRC Interpretative Guidance', *Journal of International Humanitarian Legal Studies*, 1 (2010), pp. 143–159; M. N. Schmitt, 'The Interpretative Guidance on the Notion of Direct Participation in Hostilities: A Critical Analysis', *Harvard National Security Journal*, 1 (2010), pp. 5–44 [hereinafter 'Critical Analysis'].

[20] Melzer, *The ICRC's Clarification Process on the Notion of Direct Participation in Hostilities under International Humanitarian Law*, 300. For support, see S. Pomper, 'Remarks', *Proceedings of the American Society of International Law*, 103 (2009), pp. 307–310, 307.

[21] Schmitt, *Critical Analysis*, 14–5, suggests that there is a risk that separating them off may mean that some civilians may be deprived of their rights under the Fourth Geneva Convention, but this risk has, so far, seemed to be remote. That said, he rightly criticises (17) the ICRC for then referring to provisions that relate to POW status out of context.

[22] L. Hill-Cawthorne, 'The Copenhagen Principles on the Handling of Detainees: Implications for the Procedural Regulation of Internment', *Journal of Conflict & Security Law*, 18 (2013), pp. 481–497.

[23] Article 8(2)(b)(xxvi), see W. A. Schabas, *The International Criminal Court: Commentary on the Rome Statute* (Oxford: Oxford University Press, 2010), pp. 252–255.

The second is that the various parts of the *Guidance* cannot be entirely separated out and appraised. As the commentary says: 'The sections and recommendations of the Interpretative Guidance are closely interrelated and can only be properly understood if read as a whole'.[24] As we will see, a number of commentators have taken individual parts and appraised them individually, often saying that certain parts (those they prefer) accurately reflect IHL, and others (which they are less happy with) do not. This is to misunderstand the nature of the guidance; the individual parts are like pieces of a jigsaw, and only make sense when placed together as a whole, the individual aspects are not completely severable.

It is also important to note that the *Guidance* is, as a whole, the official position of the ICRC on what constitutes DPH. As the *Guidance* itself says, it is not a proposal *de lege ferenda*:

> The purpose of the interpretative guidance is to provide recommendations concerning the interpretation of international humanitarian law (IHL) as far as it relates to the notion of direct participation in hostilities. Accordingly, the 10 recommendations made by the interpretative guidance as well as the accompanying commentary, do not endeavour to change binding rules of customary or treaty IHL, but reflect the ICRC's institutional position as to how existing IHL should be interpreted in light of the circumstances prevailing in contemporary armed conflicts.[25]

This is important for a number of reasons, amongst them is that, although it is framed as guidance, and therefore ought to be appraised as such, it is also the official position of the ICRC, therefore, like the customary law study, it is the basis upon which the ICRC will make representations to States and (perhaps) make critiques of the State's conduct. As such it cannot be ignored by States, even where they are not happy with it.[26] We will return to this presently. However, it is now time to look directly at the *Guidance* itself. It consists of ten Recommendations; given space limitations, and in spite of the previous discussion of the importance of reading

[24] Melzer, *Guidance*, 10. See also Melzer, *Keeping the Balance Between Military Necessity and Humanity*, 836.

[25] Melzer, *Guidance*, 9. Although some query this, see e.g. K. Watkin, 'Opportunity Lost: Organized Armed Groups and the ICRC "Direct Participation in Hostilities" Interpretative Guidance', *New York University Journal of International Law and Politics*, 42 (2009–2010), pp. 641–695, 643–644 [hereinafter 'Armed Groups'].

[26] As W. H. Boothby, 'Direct Participation in Hostilities – A Discussion of the ICRC Interpretative Guidance', *Journal of International Humanitarian Legal Studies*, 1 (2010), pp. 143–159, 144–145, notes though, States remain the masters of their treaty obligations, although, as we will see, this rather understates the role of the ICRC on point.

the guidance as a whole, this piece will limit itself to look at three deeply interlinked principles of the guidance, and one other, so as to understand the critiques that have been made of the *Guidance* and the nature of contemporary debates about the appropriate interpretation (and interpreters of) IHL. The first three principles are about the concept of civilians and combatants in armed conflicts and the level of force that may be used against the latter (principles I, II and IX). The final principle that is discussed is principle III, which relates to the status of private military and security companies and their employees. It is not the purpose of this chapter to write a hagiography of the *Guidance*, but engage in a friendly critique of it, and use other critiques as a means of investigating how IHL is discussed by its various interlocutors.

IV. Civilians, Combatants and the Use of Force in the Jus in Bello: Principles I, II and IX

Let us begin our investigation with principle I, which reads:

Principle I. The Concept of Civilian in International Armed Conflict

> For the purposes of the principle of distinction in international armed conflict, all persons who are neither members of the armed forces of a party to the conflict nor participants in a *levée en masse* are civilians and, therefore, entitled to protection against direct attack unless and for such time as they take a direct part in hostilities.

As can be seen, this recommendation (which draws on API) defines the civilians negatively, as not being members of the armed forces or participants in a *levée en masse* (the latter category now, to all intents and purposes having been relegated to history). The commentary, drawing on Article 43(1) of API (which, following the *Customary Study*, the ICRC considers customary) defines members of the armed forces as 'all organised armed forces, groups and units which are under a command responsible to that party for the conduct of its subordinates.'[27] Given that the *Guidance* is about targetability rather than POW status, it, rightly, does not impose the four requirements in Article 4(A)(2) of Geneva Convention III on those who are not the regular armed forces. They are targetable whether they fulfil them or not.[28]

[27] Melzer, *Guidance*, p. 21. [28] *Ibid*., p. 22.

All forces must, though, belong to a party to the conflict.[29] This, often forgotten aspect, is said by the *Guidance* to be determined by the rules of State responsibility.[30] Unfortunately, the *Guidance* does not really engage with the difficulties that surround this area, in particular owing to the disjunction between the jurisprudence of the ICJ and the international criminal tribunals. As is well known, the ICTY rejected the ICJ's *Nicaragua* test of 'effective control' in the 1999 *Tadić* Appeal.[31] The ICTY's approach (the using of the lower standard of 'overall control') was followed by the ICC in the *Lubanga* case.[32] This was in spite of the ICJ's judgment in the *Bosnian Genocide* case, which rejected the *Tadić* test in strong terms, differentiating international criminal law (and therefore, on point, IHL) and the law of State responsibility.[33] It is therefore a matter of regret that, in spite of citing *Nicaragua*, *Tadić*, and the *Bosnian Genocide* case, the *Guidance* does not explain the details of the relevant test further.[34]

Another difficulty that is perhaps not sufficiently dealt with in the *Guidance* is the question of membership. It asserts, 'For the regular armed forces of States, individual membership is generally regulated by domestic law and expressed through formal integration into permanent units distinguishable by uniforms, equipment and insignia', whilst for irregular forces, the criteria have to be more functional, akin to those used for organised armed groups in non-international armed conflicts.[35] The latter proposition is subject to similar discussion to that contained later on in relation to recommendation II, the former though is rather too sweeping, in that in modern Western armies such as those of the United States

[29] Those not doing so are civilians according to the *Guidance*, but may be parties to a separate non-international armed conflict, *ibid*., pp. 23–24. On such situations see E. Wilmshurst (ed.), *International Law and the Classification of Armed Conflict* (Oxford: Oxford University Press, 2012).

[30] Melzer, *Guidance*, p. 23.

[31] *Military and Paramilitary Activities in and Against Nicaragua (Nicaragua v. USA)* (1986) ICJ Reports 4, para. 115, *contra Prosecutor v. Tadić*, Judgment, IT-94-1-A, 15 July 1999, para. 145.

[32] *Prosecutor v. Lubanga*, Judgment, ICC-01/04–01/06, 14 March 2012, para. 541.

[33] *Case Concerning the Application of the Convention Concerning the Prevention and Punishment of the Crime of Genocide (Bosnia and Herzegovina v. Serbia and Montenegro)*, Judgment, (2007) ICJ Reports 43, paras 404–5. As Al-Khasawneh noted, however in his dissenting opinion (para. 38), on the ICTY's reasoning, the State responsibility point was crucial to the exercise of its primary, criminal, jurisdiction over grave breaches of the Geneva Conventions.

[34] For scepticism about *Tadić* in this regard see James Crawford, *State Responsibility: The General Part* (Cambridge: Cambridge University Press, 2013), pp. 146–156.

[35] Melzer, *Guidance*, p.25.

or United Kingdom, this is probably the case. However, these are not the universal norm. In the developing world, the idea of such formal criteria being determinative is optimistic to say the least. For example, the Taliban in 2002 were the national armed forces of Afghanistan, yet it seems extremely unlikely that they were appointed pursuant to a formal, legal process, and that a register of members of the armed forces were kept.

This may be an instance of a more general issue that may affect the reception of the *Guidance*, this is that it tends to assume, for both international and non-international armed conflicts, a rather traditional view of conflict, not taking into account for example, cyberwarfare, the use of autonomous weapons, intelligence officials becoming involved intimately at the coal face of targeting, and other recent developments in conflict.[36] On the other hand, care must also be taken about the illusion of novelty in international law, especially IHL, where such claims are often made to circumvent humanitarian protection.[37]

As a final comment prior to moving on to non-international armed conflicts, it is very important, and telling that the *Guidance* has taken the view that there is no 'third status' between combatant and civilian. Therefore, the *Guidance* must be taken as rejecting the idea, propagated in particular that there is such a status (often, erroneously called 'unlawful combatant') that is separate to those other two statuses. This is in accordance with ICTY jurisprudence on point and the generally accepted position.[38] The *Guidance* enters more torrid waters, however, when it deals with non-international armed conflicts, in principle II, which reads:

Principle II. The Concept of Civilian in Non-International Armed Conflict

For the purposes of the principle of distinction in non-international armed conflict, all persons who are not members of State armed forces or organized armed groups of a party to the conflict are civilians and, therefore, entitled to protection against direct attack unless and for such time as they take a direct part in hostilities in non-international armed conflict, organised armed groups constitute the armed forces of a non-State party

[36] See, e.g. H. Harrison Dinnis, *Cyber Warfare and the Laws of War* (Cambridge: Cambridge University Press, 2012); D. Cline, 'An Analysis of the Legal Status of CIA Officers Involved in Drone Strikes', *San Diego International Law Journal*, 15 (2013), pp. 51–114.

[37] See e.g. G. Schwarzenberger, *International Law and Totalitarian Lawlessness* (London: Stevens, 1943), pp. 37–39.

[38] *Prosecutor* v *Delalić, Delić, Mucić and Lanžo* (Čelebići), Judgment, IT-96–21 –A, para. 35.

to the conflict and consist only of individuals whose continuous function it is to take a direct part in hostilities ('continuous combat function').

The ICRC, therefore, in spite of the attempts of the ICTY (and others) to render IHL the same whether or not a conflict is international or non-international,[39] continues (rightly, given the *lex lata* on point) to distinguish international and non-international armed conflicts. Hence, unlike in international armed conflict, where there is generally equal applicability of IHL, in the sense of belligerent privilege for organised armed forces belonging to one side or the other,[40] in the context of non-international armed conflicts the *Guidance* distinguishes State and non-State forces. In relation to the former, the *Guidance* takes the position that such personnel are to be determined by the same test as applies in international armed conflicts.[41] As such, civilian status is only recovered when a person is discharged or becomes a deactivated reservist.[42]

Although there are those that claim that international law simply does not regulate the status of governmental armed forces,[43] the ICRC's view is the most consistent with the State practice that exists, in particular that prosecutions of State armed forces for the mere fact of participation in hostilities are, to all intents and purposes, unheard of. Equally, the test set, being the same as that for international conflicts, is subject to the same comments that were made previously in relation to Recommendation I. In the specific context of non-international armed conflicts in certain contexts, law enforcement officials may be considered members of State armed forces, even though they are not statutorily considered to be so.[44] Hence, the *Guidance* may be under-inclusive here.

[39] See, e.g. S. Boelaert-Suominen, 'The Yugoslavia Tribunal and the Common Core of Humanitarian Law Applicable to all Armed Conflicts, *Leiden Journal of International Law*, 13 (2000), pp. 619–653; E. Crawford, *The Treatment of Combatants and Insurgents under the Law of Armed Conflict* (Oxford: Oxford University Press, 2010).

[40] Attempts to alter this position have, for very good reasons, been rejected, see e.g. N. Boister and R. Cryer, *The Tokyo International Military Tribunal: A Reappraisal* (Oxford: Oxford University Press, 2008), chapter 6.

[41] Melzer, *Guidance*, pp. 30–31.

[42] *Ibid.*, p. 31.

[43] S. Watts, 'The Status of Government Armed Forces in Non-International Armed Conflict' in K. Watkin and A. J. Norris (eds.), *Non-International Armed Conflict in the Twentieth Century* (Newport, RI: US Naval War College, 2013), pp. 145–180, p. 149. Although, as he accepts, States have generally not looked to international law to legitimise their role in such conflicts.

[44] Y. Sandoz, C. Swiniarski and B. Zimmermann (eds.), *Commentary on the Additional Protocols to the Geneva Conventions of 12 August 1949*, para. 4462; see M. N. Schmitt, 'The Statute of Opposition Fighters in a Non-International Armed Conflict', in Watkin and Norris, *ibid.*, pp. 119–144, p. 126 [hereinafter 'Opposition Fighters'].

Things become far more complex, though, when it comes to determining the categorisation of non-State forces in such conflicts.[45] The *Guidance*, basing itself on the fragmentary treaty law on the subject, essentially adopts a tripartite structure for fighters in non-international armed conflicts: (1) dissident armed forces (i.e. members of what were State forces who have turned against the government), (2) members of other organised armed groups and (3) civilians who directly participate in hostilities. The first type, dissident armed forces, have their membership determined by the same criteria as the State forces that they were.[46] This has proved uncontroversial.[47]

The same cannot be said for the second category, members of other organised armed forces. Again, extrapolating from their interpretation of Common Article 3 and APII, the *Guidance* speaks of such forces as parties to armed conflicts. It was by no means clear prior to the *Guidance* that this category was clearly distinguished from civilians who directly participate in hostilities.[48] The *Guidance*'s response is that such an approach

> '[W]ould seriously undermine the conceptual integrity of the categories of persons underlying the principle of distinction, most notably because it would create parties to non-international armed conflicts whose entire armed forces remain part of the civilian population.'[49]

As a result, the *Guidance* asserts that 'civilians, armed forces, and organised armed groups of the parties are mutually exclusive categories also in non-international armed conflicts'.[50] Although there is sense in this, and it can (perhaps at a stretch) be inducted from the relevant treaties, it assumes what it needs to prove, that there is such a category (of organised armed groups) that exists to be mutually exclusive to the others.[51]

Assuming that such a distinction exists though, the *Guidance* then separates those organised groups opposing the government (or other such groups) into two subcategories. These are the armed forces of that group in the functional sense, and their political and humanitarian wings. Only the former are, according to the *Guidance*, to be considered the 'organised armed group'.[52] The others retain their civilian status. As we will see,

[45] For an overview of the topic see Schmitt, 'Opposition Fighters'.

[46] Melzer, *Guidance*, p. 32.

[47] Schmitt, 'Opposition Fighters', pp. 124–125.

[48] Schmitt, 'Opposition Fighters', p. 127.

[49] Melzer, *Guidance*, p. 28. As Rogers, 'Direct Participation', p. 158 has noted, it may just be the case that this is fine, just that the relevant civilians have lost their protection.

[50] Melzer, *Guidance*, p. 28.

[51] For very useful discussion on the nature of organised and armed in this context see Schmitt, 'Opposition Fighters', pp. 127–131.

[52] Melzer, *Guidance*, p. 32.

this is a crucial distinction from the point of view of targeting. There is an intuitive appeal to this, but it cannot be ignored that such a distinction is by no means easy to make, as the two may be interlinked. To take a UK-based example, in the 'Troubles' in Northern Ireland,[53] the political wing of the armed republican movement, *Sinn Féin*, always maintained it was a separate entity to the IRA, although it is now clear that at least some of its leadership was also active in the IRA Army Council.

Leaving this aside, the *Guidance* provides for different levels of targetability for the two types of supporters. The first (who is targetable at any time) are members of the organised armed forces of a group, and the second are civilians who remain immune from attack unless and for such time as they are directly participating in hostilities. As the *Guidance* accepts, membership of an organised armed force is more difficult to define than for State armed forces, as the membership of such forces is fluid, less binary, deformalized and often clandestine.[54] Therefore, the distinguishing criterion the *Guidance* sets out is that of a 'continuous combat function'. This requires 'lasting integration into an organised armed group acting as the armed forces of a non-State party to an armed conflict. Thus, individuals whose continuous function involved the preparation, execution or command of operations amounting to direct participation in hostilities are assuming a continuous combat function'.[55] This includes those who have assumed such a role but have not yet directly participated.[56]

There are two issues that arise with respect to this. The first is the term (and concept) itself. Even the most assiduous readers of IHL treaties will search in vain for it in the entire corpus of treaty-based IHL. It is a creation of the *Guidance*, and as such there is no real authority for it other than the alleged logic of the relevant conventions (Common Article 3 implying the existence of a category of non-State armed forces). This is not always clear. Indeed, some take the view that there is no status-based targeting in

[53] Which, at least for a time, was considered by many to be a Common Article 3 conflict, see S. Haines, 'Northern Ireland 1968–1998' in E. Wilmshurst, (ed.), *International Law and the Classification of Armed Conflict* (Oxford: Oxford University Press 2012), p. 117.

[54] Melzer, *Guidance*, pp. 32–33. Schmitt, 'Opposition Fighters' pp. 132–133, not without justification, asserts that the problems may be overstated as many organised armed groups operate in a manner similar to regular armed forces. This is true, but really identifies the necessity of avoiding totalising statements rather than a fatal objection to the *Guidance*'s point.

[55] Melzer, *Guidance*, p. 33. D. J. van der Toorn, '"Direct Participation in Hostilities": A Legal and Practical Evaluation of the ICRC Guidance' available at: works.bepress.com/damien_van_der_toorn/1, p. 29, considers integration to be synonymous with membership, but this is clearly not the intention of the *Guidance*.

[56] Van der Toorn, *ibid*.

non-international armed conflicts at all, and targetability in such contexts can only be based on behavioural tests (i.e. DPH).[57] Therefore, a strong case can be made that by adopting a concept of the continuous combat function, the ICRC has gone beyond what IHL permits in terms of targetability and expanded States' rights in this regard. This is worth bearing in mind when evaluating the critiques of the *Guidance* that are canvassed later with respect to principle IX.

The second important and difficult issue is the line between an individual act of direct participation in hostilities. Put into the interrogative, where does the line lie between a civilian who sometimes/occasionally/quite often/frequently engages in individual acts of direct participation and someone who has assumed a continuous combat function (particularly if that person has not actually undertaken any individual act of direct participation)? This critical issue is not well elaborated upon in the *Guidance*.[58] Given the importance that the distinction will have for targeting, this is, to say the least, unfortunate.

Perhaps the most stinging critique of the *Guidance* has come from Brigadier-General Kenneth Watkin.[59] Watkin asserts that in addition to departing from the existing law, overreliance on untenable general assumptions, and being unclear, the *Guidance* fails to take into account the realities of modern conflict, and unacceptably favours non-State forces.[60] With respect to this last aspect, the most important for our purposes,[61] Watkin takes the view that State armed forces are all considered targetable at any time; for non-State forces, only those exercising a continuous combat function are subject to that regime.[62] Furthermore, he is critical of the extent to which logistics and other supporting roles can be considered part of conflict, and thus argues that such roles should be included in DPH, and thus ought to form the basis for a continuous combat function,[63] as State

[57] F. J. Hampson, 'Direct Participation in Hostilities and the Interoperability of the Law of Armed Conflict and Human Rights Law', *International Law Studies Series US Naval War College*, 87 (2011), pp. 187–216, 203–205.

[58] See also W. H. Boothby, 'Direct Participation in Hostilities – A Discussion of the ICRC Interpretative Guidance', *Journal of International Humanitarian Legal Studies*, 1 (2010), pp. 143–159, 154–155. Van der Toorn, *ibid.*, p. 28 considers it a high threshold, not including regular participation, but this is not clear.

[59] Watkin, 'Armed Groups'.

[60] Watkin, 'Armed Groups', pp. 643–645.

[61] Little needs to be said about his criticism that the *Guidance* fails to take into account just war theory sufficiently (Watkin, 'Armed Groups', pp. 667–672). Such theories (there are more than one) may have had influence on IHL, but are not sources of positive law.

[62] Watkin, 'Armed Groups', pp. 649, 672–680.

[63] Watkin, 'Armed Groups', pp. 683–686. W. H. Boothby, 'Direct Participation in Hostilities – A Discussion of the ICRC Interpretative Guidance', p. 154, would only exclude 'political, diplomatic or similar functions' from DPH by members of armed groups.

forces are targetable at will. Watkin also is uncomfortable with the *Guidance* adopting a 'revolving door' approach which allows civilians to occasionally participate in combat, then become immune again after having done so.[64] His true preference though is that if there is repetitious participation (a term that is not exactly clear), then active disengagement would be required (as it is for State forces) for a person to return to civilian status and immunity.[65]

He is correct to note that there are different levels of organisation of different armed groups, such a critique has been made previously.[66] However, his views have not gone without response from the *Guidance*'s author.[67] Nils Melzer has replied that IHL (most importantly the Hague Regulations and the Third Geneva Convention of 1949) has always accepted the possibility of functional tests for non-State actors,[68] and the concept of the continuous combat function solves many of the difficulties, and indeed Watkin's critique really is about expanding that concept rather than critiquing it, and expanding it too broadly, in a manner that would not be easily applicable without being highly overinclusive.[69] Any bias against States (which Melzer denies) is, according to him, simply based in the existing law on point.[70]

There is much to this, and Melzer is by no means alone in favouring functional criteria over formal ones.[71] There may, in addition, be other arguments here that blunt Watkin's critique. The first is that Watkin may be misdirecting his critique. The law applicable to international armed conflicts (Hague Regulation 3) accepts that the armed forces of a State party to a conflict may consist of combatants and non-combatants; as Ipsen parses the situation 'armed forces are described as consisting also of "non-combatants"; this refers to the exception that, in addition to the medical and religious personnel, there may be other members of the armed forces which are not authorised to participate directly in hostilities'.[72] As such, a more pointed critique might be that principle I of the guidance is overinclusive rather than principle II being the problem.

64 Watkin, 'Armed Groups', pp. 686–690.

65 Watkin, 'Armed Groups', pp. 692–693.

66 Watkin, 'Armed Groups', pp. 672–680.

67 Melzer, *Guidance*.

68 Melzer, *Guidance*, pp. 834–836.

69 Melzer, *Guidance*, pp. 846–850.

70 Melzer, *Guidance*, pp. 850–852.

71 D. Turns, 'Targeting' in N. D. White and C. Henderson (eds.), *Research Handbook on Conflict and Security Law* (Celtenham: Edward Elgar, 2013), pp. 342–374, p. 357.

72 K. Ipsen, 'Combatants and Non-Combatants' in D. Fleck (ed.), *The Handbook of International Humanitarian Law* (Oxford: Oxford University Press, 3rd ed., 2013) pp. 79–230, p. 80. The categories of such personnel are usefully discussed in W. H. Boothby, *The Law of Targeting* (Oxford: Oxford University Press, 2012), pp. 143–144.

Furthermore, with respect to non-international armed conflicts, a distinction between State armed forces and non-State armed forces is already clearly accepted, in that the former are granted combatant immunity/belligerent privilege, whereas the latter do not; therefore, one reason for treating the two differently is that non-State forces remain domestically criminally liable for any death, injury or damage they cause whilst engaging in belligerency, a point the *Guidance* accepts in principle X.[73] So, the advisability of treating the two types of forces the same may not be a given, or reflective of the existing international law on point, which (in all likelihood) grants State armed forces belligerent privilege, but remains ecumenical on that of non-State fighters.

Notwithstanding the previous, the *Guidance*'s approach to continuous combat function and targetability, especially in non-international armed conflicts, cannot be divorced from its treatment of the level of force that may be employed against those who may be lawful targets. The ICRC's view is encapsulated in principle IX of the *Guidance*:

> *Principle IX. Restraints on the Use of Force in Direct Attack*
>
> In addition to the restraints imposed by international humanitarian law on specific means and methods of warfare, and without prejudice to further restrictions that may arise under other applicable branches of international law, the kind and degree of force which is permissible against persons not entitled to protection against direct attack must not exceed what is actually necessary to accomplish a legitimate military purpose in the prevailing circumstances.

This has, in accordance with early predictions on point,[74] proved probably the most contentious of the principles enunciated in the *Guidance*. It has been the subject of considerable, bitter and strongly expressed critique.[75] These will be canvassed next, largely to elucidate the more

[73] On which see, e.g. D. J. R. Frakt, 'Direct Participation in Hostilities as a War Crime: America's Failed Attempt to Change the Law of War', *Valparaiso Law Review*, 46 (2012), pp. 729–764. This again shows the importance of reading the *Guidance* as a whole, rather than 'cherry picking' it.

[74] D. Akande, 'Clearing the Fog of War: The ICRC's Interpretative Guidance on Direct Participation in Hostilities', *International & Comparative Law Quarterly*, 59 (2010), pp. 180–192, 191.

[75] See, e.g., Hays Parks, 'Part IX', p. 769; G. S. Corn, L. R. Blank, C. Jenks and E. Talbot Jensen, 'Belligerent Targeting and the Invalidity of a Least Harmful Means Rule' in A. Deeks (ed.), *The Geography of Cyber Conflict: Through a Glass Darkly* (Newport, RI: US Naval War College, 2013), p. 536 [hereinafter *Cyber Conflict*]. For more generous critiques see e.g. J. K.

general point to be developed, about the dispute that has arisen about who are the appropriate interpreters and guardians of IHL. To explain this principle, though, it is important to understand what the *Guidance* meant by this. The first aspect of this is that the ICRC has based this principle in part on the 'principles of distinction, precaution, proportionality, as well as the prohibitions of denial of quarter and perfidy', as well as the prohibition of particular weapons, and the prohibition of the infliction of unnecessary suffering.[76] As the *Guidance* accepts though, outside of this 'the specific provisions of IHL do not expressly regulate the kind and degree of force permissible against legitimate military targets'.[77]

The second, and in many ways more important, issue is that this principle must be read in context, i.e. that in international armed conflicts, according to the *Guidance*, all members of the armed forces, and in non-international armed conflict, all persons engaging in DPH are targetable for such time as they do so,[78] and those who have a continuous combat function,[79] are apodictically targetable. This last aspect is one which may well expand the approach to targetability that previously existed. Therefore, principle IX ought to be seen as a counterpoint to this expansion of who is targetable. Furthermore, the scope of this limitation ought to be read with respect to the commentary to this principle which states:

> The aim cannot be to replace the judgment of the military commander by inflexible or unrealistic standards; rather it is to avoid error, arbitrariness, and abuse by providing guiding principles for the choice of means and methods of warfare based on his or her assessment of the situation ... in classic large-scale confrontations between well- equipped and organized armed forces or groups, the principles of military necessity and of humanity are unlikely to restrict the use of force against legitimate military targets beyond what is already required by specific provisions of IHL. The practical importance of their restraining function will increase with the ability of a party to the conflict to control the circumstances and area in which its military operation is conducted, and may become decisive where armed forces operate against selected individuals in situations comparable

Kleffner, 'Section IX of the ICRC Interpretative Guidance on Direct Participation in Hostilities: The End of *Jus in Bello* Proportionality as we Know It?', *Israel Law Review*, 45 (2012), pp. 35–52 [hereinafter 'Section IX']; and J. D. Ohlin, 'The Duty to Capture', *Minnesota Law Review*, 97 (2013), pp. 1268–1342.

[76] Melzer, *Guidance*, pp. 77–78. [77] Melzer, *Guidance*, p. 78.

[78] See principles VI and VII.

[79] Subject to the previous commentary with respect to principles I and II.

> to peacetime policing. In practice such considerations are likely to become particularly relevant where a party to the conflict exercises effective territorial control, most notably in occupied territories and non-international armed conflicts.[80]

As such the *Guidance* ought not to be overread in terms of its ambit; it speaks to specific circumstances, and in particular those where human rights law may also be applicable.[81] Furthermore, it addresses itself largely to those higher up in the chain of command than the individual soldier being asked to make a particular call on the military necessity of engaging in lethal force.

That said, the principle is open to other interpretations, and its IHL basis has been subject to considerable critique. So, for example, the notional basis of the principle being founded on the principles of military necessity and humanity, as forming independent sources of IHL, has been excoriated by a number of the *Guidance*'s critics.[82] It is perhaps a little excessive to criticise the *Guidance* on this point, given that it expressly asserts that 'considerations of military necessity and humanity neither derogate from nor override the specific provisions of IHL, but constitute guiding principles for the interpretation of the rights and duties of belligerents within the parameters set by these provisions'.[83] That said, the reliance that seems to have been put by the *Guidance* on the Martens clause (on humanity) and its relationship to positive law, although not without precedent,[84] is a little shaky.[85]

The *Guidance* does, though, also rely on interpretations of API (in particular Articles 52, 35, 40 and 41) and the asserted State understandings of those provisions.[86] These are far from uncontroversial,[87] but, as Ryan Goodman has shown, they have more of a pedigree than the

[80] Melzer, *Guidance*, pp. 80–81.

[81] Melzer, *Guidance*, pp. 81–82. Space prohibits detailed discussion of this aspect, but see e.g. F. J. Hampson, 'Direct Participation in Hostilities and the Interoperability of the Law of Armed Conflict and Human Rights Law', *International Law Studies Series US Naval War College*, 87 (2011), pp. 187–216.

[82] Kleffner, 'Section IX', pp. 39–40; Hays Parks, 'Part IX', p. 797; Corn *et al.*, 'Cyber Conflicts', p. 552.

[83] Melzer, *Guidance*, pp. 78–79.

[84] *Ibid.*, footnote 219.

[85] See the critiques of these authorities in e.g. C. Greenwood, 'Belligerent Reprisals in the Jurisprudence of the International Criminal Tribunal for the Former Yugoslavia' in H. Fischer, C. Kreß and S. R. Lüder (eds.), *International and National Prosecution of Crimes Under International Law* (Berlin: de Gruyter, 2001), pp. 359–558.

[86] Melzer, *Guidance*, pp. 77–78.

[87] See e.g. Corn *et al.*, *Cyber Conflicts*, pp. 568ff.

critics admit.[88] The strict legal position with respect to the existing IHL on point,[89] as well as the domestic authorities, such as the *Targeted Killings* case, may be subject to legitimate debate,[90] but the *Guidance* is not, as has been implied by some of its critics, spurious as a matter of law.[91] Still further, and as will be elaborated upon later, the idea that the ICRC, in engaging in debate upon this issue is stepping outside its mandate, betrays an underlying approach to IHL that, sources doctrine (important though it is) aside, is antithetical to a pluralistic understanding of the international legal order. Prior to engaging in such a discussion, though it is worthwhile looking at one other principle in the *Guidance*, that shows how the relevant experts and critics have, in spite of some comments to the contrary, defined aspects of the debate, whilst being deeply critical of an attempt by the ICRC to seek to strike out upon their own path.

V. A Counterpoint: Private Companies in Armed Conflict

Finally, turning to a slightly different issue, albeit one that is also telling in terms of the issues this chapter seeks to investigate, let us turn to the way in which the *Guidance* deals with a matter that States, particularly, albeit by no means only, in the West are interested in, but perhaps do not wish (at least in the post-colonial era) to see regulated in detail. This is the regulation of the participation of private military and security companies in armed conflicts. In spite of their importance in modern conflicts, the *Guidance* deals with them quickly and with little commentary. The relevant principle is as follows:

Principle III. Private Contractors and Civilian Employees

> Private contractors and employees of a party to an armed conflict who are civilians (see above i and ii) are entitled to protection against direct

[88] See, for different views, R. Goodman, 'The Power to Kill or Capture Enemy Combatants', *European Journal of International Law*, 24 (2013), pp. 819–853; M. N., Schmitt, 'Wound, Capture or Kill: A Reply to Ryan Goodman's 'The Power to Kill or Capture Enemy Combatants', *European Journal of International Law*, 24 (2013), pp. 855–861; R. Goodman, 'The Power to Kill or Capture Enemy Combatants: A Rejoinder to Michael N Schmitt', *European Journal of International Law*, 24 (2013), pp. 863–866.

[89] Space prevents the detailed elaboration of the question of the relationship between IHL and human rights law on point, see though Kleffner, 'Section IX', pp. 49–52 (whose scepticism about the *Al-Skeini* decision must be doubted).

[90] See e.g. Hays Parks, 'Part IX', pp. 788ff, *contra* Melzer, *Guidance*, pp. 911–912.

[91] See, albeit critically, Kleffner, 'Section IX', p. 39.

> attack unless and for such time as they take a direct part in hostilities. Their activities or location may, however, expose them to an increased risk of incidental death or injury even if they do not take a direct part in hostilities.

This principle has been the subject of relatively little critical attention in the debate on the *Guidance*. This is in spite of the fact of the fact that such contractors are now a major part of the way in which Western States undertake armed conflict,[92] and the tasks such employees are asked to undertake raise significant issues with respect to the extent to which they may DPH.[93]

It may be the case that it is a specific application of the previously discussed principles to such actors, but it is notable that, in spite of the detailed critiques which military sources have engaged in with respect to the *Guidance* with regard to rebel forces, there has been little discussion of these non-State actors in this regard.[94] There are two linked aspects to this, the first is that although States frequently employ such actors, their responsibility for them is by no means easy to establish.[95] This is, of course, a source of attraction for States. The second is related to the approach of the experts that were consulted by the ICRC. As Michael Schmitt, one of the experts, and a friendly critic of the *Guidance*, has said, the issue of private military companies was looked at in the early days of the development of the *Guidance*; however, the experts moved the debate on to irregular forces such as Hamas and al-Qaeda, as this was more central to State[96] concerns than private contractors.[97] Experts from States where such

[92] Schmitt, 'Critical Analysis', pp. 9–10. Reports that there were more privately contracted staff in Iraq in 2009 than any State forces other than US service members. As he says, at pp. 9–10, 'Contractors also have been involved in numerous incidents involving civilian deaths, the most notorious being the 2007 killing of seventeen Iraqis by Blackwater employees while escorting a US Department of State convoy [. . .] Contractor participation in operations extends beyond providing security. For instance, Blackwater employees have reportedly participated in both CIA-led Predator strikes against al Qaeda operatives and 'capture or kill' operations conducted in Iraq and Afghanistan. The precise nature of Blackwater's involvement, however, remains murky'.

[93] H. Tonkin, *State Control over Private Military and Security Companies in Armed Conflict* (Cambridge: Cambridge University Press, 2011), pp. 50–52.

[94] This is not to say that only States employ such contractors, see e.g. Tonkin, *ibid.*, chapter 1, and p. 37.

[95] See Tonkin, *ibid.*, chapter 1; L. Cameron and V. Chetail, *Privatizing War: Private Military and Security Companies under Public International Law* (Cambridge: Cambridge University Press, 2013), chapter 2.

[96] I.e. those States the experts took as representing the general interest in this regard.

[97] Schmitt, 'Critical Analysis', pp. 10–11.

contractors have been deployed may have had other views on this,[98] as might others who view such actors with considerable suspicion.[99] The fact that the experts steered discussion away from this shows that the ICRC was not unsolicitous of their views.

VI. Direct Participation and/in the Struggle for Interpretation

In their insightful introduction to the symposium that has largely defined the debate about the *Guidance*, Ryan Goodman and Derek Jinks noted that there can be critiques of it from both sides, i.e. human rights and from the point of view of military personnel.[100] As they say, both have their legitimate points: the law ought to be humane but also implementable, but to take either side's points to their (il)logical conclusion would lead to results that would not be acceptable to each.[101] That said, there is no question that 'humanising' developments have had a surprising record in IHL in the last few decades, beyond what many on the military necessity/law of war end of the equation would accept.[102] The rapid acceptance by States of the now seminal decision of the ICTY in the 1995 *Tadić* appeal is an exemplar in this regard.[103] It is true that thoughtful and humane scholars such as Schmitt and others have criticised the ICTY for being too much on the humanity side of IHL,[104] but the work of Antonio Cassese and the jurisprudence of the ICTY on many issues (although not all) have been on the kind end of the judgment of history,[105] so care ought to be taken

98 It is notable that the experts, insofar as can be deduced (their names and affiliations have not been officially released) seem to have been primarily, if not solely from four States (the United States, United Kingdom, Canada and Israel) see, Hays Parks, 'Part IX', p. 795.

99 The overlap with what many would consider mercenarism, at least *lato sensu*, cannot be ignored here.

100 R. Goodman and D. Jinks, 'The ICRC Interpretive Guidance on the Notion of Direct Participation in Hostilities Under International Humanitarian Law: An Introduction to the Forum', *New York University Journal of International Law and Politics*, 42 (2009–10), pp. 637–640, 639.

101 *Ibid.*

102 See e.g. T. Meron, 'The Humanization of International Humanitarian Law', *American Journal of International Law*, 94 (2000), pp. 239–278.

103 See generally, S. Darcy, *Judges, Law and War: The Judicial Development of International Humanitarian Law* (Cambridge: Cambridge University Press, 2014).

104 M. Schmitt, 'Military Necessity and Humanity in International Humanitarian Law: Preserving the Delicate Balance, *Virginia Journal of International Law*, 50 (2010), pp. 795–839.

105 *Ibid.*, See also R. Cryer, 'International Criminal Tribunals and The Sources of International Law: Antonio Cassese's Contribution to the Canon', *Journal of International Criminal Justice*, 10 (2012), pp. 1045–1061; although the rejection of the *Kupreškić* decision in this regard cannot be ignored, not least given its controversial interpretation of the

before the ICRC's work on DPH is dismissed, as some have done, on the basis that, in the words of one critic (speaking in relation to principle IX), has 'failed to heed [its] expert advice, constructing a theory not supported by treaty law, State practice or court decisions. Its ill-constructed theory is flawed beyond repair'.[106] As explained earlier, although the *Guidance* is not beyond reproach, it represents a significant development in the framework of debate on what has, and is, a hugely difficult area of IHL;[107] a point accepted by many of its critics.[108]

This said, the *Guidance* and the response to it is an instantiation of a broader conflict over the ownership of IHL and its interpretation, between those who are, or have been, involved with IHL as members of (Western) armed forces, and others.[109] The critiques of the *Guidance* have tended to come from the military law side of IHL. As mentioned earlier, it is important to remember that IHL is intended to be a practical, implementable law. As such, military perspectives are indispensable in its formulation and application. But that is not the whole of the law, so to speak. There is a risk of this type of reasoning falling into *Kriegsraison*, a position that was rejected, at the very latest, by the end of the nineteenth century. If the human rights law critiques can be criticised for being a little utopian, the military critiques can also be sometimes a little apologetic, to adopt Koskenniemi's famous formula.[110]

The issue of DPH is one where the strict written (and probably customary) law is one which is Delphic. As such (even if not elsewhere) interpretation is the life of the law here. As Martti Koskenniemi has said, '[l]egal argument is never deduction from self-evident rules. It always adds to our

Martens clause, that does have relevance with respect to PDH and the ICRC *Guidance*, see, C. Greenwood, 'Belligerent Reprisals in the Jurisprudence of the International Criminal Tribunal for the Former Yugoslavia'.

106 Hays Parks, 'Part IX', p. 828.

107 Lauterpacht may be quoted in aid of such a point: H. Lauterpacht, 'The Problem of the Revision of the Law of War, *British Yearbook of International Law*, 29 (1952), pp. 360–382, 382.

108 See Schmitt, 'Critical Analysis', p. 6; W. H. Boothby, *The Law of Targeting* (Oxford: Oxford University Press, 2012) p. 146; and van der Toorn, 'Direct Participation in Hostilities: A Legal and Practical Evaluation of the ICRC Guidance', p. 22.

109 It must be noted at this juncture that the point of this part is not to traduce military lawyers, who have (as the 'War on Terror' has shown) often operated as a considerable brake on unfortunate civilian interpretations of IHL, and whose expertise is undoubtedly important in the development of the law here. The point is more limited, being that such actors are not the sole appropriate authors and interpreters of the law in this regard.

110 M. Koskenniemi, *From Apology to Utopia* (Cambridge: Cambridge University Press, reprint with new epilogue, 2005). Kleffner, 'Section IX', p. 39, also references such a point.

understanding of the law, and thus to the identity, objective and principles of the community.'[111] Furthermore, as Friedrich Kratochwil has noted, the life of law, and indeed its meaning is embodied in the use that is made of rules more than the rules themselves.[112] This is fundamentally important in areas such as this, where it is not necessary to subscribe to the tenets of radical indeterminacy to accept that there are contesting, plausible interpretations of the law.

It is against this background that discussions of the *Guidance* ought to be seen as an embodiment of the life of law and indeed its meaning. This is because, at least here, the meaning of DPH is embodied in the use that is made of the skeletal rules that exist more than the rules themselves. As Carlo Focarelli has said:

> If law is a social construct ultimately founded in mythic belief, there must be a constant struggle engaged by different groups to control the generation and prevalence about its belief and reality. While science looks for truth in the world 'before us', like mountains, law is 'among us'. Scientists are not part of the process of creating mountains but jurists and people do participate in the making and unmaking of law. Law is mythic because we are a part thereof. When dealing with law 'observers' become 'agents' whether they like it or not. The 'we' who make or unmake law is in constant struggle, whether actively or tacitly, to shape the law one way or another.[113]

In a similarly general manner (whether or not such a manner is generalizable or not need not concern us here) Ingo Venzke has commented that actors in international law through interpretation try to seek semantic authority and influence discourse to their own ends.[114] Some of the military critics of the *Guidance* show this in no short order. For example, Corn *et al.* make such a commitment open, stating that:

> We are under no illusion that we will persuade proponents of this least harmful means rule to reconsider their position. Nor are we insensitive to the profound human consequences of a rule that legally authorises attack with methods and means of warfare that are likely to cause death as a measure of first resort with no obligation to consider lesser means to incapacitate the target – even against an individual who may in fact pose little or no threat to an attacking force at that precise moment. If anything,

[111] M. Koskenniemi, 'The Place of Law in Collective Security', *Michigan Journal of International Law*, 17 (1996), pp. 455–490, 480.

[112] See e.g. F. Kratochwil, *The Status of Law in World Society: Meditations on the Role and Rule of Law* (Cambridge: Cambridge University Press, 2014).

[113] C. Focarelli, *International Law as Social Construct: The Struggle for Global Justice* (Oxford: Oxford University Press, 2012), pp. 55–56.

[114] I. Venzke, *How Interpretation Makes International Law: On Semantic Change and Normative Twists* (Oxford: Oxford University Press, 2012), p. ix.

> the combined sixty-two years of military experience shared by three of the authors – experience that required a very personal sensitivity to the human dimension of warfare – makes it impossible for us not to appreciate these consequences. But this experience, and our continued collective experience of working closely with those who remain engaged in the physically, mentally, and morally demanding business of fighting our nations' wars, also informs our view that the LOAC must, as it historically has, remain rationally grounded in the realities of warfare. We are confident that anyone grappling with this issue understands that decisions related to the employment of combat power are not resolved in the quiet and safe confines of law libraries, academic conferences, or even courtrooms, they are resolved in the intensely demanding situations which our nation thrusts our armed forces.[115]

Their approach is not an isolated one.[116] It can, with little extension, be seen as an attempt to create or maintain an interpretative hegemony over IHL, by the assertion of special expertise, relying on a form of military 'common sense' approach to IHL which cannot go unchallenged. As Bonaventura de Sousa Santos has shown, legal 'common sense' is as constructed as any other form of knowledge,[117] and, as Cemenceau famously put it, war is far too important to be left to the military on their own.

This leads to a more general point, that IHL is not simply the purview of the military. Michael Bothe has made the very important point that there needs to be civilian control over the military: 'In democratic systems, the values pursued by the military and those by society cannot be far apart. The value system on the basis of which the military is operating has to conform to that of the civil society and not *vice versa*'.[118] After all, what is done by the military is done in the name of the State, and therefore the name of its citizens, who have a right to a say in the laws that govern those who at some level act for them. Indeed, it is possible to go further to say that IHL, of necessity, has to have an external evaluative element if it is to be law worthy of the name, in that it is not simply a system of self-regulation. There is a risk, if the interpretation of IHL is left entirely

[115] G. S. Corn, L. R. Blank, C. Jenks and E. Talbot Jensen, 'Belligerent Targeting and the Invalidity of a Least Harmful Means Rule' in A. Deeks (ed.), *The Geography of Cyber Conflict: Through a Glass Darkly* (Newport, RI: US Naval War College, 2013), pp. 536–626, the use of 'our' in the quote further shows the specific milieu in which the authors write, and who their intended audience are.

[116] See also, e.g. Hays Parks, 'Part IX', p. 796.

[117] B. de Sousa Santos, *Towards a New Legal Common Sense* (Cambridge: Cambridge University Press, 2nd ed., 2002).

[118] M. Bothe, 'The Protection of the Civilian Population and the NATO Bombing of Yugoslavia: Comments on a Report to the ICTY Prosecutor', *European Journal of International Law*, 12 (2001), pp. 531–536, 535.

to military practitioners (although again, experience shows the many are *bona fide* supporters of what they would call the LOAC (although the terminology on both sides is telling), that IHL becomes simply a meek form of self-regulation. The banking crisis has shown us that, although expertise in the area is very important for ensuring that the law is relevant, it cannot be the sole source of reference.

All constituencies have their own conscious or unconscious interest, and IHL is no exception. Given that indeed the rights that combatants are granted under IHL to do what would otherwise clearly be a domestic crime, careful scrutiny needs to be engaged in unless a consumerist attitude is taken on the part of those IHL empowers to kill. Sadly, consumerist attitudes to IHL, especially in the 'war on terror', cannot be ruled out.

What the ICRC has provided us with is a framework in which to evaluate such matters, and what is notable is that the critics have tended not to provide coherent alternatives, and in their absence, we are thrown back to ad hoc determinations, which do not advance the rule of law, but privilege deformalised decision makers, who are empowered, not limited by law. Thus, although the *Guidance* is not unimpeachable, it is far better than the alternative. Free interpretation all too often becomes a free-for-all, and in armed conflict, that is not a good thing. Although some military critics of the *Guidance* have complained (unfairly) that the ICRC have stepped outside its mandate in promulgating the *Guidance*,[119] the ICRC is a huge operator in the area of IHL,[120] and its views cannot simply be dismissed on the basis of an alleged lack of expertise. Even were it to lack such expertise, it is also important to accept that not all legitimate participants in the development of law are necessarily experts, and to define such a concept in and of itself may be problematic.

VII. Conclusion

The point of the chapter is not to eulogise the *Guidance* but to show how, although it is not beyond critique, it represents an important contribution to the development of IHL. Such developments are not solely, if they ever were, the remit of States, or more narrowly, the military representatives of those States. One well-regarded military critic of the *Guidance* has said

[119] Hays Parks, 'Part IX', pp. 794–796. See the convincing response by Melzer, *Guidance*, pp. 893–894 and W. H. Boothby, *The Law of Targeting* (Oxford: Oxford University Press, 2012), p. 146.

[120] S. R. Ratner, 'Persuading to Comply: On the Deployment and Avoidance of Legal Argumentation.' in J. L. Dunoff and M. A. Pollack (eds.), *Interdisciplinary Perspectives on International Law and International Relations: The State of the Art* (Cambridge: Cambridge University Press, 2012), pp. 568–590.

that 'the deficiencies identified [in the *Guidance*] demonstrate a general failure to fully appreciate the operational complexity of modern warfare. Accordingly, States involved in twenty-first-century warfare are unlikely to view the document favourably, let alone use it to provide direction to their forces in the field.'[121] This comment reflects a rather unreflective and insular view of how IHL works, and one that assumes that military legal advisors, and their view of IHL is the be-all-and-end-all of IHL. Such a view is inadequate. It forgets that IHL is not an entirely self-referential system, and there is a plurality of interpreters of the law, admittedly of varying levels of authority, but such authority is not entirely binary, and the ICRC has a strong, State-mandated role in this respect.

Indeed, in spite of the critiques that have come from some commentators, the *Guidance* is likely to become the frame of reference for discussing the issues it raises. At the very least, it represents the ICRC's official view on point, and, as such where it is making representations to national interlocutors about targeting, this is what the ICRC will use. Whether such interlocutors agree or not is relevant, but the terms of the debate, and the standards upon which the ICRC will take a view on compliance, will now be those contained in the *Guidance*. Therefore, States would be ill-advised to ignore them.

The ICRC has now set out its institutional view on the law. If the experience of the commentaries to the Geneva Conventions, and Additional Protocols, as well as the *Customary Humanitarian Law* study, is anything to go by, it will become increasingly difficult to reject the *Guidance* as an accurate interpretation of the law without strong reasoning.[122] As was noted by David Caron with regard to the ILC draft Articles on State Responsibility, the simple fact of reducing controversial issues to propositions of law, in writing, has its own inertia, and States come to discuss even controversial issues in the terms that have been written down rather than deny the terms of reference that have been set.[123] Anecdotal evidence is that some States are already treating the *Guidance* as the law on point. This

[121] Hays Parks, 'Part IX', p. 699.

[122] On the customary study see E. Wilmshurst and S. Breau (eds.), *Perspectives on the ICRC Study on Customary International Humanitarian Law* (Cambridge: Cambridge University Press, 2007); for the US response see Letter from John Bellinger III, Legal Advisor, US Department of State, and William J. Haynes, General Counsel, US Department of Defense, to Jakob Kellenberger, President, International Committee of the Red Cross, Regarding Customary International Law Study (Nov. 3, 2006), *International Legal Materials*, 46 (2007), 514–531.

[123] D. D. Caron, 'The ILC Articles on State Responsibility: The Paradoxical Relationship Between Form and Authority', *American Journal of International Law*, 96 (2002), pp. 857–873, 867–870.

is not to say that the *Guidance* is the alpha and omega of the law on DPH, but that it is already having an impact in practice, and the more practice that accumulates that conforms with the *Guidance*, the more difficult it may be to deny its normative status.[124] The *Guidance* is not perfect, but it is now what we have. Governments have so far shown themselves incapable of writing a similar piece of guidance, and so if they wish to reject the ICRC's views, the impetus is now for them to show that they can create (and get broad agreement thereupon) something better.

[124] See the discussion on previous practice and its relationship to *opinio juris* in Corn *et al.*, Cyber Conflicts, pp. 608–609; and C. Goodman, 'The Power to Kill or Capture Enemy Combatants', *European Journal of International Law*, 24 (2013), pp. 819–853, 825–826. I am grateful for the discussions I have had on this point with Dapo Akande, who has, to say the least, considerably influenced my views on how practice had solidified what is initially asserted to be a matter of policy. See also on point F. Kirgis, 'Custom on a Sliding Scale', *American Journal of International Law*, 81 (1987), pp. 146–151.

PART III

The International Committee of the Red Cross' Influence on Related Areas of International Law

5

Development of Treaties Limiting or Prohibiting the Use of Certain Weapons: The Role of the International Committee of the Red Cross

KATHLEEN LAWAND AND ISABEL ROBINSON*

I. Introduction

In the course of its 150-year history, the International Committee of the Red Cross (ICRC) has played a significant role in the development of many of the international humanitarian law (IHL) rules limiting or prohibiting the use of weapons of concern. By drawing the attention of states and the public to the unacceptable effects of certain weapons on combatants and civilians, the ICRC has helped to create the conditions for development of the law in this area, notably with regard to chemical and biological weapons, blinding laser weapons, as well as anti-personnel mines, explosive remnants of war and cluster munitions, to give but a few examples. The ICRC's work towards the development of IHL applicable to weapons is firmly grounded in its historical tradition of promoting the reaffirmation, clarification and development of the law in response to gaps in legal protection, which the organisation has observed in armed conflicts or anticipated from evolving technologies of warfare. Today, the legal basis of this work is derived notably from the responsibilities that States have entrusted to the ICRC under IHL, the Statutes of the International Red Cross and Red Crescent Movement and the resolutions of the International Conference of the Red Cross and Red Crescent,[1] which

* The research assistance of Kristina Nechayeva is gratefully acknowledged. This chapter was written in a personal capacity and does not necessarily reflect the views of the ICRC.

[1] The International Conference of the Red Cross and Red Crescent meets every four years and is composed of the States' Parties to the 1949 Geneva Conventions and the components of the International Red Cross and Red Crescent Movement, namely National Red Cross and Red Crescent Societies, the ICRC and the International Federation of Red Cross and Red Crescent Societies. The International Conference is 'the supreme deliberative body for the Movement' and its members together 'examine and decide upon humanitarian matters

underpin the ICRC's role as 'guardian of international humanitarian law'.[2]

The ICRC's approach to each weapon of humanitarian concern has typically been based on a combination of elements. First, the organisation has witnessed first-hand the effects of the weapon on combatants and/or on civilians, as observed in its field operations. Indeed, as a humanitarian organisation mandated to protect and assist the victims of armed conflict, the ICRC deals with the humanitarian consequences of the use of weapons on a daily basis. Second, it has facilitated specialist discussions, by convening meetings of government and independent experts from a range of professional backgrounds – including military, legal, medical and policy – to examine the different aspects of the weapon.[3] Third, the ICRC has brought its own health, technical and legal expertise to inform discussions on the weapon. Together with the organisation's experience in situations where the weapon has been used and its proximity to the victims, this expertise has aimed to ensure that its recommendations to States regarding the weapon would be practical and relevant, also taking into account the weapon's military purpose and weighing it against its human costs. Finally, the ICRC has engaged in humanitarian advocacy by informing public perceptions and appealing directly to States to take action on the weapon, including through the development of new rules to limit its use or prohibit it altogether where its human costs clearly outweigh its military utility. In this humanitarian advocacy on weapons, the ICRC has worked in close cooperation with National Red Cross and Red Crescent Societies.

of common interest and any other related matter': *Statutes of the International Red Cross and Red Crescent Movement*, adopted by the 25th International Conference of the Red Cross in 1986 (Resolution XXXI), amended in 1995 (Resolution 7 of the 26th International Conference) and 2006 (Resolution 1 of the 29th International Conference), Article 8.

[2] Pursuant to Art 5(2)(g) of the Statutes of the International Red Cross and Red Crescent Movement, the role of the ICRC includes 'to work for the understanding and dissemination of knowledge of international humanitarian law applicable in armed conflicts and to prepare any development thereof'. See also: Y. Sandoz, *The International Committee of the Red Cross as Guardian of International Humanitarian Law*, (Geneva: *ICRC*, 31 December 1998), available at: www.icrc.org/eng/resources/documents/misc/about-the-icrc-311298.htm; J.-P. Lavoyer and L. Maresca, 'The Role of the ICRC in the Development of International Humanitarian Law', *International Negotiation* 4 (1999), p. 504; F. Bugnion, 'The International Committee of the Red Cross and the Development of International Humanitarian Law', *Chicago Journal of International Law* 5 (1) (2004), pp. 191–215. On the nature of the ICRC's work and its mandate, see ICRC, *The ICRC: Its Mission and Work* (Geneva, ICRC: March 2009), pp. 6–8.

[3] In this regard, Sandoz refers to the ICRC's 'catalysing role' (translated from French). See Y. Sandoz, 'Interdiction et restriction de l'usage de certains armes: trois questions clés', *International Review of the Red Cross*, 76(806) (1994), p. 105.

Together, these elements have driven the organisation's 'effects-based' approach to the regulation of weapons. This approach observes the actual and, in the case of new weapons not yet deployed, foreseeable effects of the use of weapons – including their long-term impact – on civilians and on the health of combatants. Drawing attention to the level of suffering caused by a weapon, unjustified by military considerations and unacceptable in moral and social terms – in other words abhorrent to the 'public conscience' – has led to the development of new IHL rules limiting or prohibiting the use of the weapon.[4]

In this respect, over the last century and a half, the 'principles of humanity' and the 'dictates of public conscience', as codified in the 'Martens Clause',[5] have underpinned the development of IHL applicable to weapons.[6] Recent treaties have explicitly recognised 'the role of public conscience in furthering the principles of humanity' and the efforts to this end undertaken by the International Red Cross and Red Crescent Movement and other organisations.[7]

Furthermore, IHL's specific limits and prohibitions on the use of certain weapons have been grounded on two 'cardinal' rules of IHL

[4] See P. Herby and K. Lawand, 'Unacceptable Behaviour: How Norms are Established' in J. Williams, S. Goose and M. Wareham (eds.), *Banning Landmines: Disarmament, Citizen Diplomacy and Human Security* (Lanham, MD: Rowman & Littlefield Publishers, 2008), p. 202.

[5] The 'Martens Clause' was first codified in the preambles of the Hague Conventions of 1899 and 1907. It later appeared in Article 1(2) of *Additional Protocol I*, (Protocol Additional to the Geneva Conventions of 1949 and Relating to the Protection of Victims of International Armed Conflicts (Additional Protocol I), Geneva, 8 June 1977, in force 7 December 1978, 1125 UNTS) and in the preamble of the *Protocol Additional to the Geneva Conventions of 1949 and Relating to the Protection of Victims of Non-International Armed Conflicts (Additional Protocol II)*, Geneva, 8 June 1977, in force 17 December 1978, 1125 UNTS 609. Article 1(2) of Additional Protocol I reads: 'In cases not covered by this Protocol or by other international agreements, civilians and combatants remain under the protection and authority of the principles of international law derived from established custom, from the principles of humanity and from the dictates of public conscience'. Beyond these general IHL treaties, the Martens Clause was most recently recalled in the 11th preambular paragraph of the *Convention on Cluster Munitions (CCM)*, Dublin, 30 May 2008, in force 1 August 2010, 2688 UNTS 39.

[6] The International Court of Justice has stressed that the Martens Clause has 'proved to be an effective means of addressing the rapid evolution of military technology' and represents customary international law: *Legality of the Threat or Use of Nuclear Weapons*, Advisory Opinion, I.C.J. Rep. 1996 (July 8), paras 78–9.

[7] *Convention on the Prohibition of the Use, Stockpiling, Production and Transfer of Anti-Personnel Mines and on their Destruction* (APMBC), Oslo, 18 September 1997, in force 1 March 1999, 2056 UNTS 211, 8th preambular paragraph; CCM, 17th preambular paragraph.

applicable to all weapons: the prohibition of indiscriminate attacks,[8] including the customary law prohibition to use weapons that are by nature indiscriminate,[9] which aims to protect civilians; and the prohibition to employ weapons of a nature to cause superfluous injury or unnecessary suffering,[10] which aims to protect combatants. Along with the Martens Clause, these rules are, in the words of the International Court of Justice, 'fundamental to the respect of the human person and "elementary considerations of humanity"'.[11] It is these 'elementary considerations of humanity' that have driven the ICRC's work towards limits or prohibitions on the use of specific weapons and towards stricter controls on arms availability.

This chapter will examine more closely the ICRC's role in the development of IHL applying to chemical and biological weapons, anti-personnel mines, cluster munitions and explosive remnants of war, blinding laser weapons, and arms transfers. In each of these cases, the typical features of the ICRC's approach to weapons of concern will be discussed, along

[8] The prohibition of indiscriminate attacks is articulated in Article 51(4) and (5) of the *Additional Protocol I*. The prohibition is considered customary law in both international and non-international armed conflicts: see J.-M. Henckaerts and L. Doswald-Beck (eds.), *Customary International Humanitarian Law, Volume I: Rules* (Cambridge: Cambridge University Press/ICRC, 2005), pp. 37–45 (Rules 11–13).

[9] See Henckaerts and Doswald-Beck, *Customary International Humanitarian Law, Volume I*, pp. 244–250 (Rule 71). The prohibition is considered customary law in both international and non-international armed conflicts.

[10] The prohibition of weapons, projectiles and material and methods of warfare of a nature to cause superfluous injury or unnecessary suffering was codified in Article 35(2) of Additional Protocol I, as well as in Article 23(e) of *Convention (II) with Respect to the Laws and Customs of War on Land and its annex: Regulations concerning the Laws and Customs of War on Land* (1899 Hague Convention), The Hague, 29 July 1899, in force 4 September 1900, 26 Martens Nouveau Recueil (ser. 2) 949; 187 Consol. T.S. 429; and in Article 23(e) of *Convention (IV) respecting the Laws and Customs of War on Land and its annex: Regulations concerning the Laws and Customs of War on Land* (1907 Hague Convention), The Hague, 18 October 1907, in force 26 January 1901, 3 Martens Nouveau Recueil (ser. 3) 461; 205 Consol. T.S. 277. The rule is considered customary law in both international and non-international armed conflicts: see Henckaerts and Doswald-Beck, *Customary International Humanitarian Law, Volume I*, pp. 237–244 (Rule 70).

[11] In its Advisory Opinion on the *Legality of the Threat or Use of Nuclear Weapons*, the International Court of Justice found that pursuant to the Martens Clause and the 'cardinal principles' of IHL, 'humanitarian law, at a very early stage, prohibited certain types of weapons either because of their indiscriminate effect on combatants and civilians or because of the unnecessary suffering caused to combatants, that is to say, a harm greater than that unavoidable to achieve legitimate military objectives. If an envisaged use of weapons would not meet the requirements of humanitarian law, a threat to engage in such use would also be contrary to that law' (para. 78).

with some of the challenges the organisation has faced. The cases presented are some of the more prominent areas where the ICRC has played an important role in developing the law. It should be stressed that this chapter focuses primarily on development of the law, and does not address the work of the ICRC in promoting implementation of weapons treaties.[12] On the basis of the cases studied, the chapter will draw some concluding observations on the ICRC's role in the development of IHL applying to weapons, on changes in the landscape of humanitarian diplomacy in recent years, and on areas of possible future normative developments.

II. Chemical and Biological Weapons

In February 1918, faced with the growing use of asphyxiating and poisonous gases on the battlefields of Europe, the ICRC publicly demanded 'a ban on this appalling method of waging war'.[13] In its appeal – which was sent not only to the heads of belligerent and neutral countries, but also to national Red Cross societies of the day, various religious leaders and the press – the ICRC testified about the 'terrible suffering caused by these gases' which were being witnessed by the ICRC medical personnel who were treating the victims.[14] It described these weapons as 'barbaric', 'cruel', and 'murderous'. In addition, the ICRC invoked existing law, in particular the Hague Regulations of 1899 and 1907, which prohibit the use of poison or poisonous weapons and weapons of a nature to cause unnecessary

[12] For example, the Maputo Action Plan 2014–2018 for the APMBC recognises 'the special partnerships in the universalization and implementation of the Convention with . . . the International Committee of the Red Cross . . . ' See *Anti-Personnel Mine Ban Convention*, (Geneva: Implementation Support Unit, September 2014), p. 21. See also, 'Final Declaration', CCW/CONF.IV/4/Add.1, 15 December 2011, final document of the Fourth Review Conference of the CCW, p. 3. Regarding the role of the ICRC, among others, in efforts to universalise and implement the CCM, see paragraphs 3, 5, 16, 23, 68, 69 and 82 of the *Lusaka progress report, Monitoring progress in implementing the Vientiane Action Plan between the Third and Fourth Meetings of States Parties*, in Annex I of the Final Document of the Fourth Meeting of States Parties, CCM/MSP/2013/6, 23 September 2013. For a discussion of the role of the ICRC in promoting the implementation of the APMBC, see K. Lawand, 'The Convention on the Prohibition of the Use, Stockpiling, Production and Transfer of Anti-Personnel Mines and on their Destruction (Ottawa Convention)' in G. Ulfstein, T. Marauhn and A. Zimmerman (eds.), *Making Treaties Work – Human Rights, Environment and Arms Control*, (Cambridge: Cambridge University Press, 2007), pp. 324–347.

[13] ICRC, 'Appel contre le gas vénéneux', *Bulletin International des Sociétés de la Croix-Rouge* 49 (1918), p. 187 (translated from French).

[14] *Ibid.*, 188.

suffering. Significantly, the ICRC also explicitly appealed to the belligerents' 'feeling of humanity, which we do not believe is extinguished even after three years of war'.[15] In so doing, the ICRC was invoking the principles of humanity and the dictates of public conscience, to put an end to the use of poisonous and asphyxiating gases.

The ICRC appeal in the final year of World War I was significant for the organisation as it was the first time ever that the ICRC called on States to prohibit the use of a weapon.[16] In effect, this marked an expansion in the focus of the ICRC from its traditional domain of so-called 'Geneva Law' to more active engagement on issues of 'Hague Law'.[17] This decision did not come lightly for the organisation, particularly as the use of poisonous weapons was a very controversial issue at the time and had been the subject of mutual accusations on the part of the belligerent States. Still, in deciding to launch the appeal, the ICRC was embarking on a new course of action which went beyond assisting victims and ventured into pronouncing itself on the acceptability of means and methods of warfare, a course of action that was consolidated and strengthened over the years, as the ICRC etched out an increasingly important role in normative development to address the unacceptable human cost of certain weapons.[18]

The 1918 appeal received mixed responses: on the one hand, the appeal received support from a number of States and national Red Cross societies; on the other hand, the parties to the conflict accused the ICRC of partiality and acting with political motives.[19] Yet the ICRC continued its

[15] *Ibid.*, 186.

[16] Bugnion, 'The International Committee of the Red Cross and the Development of International Humanitarian Law', pp. 200–201.

[17] The term 'Geneva Law' has been used to refer to the part of IHL that covers protection of persons when in the power of the enemy, whereas 'Hague Law' refers to IHL rules on the conduct of hostilities. Geneva Law was driven by the ICRC and became known as such given that all significant steps in developing this branch of IHL took place in Geneva, starting with the Geneva Convention of 1864. Hague Law was initiated with the Saint Petersburg Declaration of 1868 and the International Peace Conferences in The Hague in 1899 and 1907. Eventually, both bodies of law converged in the 1977 Additional Protocols to the Geneva Conventions. See F. Bugnion, 'Droit de Genève et droit de la Haye', *International Review of the Red Cross*, 83(844) (2001), pp. 901–905.

[18] For the internal and external tensions regarding this 'new' role of the ICRC in matters of 'Hague Law', see L. V. Bergen and M. Abbenhuis, 'Man-monkey, monkey-man: neutrality and the discussions about the "inhumanity" of poison gas in the Netherlands and the International Committee of the Red Cross', *First World War Studies*, 3(1) (2012), pp. 1–23. Regarding the ICRC's role in weapons issues more generally, see R. Mathur, *The International Committee of the Red Cross and Humanitarian Practices of Arms Control and Disarmament* (Toronto: York University, 2011).

[19] A. Durand, *History of the International Committee of the Red Cross: From Sarajevo to Hiroshima* (Geneva: Henry Dunant Institute, 1978), pp. 93–95.

work towards the goal of banning poison gas by seeking support from academic and military circles, as well as national Red Cross societies, with a view to facilitating exchange of expertise. Importantly, the appeal fuelled heated debate between those who saw gas warfare as barbaric, and those who insisted on its military value and maintained a position that gas was somehow an acceptable weapon.[20] In this regard, the ICRC continued to facilitate expert discussion, publishing an article in the *International Review of the Red Cross*[21] in 1919, which outlined the horrendous suffering caused by poison gas.[22] Further, the ICRC requested the League of Nations in 1920 to prohibit the use of asphyxiating gas,[23] and raised the issue before the 10th International Conference of the Red Cross and Red Crescent in 1921. As a result, the Conference adopted a resolution asking governments to amend the Fourth Hague Convention of 1907 to include, among others, 'an absolute prohibition of the use of gases as a means of combat'.[24] Measures such as this helped to ensure that gas weapons became an issue of both public and government concern.[25]

In 1925, the call of the ICRC was finally answered when a League of Nations conference on the international trade in weapons adopted the *Geneva Protocol for the Prohibition of the Use in War of Asphyxiating, Poisonous or other Gases and Bacteriological Methods of Warfare (Geneva Protocol)*.[26] By virtue of its 'moral prestige',[27] the ICRC was invited to attend the conference as an observer, although at the time, the role of observers was much more limited than the dynamic role played by the ICRC in contemporary diplomatic conferences. Nevertheless, it is clear that the ICRC played a significant role in triggering the political will for such a conference and in building momentum for the eventual ban on

20 L. V. Bergen, 'The Poison Gas Debate in the Inter-War Years', *Medicine Conflict and Survival*, 24(3) (2008), pp. 175–182.

21 Established in 1869, the *Review* has proven to be an important launch pad for disseminating expert views on IHL issues, including with regard to the effects of certain weapons.

22 H. Staudinger, 'La Technique Moderne', *International Review of the Red Cross*, 1(5) (1919), pp. 508–515.

23 ICRC, 'Limitation de la guerre: Lettre du Comité international de la Croix-Rouge à l'Assemble de la Société des Nations', reproduced in *International Review of the Red Cross*, 2(24) (1920), p. 1348.

24 10th International Conference of the Red Cross and Red Crescent, Geneva, 30 March – 7 April 1921, Resolution XII on 'Limitation de la Guerre'.

25 R. Price, *The Chemical Weapons Taboo* (London and Ithaca: Cornell University Press, 1997), p. 71.

26 *Protocol for the Prohibition of the Use of Asphyxiating, Poisonous or Other Gases, and of Bacteriological Methods of Warfare*, Geneva, 17 June 1925, in force 8 February 1928.

27 Mathur, *The International Committee of the Red Cross and Humanitarian Practices of Arms Control and Disarmament*, pp. 265–266.

these weapons. Indeed, 'the ICRC was instrumental in the adoption of the Protocol by its appeals, by its approaches to governments and by mobilization of public opinion'.[28]

Yet the ICRC's commitment to ban chemical warfare did not stop there. Following the adoption of the Geneva Protocol, the ICRC continued encouraging States to accede to the Protocol through multiple resolutions of the International Conferences of the Red Cross and Red Crescent,[29] and through subsequent appeals to States. For example, in July 1966, the ICRC called on 80 governments to accede to the Geneva Protocol, which resulted in a number of new accessions.[30] The ICRC also raised awareness on this issue through the establishment of a Documentation Centre in 1928, charged with the task of distributing information to national Red Cross societies and informing the public about the dangers of chemical warfare.[31]

Further, the ICRC was mandated by the International Conference to convene an International Commission of Experts for the Legal Protection of Civilian Populations against Aero-Chemical Warfare.[32] This request responded directly to public concerns that future conflicts would be characterised by aero-chemical warfare, and that there was thus still a need to develop additional legal protections. Following two meetings of technical experts, in 1931, the ICRC brought together legal experts from twelve national Red Cross societies to consider a potential treaty regulating aero-chemical warfare. This Commission of Experts underlined the

[28] Bugnion, 'The ICRC and the Development of International Humanitarian Law', p. 201.

[29] See, for example, 12th International Conference of the Red Cross and Red Crescent in October, Geneva, 7–10 October 1925, Resolution V on 'Guerre Chimique'; 17th International Conference of the Red Cross and Red Crescent, Stockholm, 20–30 August 1948, Resolution XXIV on 'Non-Directed Weapons'.

[30] ICRC, 'Le Protocole de Geneve', *International Review of the Red Cross*, 49(578) (1967), pp. 51–57; J. Mirimanoff, 'The Red Cross and Biological and Chemical Weapons', *International Review of the Red Cross*, 52(618) (1970), p. 3.

[31] Establishment of a Documentation Centre was one of the recommendations of the Commission of Experts for the Protection of the Civilian Population Against Chemical Warfare. The Centre was mandated to house all relevant publications on protection against gas warfare, progress achieved by governments on this issue and measures taken to protect industrial workers exposed to harmful substances. See Annex to Resolutions adopted by the International Commission of Experts for the Protection of the Civilian Population against Chemical Warfare, in *Document Relatifs à la Guerre Chimiques et Aérienne présenté aux membres de la Conférence pour la réduction et la limitation des armements par la Comité International de la Croix Rouge* (Geneva: ICRC, 1932), p. 18.

[32] 14th International Conference of the Red Cross and Red Crescent, Brussels, 6–11 October 1930, Resolution V on 'Protection des Populations Civiles Contre la Guerre Chimique'.

need for further development of the law, primarily because not all States were party to the Geneva Protocol, and previous legal documents were not sufficient to regulate air warfare.[33] The Report of the Commission of Experts was submitted to the Disarmament Conference on the Reduction and Limitation of Weapons, organised by the League of Nations in 1932, which discussed the issue of legal regulation of chemical, bacteriological and incendiary weapons.[34] This did not, however, lead to further normative development.

While a ban on the use of asphyxiating, poisonous or other gases was achieved in 1925, it took a further forty-seven years to adopt a legal instrument – the 1972 *Biological Weapons Convention* (BWC)[35] – which requires complete elimination of biological weapons. Likewise, the requirement to eliminate chemical weapons was not agreed until sixty-eight years later with the 1993 *Chemical Weapons Convention* (CWC).[36] A comprehensive and unconditional ban of these weapons was required because, despite the clear prohibition on their use in the 1925 *Geneva Protocol*, several States continued to weaponize toxic chemicals and amass vast stockpiles of chemical weapons, and to carry out research programmes in biological weapons. At the time, this seemed justified for States by the fact that the Geneva Protocol did not prohibit these activities and more importantly, by the reservations that many States had made upon ratification of the Protocol, whereby they reserved themselves the possibility to use chemical or biological weapons in retaliation to a first use by an enemy. The Geneva Protocol therefore had become *de facto* a no-first-use treaty.

The ICRC played a more modest role in the development of the Chemical and Biological Weapons Conventions, for example, by calling on States at the 1989 Paris Conference on the Prohibition of Chemical Weapons to

[33] 'Rapport adopté par la Commission Internationale d'Experts pour la protection juridique des populations civiles contre les dangers de la guerre aéro-chimique' in *Document Relatifs à la Guerre Chimiques et Aérienne présenté aux membres de la Conférence pour la réduction et la limitation des armements par la Comité International de la Croix Rouge* (Geneva: ICRC, 1932), p. 35.

[34] In May 1932, the Conference created a Special Committee on technical questions arising from chemical, bacteriological and incendiary weapons. See League of Nations Archives, Doc. Conf.D.120, 10 May 1932.

[35] *The Convention on the Prohibition of the Development, Production and Stockpiling of Bacteriological (Biological) and Toxin Weapons and on their Destruction*, 10 April 1972, in force 26 March 1975, 1015 UNTS 163.

[36] *The Convention on the Prohibition of the Development, Production, Stockpiling and Use of Chemical Weapons and on Their Destruction*, Geneva, 8 February 1993, in force 29 April 1994, 1974 UNTS 45.

'eliminate the use of chemical weapons in all circumstances and ... abolish them completely'.[37] In addition, the ICRC has actively promoted adherence to these treaties and implementation of the norm of non-use embodied in the framework of the Geneva Protocol, the BWC and the CWC, including through public expression of concern in cases of alleged or confirmed use of such weapons.[38]

Since entry into force of the BWC and CWC, the ICRC has sought to safeguard the prohibitions set out in these treaties by recalling that the existing legal frameworks remain applicable to new technologies. In 2002, the ICRC launched an appeal on 'Biotechnology, Weapons and Humanity' which involved two tracks.[39] On the one hand, the ICRC called on the scientific community to consider the risks, rules and responsibilities related to advances in biotechnology, and to 'remember our common humanity'.[40] On the other hand, it called on States to adopt a high-level political declaration on biotechnology, weapons and humanity. Although this second objective was not supported at the time by some States, a number of ideas from the appeal were taken up by States' parties to the BWC and by prominent actors in the life sciences community.[41]

[37] ICRC, 'Message to the Chairman of the Paris Conference on the Prohibition of Chemical Weapons (7–11 January 1989)', reproduced in *International Review of the Red Cross*, 71(775) (1989), p. 74.

[38] In 1967, the ICRC publically condemned the use of chemical weapons in the non-international armed conflict in Yemen. See ICRC, Press Release No. 829b, 'The ICRC and the Yemen Conflict', 2 June 1967. In 1988, the ICRC also spoke publically about the use of chemical weapons in the international armed conflict between Iran and Iraq. See ICRC, Press Release No. 1567, 'Iran-Iraq conflict', 23 March 1988. More recently the ICRC expressed its shock at the use of chemical weapons in Syria in 2013 and 2014, which it called a serious violation of IHL. See the statements of the ICRC at the Eighteenth (2013) and Nineteenth (2014) Sessions of the Conferences of the States Parties to the Chemical Weapons Convention. This said, during the Italian–Ethiopian War in the 1930s, the ICRC refrained from handing over to the League of Nations its findings about the use of mustard gas by Italian forces, because it feared 'claims of partiality', as had been made by some States following its 1918 Appeal: see v. Bergen and Abbenhuis, 'Man-monkey, monkey-man', 14. See also R. Baudendistel, *Between Bombs and Good Intentions: The Red Cross and the Italian-Ethiopian War 1935 – 1936* (New York: Berghahn Books, 2006), pp. 279 and 310.

[39] The appeal was launched publically on 25 September 2002 and at a Meeting of Government Experts in Montreux on 23–24 September 2002. See ICRC, *Biotechnology, Weapons and Humanity. An informal meeting of government experts and independent experts: Summary Report*, available at: www.icrc.org/eng/assets/files/other/montreux_report.pdf.

[40] ICRC, 'Biotechnology, weapons and humanity', *International Review of the Red Cross*, 84 (848) (2002), p. 903.

[41] For example, the BWH appeal introduced the idea of a 'web of prevention', which involved different measures at various levels to prevent the misuse of biotechnology and the use of biological weapons. This notion was later taken up by the US National Academies of

As for the prohibition of chemical weapons, since 2003, the ICRC been expressing its concerns regarding the threats to this prohibition, and more generally the serious risks to life and health posed by the development and use of toxic chemicals as weapons for law enforcement, referred to by some as 'incapacitating chemical agents'. In recent years, the ICRC convened two expert meetings to explore further the implications of the development of such weapons for existing international law, including the CWC.[42] In addition to these expert meetings, in February 2013, the ICRC published its position on the matter, stating that the use of toxic chemicals as weapons for law enforcement should be limited exclusively to riot control agents.[43] In this regard, the ICRC has called on States to reaffirm their national policies and legislation limiting the use of toxic chemicals in law enforcement to riot control agents only. In response, a small but growing number of States are doing so, or are at least calling for discussions on the issue in the policy-making organs of the Organisation for the Prohibition of Chemical Weapons.[44]

III. Weapons that 'Keep on Killing'

The ICRC has had long-standing concerns regarding conventional weapons that remain activated and ready to strike long after the end of active hostilities – weapons that 'keep on killing'. These include anti-personnel and anti-vehicle mines, cluster munitions and unexploded ordnance. The post-conflict dangers to civilians caused by these weapons are today well known. Hundreds of thousands of civilians have been killed or maimed as a consequence of the widespread use of these weapons over decades. They inflict horrific injuries, leaving disabled survivors in need of lifetime rehabilitation and socioeconomic support, while contamination of land with these weapons creates severe economic consequences for affected communities.

Science. See *Globalisation, Biosecurity and the Future of the Life Sciences* (Washington: US National Academies of Science, 2006).

42 See ICRC, *Expert Meeting: Incapacitating Chemical Agents, Implications for International Law, Montreux, 24–26 March 2010* (Geneva: ICRC, 2010); and ICRC, *Expert Meeting: 'Incapacitating Chemical Agent', Law Enforcement, Human Rights Law and Policy Perspectives, Montreux, 24–26 April 2012* (Geneva: ICRC, 2013).

43 ICRC, 'ICRC position on the use of toxic chemicals as weapons for law enforcement', 6 February 2013. Available at: www.icrc.org/eng/assets/files/2013/2013–02-toxic-chemicals-icrc-position-eng.pdf.

44 See Australia, 'Weaponisation of Central Nervous System Acting Chemicals for Law Enforcement Purposes', C-19/NAT.1 (14 November 2014), paper presented to the Nineteenth Session of the OPCW Conference of the States Parties.

The current treaty framework[45] regulating such weapons includes the *Anti-Personnel Mine Ban Convention* (APMBC) and the *Convention on Cluster Munitions* (CCM)[46], both of which impose absolute bans on the use, production and transfer of such weapons. For States that are not party to the APMBC, the use of anti-personnel landmines is regulated principally by *Amended Protocol II*[47] of the *Convention on Certain Conventional Weapons* (CCW),[48] which also regulates the use of anti-vehicle mines. Responsibilities for protecting civilians from the effects of explosive remnants of war (ERW) are established in *Protocol V* to the CCW.[49]

The ICRC played an important role in the development of each of these treaties. Similar to its work on chemical weapons, its approach included raising awareness of the unacceptable human cost of the weapons of concern, and facilitating expert discussions concerning legal and technical issues, as well as the impact of these weapons on health. In sensitizing governments and the public to the effects of these weapons, the ICRC worked alongside national Red Cross and Red Crescent societies. The efforts and 'role of public conscience' of the International Red Cross and Red Crescent Movement are recognised in the preambles of the APMBC and of the

[45] For States not party to the treaties discussed in this section, the use of landmines, cluster munitions and other explosive munitions is governed by the general rules of treaty and customary IHL applicable to the conduct of hostilities (notably the rules of distinction, proportionality and precautions in attack), as well as the specific rules of customary IHL applicable to landmines. The latter requires that when landmines are used: 'particular care' is taken to minimise their indiscriminate effects; their placement is recorded 'as far as possible'; and at the end of active hostilities, the party that has used landmines remove or otherwise render them harmless to civilians, or facilitate their removal. See Henckaerts and Doswald-Beck (eds.), *Customary International Humanitarian Law*, pp. 3–67 (Rules 1–21) and 280–6 (Rules 81–3).

[46] The APMBC and CCM are cited in footnote 7.

[47] *Amended Protocol on Prohibitions on Restrictions on the Use of Mines, Booby-Traps and Other Devices (Amended Protocol II)*, Geneva, 3 May 1996, in force 3 December 1998, 2048 UNTS 93. *Amended Protocol II* was adopted to strengthen the rules in the original *Protocol II*. See *Protocol on Prohibitions or Restrictions on the Use of Mines, Booby-Traps and Other Devices (Protocol II)*, Geneva, 10 October 1980, in force 2 December 1983, 1342 UNTS 137. Today only nine States remain party to the original *Protocol* without having adhered to *Amended Protocol II*.

[48] *Convention on Prohibition or Restrictions on the Use of Certain Conventional Weapons which May be Deemed to be Excessively Injurious or to Have Indiscriminate Effects (CCW)*, Geneva, 10 October 1980, in force 2 December 1983, 1342 UNTS 137.

[49] *Protocol on Explosive Remnants of War (Protocol V)*, Geneva, 28 November 2003, in force 12 November 2006, 2399 UNTS 100.

CCM, as are the contributions of the UN and the NGO campaigns that helped bring about these treaties.[50]

1. *Anti-Personnel Mines*

The AMPBC – often referred to as the 'Ottawa treaty' – is widely regarded as one of the most successful treaties to address the humanitarian impact of a weapon, having achieved significant results in reducing the numbers of new victims worldwide. Yet behind this success story lies decades of awareness-raising and humanitarian advocacy and diplomacy, which from the ICRC's perspective, began in the 1950s. At this stage, the organisation drafted rules that aimed to prohibit 'delayed-action' weapons and obliged States to record and share information regarding the location of minefields.[51] Although the draft rules were presented to States at the 19th International Conference of the Red Cross in New Delhi in 1957, no action was taken to develop the rules into a binding legal instrument. Thus, the ICRC again raised the issue of landmines in the context of the Diplomatic Conference on Reaffirmation and Development of International Humanitarian Law Applicable in Armed Conflict, which took place from 1974 to 1977 and led to the adoption of the Additional Protocols to the 1949 Geneva Conventions.

In 1972, in the lead up to the Diplomatic Conference, States requested the ICRC to convene a consultation with legal, military and medical experts on 'conventional weapons that may cause unnecessary suffering or have indiscriminate effects'.[52] Accordingly, the ICRC convened expert

[50] In addition, the APMBC, the CCM and *Protocol V*, in their provisions on international cooperation and assistance, recognise the components of the International Red Cross and Red Crescent Movement, among other organisations, as actors through which States' parties 'in a position to do so' can provide assistance for risk education to civilians and for the care and rehabilitation of victims of these weapons: APMBC, Art 6(3); *Protocol V*, Art 8(1) and (2); and CCM, Art 6(7).

[51] ICRC, *Final Record concerning the Draft Rules for the Limitation of the Dangers incurred by the Civilian Population in Time of War*, (Geneva: ICRC, April 1958). Draft Article 14 prohibited 'delayed-action weapons, the dangerous effects of which are liable to be felt by the civilian population', among other weapons whose harmful effects could 'escape, either in space or in time, from the control of those who employ them'. Draft Article 15 required parties to armed conflicts to chart minefields and provide these charts to the opposing side or authorities following the end of hostilities.

[52] ICRC, *Conference of Government Experts on the Reaffirmation and Development of International Humanitarian Law Applicable in Armed Conflict (Second Session 3 May – 3 June*

meetings in Geneva in 1973,[53] in Lucerne in 1974,[54] and in Lugano in 1975[55] with the aim of developing detailed reports to support discussions in the event that these weapons would be addressed at the Diplomatic Conference and regulated in the Additional Protocols.[56] Ultimately, the Diplomatic Conference did not include specific regulation of landmines in the Additional Protocols. However, it requested that this issue be considered in the context of the UN, which subsequently launched a process that led to the adoption of the CCW and its three protocols, including *Protocol II* on mines, booby traps and other similar devices.[57] Discussions at the diplomatic conferences that negotiated and adopted the CCW were based on the reports of the ICRC's previously mentioned expert meetings.[58]

As of the late 1980s, ICRC surgeons and medical personnel were observing dramatic increases in the number of civilian casualties due to anti-personnel mines, many of which were occurring long after hostilities had ended.[59] The Medical Division of the ICRC began collecting data on the number of victims, as well as the effects of anti-personnel mines on victims, including death and traumatic amputation of limbs as well as

1972): Report of the Work of the Conference Volume II (Geneva: ICRC, 1972), Proposal CE/SPF/2, p. 115.

53 ICRC, *Weapons that may Cause Unnecessary Suffering or have Indiscriminate Effects: Report on the Work of Experts* (Geneva: ICRC, 1973).

54 ICRC, *Conference of Government Experts on the Use of Certain Conventional Weapons (Lucerne 24 September – 18 October 1973): Report* (Geneva: ICRC, 1975).

55 ICRC, *Conference of Government Experts on the Use of Certain Conventional Weapons (Lugano 28 January– 26 February 1976): Report* (Geneva: ICRC, 1976).

56 The reports of the expert meetings were submitted to the Diplomatic Conference in 1977.

57 Although *Protocol II* to the CCW was an important first step in developing the law on landmines, the regulation in the Protocol is rudimentary. It prohibits indiscriminate use of anti-personnel and anti-vehicle mines, as well as their manual emplacement in populated areas, unless combat is taking place or is imminent or the mined areas are clearly marked. Remotely delivered mines are prohibited unless they are used in the vicinity of a military objective and their location can be accurately recorded or they possess an effective neutralising mechanism. In addition, all pre-planned minefields must be recorded. Regarding all other minefields, parties to the conflict are to endeavour to record their locations.

58 ICRC, 'Rapport du Comité International de la Croix-Rouge pour la Conférence d'Examen de la Convention de 1980 des Nations Unies sur L'interdiction ou la Limitation de L'emploi de certaines armes classiques qui peuvent être considérées comme produisant des effets traumatiques excessifs ou comme frappant sans discrimination', *International Review of the Red Cross*, 76 (806) (1994), pp. 131–201.

59 For example, the ICRC surgical team in Jalalabad University Hospital in Afghanistan, recorded an increase in landmine injuries in early 1993 from 35 per cent to 60 per cent of all war-wounded. ICRC, *The Worldwide Epidemic of Landmine Injuries: The ICRC's Health Oriented Approach* (Geneva: ICRC, 1995), p. 2. See also ICRC, *Mines: A Perverse Use of Technology* (ICRC: Geneva, 1992).

longer-term effects such as rehabilitation, social and economic effects and loss of access to land.[60] The ICRC estimated that approximately 24,000 persons, mostly civilians, were being killed and wounded each year by anti-personnel mines,[61] leading the organisation to characterise the issue as a 'worldwide epidemic of landmine injuries'.[62] Given the strong evidence base demonstrating the effects of anti-personnel mines, the ICRC was once again well placed to call for development of the law regulating the use of this weapon. However, the challenge remained as to how to engage with States and translate medical field experience into new legal norms.

In 1993, the ICRC organised the Montreux Symposium, which brought together government and independent experts from various fields including military, technical, surgical, rehabilitation and legal experts, as well as demining organisations and non-governmental organisations, with a view to developing as accurate a picture as possible of the scope of the problem and the measures available to alleviate the suffering of mine victims.[63] The report of the Symposium was sent to all governments,[64] and influenced the decision of eighteen landmine-producing countries to enact national moratoria on the transfer and use of anti-personnel mines.[65]

In February 1994, in a manner reminiscent of its 1918 call on chemical weapons, the ICRC launched an appeal to States for a comprehensive ban on anti-personnel mines.[66] The ICRC followed this appeal in

60 R. Coupland and A. Korver, 'Injuries from antipersonnel mines: the experience of the International Committee of the Red Cross', *British Medical Journal*, 303 (1991), p. 1509.

61 C. Giannou. 'Antipersonnel landmines: facts, fictions and priorities', *British Medical Journal* 315 (1997), p. 1454.

62 ICRC, *The Worldwide Epidemic of Landmine Injuries.*

63 ICRC, Report of the Montreux Symposium (21–23 April 1993), reproduced in Maresca and Maslen (eds.), *The Banning of Anti-Personnel Landmines: The Legal Contribution of the International Committee of the Red Cross 1955–1999* (Cambridge: Cambridge University Press, 2000), p. 130.

64 *Ibid.*, p. 129.

65 A. Parlow, 'Towards a global ban on landmines', *International Review of the Red Cross*, 35(307) (1995), p. 391. Even before the adoption of the APMBC in 1997, some thirty States had already unilaterally renounced or suspended the future use of anti-personnel mines: Herby and Lawand, 'Unacceptable Behaviour', p. 202.

66 'ICRC: A total ban on anti-personnel mines and blinding weapons is the best option', Statement by President Cornelio Sommaruga, President of the ICRC, ICRC Press Conference, Geneva, 24 February 1994, available at: www.icrc.org/eng/resources/documents/misc/57jmpb.htm.The ICRC's appeal had followed a similar call by the International Campaign to Ban Landmines (ICBL) a year earlier. See ICBL, 'Joint Call to Ban Antipersonnel Landmines', May 1993, cited in J. Williams and S. Goose, 'The International Campaign to Ban Landmines' in M. Cameron, R. Lawson and B. Tomlin (eds.), *To Walk without Fear: The Global Movement to Ban Landmines* (Oxford: Oxford University Press, 1998).

November 1995, with an international media campaign premised on exposure of its eyewitness accounts of 'landmine carnage'.[67] Print and television advertisements appeared *pro bono* in international media with an estimated audience of 700 million people.[68] In addition, ICRC delegations around the world facilitated visits of journalists to mine-affected areas, as well as to medical and rehabilitation clinics where mine victims were being treated.[69] Finally, the international media campaign involved medical experts speaking at meetings and conferences in order to highlight the organisation's firsthand experience in treating landmine victims.[70] Importantly, the international media campaign was launched in cooperation with national Red Cross and Red Crescent societies,[71] a trend that has continued in the work of the ICRC on weapons issues.

Expanding its public communication strategy was a major step for the ICRC as it was the first time that the organisation had used a media campaign to promote the development of IHL, using powerful images depicting the effects of these weapons in order to inform societal perceptions.[72] Fundamentally, as with its call to ban poison gas in 1918, the ICRC's campaign against anti-personnel mines was grounded on 'the principles of humanity' and 'the dictates of public conscience',[73] reaffirming the ongoing importance of the 'Martens Clause' in shaping the development of the law on weapons of humanitarian concern.[74]

In addition, the ICRC sought to address the question of the military utility and effectiveness of anti-personnel mines. It commissioned a study on the matter, which was published in 1996, and concluded that 'the limited military utility of anti-personnel mines is far outweighed by the appalling humanitarian consequences of their use in actual conflicts'.[75]

[67] See 'Statement of Cornelio Sommaruga, President of the ICRC', ICRC Press Conference, Geneva, 22 November 1995, reproduced in Maresca and Maslen (eds.), *The Banning of Anti-Personnel Landmines*, pp. 404–406.

[68] Lavoyer and Maresca, 'The Role of the ICRC', p. 516. [69] *Ibid.*, 517. [70] *Ibid.*, 516.

[71] For example, the British Red Cross organised a visit to Angola by Princess Diana in January 1997.

[72] Herby and Lawand, 'Unacceptable Behaviour', pp. 202–203.

[73] ICRC, 'A total ban on anti-personnel mines'.

[74] The preamble of the APMBC stresses 'the role of public conscience in furthering the principles of humanity, as evidenced by the call for a total ban on anti-personnel mines and recognising the efforts to that end undertaken by the International Red Cross and Red Crescent Movement, the International Campaign to Ban Landmines and numerous other non-governmental organisations around the world'. See also Herby and Lawand, 'Unacceptable Behaviour', p. 212.

[75] ICRC, *Anti-Personnel Landmines: Friend or Foe? A study of the military use and effectiveness of anti-personnel mines* (Geneva: ICRC, 1996), p. 7. The Study examined the effectiveness

This finding was developed further at a meeting of military experts, and eventually endorsed by fifty-five senior military commanders from nineteen countries, which helped to influence how anti-personnel mines were perceived amongst the military.[76]

Meanwhile, in light of the growing pressure on States to address the devastating human cost of anti-personnel mines, the CCW Review Conference of 1996 agreed to strengthen the rules on the use of landmines in a new treaty, *Amended Protocol II* on the use of mines, booby traps and similar devices.[77] The ICRC played an active role before and during the CCW Review Conference by submitting a background document and commenting on the draft text of the treaty.[78] However, the result fell far short of the ban on anti-personnel mines sought by the ICRC, the International Campaign to Ban Landmines (ICBL) and many States. According to an ICRC press release at the time, *Amended Protocol II* was 'woefully inadequate'.[79]

What took place following the CCW Review Conference is by now well known: within five months, forty States led by Canada took the issue out of the consensus-based CCW, adopting the Ottawa Declaration on 5 October 1996 which committed participants to work to achieve a comprehensive ban on anti-personnel mines as soon as possible. Following two diplomatic conferences in Oslo and Brussels, the APMBC was adopted in September 1997 and entered into force in March 1999. Again, the ICRC played an active role throughout the 'Ottawa process', working closely with governments, NGOs and national Red Cross and Red Crescent societies. States negotiating the text of the treaty agreed to incorporate the

of anti-personnel landmines in 26 conflicts since World War II. Its finding was reaffirmed in 2004 at the First Review Conference of the AMPBC on the basis of information from an additional 10 conflicts. See ICRC, *Report on observations and conclusions from a review of the ICRC study on Anti-personal landmines, Friend or Foe?*, 2004. Available at: www.icrc.org/eng/assets/files/other/friendfoereportobservations30nov1dec2004.pdf.

[76] Lavoyer and Maresca, 'The Role of the ICRC', p. 516.

[77] See footnote 53. *Amended Protocol II* sets out restrictions on the use of anti-personnel and anti-vehicle mines, including requirements that anti-personnel mines are detectable and have self-destruct or self-deactivating features, that all feasible precautions are taken to protect civilians from the effects of these weapons, and that landmines are cleared, destroyed or removed after the end of active hostilities.

[78] See 'The rationale for amending and the ways and means of improving Protocol II of the Convention as well as the military and humanitarian perspectives concerning the amendment of Protocol II of the Convention', CCW/CONF.I/GE/6, April 1994, background document prepared by the ICRC at the request of the Group of Government Experts (GGE) established to prepare the First Review Conference of the CCW.

[79] ICRC, 'ICRC views Amended Landmines Protocol as "Woefully Inadequate"', Press Release 96/16, 3 May 1996.

three key elements of the ICRC's position: first, an unambiguous definition of anti-personnel mines; second, a comprehensive prohibition of the use, production, stockpiling and transfer of anti-personnel mines; and third, requirements relating to victim assistance, mine clearance and mine awareness.[80]

The adoption of the APMBC represented a milestone for IHL for a number of reasons, two of which are mentioned here. To begin with, it was the first multilateral treaty to comprehensively prohibit a weapon that was already in widespread use. Whereas the complete prohibition of chemical weapons came decades after their use was banned, the APMBC was the first treaty to combine the classical IHL aim of regulating the use of a weapon with the disarmament goal of removing and eliminating the weapon, in both cases for humanitarian reasons. The second reason that the APMBC represented a milestone for IHL is that it was the first time that a treaty regulating a weapon required that assistance be provided to the weapon's victims, a feature that was later replicated in *Protocol V* to the CCW and in the *CCM*.[81] Throughout the negotiations of the APMBC, the ICRC had advocated for the treaty to include both a comprehensive prohibition and a provision on victim assistance.

2. *Explosive Remnants of War*

In the course of documenting the effects of anti-personnel mines, the ICRC was also observing the devastating impact of other kinds of 'weapons that keep on killing' and began recording these effects as well. Although part of the problem had been addressed through the APMBC, the armed conflict in Kosovo in 1999 highlighted that there was still work to be done to protect civilians from the threat posed by other explosive remnants of war. Based on two key studies – the first documenting the extent of the problem in Kosovo[82] and the second examining the

[80] ICRC, Position Paper No. 4, December 1997, reproduced in Maresca and Maslen (eds.), *The Banning of Anti-Personnel Landmines*, p. 495.

[81] See APMBC, Article 6(3), which formulates victim assistance as an obligation of means: 'Each State Party in a position to do so shall provide assistance for the care and rehabilitation, and social and economic reintegration, of mine victims (. . .)' A virtually identical requirement is found in Article 8(2) of *Protocol V*. For its part, Article 5 of the CCM is fully dedicated to victim assistance requirements.

[82] S. Maslen, *Cluster Bombs and Landmines in Kosovo* (Geneva: ICRC, August 2000, revised in June 2001). According to NATO forces, approximately 10 per cent of NATO-dropped bomblets would not explode on impact, resulting in an estimated 289,536 unexploded bomblets in Kosovo after the end of the conflict.

technical aspects of explosive munitions[83] – and in view of the Second Review Conference of the CCW in December 2001, the ICRC convened a meeting of government and other experts to examine the problems associated with weapons threatening civilians after the end of active hostilities, including unexploded and abandoned ordnance. The meeting addressed a number of aspects, and provided an opportunity for the ICRC to present its preliminary proposal for a new CCW protocol on explosive remnants of war.[84] According to one author, this was a 'key event' that served 'to elevate the post-conflict impacts of ERW from a like-minded concern to that of a CCW priority . . . '.[85]

After receiving positive reactions from governments, the ICRC submitted a formal proposal to the First Preparatory Meeting for the CCW Review Conference, which set out the ICRC's view on the main elements of a future protocol.[86] In this proposal, the ICRC sought to take a comprehensive approach to explosive remnants of war rather than 'a weapon by weapon or "*à la carte*" approach'.[87] The proposal contained obligations addressing contamination similar to those set out in *Amended Protocol II* relating to mines, booby traps and similar devices. In addition, the proposal contained a prohibition on the use of submunitions against military objectives located in areas with a concentration of civilians, but this element did not receive sufficient support from States.[88] Still, the ICRC's call to regulate explosive remnants of war triggered discussions on the issue at the CCW's Second Review Conference, which then established a Group of Governmental Experts (GGE) to examine the issue further.[89]

[83] C. King, *Explosive Remnants of War* (Geneva: ICRC, August 2000), reproduced in ICRC, *Cluster munitions: statements and materials of the ICRC (1976–2009)* (Geneva: ICRC, 2010).

[84] ICRC, *Expert Meeting on Explosive Remnants of War: A Summary Report, 18–19 September 2000, Nyon Switzerland* (Geneva: ICRC, 2000).

[85] J. Borrie, *Unacceptable Harm: A History of How the Treaty to Ban Cluster Munitions Was Won* (Geneva and New York: UNIDIR, 2009).

[86] 'Scope of Application of the CCW and Explosive Remnants of War', CCW/CONF.II/PC.1/WP.1, 11 December 2000, report of the ICRC to the Preparatory Committee for the 2001 Review Conference of the CCW.

[87] *Ibid.*, p. 39.

[88] Some government experts supported this proposal (including from Norway, China, Mexico), as well as, Human Rights Watch and Landmine Action, however others were against, primarily on the basis that the rules in Additional Protocol I on the conduct of hostilities were adequate to address this issue. See L. Maresca, 'Regulating Explosive Remnants of War', *Yearbook of International Humanitarian Law*, 5 (2002), p. 372.

[89] The GGE was also mandated to consider proposals put forward by Switzerland on mandatory self-destruct and self-deactivation features of submunitions, and by the United States, on anti-vehicle mines.

Following three sessions of the GGE in 2003, to which the ICRC contributed both legal and technical expertise,[90] *Protocol V* on ERW was adopted by the CCW Meeting of States' Parties in November 2003.[91]

In contrast with other CCW Protocols dealing with the humanitarian consequences of certain conventional weapons, *Protocol V* does not prohibit nor limit the use of a weapon, but instead provides a framework for reducing the threat to civilians caused by ERW, defined for the purposes of the treaty as unexploded ordnance and abandoned explosive ordnance.[92] Among other obligations, the Protocol requires each party to an armed conflict to mark and clear ERW in the territory it controls 'as soon as feasible' after cessation of active hostilities.[93] In addition, the user of explosive ordnance is required to provide assistance 'where feasible' to facilitate the removal of ERW left over from its operations and situated in areas it does not control, either directly to the party in control of the territory or through a mutually agreed-upon third party.[94] Critically, each State party is required 'to the maximum extent possible and as far as practicable' to record information on the explosive ordnance used by its armed forces during active hostilities and share that information afterwards with the party in control of the affected area or through a third party, with a view to facilitating the rapid marking and removal of ERW.[95] These requirements essentially echo the elements that the ICRC had put forth in 2000 in its proposal for a new Protocol on ERW.

While the adoption of *Protocol V* was an important step to protect civilians from 'weapons that keep on killing', it had not resolved the specific patterns of harm caused by cluster munitions.

[90] 'The types of munitions which become explosive remnants of war. Factors which contribute to the occurrence of explosive remnants of war', CCW/GGE/I/WP.5, 14 May 2002, working paper prepared by the ICRC and Geneva International Centre for Humanitarian Demining for the GGE; 'Explosive Remnants of war: an examination of legal issues raised in the ERW discussions', CCW/GGE/II/WP.8, 15 July 2002, working paper prepared by the ICRC for the GGE. Both documents are reproduced in ICRC, *Cluster munitions: statements and materials.*

[91] *Protocol V* is cited in footnote 48.

[92] *Protocol V*, Art. 2(4). Unexploded ordnance is defined as explosive ordnance that have been used or fired but that fail to explode as intended (Art. 2(2)), while abandoned explosive ordnance refers to unused explosive ordnance dumped or left behind by a party to an armed conflict and which are no longer under the control of that party (Art. 2(3)). Explosive ordnance 'means conventional munitions containing explosives, with the exception of mines, booby traps and other devices as defined in Protocol II of this Convention as amended on 3 May 1996' (Art. 2(1)).

[93] *Ibid.*, Art. 3(1). [94] *Ibid.* [95] *Ibid.*, Art. 4.

3. *Cluster Munitions*

In the years that followed the adoption of *Protocol V*, a number of armed conflicts highlighted the ongoing problem with cluster munitions, in particular in Afghanistan,[96] Iraq,[97] and Lebanon.[98] Despite the reluctance of several States' parties to the CCW to specifically address cluster munitions,[99] the ICRC remained committed to the CCW as the most appropriate forum in which to pursue development of the law on these weapons. Accordingly, the day before the opening of the Third Review Conference of the CCW in November 2006, the ICRC publicly called on all States to immediately end the use of inaccurate and unreliable cluster munitions, to prohibit the targeting of cluster munitions against any military objective located in a populated area, to eliminate stocks of inaccurate and unreliable cluster munitions, and, pending their destruction, not to transfer such weapons to other countries.[100]

By the time of the CCW's Third Review Conference, there was clear momentum for development of the law on cluster munitions, supported not only by the ICRC, but also by the Cluster Munitions Coalition, the UN Secretary General, and an initial group of interested States.[101] Echoing part of the ICRC proposal that States had rejected a few years earlier in the lead up to the *Protocol V* negotiations, the UN Secretary General challenged CCW States' parties to 'devise effective norms' to address the humanitarian impact of cluster munitions and to freeze the use of cluster munitions against military objectives located in or near populated areas.[102] Despite the evidence of the pattern of harm caused by cluster

[96] Human Rights Watch, *Fatally Flawed: Cluster Bombs and their use by the United States in Afghanistan* (New York: HRW, 2002).

[97] Borrie, *Unacceptable Harm*, p. 50.

[98] T. Nash, *Foreseeable Harm: The use and impact of cluster munitions in Lebanon* (London: Landmine Action, 2006). The conflict lasted only one month but resulted in contamination of an area estimated at 37 million square metres with close to one million unexploded submunitions.

[99] During the negotiations of *Protocol V*, several States had made clear that they opposed a legally binding prohibition on the use of cluster munitions. See G. Nystuen and S. Casey-Maslen (eds.), *The Convention on Cluster Munitions: A Commentary* (Oxford: Oxford University Press, 2010), p. 13.

[100] 'The need for urgent international action on cluster munitions', Statement by Philip Spoerri, Director of International Law and Cooperation within the Movement, ICRC, ICRC Press Conference, Geneva, 6 November 2006, available at: www.icrc.org/eng/resources/documents/statement/cluster-munition-statement-061106.htm.

[101] Borrie, *Unacceptable Harm*, pp. 134 and 140–141.

[102] 'Secretary-General's message to the Third Review Conference of the Convention on Certain Conventional Weapons', Geneva, 7 November 2006. Available at: www.un.org/sg/statements/?nid=2289.

munitions and the calls for action made by the ICRC, the UN, NGOs and several States,[103] the Review Conference could only agree to continue discussions in a GGE set up for this purpose.[104] As had been the case with anti-personnel mines, the failure of the CCW States' parties to take more decisive action on cluster munitions triggered a process outside of the CCW towards an international ban on cluster munitions.[105] This process began in Oslo, Norway, in February 2007 and concluded in May 2008 with the adoption of the Cluster Munitions Convention (CCM) by 107 states.[106]

In parallel to the Oslo process, the ICRC convened an expert meeting in April 2007 to examine the humanitarian, military, technical and legal issues related to cluster munitions and to consider all possible means of reducing their negative impact on civilian populations.[107] On the basis of this meeting, the ICRC concluded that concrete evidence had not been produced to show that the military results achieved by cluster munitions outweighed the well-documented humanitarian concerns. In October 2007, in an official statement to the Geneva-based diplomatic missions, the ICRC's president called upon States to 'urgently' conclude a new treaty to address the humanitarian consequences of cluster munitions, including to prohibit the use, development, production, stockpiling and transfer of 'inaccurate and unreliable' cluster munitions.[108] While noting

[103] See in particular Sweden's declaration on behalf of twenty-five States' parties, delivered on the last day of the Third Review Conference, calling for an 'agreement' to ban the use of cluster munitions within concentrations of civilians, and for the prohibition and elimination of cluster munitions 'that pose serious humanitarian hazards': 'Final Declaration on Cluster Munitions', CCW/CONF.III/WP.18, 20 November 2006, presented to the Third Review Conference of the CCW by Austria, Belgium, Bosnia-Herzegovina, Croatia, Costa Rica, Czech Republic, Denmark, Germany, Holy See, Hungary, Ireland, Lichtenstein, Lithuania, Luxemburg, Malta, Mexico, New Zealand, Norway, Peru, Portugal, Serbia, Slovakia, Slovenia, Sweden and Switzerland.

[104] 'Final Declaration', CCW/CONF.III/11 (Part II), 17 November 2006, final document of the Third Review Conference of the CCW, Decision 1.

[105] On the penultimate day of the CCW's Third Review Conference, the government of Norway invited all interested States and civil society to attend an international conference in Oslo in February 2007. The Oslo Conference ended with a declaration signed by 46 participating States, committing them to conclude by 2008 a 'legally binding international instrument' to comprehensively ban cluster munitions 'that cause unacceptable harm to civilians'. See Borrie, *Unacceptable Harm*, p. 156.

[106] For a brief summary of the 'Oslo process', see L. Maresca, 'Introductory Note to the Convention on Cluster Munitions', *International Legal Materials*, 48(2) (2009), p. 354.

[107] ICRC, *Humanitarian, military, technical and legal challenges of cluster munitions: expert meeting*, Montreux, Switzerland, 18–20 April 2007 (Geneva: ICRC, 2008).

[108] 'The ICRC's position on cluster munitions and the need for urgent action', Statement to Geneva Diplomatic Missions by J. Kellenberger, President of the ICRC, Geneva, 25 October 2007, reproduced in ICRC, *Cluster munitions: statements and materials*. See also,

the Oslo Declaration and CCW discussions, the ICRC's statement took care not to favour either forum.

According to one author, the ICRC's appeal had been particularly important in contributing to the credibility to the Oslo process,[109] in which the ICRC actively participated. Modelled on the approach of the APMBC, the CCM provides for the comprehensive ban of cluster munitions, clearance of land contaminated with cluster munition remnants, and measures to protect civilians from the dangers of these remnants pending their clearance, as well as assistance to the victims of these weapons.

Although a new treaty comprehensively prohibiting cluster munitions had been adopted, States party to the CCW, among them states that had agreed to the treaty in Dublin, in parallel continued to 'negotiate a proposal' to address the humanitarian impact of cluster munitions, pursuant to a mandate of the November 2007 CCW annual meeting of States' parties.[110] The ICRC initially supported this process, on the basis that a new CCW protocol could potentially be of added value by establishing rules on cluster munitions for those States not ready to accede to the CCM. But at all times during the CCW discussions, the ICRC stressed that any new rules on cluster munitions in the CCW framework must address the humanitarian concerns associated with these weapons, notably by not allowing the continued production and use of cluster munitions that were known to be inaccurate and unreliable. The draft protocol submitted to the CCW's Fourth Review Conference in 2011 fell significantly short of this standard.[111] Consequently, the ICRC opposed the draft protocol, as

J. Kellenberger, 'States must act now to prevent cruel toll of cluster munitions', Reuters AlertNet, 17 February 2008, reproduced in ICRC, *Cluster munitions: statements and materials*. In November 2007, the Council of Delegates of the International Red Cross and Red Crescent Movement made a similar call, which included urging governments that had adhered to the Oslo Declaration to fulfil their commitment to conclude a treaty in 2008, and urging CCW States' parties 'to develop legally binding rules on cluster munitions as a matter of urgency'. See Council of Delegates of the International Red Cross and Red Crescent Movement, Geneva, 23–24 November 2007, Resolution 8 on 'International humanitarian law and Cluster Munitions', paras 5–6.

109 According to Alexander Breitegger, '[w]ith the guardian of IHL being that outspoken, it was difficult for opponents to (continue to) argue that the Oslo process was merely a "feel good" exercise mainly for those not stockpiling, producing or using cluster munitions'. See A. Breitegger, *Cluster Munitions and International Law: Disarmament with a human face?* (Oxon: Routledge, 2012), p. 216.

110 See 'Report', CCW/MSP/2007/5,3 December 2007, final document of the Meeting of States Parties to the CCW, para. 37.

111 Among other weaknesses, the draft protocol would have permitted the continued use of all cluster munitions produced after 1980 for up to 12 years after its entry into force, as

it could not support the adoption of a treaty that provided less protection for civilians than a treaty already in force.[112] In the end, the Review Conference could not agree on the text of the draft protocol, as fifty States expressly opposed it.[113] Undoubtedly, these States' positions were influenced in part by the ICRC's views and those of other humanitarian organisations.

4. *Remaining Challenges*

Almost sixty years since the ICRC first raised concerns about 'delayed action' weapons, there is a strong treaty framework governing anti-personnel mines, cluster munitions and explosive remnants of war.[114] Today, at the diplomatic level, the ICRC's work on these weapons focuses on promoting universal adherence to these treaties and their faithful implementation, in addition to its field work supporting implementation of risk-reduction activities, clearance of contaminated areas and victim assistance, a role recognized by States' parties to these treaties.[115]

Despite the achievements of the last two decades, development of the law regulating 'weapons that keep on killing' is incomplete, particularly regarding anti-vehicle mines. Since the early 2000s, in response to the

well as indefinite use of cluster munitions fitted with a single safety feature, even though munitions with such features have been known to fail in significant numbers. During the negotiations of the draft protocol in the GGE, the ICRC made a number of proposals including a prohibition on the use of all cluster munitions in populated areas, but this was not accepted.

112 'ICRC comments on the draft protocol on cluster munitions and other issues for the CCW Review Conference', Statement of the ICRC delivered by J. Kellenberger, President of the ICRC, Fourth Review Conference of the CCW, Geneva, 15 November 2011, available at: www.icrc.org/eng/resources/documents/statement/ccw-statement-2011-11-15.htm.

113 The proposal was expressly rejected in a group statement read by Costa Rica on 14 November 2011, to which the following States associated themselves: Afghanistan, Angola, Austria, Bolivia, Burkina Faso, Chile, Colombia, Congo, Democratic Republic of Congo, Denmark, Djibouti, Ecuador, El Salvador, Ghana, Guatemala, Guinea, Guinea-Bissau, Haiti, Holy See, Honduras, Iceland, Laos, Lebanon, Lesotho, Liberia, Liechtenstein, Madagascar, Mali, Mexico, Mozambique, Namibia, Nicaragua, Niger, Nigeria, Norway, Panama, Paraguay, Senegal, Slovenia, South Africa, Spain, Sudan, Togo, Tunisia, Uganda, Uruguay, Venezuela, Zambia and Zimbabwe.

114 At time of writing, there were 162 States party to the APMBC, 87 States party to *Protocol V*, and 91 States party to the CCM.

115 See footnote 10.

humanitarian consequences of anti-vehicle mines in conflict and post-conflict situations, including staff casualties caused by these weapons, the ICRC has been calling for new rules to limit their indiscriminate effects.[116] Some limitations on the use of anti-vehicle mines exist in *Amended Protocol II* to the CCW, but they are weak: the treaty does not require that anti-vehicle mines be made detectable, nor that they be fitted with self-destruct and self-deactivation features as it does for anti-personnel mines.[117] Attempts by some States' party to the CCW to achieve normative development on the use of anti-vehicle mines have failed[118] – despite abundant evidence of the indiscriminate effects of anti-vehicle mines[119] – although a group of States have reached agreement on unilateral 'best practice' standards.[120] One reason for this lack of progress may be a perception that the humanitarian consequences of anti-vehicle mines are of lesser significance when compared to the scale of the effects of anti-personnel mines. Today, persuading all States in the CCW that strengthening IHL rules on anti-vehicle mines is a humanitarian imperative remains a challenge. In this respect, the ICRC and other humanitarian organisations continue to build the case of the indiscriminate effects of these weapons, based on evidence of their actual impact in the field.

116 See e.g. 'ICRC Statement to the Third Review Conference of the Convention on Certain Conventional Weapons', Statement of the ICRC delivered by P. Spoerri, Director of International Law and Cooperation within the Movement, ICRC, Third Review Conference of the CCW, Geneva, 7 November 2006, available at: www.icrc.org/eng/resources/documents/statement/conventional-weapons-statement-071106.htm.

117 See Articles 4 to 6 and Technical Annex of *Amended Protocol II*.

118 For a summary review of efforts of States' parties to the CCW, over the last decade and a half, to develop the law on anti-vehicle mines, including through a new protocol on 'mines other than anti-personnel mines', see United Nations Office at Geneva, *Mines other than antipersonnel mines (MOTAPM)*, available at: www.unog.ch/80256EE600585943/(httpPages)/7FAEF7CE8B841EFAC12579C1002CAF88?OpenDocument. A more detailed account can be found in the United Nations Disarmament Yearbooks from 2000 to 2014, available at: www.un.org/disarmament/publications/yearbook/.

119 See e.g. 'Rules of international humanitarian law applicable to anti-vehicle mines', CCW/MSP/2012/WP.1, 29 May 2012, working paper submitted by the ICRC to the Meeting of States Parties to the CCW; 'Report of the 2012 Meeting of Experts on Mines other than anti-personnel mines (MOTAPM)', CCW/MSP/2012/4, 29 May 2012, para. 12; Geneva International Centre for Humanitarian Demining (GICHD) and Stockholm International Peace Research Institute (SIPRI), *The Humanitarian and Developmental Impact of Anti-Vehicle Mines* (Geneva: GICHD and SIPRI, 2014).

120 'Declaration on Anti-Vehicle Mines', CCW/CONF.III/WP.16, 16 November 2006, document presented to the Third Review Conference of the CCW by: Australia, Canada, Croatia, Denmark, Estonia, Lithuania, The Netherlands, New Zealand, Norway, Slovenia and the United States.

IV. Blinding Laser Weapons

The prohibition of blinding laser weapons in 1995 was a significant legal development as it was the first time since the 1868 Saint Petersburg Declaration[121] that States had acted preventatively – rather than reactively – to ban a weapon of concern. For the ICRC, contrary to its work on chemical weapons and 'weapons that keep on killing', its work on blinding laser weapons involved for the first time a new technology of warfare that had not yet been used on the battlefield. Preventative regulation posed a number of challenges to the organisation's traditional approach to weapons of concern. First, it was simply not possible to draw on first-hand evidence from field delegations of the actual consequences of the weapon's use. Second, the ICRC faced a greater level of indifference on the part of States, with many governments remaining aloof to regulation of a weapon that was not yet in use. Despite these challenges, the organisation was still able to play an important role in drawing attention to the foreseeable harmful effects of this new technology, and harnessing sufficient political will for a preventative ban on blinding laser weapons, achieved in *Protocol IV* to the CCW (1995).[122]

The ICRC first became active on blinding laser weapons by raising its concerns at the 25th International Conference of the Red Cross and Red Crescent in 1986, where it expressed support for a draft resolution submitted by Sweden and Switzerland, which would have pronounced the anti-personnel use of laser weapons illegal on the basis that they would cause unnecessary suffering or superfluous injury.[123] In particular, the resolution noted the risk posed by the development of laser technology for military use, including anti-personnel use on the battlefield which could cause permanent blindness. However, the resolution was not adopted due to opposition from several States interested in the development of such

[121] Declaration Renouncing the Use, in Time of War, of Certain Explosive Projectiles (Saint Petersburg Declaration), Saint Petersburg, 11 December 1868, in force 11 December 1868, 18 Martens Nouveau Recueil (ser. 1) 474; 138 Consol. T.S. 297. The Declaration prohibits the use of explosive projectiles of a weight below 400 grammes. Developed by the Russian military in 1867 but never deployed in battle, these projectiles were designed to explode on contact with an individual. These abhorrent effects prompted the Russian government to propose that these projectiles be banned by international agreement. The Saint Petersburg Declaration is considered the first treaty prohibiting the use of a weapon in armed conflict, and the first treaty to codify the prohibition to use arms, projectiles and material of a nature to cause superfluous injury or unnecessary suffering.

[122] *Protocol on Blinding Laser Weapons (Protocol IV)*, in force 30 July 1998, 1380 UNTS 370.

[123] 'Draft Resolution: Further work relating to the law of sea warfare and land warfare', CI 2.6 PR3, 27 October 1986, Section B, para. 4. The resolution also invited the ICRC to follow these matters and keep the International Conference of the Red Cross informed.

weapons, and a lack of awareness by other States, who regarded blinding laser weapons as science fiction.[124] Similar reactions were triggered by an ICRC report and draft resolution[125] prepared for the 26th International Conference.[126]

Similar to its approach with other weapons, the ICRC approached this issue with a series of four expert meetings between 1989 and 1991. Essentially, the meetings sought to address the knowledge gap regarding blinding laser weapons and to engage States on the issue. They also allowed the ICRC to consolidate the evidence base supporting its call for action on these weapons. The meetings brought together technical, military and IHL experts, as well as medical specialists, to examine the various issues arising from development of blinding laser weapons.[127] In particular, medical specialists analysed the longer-term functional and psychological effects of battle-induced blindness compared to other battle injuries, thereby allowing for a more informed response to the claim that 'blinding was better than death'.[128] The last of the four ICRC expert meetings examined whether blinding lasers might already be prohibited as weapons of a nature to cause superfluous injury or unnecessary suffering, and whether treaty regulation of such weapons was desirable for policy reasons.[129] Although there was no agreement on the former question, the majority of experts thought that specific legal regulation was advisable and proposed an additional Protocol to the CCW as the most appropriate way forward.[130]

When a CCW Review Conference was initially proposed in 1993, the primary goal was an amended Protocol on landmines. As noted earlier, the ICRC was heavily engaged in these efforts, yet in the view of the

[124] At the time, the possible use of lasers in outer space was generally known, but not the developments for battlefield anti-personnel use. See L. Doswald-Beck, 'New Protocol on Blinding Laser Weapons', *International Review of the Red Cross*, 36(312) (1996), pp. 273–274.

[125] See ICRC, *Reaffirmation of Development of International Humanitarian Law: Prohibition or Restriction on the Use of Certain Weapons and Methods of Armed Conflicts: Developments in Relation to Certain Conventional Weapons and New Weapons Technologies*, Doc. C.1/6.3.2/1, Geneva, 1991, pp. 6–18. The draft resolution condemned blinding as a method of warfare, considered that the use of weapons with the sole purpose of blinding was unacceptable, and urged States not to produce such weapons: see Doc. C.1/6.3.2/Res.1, November 1991.

[126] The ICRC's proposed resolution was never discussed as the 26th International Conference, which was meant to take place in 1991, but which was suspended to 1995.

[127] See L. Doswald-Beck (ed.), *Blinding Weapons: Reports of the Meetings of Experts Convened by the International Committee of the Red Cross on Battlefield Laser Weapons 1989–1991*, (Geneva: ICRC, 1993).

[128] Doswald-Beck, 'New Protocol on Blinding Laser Weapons', p. 275.

[129] Doswald-Beck (ed.), *Blinding Weapons*, p. 321.

[130] *Ibid.*, pp. 358–360.

organisation, the Review Conference was also a prime opportunity to push for a ban on blinding laser weapons. For the most part, States were unwilling to divert attention away from landmines and many remained indifferent to the issue of blinding laser weapons, because of a perceived lack of urgency to regulate a weapon that was not yet being used. Despite this reluctance, both the ICRC and Sweden submitted draft proposals for a Protocol on Blinding Laser Weapons to the third preparatory meeting of the Review Conference. The ICRC's proposal in particular sought to prohibit 'blinding as a method of warfare', rather than taking the more familiar approach of seeking regulation of a specific weapon or means of warfare.[131] However, States were uncomfortable with this proposal, and insisted that any future Protocol would have to prohibit a specific weapon. Consequently, the Chairman of the last preparatory meeting submitted a new draft proposal which, along with other State proposals, formed the basis for negotiations at the Review Conference.

In light of the ongoing indifference or opposition of some States, the ICRC commenced major efforts in the lead-up to the Review Conference to gain support for a ban from governments and national Red Cross and Red Crescent societies.[132] In addition to publishing the reports of its four expert meetings and sending them to all States, the organisation intensified its discussions with government officials in capitals, and reached out to NGOs and medical associations already active on the human cost of weapons.[133] To get its message across to a broad range of stakeholders and the public, the ICRC launched a public campaign on blinding laser weapons, which presented information from the ICRC expert meetings in a more digestible, public-friendly form,[134] appealing to 'all citizens, militaries, parliamentarians and organisations interested in the protection of humanity', and more generally to the 'conscience of humanity'.[135]

131 The ICRC proposal was as follows: '1. Blinding as a method of warfare is prohibited; 2. Laser weapons may not be used against the eyesight of persons.' See CCW/CONF.1/GE/CRP.28, 12 August 1994, document submitted by the ICRC to the GGE established to prepare the First Review Conference of the CCW.

132 A large number of National Societies gave active support by contacting political figures and generating public debate. See Doswald-Beck, 'New Protocol on Blinding Laser Weapons', p. 281.

133 *Ibid.*, 277.

134 See ICRC, *Blinding Weapons: Gas 1918. . . . Lasers 1990s* (Geneva: ICRC, September 1994); and ICRC, 'Blinding laser weapons: questions and answers', 16 November 1994, available at: www.icrc.org/eng/resources/documents/misc/57jmcz.htm. These resources were distributed to States, NGOs and intergovernmental organisations.

135 The ICRC called on States to 'ensure that a flood of blinded soldiers or civilians will not be needed before intentional blinding is also outlawed'. See ICRC, *Blinding Weapons: Gas 1918. . . . Lasers 1990s*. See also 'ICRC: A total ban on anti-personnel mines'.

NGOs and intergovernmental organisations echoed the ICRC's call for a ban on blinding laser weapons.[136] In particular, Human Rights Watch was instrumental in prompting a high-level study by the United States Department of Defence on the acceptability of blinding laser weapons.[137] As a result, just three weeks out from the CCW Review Conference, the US government announced a new national policy prohibiting lasers specifically designed to cause permanent blindness.[138] There is no doubt that this policy influenced States at the CCW Review Conference to agree to a legal prohibition on such weapons.

The ICRC actively participated in the negotiations of the Protocol during the Review Conference, putting forward its views notably on the need for an unambiguous definition of the weapon to be banned by the new treaty and on the scope of the prohibition.[139] On 13 October 1995, the CCW Review Conference agreed to the adoption of *Protocol IV*, which prohibits the use and transfer of 'laser weapons specifically designed, as their sole combat function or as one of their combat functions, to cause permanent blindness to unenhanced vision'. It also requires precautions in the use of laser systems to avoid incidental permanent blindness to unenhanced vision. Though *Protocol IV* does not expressly prohibit blinding as a method of warfare as the ICRC had originally called for, in effect it stigmatizes deliberate blinding.[140] Accordingly, the ICRC welcomed the new Protocol as 'a victory of civilization over barbarity'.[141] Today, the

[136] The European Parliament, the Organisation of African Unity and the Inter-Parliamentary Union adopted resolutions referring to a protocol to ban laser weapons. See European Parliament, Resolution A4–0119/95, 29 June 1995, para. 6(a)(iii); Council of Ministers of the Organisation for African Unity, Resolution on the 1980 United Nations Convention on Certain Conventional Weapons and problems posed by the proliferation of anti-personnel mines in Africa, 23 June 1995, para. 7; 93rd Inter-Parliamentary Conference, Resolution on the international community in the face of the challenges posed by calamities arising from armed conflicts and by natural man-made disasters, 1 April 1995, para. 16.

[137] See Human Rights Watch Arms Project, *U.S. Blinding Laser Weapons* (New York/Washington, DC: HRW, May 1995); Human Rights Watch Arms Project, *Blinding Laser Weapons: The Need to Ban a Cruel and Inhumane Weapon*, (New York/Washington, DC: HRW, September 1995).

[138] US Department of Defence, 'DoD Announces Policy on Blinding Lasers', News Release No. 482–95, 1 September 1995, available at: www.defense.gov/Releases/Release.aspx?ReleaseID=608.

[139] For a detailed summary of the negotiating process see Doswald-Beck, 'New Protocol on Blinding Laser Weapons', pp. 285–296.

[140] *Ibid.*, 297.

[141] 'Statement of Yves Sandoz, Director of International Law and Policy, ICRC', Final Plenary of the Review Conference of the CCW, Vienna, 13 October 1995, cited in Doswald-Beck, 'New Protocol on Blinding Laser Weapons', p. 297.

Protocol's success is evident in the fact that its prohibition has been universally respected, though many States are yet to adhere to it.[142]

V. The Arms Trade Treaty

A review of the ICRC's role in the development of IHL applicable to weapons would not be complete without mention of the *Arms Trade Treaty* (ATT), which was adopted by the UN General Assembly in March 2013 and entered into force on 24 December 2014.[143] In the pantheon of humanitarian treaties applying to weapons, the ATT is unique in that it does not govern the use of weapons; instead it regulates their trade, in particular the international trade in conventional arms, their parts and components and ammunition, with the key objective of 'reducing human suffering'.[144] At the heart of the treaty are its transfer criteria, which include the prohibition to transfer the weapons and items covered by the treaty if the transferring State has knowledge that they would be used to commit genocide, crimes against humanity or a number of specified war crimes,[145] or if a risk assessment determines that there is an 'overriding' risk that the weapons could be used to commit or facilitate serious violations of IHL, serious violations of international human rights law, or other international crimes.[146]

As discussed earlier, IHL treaties applying to weapons are typically based on one of two IHL rules: protecting civilians from weapons that have indiscriminate effects and protecting combatants from unnecessary suffering. The IHL basis of the ATT is altogether different. In effect, it regulates the trade in weapons that are *per se* lawful with the purpose of preventing their unlawful use by an end user. Thus, the rule underlying the ATT's IHL-based transfer criteria is the obligation of the transferring State to respect and ensure respect for IHL, as codified in Common Article 1 of the *Geneva Conventions of 1949*. This is recognised in the preamble to the ATT, which identifies this obligation as one of the treaty's guiding principles.[147]

[142] As of April 2015, there are 104 States' parties to *Protocol IV*.

[143] *Arms Trade Treaty (ATT)*, New York, 2 April 2013, in force 24 December 2014. The ATT was adopted by UN Doc. GA Res 67/234B, 2 April 2013.

[144] Pursuant to Article 1 of the ATT, the 'object' of the treaty is to 'establish the highest possible common international standards for regulating or improving the regulation of the international trade in conventional arms' for the 'purpose' of *inter alia* 'reducing human suffering'.

[145] ATT, Art 6(3).

[146] *Ibid.*, Art 7.

[147] *Ibid.*, 5th preambular paragraph of the 'Principles'.

The ICRC's active involvement in the diplomatic process leading to the adoption of the ATT has its roots in the early 1990s, when the organisation was observing the human cost of the widespread and uncontrolled availability of small arms that had been steadily increasing since the end of the Cold War. Based on what it was observing in the field, the ICRC sensed a correlation between the proliferation of cheap and readily available 'light weapons' and the extent of IHL violations during armed conflicts, as well as the high levels of insecurity and armed violence that continued even after conflicts had ended. This link was recognised in 1995 by the 26th International Conference of the Red Cross and Red Crescent, which endorsed a series of recommendations aimed at enhancing respect for IHL, including a call on the ICRC 'to examine, on the basis of firsthand information available to it, the extent to which the availability of weapons is contributing to the proliferation and aggravation of violations of IHL in armed conflicts and the deterioration of the situation of civilians'.[148]

In fulfilment of this mandate,[149] the ICRC published a study in 1999 entitled *Arms Availability and the Situation of Civilians in Armed Conflict*,[150] which presented empirical data establishing a link between uncontrolled arms availability, violations of IHL and the deterioration of the situation of civilians in armed conflicts. Based on its 'field experience and its mandate as guardian of IHL', the ICRC concluded in the study,

[148] 26th International Conference of the Red Cross and Red Crescent, Geneva, 3–7 December 1995, Resolution 1 on 'International humanitarian law: From law to action: Report on the follow-up to the International Conference for the Protection of War Victims'; Meeting of the Intergovernmental Group of Experts for the Protection of War Victims, Geneva, 23–27 January 1995, 'Annex II: Recommendations', Recommendation VIII(c), both reproduced in *International Review of the Red Cross*, 36(310) (1996), pp. 58–60 and 88. The Intergovernmental Group of Experts was convened by the Swiss government at the request of the International Conference for the Protection of War Victims. See International Conference of the Protection of War Victims, Geneva, 30 August – 1 September 1993, 'Final Declaration of the Conference', reproduced in *International Review of the Red Cross*, 33(296) (1993), p. 381.

[149] In parallel to and supporting the ICRC's efforts, National Red Cross and Red Crescent Societies were involved early on. In 1998, the ICRC organised jointly with the Norwegian Red Cross a Meeting of Experts in Oslo, gathering a group of government, military and non-governmental experts, which proposed a number of measures including the devising of 'effective strategies to develop norms for the transfer of arms and ammunition and to put an end to illicit transfers'. See J. Egeland, 'Arms availability and violations of international humanitarian law', *International Review of the Red Cross*, 81(835) (1999), pp. 673–677; P. Herby, 'Arms availability and the situation of civilians in armed conflict: Summary of an ICRC Study for the 27th International Conference of the Red Cross and Red Crescent', *International Review of the Red Cross*, 81(835) (1999), pp. 669–672.

[150] ICRC, *Arms Availability and the Situation of Civilians in Armed Conflict*, (Geneva: ICRC, 1999).

that States should *inter alia* review their arms transfer policies in light of their obligation to respect and ensure respect for IHL and 'urgently consider the establishment of rules, based on humanitarian law, human rights and other criteria, governing the transfer of arms and ammunition'.[151] The same year, whilst seized of the ICRC's study, the 27th International Conference of the Red Cross and Red Crescent called on States to 'enhance the protection of civilians in armed conflict and post-conflict situations' notably through strengthened controls on arms exports, including at the international level. Crucially, the Conference also called on States to look at ways 'to integrate consideration of respect for [IHL] into national decision-making on transfers of arms and ammunition'.[152] This call was echoed by the following three International Conferences of the Red Cross and Red Crescent, which urged States to make respect for IHL a key consideration in controls on arms availability and arms transfer decisions, on the basis of States' obligation to ensure respect for IHL.[153]

Against the backdrop of States' commitments at the International Conferences of the Red Cross and Red Crescent, the ICRC began actively participating in inter-governmental meetings at the United Nations aimed at addressing the poorly regulated arms trade.[154] At the 2001 UN

[151] *Ibid.*, pp. 28–29.

[152] 27th International Conference of the Red Cross and Red Crescent, Geneva, 31 October – 6 November 1999, Resolution 1 on 'Adoption of the Declaration and Plan of Action' and Annex II, 'Plan of Action for the years 2000–2003', Final goal 1.5, para. 23, reproduced in *International Review of the Red Cross*, 81(836) (1999), p. 850 and 853. Meeting just prior to the International Conference, the Council of Delegates of the International Red Cross and Red Crescent Movement called on States 'to elaborate rules based on respect for [IHL] ... governing the transfer and availability of arms and ammunition' and 'as a first step, to halt arms transfers to parties committing or tolerating serious violations of human rights or of [IHL]': Council of Delegates, Geneva, 29–30 October 1999, Resolution 12 on 'Arms Availability and the Situation of Civilians in Armed Conflict and in Post-conflict Situations', para. 3, available at: www.icrc.org/eng/resources/documents/resolution/council-delegates-resolution-12–1999.htm.

[153] 28th International Conference of the Red Cross and Red Crescent, Geneva, 2–6 December 2003, Resolution 1 on 'Adoption of the Declaration and Agenda for Humanitarian Action', Final Goal 2.3; 30th International Conference of the Red Cross and Red Crescent, Geneva, 26–30 November 2007, Resolution 3 on 'Reaffirmation and Implementation of International Humanitarian Law: Preserving Human Life and Dignity in Armed Conflict' para. 20; 31st International Conference of the Red Cross and Red Crescent, Geneva, 28 November – 1 December 2011, Resolution 2 on '4-Year Action Plan for the Implementation of International Humanitarian Law', Annex 1, Objective 5.

[154] While the ICRC was speaking in these meetings on its own behalf, it also engaged in joint initiatives with other components of the International Red Cross and Red Crescent Movement. For example, in July 2001, at the UN Conference on the Illicit Trade in Small Arms and Light Weapons in All its Aspects, the ICRC, together with the International Federation

Conference on the Illicit Trade in Small Arms and Light Weapons, States agreed to wording proposed by the ICRC recognising that 'the illicit trade in small arms and light weapons in all its aspects (. . .) undermines respect for [IHL and] impedes the provision of humanitarian assistance to victims of armed conflict'. However, the non-binding Programme of Action adopted by the Conference, in which this language appeared, contained no clear acknowledgement of the close links between the 'licit' and 'illicit' trade, and the importance of taking IHL into account in 'licit' arms transfer decisions. For the ICRC, the outcome of the Conference was therefore disappointing insofar as it did not regulate arms transfers.[155]

Also in 2001, a group of Nobel Peace Laureates circulated a Draft Framework Convention on International Arms Transfers.[156] Two years later, a group of NGOs launched the Control Arms campaign, for the purpose of promoting the adoption of such a treaty, which aimed to establish common minimum standards for arms transfer decision-making for all States based on their existing commitments under international law.[157] As of mid-2005, the ICRC began publicly expressing its support for the goal of an arms trade treaty, along with a growing number of States.

By December 2006, the issue finally gained traction in the UN General Assembly, which requested that Member States submit their views on an

of Red Cross and Red Crescent Societies and the Norwegian Red Cross, organised a briefing for conference delegates on the human cost of widespread arms availability, including firsthand accounts by representatives of the Yugoslavian and Malian Red Cross Societies: see L. Eskeland and P. Herby, 'UN Conference on the Illicit Trade in Small Arms and Light Weapons in All its Aspects', *International Review of the Red Cross*, 83(843) (2001), p. 864.

155 *Ibid.*, 866. In its statements to the Conference's Preparatory Committee sessions and during the Conference's general debate, the ICRC had called on States 'in view of their responsibility under Article 1 common to the Geneva Conventions "to respect and ensure respect" for [IHL], to take urgent action to strengthen controls on the transfer of small arms and light weapons'. Likewise, at the 2006 Review Conference, the ICRC suggested that in elaborating 'adequate' elements for national arms transfer procedures, as called for in the Programme of Action, the Review Conference 'include requirements intended to evaluate respect by the recipient for existing international agreements and norms relevant to the use of arms, including the rules of [IHL]': 'Statement by the ICRC', 29 June 2006, United Nations Conference to Review Progress Made in the Implementation of the Programme of Action to Prevent, Combat and Eradicate the Illicit Trade in Small Arms and Light Weapons in All its Aspects, New York, 26 June – 7 July 2006, available at: www.un.org/events/smallarms2006/organizations.html. The Review Conference did not take up the ICRC's proposal.

156 See SIPRI, 'Arms Trade Treaty', available at: www.sipri.org/research/armaments/transfers/controlling/att.

157 See A. Boivin, 'Complicity and beyond: International law and the transfer of small arms and light weapons', *International Review of the Red Cross*, 87(859) (2005), p. 492.

'arms trade treaty'.[158] This launched a process[159] which culminated in two UN Conferences in New York on the ATT: the first in July 2012 'to elaborate a legally binding instrument on the highest possible common international standards for the transfer of conventional arms';[160] and the second in March 2013 'to finalize the elaboration of the Arms Trade Treaty'.[161]

The ICRC actively participated in the various diplomatic meetings leading to the adoption of the ATT, with the objective of ensuring that the treaty reflected States' obligations to ensure respect for IHL. In particular, the ICRC advocated that respect for IHL must be one of the fundamental criteria on which arms transfer decisions are made, so that transferred weapons do not end up in the hands of those who may be expected to use them to commit serious violations of IHL. This objective was in keeping with the commitments made by States at the International Conferences of the Red Cross and Red Crescent.[162] The ICRC also called for the scope of weapons and activities covered by the treaty to be comprehensive, and in particular, that the treaty also cover ammunition and all forms of arms transfers. These objectives were generally achieved in the text of the treaty.[163]

158 'Towards an arms trade treaty: establishing common international standards for the import, export and transfer of conventional arms', UN. Doc GA Res 61/89, 6 December 2006.

159 UN GA Resolution 61/89 called for the establishment of a GGE to examine 'the feasibility, scope and draft parameters for a comprehensive, legally binding instrument establishing common international standards for the import, export and transfer of conventional arms'. *Ibid.*, para. 2. The GGE met three times in 2008. At the end of that year, the UN General Assembly (by resolution GA Res 63/240, 24 December 2008) endorsed the GGE's report and established an Open-ended Working Group, which held two meetings in 2009. For a summary of the negotiating history of the ATT, see P. Woolcott, 'The Arms Trade Treaty', *United Nations Audio Visual Library of International Law* (2014) available at: legal.un.org/avl/pdf/ha/att/att_e.pdf.

160 UN Doc. GA Res 64/48, *The arms trade treaty*, 2 December 2009, para. 4. A Preparatory Committee for the UN Conference held four sessions in 2010, 2011 and early 2012. The UN Conference on the ATT itself was held in New York on 7–27 July 2012.

161 UN Doc. GA Res 67/234A, *The arms trade treaty*, 24 December 2012, para. 2. The Final UN Conference on the ATT was held in New York on 18–28 March 2013.

162 In order to provide practical guidance for States on how to assess respect for IHL in arms transfer decision-making, in June 2007 the ICRC published the *Arms Transfer Decisions: Applying international humanitarian law criteria – A Practical Guide*, which provides a guideline for assessing the risk of arms transfers being used to violate international humanitarian law, outlining a set of indicators that can be used as a basis for such exercises. This publication served as an important reference tool for the ICRC's positioning in the ATT negotiations.

163 See in particular Article 2 on 'Scope', Article 3 on 'Ammunition/Munitions', Article 4 on 'Parts and Components', Article 6 on 'Prohibitions', and Article 7 on 'Export and Export Assessment'.

Throughout the ATT negotiation process, the ICRC offered its IHL expertise and views, in order to ensure that existing IHL was correctly reflected in the treaty and that the treaty's transfer criteria were effective. In particular, the ICRC made two substantive contributions which impacted on government delegations' thinking and positions. First, at the July 2012 UN Conference on the ATT, the ICRC circulated an explanatory note on the meaning of 'serious violations of IHL', which aimed to address a lack of clarity regarding the relationship between 'serious violations' and 'war crimes'.[164] Second, in the lead-up to the March 2013 Final UN Conference on the ATT, the ICRC circulated its analysis of key provisions of the draft text of the treaty, which included concerns about the standard of knowledge and scope of war crimes in the draft criteria to prohibit arms transfers.[165] Most of these concerns were addressed during the March 2013 Diplomatic Conference. Indeed, government delegations working on the draft text of the ATT's transfer criteria – what are now Articles 6 and 7 of the treaty – actively consulted the ICRC for its views and associated the ICRC to their deliberations.

The ICRC has welcomed the adoption of the ATT and its entry into force.[166] In cooperation with national Red Cross and Red Crescent societies, it continues to promote the treaty's faithful implementation in a 'consistent, objective and non-discriminatory manner' in keeping with its humanitarian purpose.[167]

[164] ICRC, 'What are 'serious violations of international humanitarian law'? Explanatory Note', available at: www.icrc.org/eng/resources/documents/statement/2012/att-arms-availability-statement-2012–07–12.htm. This paper notably stresses that the terms 'serious violations of IHL' and 'war crimes' are synonymous and it lists in annexes specific 'war crimes' and 'serious violations of IHL', indicating their legal sources. The ICRC introduced the explanatory note in: 'ICRC Statement on transfer criteria', UN Conference on the Arms Trade Treaty, New York, 12 July 2012, available at: www.icrc.org/eng/resources/documents/statement/2012/att-arms-availability-statement-2012–07–12.htm.

[165] ICRC, 'ICRC Analysis of Articles 2, 3, 4, and 5 of the July 2012 Draft Arms Trade Treaty', 12 March 2013, available at: www.icrc.org/eng/assets/files/2013/icrc-analysis-draft-att.pdf. The ICRC's analysis was informed in part by a closed-door expert meeting organised by the ICRC in Geneva on 6–7 February 2013, attended by representatives of 18 governments, to discuss the legal and policy aspects of the draft ATT text. The ICRC also commented on subsequent drafts of the treaty circulated during the Final UN Conference on the ATT: see e.g. 'Statement of the ICRC', Final Diplomatic Conference on the Arms Trade Treaty, New York, 21 March 2013', available at: www.icrc.org/eng/resources/documents/statement/2013/03–21att-arms-availability-statement.htm.

[166] See e.g. 'The Arms Trade Treaty: Towards entry into force', Statement of the ICRC delivered by P. Maurer, President of the ICRC, ATT High-Level Event, New York, 25 September 2013, available at: www.icrc.org/eng/resources/documents/statement/2013/09–25-att-arms-trade-treaty-maurer.htm.

[167] As required by Article 5(2) of the ATT.

VII. Concluding Observations and Possible Future Developments

This chapter has examined the most notable cases of the ICRC's humanitarian advocacy in favour of the development of IHL to address the unacceptable effects of certain weapons, in particular chemical and biological weapons, blinding laser weapons and 'weapons that keep on killing', and to prevent the suffering caused by the widespread availability of conventional arms. This chapter has also referred to some current challenges in the organisation's efforts to strengthen the law applicable to certain weapons, such as anti-vehicle mines.[168]

The main elements of the ICRC's humanitarian approach to weapons of concern, described in the introduction and examined in the studied cases, draw from the organisation's lengthy experience protecting and assisting the victims of armed conflicts, its multi-disciplinary expertise and its stature as 'guardian of IHL'. With this in mind, a number of concluding observations can be made about the ICRC's role in the development of limits or prohibitions on the use of certain weapons for humanitarian reasons.

First, it must be emphasised that the ICRC has never taken lightly its decisions to call for the development of the law in respect of a specific weapon. The organisation's preference is to rely on States' faithful implementation of the 'cardinal' rules of IHL as they apply to all weapons,[169] to limit or prevent the deployment of new weapons which would have unacceptable effects in some or all circumstances, and to limit or cease the use of existing weapons which have such effects. The requirements of States to carry out legal reviews of any new weapons they develop or acquire,[170] and more generally to 'respect and ensure respect' for IHL[171] in the conduct of hostilities, are meant to safeguard against such development and use of weapons. In the cases where the ICRC took the step of calling for

[168] See above, text accompanying footnotes 116 to 120. Regarding challenges in respect of new developments that may threaten the prohibitions of biological and chemical weapons, see text accompanying footnotes 39 to 44 above.

[169] See text accompanying footnotes 8 to 11 above.

[170] As codified in Article 36 of *Additional Protocol I*, which reads: 'In the study, development, acquisition or adoption of a new weapon, means or method of warfare, a High Contracting Party is under an obligation to determine whether its employment would, in some or all circumstances, be prohibited by this Protocol or by any other rule of international law applicable to the High Contracting Party.'

[171] As codified in Common Article 1 of the *Geneva Conventions of 1949*, and Article 1(1) of *Additional Protocol I*, and considered customary law in both international and non-international armed conflicts.

weapon-specific rules, it did so in response to the weapon's severe human costs and to the inconsistent application of IHL's general rules to the weapon.[172]

Second, it is important to stress that the ICRC's historic role in the development of IHL treaties limiting or prohibiting to weapons has essentially been one of catalyst,[173] and nothing more. Although in respect of the weapons presented in this chapter, the ICRC urged States to develop new rules and actively participated in the processes leading to such development, it is States themselves that took the decisions to strengthen the law and led the negotiation processes. Indeed, States make law, not the ICRC. Weapons have been prohibited or their use limited because of the will of a critical mass of States to agree on new rules. The humanitarian advocacy of the ICRC, of national Red Cross and Red Crescent societies, and of civil society organisations undoubtedly influenced governments, but so did factors outside the control of these actors linked to the multilateral politics prevailing at the time.[174] For example, the decade that followed the end of the Cold War saw a multilateral environment conducive to achieving the agreements to ban blinding lasers and anti-personnel mines, among other weapon-specific treaties. In today's 'less hospitable world order',[175] the ICRC and other actors face greater challenges in convincing a significant number of States to develop the law to address the unacceptable consequences of weapons, though the 2013 Arms Trade Treaty has shown that it remains possible where humanitarian and political interests are aligned.

Third, as the cases studied in this chapter have shown, the ICRC has never been alone among 'non-State' actors in raising concerns about the humanitarian consequences of certain weapons, even less so in recent years. National Red Cross and Red Crescent societies have engaged their respective governments and the public at domestic levels in support of the ICRC's efforts, a recurring feature ever since the ICRC's early call for the prohibition of chemical weapons. Doctors and civil society organisations have also been key actors in historic efforts to regulate weapons of humanitarian concern, in some cases without ICRC involvement.[176]

[172] See e.g. Spoerri, 'The need for urgent international action on cluster munitions'.

[173] See Sandoz, 'Interdiction et restriction de l'usage de certaines armes', p. 103.

[174] See D. Hubert, *The Landmine Ban: A Case Study in Humanitarian Advocacy* (Providence: Thomas J. Watson Institute for International Studies, 2000), at p. xviii.

[175] *Ibid.*, at p. 71.

[176] Efforts in the late nineteenth century to ban bullets that expand or flatten easily in the human body – so-called 'dum-dum' bullets – began when doctors reporting on wounds

But in recent decades, there has been a notable increase in the knowledge, competence and involvement of civil society, as well as UN agencies, regarding weapons and their effects. NGOs with firsthand experience of the humanitarian consequences of weapons[177] and with relevant technical expertise[178] have been increasingly present in the landscape of humanitarian diplomacy.[179] In parallel to the work of the ICRC, their evidence-based reports and advocacy campaigns have also had a significant impact on shaping public perceptions, government positions and multilateral debates about the acceptability of certain weapons in humanitarian terms. In this respect, the ICRC and NGOs have distinct but complementary approaches. The focus of advocacy NGOs has been on stigmatisation of the weapons of concern, in particular of its producers and users, through public 'education and shaming campaigns'.[180] While the ICRC has

encountered during fighting in India drew attention to the issue in the medical community in Europe. This led peace activists of the day to engage governments in advance of the 1899 Hague Peace Conference, calling for the prohibition of these bullets: see Hubert, 'The Landmine Ban', pp. 2–3. The ICRC was not involved in these efforts. States prohibited the use of these projectiles in the *1899 Hague Declaration*.

[177] A prominent example is the International Campaign to Ban Landmines (ICBL), founded in 1992 by six non-governmental organisations – Handicap International, Medico International, Vietnam Veterans of America Foundation, Human Rights Watch (HRW), Physicians for Human Rights, and Mines Advisory Group – that had been providing relief to and recording the plight of civilians affected by anti-personnel mines in contexts such as Cambodia, Afghanistan and Somalia: Williams and Goose, 'The International Campaign to Ban Landmines', pp. 21–22. Today, the ICBL has merged with the Cluster Munitions Coalition and consists of NGOs active in more than 100 countries: www.icbl.org/en-gb/about-us.aspx. Also of note is the work of HRW, with the expertise of its Arms Division, which has very effectively documented the use and devastating impact of weapons of humanitarian concern in a variety of contexts, analysed their technical functions and legal implications and called for normative development. See e.g. *Fatally Flawed: Cluster bombs and their use by the United States in Afghanistan*, 18 December 2002, www.hrw.org/reports/2002/12/18/fatally-flawed, *Cluster Munitions a Foreseeable Hazard in Iraq*, 18 March 2003, www.hrw.org/reports/2003/03/18/cluster-munitions-foreseeable-hazard-iraq, and *Cluster Munitions and International Humanitarian Law*, 1 July 2004, www.hrw.org/reports/2004/07/01/cluster-munitions-and-international-humanitarian-law.

[178] See e.g. the work of the Geneva International Center for Humanitarian Demining (GICHD) in relation to calls for new rules to address the indiscriminate effects of anti-vehicle mines: *The Humanitarian and Developmental Impact of Anti-Vehicle Mines* (Geneva: GICHD and SIPRI, 2014).

[179] To give a recent example, 17 NGOs attended the four-day 2014 Meeting of Experts on autonomous weapon systems held by the States' party to the CCW, 12 of which were under the umbrella of the Campaign to Stop Killer Robots: see *Report of the informal Meeting of Experts on Lethal Autonomous Weapon Systems (LAWS)*, CCW/MSP/2014/3, para. 7.

[180] See L. Wexler, 'The International Deployment of Shame, Second-Best Responses and Norm Entrepreneurship: The Campaign to Ban Landmines and the Landmine Ban Treaty',

successfully used public communication strategies to raise awareness of the effects of specific weapons, it has been careful to avoid singling out certain States or 'naming and shaming', in keeping with its traditional modes of action. Moreover, consistent with its preferred method of working, the organisation has put equal emphasis on discreet advocacy, engaging States through bilateral dialogue and through discussions with groups of experts and policy-makers. Mindful that its IHL-based responsibilities to protect and assist the victims of armed conflict and to promote and strengthen IHL give it unique and significant weight among the chorus of those that call for State action to address the human costs of certain weapons, the ICRC has been circumspect in its use of this leverage.

Fourth, the ICRC's chief concern has been with the humanitarian consequences of the *use* of weapons, as it has witnessed firsthand in the course of its field work (as in the cases of chemical weapons, anti-personnel mines, cluster munitions and explosive remnants of war) or, in respect of new weapons not yet deployed, as it has assessed based on expert analysis of the weapons' foreseeable design-dependent effects (as in the case of blinding lasers). This is consonant with the aim of IHL, which is to limit the effects of armed conflict, notably through restrictions on means and methods of warfare. IHL has mostly prohibited the use of weapons for humanitarian reasons, without explicitly banning their possession or proliferation, or otherwise requiring their elimination. For example, the 1925 Geneva Protocol prohibited only the use of chemical and biological weapons.[181] The comprehensive prohibition of these weapons, including the prohibition to develop, produce and transfer them, and the requirement to destroy existing stockpiles – in other words the *disarmament*[182]

Arizona Journal of International and Comparative Law 20 (2003), pp. 561–606. On ICBL strategy and the 'mobilization of shame', see D. R. Dechaine, *Global Humanitarianism: NGOs and the Crafting of Community*, (Lanham, MD: Lexington Books, 2005), pp. 115–129.

181 Earlier examples of IHL prohibiting only the use of a weapon include the prohibition to employ exploding bullets in the *1868 Saint Petersburg Declaration*, and the prohibition to use expanding ('dum-dum') bullets in the *1899 Hague Declaration*. More recent examples include the *Protocol on Non-Detectable Fragments (Protocol I)* of the 1980 CCW, which prohibits the use of weapons the primary effect of which is to injure by undetectable fragments, and Protocol IV of 1995 which prohibits the use and transfer of blinding laser weapons, but not their development or production.

182 'Disarmament' is described by two authors as 'the traditional term for the elimination, as well as the limitation or reduction (through negotiation of an international agreement) of the means by which nations wage war.' R. J. Matthews and T. L. H. McCormack, 'The influence of humanitarian principles in the negotiation of arms control treaties', *International Review of the Red Cross*, 81(834) (1999), at p. 333.

of these weapons – only came forty-seven and sixty-eight years later, with the Biological and Chemical Weapons Conventions, respectively.[183] However, the adoption of the APMBC in 1997 marked the first time that IHL and disarmament aims converged in the same treaty: States were comprehensively prohibiting a weapon and requiring its complete elimination, what is more on humanitarian grounds.[184] Likewise, the ICRC's humanitarian advocacy on anti-personnel mines represented the first time the organisation called for the comprehensive prohibition of a weapon, extending from the traditional IHL prohibition on use to responsibility to remove the threat posed by deployed weapons through mine clearance, to complete disarmament through destruction of stockpiled weapons.[185] The prohibition of cluster munitions in the CCM in 2008 again brought together IHL and disarmament objectives in a single treaty, for primarily humanitarian reasons. In other respects, the ICRC's advocacy in favour of IHL-based arms transfer criteria in the ATT also represented a precedent for the organisation to the extent that it was addressing controls on the proliferation of otherwise lawful weapons, as always for humanitarian reasons.

Though the convergence of the classical IHL and disarmament approaches to the regulation of weapons is a recent phenomenon, the potential indirect impact of the ICRC's humanitarian advocacy on disarmament was not lost on the organisation's founders. In 1863, Gustave Moynier declared that:

> . . . in organizing succour for the wounded, in addressing fervent appeals in their favour to the various nations, in exciting pity by the relation of their miseries, and in laying bare, with a view to help our cause, the lamentable spectacle of a field of battle, in unveiling the terrible realities of war, and in proclaiming, in the name of charity, that which policy has often an interest to keep concealed, we shall do more for the disarmament of nations than those who have recourse to economic arguments or to the declamations of a sterile sentimentalism.[186]

As shown in this chapter, among the successful instances of the ICRC's advocacy for regulation of weapons, most have drawn from its direct testimony to their humanitarian consequences. However, some of the

[183] See above, text accompanying footnotes 35 and 36.
[184] Matthews and McCormack, 'The influence of humanitarian principles', p. 347.
[185] See *Ibid.*, p. 351.
[186] J. F. Hutchison, *Champions of Charity: War and the Rise of the Red Cross*, (Boulder: Westview Press, 1996), p. 68.

ICRC's 'fervent appeals' in this regard have remained unheeded, perhaps most notably that on nuclear weapons. Since 1945, when the ICRC witnessed firsthand the 'lamentable spectacle' at Hiroshima shortly after the atomic bombing, the entire International Red Cross and Red Crescent Movement has repeatedly called for the prohibition of nuclear weapons.[187] In 2011, in a historic resolution, the Movement emphasized 'the incalculable human suffering that can be expected to result from any use of nuclear weapons' as well as 'the lack of any adequate humanitarian response capacity', and stated that it found it 'difficult to envisage how any use of nuclear weapons could be compatible with the rules' of IHL.[188] Today, nuclear weapons are the only weapon of mass destruction not explicitly and completely prohibited. It is this 'legal gap'[189] that the ICRC and the Movement have been urging States to fill through the negotiation of a legally binding international agreement that would prohibit the use of and completely eliminate nuclear weapons.[190] The growing attention being paid by States, international organisations and NGOs to the 'humanitarian impact' of nuclear weapons, which is reframing the debate on nuclear disarmament in humanitarian terms instead of the narrow military–security considerations that have prevailed until now, may very well trigger the

[187] Notably in resolutions of the International Conferences of the Red Cross of 1948 (Resolution XXIV of the 17th International Conference, Stockholm), 1952 (Resolution XVIII of the 18th International Conference, Toronto), 1957 (Resolution XVIII of the 19th International Conference, New Delhi), 1965 (Resolution XXVIII of the 20th International Conference, Vienna), 1969 (Resolution XIV of the 21st International Conference, Istanbul), 1977 (Resolution XII of the 23rd International Conference, Bucharest), and 1981 (Resolution XIII of the 24th International Conference, Manila).

[188] Council of Delegates of the International Red Cross and Red Crescent Movement, *Working towards the elimination of nuclear weapons*, Resolution 1 (26 November 2011), paras 1 and 2.

[189] In an address to the Geneva-based diplomatic corps on 18 February 2015, the President of the ICRC, P. Maurer, stated that '70 years after Hiroshima and Nagasaki – names that recall humanitarian disasters like no other – clear progress towards the prohibition and elimination of nuclear weapons is still lacking. Nuclear weapons are the one weapon of mass destruction on which we are still confronted with a legal gap': www.icrc.org/en/document/nuclear-weapons-ending-threat-humanity. This address followed from the historic appeal, five years earlier, on 20 April 2010, of then President of the ICRC, J. Kellenberger, to all States 'and to all in a position to influence them, to seize with determination and urgency the unique opportunities now at hand to bring the era of nuclear weapons to an end': www.icrc.org/eng/resources/documents/statement/nuclear-weapons-statement-200410.htm.

[190] Council of Delegates, *Working towards the elimination of nuclear weapons*, para. 3.

paradigm shift needed to achieve tangible progress towards the elimination of nuclear weapons.[191]

Autonomous weapon systems, on which there is currently much international debate thanks notably to an NGO campaign launched in 2013 to 'Stop Killer Robots',[192] represent another area of possible future regulation of weapons under IHL. This new technology of warfare has already been deployed on the battlefield, though in rudimentary form.[193] The issue has a degree of complexity in that it does not concern a specific weapon system, but refers to autonomy in the 'critical functions' of selecting and attacking targets[194] in any kind of

[191] Attention of the international community to the humanitarian impact of nuclear weapons has been building since the May 2010 Review Conference of the Treaty on the Non-Proliferation (NPT), when the States' party to the treaty unanimously expressed 'deep concern at the catastrophic humanitarian consequences of any use of nuclear weapons': *2010 Review Conference of the Parties to the Treaty on the Non-Proliferation of Nuclear Weapons, Final Document*, NPT/CONF.2010/50 (Vol. I), para. 80 and Conclusion I.A.v. Since then, Norway, Mexico and Austria have hosted three inter-governmental conferences gathering up to 158 States to engage in a 'fact-based discussion' on the humanitarian impact of nuclear weapons. See N. Ritchie, *The Story So Far: The humanitarian initiative on the impacts of nuclear weapons*, ILPI-UNIDIR Vienna Conference Series, Paper no. 1 of 6. In April 2015, in a joint statement to the 2015 NPT Review Conference, 159 States emphasized that 'awareness of the catastrophic consequences of nuclear weapons must underpin all approaches and efforts towards nuclear disarmament' and that the 'only way to guarantee that nuclear weapons will never be used again is through their total elimination'. The statement also welcomed the role of the ICRC, among other actors, in working to raise awareness of the catastrophic humanitarian consequences of nuclear weapons. See 2015 Review Conference of the Parties to the Treaty on the Non-Proliferation of Nuclear Weapons, *Joint Statement on the Humanitarian Consequences of Nuclear Weapons*, delivered by S. Kurz, Federal Minister for Europe, Integration and Foreign Affairs of Austria, (New York, 28 April 2015).

[192] The Campaign to Stop Killer Robots is a coalition of NGOs launched in April 2013 and led by among others Human Rights Watch, Article 36, the International Committee for Robotic Arms Control, the Nobel Women's Initiative, and Women's International League for Peace and Freedom. The Campaign's objective is a preemptive ban on 'fully autonomous weapons': www.stopkillerrobots.org/.

[193] See ICRC, *Expert Meeting, Autonomous Weapon Systems: Technical, Military, Legal and Humanitarian Aspects (Geneva, 26–28 March 2014)* (Geneva: ICRC, 2014), pp. 14–15 and 65–69.

[194] There is no universally accepted definition of autonomous weapon systems. At the first informal Meeting of Experts of the CCW in May 2014, the ICRC proposed that 'autonomous weapon systems' are 'weapons that can independently select and attack targets, that is, they have autonomy in the 'critical functions' of acquiring, tracking, selecting and attacking targets': Convention on Certain Conventional Weapons (CCW) Meeting of Experts on Lethal Autonomous Weapons Systems (LAWS), 13–16 May 2014, Geneva, Statement of the International Committee of the Red Cross (ICRC) 13 May 2014. See ICRC, *Expert Meeting, Autonomous Weapon Systems: Technical, Military, Legal and*

weapon.[195] In this respect, as when blinding laser weapons were initially discussed by the international community in the early 1990s, the focus has been on better understanding the military applications and the legal, ethical and societal implications of this new technology of warfare, with a view to raising the awareness of diplomats, policy-makers and the public. The ICRC has since 2011 been calling for careful consideration of the issues raised by autonomous weapon systems before they are further developed and deployed, and in March 2014 it held a meeting of government and independent experts to help inform discussions on these weapons.[196] States have held two informal 'Meetings of Experts' on these weapons within the framework of the CCW, in which the ICRC, other international organisations and NGOs have actively participated.[197] It is too early to tell whether normative development on autonomous weapon systems will ensue in the CCW or elsewhere, but as most States appear to acknowledge the need to retain human control over the critical functions of weapon systems, a number of stakeholders including the ICRC have proposed that discussions now focus on what level of human control would be 'meaningful' or appropriate,[198] as a matter of law and policy, but also as a matter of ethics. Indeed, the ICRC among others has

Humanitarian Aspects (Geneva, 26–28 March 2014) (Geneva: ICRC, 2014), pp. 7, 14–15, 57 and 63–64.

195 As explained by the UN Institute for Disarmament Research (UNIDIR), which has taken up the definition of autonomous weapon systems proposed by the ICRC, autonomy is a characteristic of a technology, attached to a function or functions of a weapon system, and not the weapon system itself: see UNIDIR, *Framing Discussions on the Weaponization of Increasingly Autonomous Technologies, No.1 UNIDIR Resources*, (Geneva: UNIDIR, 2014), pp. 4–5.

196 See report of the meeting in ICRC, *Expert Meeting, Autonomous Weapon Systems.*

197 A first 'informal' CCW meeting on autonomous weapons took place in Geneva from 13 to 16 May 2014: see Meeting of the High Contracting Parties to the CCW, *Report of the 2014 informal Meeting of Experts on Lethal Autonomous Weapons Systems (LAWS)*, CCW/MSP/2014/3, 11 June 2014. A second 'informal' meeting took place from 13 to 17 April 2015 (report not available at time of writing). It should also be noted that the Human Rights Council has also been debating 'Lethal Autonomous Robotics', notably around the reports on this issue submitted by the UN Special Rapporteur on extrajudicial, summary or arbitrary executions, C. Heyns: see e.g. A/HRC/27/47 (9 April 2013).

198 See e.g.: M. C. Horowitz and P. Scharre, *Meaningful Human Control in Weapon Systems: A Primer* (Washington, DC: Center for a New American Security, March 2015); UNIDIR, *The Weaponization of Increasingly Autonomous Technologies: Considering how Meaningful Human Control might move the discussion forward, No.2 UNIDIR Resources*, (Geneva: UNIDIR, 2014); Remarks by T. Nash, Director, Article 36, Informal Meeting of Experts on Lethal Autonomous Weapon Systems, CCW, Geneva, Thursday 15 May 2015; N. Sharkey, 'Towards a principle for the human supervisory control of robot weapons', *Politica & Società* 2 (May–August 2014). See also ICRC, Closing Statement, CCW Informal Meeting of

called on States to consider not just whether the development and use of autonomous weapon systems may affect the ability of parties to armed conflicts to respect IHL, but also whether these developments are acceptable in moral terms. Even if weapons that autonomously select and attack targets, including human targets, are capable of being used in accordance with IHL, such machines making life and death decisions on the battlefield without human control may be considered abhorrent to the principles of humanity and the dictates of public conscience.[199] As guardian of IHL and a voice of the public conscience, the ICRC will continue to make known its views on these and other new weapons which raise questions of crucial importance to the future of warfare, and indeed to the future of humanity.

Experts on Lethal Autonomous Weapon Systems (LAWS), 17 April 2015: 'To move forward, there is now a need for States to address where the limits should lie, in order to ensure that meaningful, adequate and effective human control is maintained over weapon systems.'

[199] See ICRC, *Expert Meeting, Autonomous Weapon Systems*, pp. 23–24 and 92–94; ICRC, Statement to Concluding Session, CCW Expert Meeting on 'Lethal Autonomous Weapons Systems', Geneva, 16 May 2014.

6

Between 'Constructive Engagement', 'Collusion' and 'Critical Distance': The International Committee of the Red Cross and the Development of International Criminal Law

CARSTEN STAHN

I. Introduction

The International Committee of the Red Cross (ICRC) is a unique legal creature.[1] Its relationship to International Criminal Law (ICL) is equally unique. It is shaped by antinomies. It is not 'love at first sight', like the idealistic match between ICL and human rights in the 'honeymoon' phase of ICL, but rather a relationship which has evolved over time and grown with time. It is shaped by pragmatism and constructive engagement. There are significant points of convergence. But there are also marked divergences. This may be part of the strength of the mutual relationship.

There is a natural correlation between the ICRC and International Humanitarian Law (IHL). This connection is less evident in the relationship to ICL. ICL has grown rapidly over the past decades. In its process of maturation, it has absorbed influences from different and sometimes competing bodies of law: IHL, public international law, criminal law and human rights. It thus is to some extent a 'jack-in-the-box' in the landscape

[1] The ICRC has features of a public and private international organisation. It is formally a private association incorporated in Switzerland, but it also enjoys international legal personality. See H.-P. Gasser, 'International Committee of the Red Cross' in R. Wolfrum (ed.), *The Max Planck Encyclopedia of Public International Law*, Vol. V (Oxford: Oxford University Press, 2012), pp. 452–453. See generally D. P. Forsythe, 'The ICRC: A Unique Humanitarian Protagonist', *International Review of the Red Cross*, 89(865) (2007), pp. 63–96; D. P. Forsythe, *The Humanitarians: The International Committee of the Red Cross* (Cambridge: Cambridge University Press, 2005); S. R. Ratner, 'Law Promotion Beyond Law Talk: The Red Cross, Persuasion, and the Laws of War', *European Journal of International Law*, 22 (2011), pp. 459–506; D.-E. Khan, *Das Rote Kreuz: Geschichte einer humanitären Weltbewegung* (München: C. H. Beck, 2013).

of international law. It is an amalgam of vastly different areas of law, and different legal cultures.[2] It is thus inherently pluralistic in nature. IHL is only part of a broader puzzle in its systemic framework. A terminological branding of international criminal courts as 'war crimes' courts or 'military tribunals' is today almost a misnomer to members of the profession.

The ICRC has supported the 'growth' of international criminal law. But its role has been distinct and specific. The ICRC has focused its contribution mainly on the norm-creating process and implementation. It has been less forceful and more cautious in the creation of ICL than the 'human rights' movement in terms of advocacy. This is the result of two factors: its specific focus as 'promoter' and 'guardian' of international humanitarian law, and its partly different normative agenda and institutional mandate.[3]

IHL and ICL share certain synergies, but they differ in standards, methods and culture.[4] ICL is a project with a vested interest in specific normative goals. These include, first and foremost, accountability, transparency and fair and effective investigation and prosecution of individuals. It is focused on individual responsibility for violations, rather than primary rules of behaviour. IHL is shaped by different prerogatives (e.g. humanizing warfare, balancing 'military necessity' and concerns of 'humanity'). They are reflected in the role of the ICRC. Its work is shaped by broader humanitarian concerns. Its authority and practice is founded on the principles of humanity, impartiality, neutrality, independence, voluntary service, unity, and universality.[5] The ICRC has the mandate to protect and assist military and civilian victims in ongoing conflict and crisis.[6] This

[2] See C. Stahn and L. van den Herik, 'Fragmentation, Diversification and 3D Legal Pluralism: International Criminal Law as Jack-in-the-Box?' in L. van den Herik and C. Stahn (eds.), *The Diversification and Fragmentation of International Criminal Law*, (Leiden, MA: Brill/Martinus Nijhoff, 2012), pp. 21–87.

[3] Ratner lists at least six types of non-legal arguments advanced by the ICRC: 'humanitarian arguments', 'political arguments', 'economic arguments', 'pragmatic arguments', 'moral arguments' and 'customary arguments'. See Ratner, 'Law Promotion Beyond Law Talk', at p. 478.

[4] For a study, see S. Sivakumaran, *The Law of Non-International Armed Conflict* (Oxford: Oxford University Press, 2012), pp. 77–83; R. Cryer, 'The Interplay of Human Rights and Humanitarian Law: The Approach of the ICTY', *Journal of Conflict and Security Law*, 14 (2000), p. 511, 516; D. Robinson, 'The Identity Crisis of International Criminal Law', *Leiden Journal of International Law*, 21 (2008), pp. 946–955.

[5] Fundamental Principles of the International Red Cross and Red Crescent Movement proclaimed by the 20th International Conference of the Red Cross, Vienna, 1965, as revised during the 25th International Conference of the Red Cross, Geneva, 1986, contained in the Statutes of the International Red Cross and Red Crescent Movement.

[6] The mission statement of the ICRC captures the main rationales as follows: 'The International Committee of the Red Cross (ICRC) is an impartial, neutral and independent organisation whose exclusively humanitarian mission is to protect the lives and dignity of victims

requires different methodologies, which are more akin to conflict management, i.e. the preservation of a 'constructive relationship' to States and actors involved in the violence and 'quiet diplomacy'.[7] The 'confidentiality rule' is a hallmark of the ICRC and essential in maintaining relationships with warring parties.

These differences have shaped the engagement with ICL. The ICRC has played different roles in the development of international criminal law. It has pursued a policy of 'strategic engagement'. It has acted as a gentle driving force or 'modernizer of ICL' in some areas. In other areas, it has voiced concern or dissent.

This contribution examines several dimensions of this relationship. It starts with an analysis of specific ICRC lenses and approaches towards ICL. It argues that the approach of the ICRC to ICL is marked by three overarching principles: (i) 'structural independence', (ii) 'strategic engagement' and (iii) systemic support for implementation. It then analyses (iv) potential areas of 'shared understanding' in interaction, before concluding (v) with some final observations on rethinking existing relations.

II. The ICRC and Structural Independence

A first distinctive feature, characterizing the ICRC's approach to ICL, is its principled focus on structural and normative independence. Unlike other organisations, and particularly some non-governmental organisations (NGOs; e.g. the Coalition for the International Criminal Court), the ICRC has not become immersed in the project and purposes ICL. It has supported the creation of International Criminal Courts and Tribunals (ICCTs). It has welcomed the adoption of their respective Statutes. But it has continued to stress the autonomous and separate nature of its own mandate vis-à-vis ICCTs. It kept a 'critical stance' towards a 'merger of ICL and IHL'. The divide is rooted in the tensions of the ICRC's own mandate.

of armed conflict and other situations of violence and to provide them with assistance. The ICRC also endeavors to prevent suffering by promoting and strengthening humanitarian law and universal humanitarian principles.' See ICRC, 'The mandate and mission of the ICRC', at www.icrc.org/eng/who-we-are/mandate/.

[7] See generally J.-P. Lavoyer and L. Maresca, 'The Role of the ICRC in the Development of International Humanitarian Law', *International Negotiation*, 4 (1999), pp. 501–525. As W. J. Fenrick notes: 'The success or failure of international humanitarian law must be measured in terms of lives saved and injuries not suffered. It is not measured by the number of prosecutions or the number of convictions.' See W. J. Fenrick, 'The Law Applicable to Targeting and Proportionality after Operation Allied Force: A View from the Outside', *Yearbook of International Humanitarian Law*, 3 (2000), pp. 79–80.

It has *inter alia* three cardinal functions which may compete with each other:

(i) The 'guardian role' of the ICRC, i.e. 'to work for the faithful application of international humanitarian law applicable in armed conflicts and to take cognizance of any complaints based on alleged breaches of that law'.[8] It involves monitoring of compliance with IHL and sharing of information on alleged violations of IHL primarily with the party responsible.

(ii) Its 'protective role', i.e. 'to endeavour at all times – as a neutral institution [. . .] to ensure the protection of and assistance to military and civilian victims of such events and of their direct results'.[9] This may entail action to serve as intermediary between parties to a conflict;[10] and

(iii) its 'advocacy' and 'dissemination' role, i.e. to 'work for the understanding and dissemination of knowledge of international humanitarian law applicable in armed conflicts and to *prepare any development* thereof'.[11] It has interpreted this role as a mandate to develop the law.[12]

The practice of the ICRC, including the dilemmas of the Holocaust[13], have shown that these three functions do not always coincide with each other.[14] They have different degrees of convergence/divergence with the purposes and principles of ICL. Most synergies appear to exist in relation to the first and the last role, i.e. monitoring of violations, and dissemination and development of the law. But this 'dédoublement fonctionnel' has also created tensions. This is evident in relation to roles (i) and (ii).

1. *Guardianship*

Historically, 'guardianship' (i.e. scrutiny over the application of IHL) used to be predominantly in the realm of the Conventions and the ICRC. This prerogative has been eroded by the growing application and interpretation

[8] See Art. 4 (1) (c) Statutes of the International Committee of the Red Cross.

[9] *Ibid.*, Art. 4 (1) (d). [10] *Ibid.*, Art. 4 (2). [11] *Ibid.*, Art. 4 (1) (g).

[12] See Lavoyer and Maresca, 'The Role of the ICRC', at p. 506.

[13] See J.-C. Favez, *The Red Cross and the Holocaust* (Cambridge: Cambridge University Press, 1999).

[14] For an illustration of conflicts between the 'protection rationale' and the commitment to uphold rules and principles of IHL, see Ratner, 'Law Promotion Beyond Law Talk', at pp. 501–502.

of IHL by ICCTs. It thus plays now partially a 'shared' role. This has led to a plurality of voices, and occasionally an 'estrangement' between the law found in the 'Hague' and the 'Geneva' Law, and its application and interpretation by the tribunals.

On the positive side, engagement with ICCTs has strengthened the leverage of the ICRC. For instance, the ICRC Study on Customary International Law relied heavily on findings of the ICTY, in order to elucidate practice.[15] Some critics argue that the ICRC might have given too much weight to influences from ICCTs.[16] ICCTs have clarified essential elements of war crimes law. The ICRC Study has taken into account various developments in ascertaining rules and practice.

The basic rules on conduct of hostilities (Rules 1 to 24) and treatment of civilians and persons *hors de combat* (Rules 32 to 39) are essentially the same in relation to international and non-international armed conflict. This is largely a result of the *Tadić* jurisprudence, and its ramifications in practice, which diminished the boundaries between the law relating to international and non-international armed conflict, with its famous *dictum* that

> what is inhumane, and consequently proscribed, in international wars, cannot be but be inhumane and inadmissible in civil strife.[17]

The ICRC Study takes into definitions of crimes and concepts of responsibility shaped by ICCTs. There are various examples of cross-fertilisation. For instance, the prohibition of spreading terror among the civilian population (Rule 2) has been influenced by ICTY case law, in particular the *Galić* jurisprudence[18] which established infliction of terror as a war crime.

[15] See J.-M. Henckaerts and L. Doswald-Beck (eds.), *Customary International Humanitarian Law* (Cambridge: Cambridge University Press, 2005). For analysis, see E. Wilmshurst and S. Breau, *Perspectives on the ICRC Study on Customary Law International Humanitarian Law* (Cambridge: Cambridge University Press, 2007).

[16] See R. Cryer, 'On Custom, Treaties, Scholars and the Gavel: The Influence of the International Criminal Tribunals on the ICRC Customary Law Study', *Journal of Conflict and Security Law*, 11 (2006), p. 251.

[17] See ICTY, Appeals Chamber, *Prosecutor* v. *Tadić*, Decision on Defence Motion for Interlocutory Appeal on Jurisdiction (IT-94–1-AR72), 2 October 1995, para. 119. Subsequent instruments, such as the ICC Statute, the Statute of Special Court for Sierra Leone, The Hague Protocol on Cultural Property (1999), and the Convention on Cluster Munitions apply to non-international armed conflict.

[18] See ICTY, Appeals Chamber, *Prosecutor* v. *Galić*, (IT-98–29-A), 30 November 2006, para. 104. Judge Nieto-Navia dissented at trial, arguing that a Court may under no circumstance create 'new criminal offences'. For a discussion, see R. Cryer, '*Prosecutor* v. *Galić* and the War Crime of Terror Bombing', *Israel Defence Force Law Review*, 2 (2005–2006), p. 73.

It held that the actual terrorisation is not a required element of the offence, but part of the intent to spread terror which can be inferred by circumstances (e.g. acts or threats of violence), including direct attacks or indiscriminate attacks. The Tribunals gave new impulses relating to the protection of cultural property (Rules 38 to 41)[19] and other war crimes which are reflected in the Study (Rules 156–161). Rape is prohibited by the Geneva Conventions, but not explicitly listed as a grave breach in Conventions or Additional Protocol I. The *Furundzija* and *Kunarac* (Trial and Appeals Chamber) decisions of the ICTY set new footprints by defining elements of rape and sexual violence.[20] *Stakić* identified the cross-border requirement as an element of deportation, i.e. transfer across a *de jure* or *de facto* State border.[21] *Hadzihasanović* applied the doctrine of command responsibility to non-international armed conflicts.[22]

This interaction is conducive to the development and adaptation of the law. But it also has its downsides. The emerging jurisprudence of ICCTs has made it more difficult to determine what is a 'faithful' application of IHL. There are growing areas of divergence and risks arising out of a rewriting of war crimes law by ICCTs.[23]

In some areas, interpretations in ICL have significantly narrowed conceptions under IHL. A famous example is the ban of belligerent reprisals by the *Kupreskić* Trial Judgment. The Trial Chamber argued that the prohibition of IHL has been altered through developments in ICL. It held:

> while reprisals could have had a modicum of justification in the past, when they constituted practically the only effective means of compelling the enemy to abandon unlawful acts of warfare and to comply in future with international law, at present they can no longer be justified in this manner. A means of inducing compliance with international law is at present more

19 See generally R. O'Keefe, *The Protection of Cultural Property in Armed Conflict* (Cambridge: Cambridge University Press, 2006).

20 See ICTY, Appeals Chamber, *Prosecutor* v. *Kunarac* (IT-96–23/1-A), 12 June 2002, paras 128, 195; ICTY Trial Chamber, *Prosecutor* v. *Furundzija* (IT-95–17/1-T), 10 December 1998, paras 176 et seq.

21 See ICTY, Appeals Chamber, *Prosecutor* v. *Stakić* (IT-97–24-A), 22 March 2006, paras 300–8.

22 See ICTY, Appeals Chamber, *Prosecutor* v. *Hadzihasanović*, Decision on Interlocutory Appeal Challenging Jurisdiction in Relation to Command Responsibility (IT-01–47-AR72), 16 July 2003, paras 11–31.

23 See generally S. Darcy, 'The Reinvention of War Crimes by the International Criminal Tribunals' in S. Darcy and J. Powderly (eds.), *Judicial Creativity at the International Criminal Tribunals* (Oxford: Oxford University Press), pp. 106–128.

> widely available and, more importantly, is beginning to prove fairly efficacious: the prosecution and punishment of war crimes and crimes against humanity by national or international courts.[24]

This finding contrasts with later case law in *Martić*, in which the Trial Chamber held that belligerent reprisals may 'be considered lawful', subject 'to strict conditions'[25], and Rule 145 of the Customary Law Study which States that '[w]here not prohibited by international law, belligerent reprisals are subject to stringent conditions'.[26]

In other contexts, ICL has challenged fundamental conceptions relating to the applicability of IHL. ICCTs have developed a rich, yet partially controversial jurisprudence on 'internationalization' of non-international armed conflicts (e.g. 'effective' v. 'overall control').[27] This jurisprudence was not taken up in the Customary Law Study. Questions relating to the definition of 'armed conflict' are addressed in less formalized policy documents of the ICRC.[28] This creates doubts to what extent some of these findings might be taken not to reflect customary law.[29] For instance, following the *Genocide* case at the International Court of Justice, there are at least three divergent positions on criteria for the internationalisation of armed conflict. Some claim that the 'overall control' test retains validity in general international law, not to determine State responsibility, but under the specific rules of international humanitarian (*lex specialis*).[30]

[24] ICTY, *Prosecutor* v. *Kupreskić* (IT-95–16-T), Judgment, 14 January 2000, para. 530.

[25] ICTY, *Prosecutor* v. *Martić*, (IT-95–11-T), Judgment, 12 June 2007, para. 465.

[26] Rule 145, 'Reprisals', at www.icrc.org/customary-ihl/eng/docs/v1_rul_rule145.

[27] *Prosecutor* v. *Tadić* (IT-94–1-AR72), at para. 139. The 'overall control test' was endorsed by the ICC in *Lubanga*. See ICC, Pre-Trial Chamber, *Prosecutor* v. *Lubanga*, Decision on Confirmation of Charges (ICC-01/04–01/06), 27 February 2007, paras 210–1, Judgment under Art. 74, March 2012, para. 541. For a discussion, see S. Sivakumaran, 'Identifying an Armed Conflict Not of an International Character' in C. Stahn and G. Sluiter (eds.), *The Emerging Practice of the International Criminal Court* (Leiden, MA: Brill/Martinus Nijhoff, 2009); D. Akande, 'Classification of Armed Conflicts: Relevant Legal Concepts' in E. Wilmshurst (ed.), *International Law and the Classification of Conflicts* (Oxford: Oxford University Press, 2012), pp. 32–79.

[28] See e.g. ICRC, Opinion Paper March 2008, at www.icrc.org/eng/assets/files/other/opinion-paper-armed-conflict.pdf.

[29] See ICJ, *Case Concerning the Application of the Convention on the Prevention and Punishment of the Crime of Genocide* (*Bosnia and Herzegovina* v. *Serbia and Montenegro*), Judgment of 26 February 2007, paras 404–5.

[30] Support for this argument may be found in Art. 55 of the ILC Articles on State Responsibility. It reads: 'These articles do not apply where and to the extent that the conditions for the existence of an internationally wrongful act or the content or implementation of the international responsibility of a State are governed by special rules of international law which allow for different rules in separate areas.'

Others regard the test as a simple application of international humanitarian law. Again others claim that the reasoning in *Tadić* was misguided in the first place, since internationalisation of internal armed conflict should be decided according to criteria governing recourse to force, i.e. *jus ad bellum*, rather than *jus in bello*.[31]

The ICRC study and ICCTs differ in relation to some concepts of criminal responsibility. One example is superior order. The Study follows the permissive approach of Article 33 of the ICC Statute in relation to war crimes[32], rather than the clear-cut rejection of superior order as a defence in the Statutes of UN tribunals (ICTY, ICTR, SCSL).[33]

There are various examples of 'progressive development of the law' in the case law of ICCTs. The *ad hoc* tribunals have adopted an extended definition of the concept of 'protected persons' under the Fourth Geneva Convention by relying on ethnicity rather than nationality.[34] They have identified contours of new war crimes, such as terrorizing the civilian population (*Galić*) or new categories of sexual violence. Individual Chambers have occasionally developed new standards affecting the application of primary rules of IHL. In *Martić*, the Prosecution argued on appeal that the expression 'civilian population' in crimes against humanity should not be limited to its meaning under international humanitarian law, i.e. individuals who are not members of armed forces, but should include other categories of non-combatants such as persons *hors de combat*.[35] This definition of the notion of 'civilian' was rejected by the Appeals Chamber. It invoked the ordinary meaning of the term 'civilian' in Article 50(1) of Additional Protocol I to conclude that this only includes persons who are not members of the armed forces.[36]

[31] See Akande, 'Classification of Armed Conflicts', at pp. 61–62, relying on para. 7, Separate Opinion of Judge Shahabuddeen in *Tadić*.

[32] See Henckaerts and Doswald-Beck (eds.), *Customary International Humanitarian Law*, Rules 153–5.

[33] See Art. 7 (4) ICTY Statute, Art. 6 (4) ICTR Statute and Art. 6 (4) of the Statute of the Special Court for Sierra Leone.

[34] ICTY, Appeals Chamber, *Prosecutor* v. *Tadić* (IT-94–1-A), 15 July 1999, para. 166. The Appeals Chamber concluded that 'not only the text and the drafting history of the Convention but also, and more importantly, the Convention's object and purpose suggest that allegiance to a Party to the conflict and correspondingly, control by this Party over persons in a given territory, may be regarded as the crucial test'.

[35] ICTY, Appeals Chamber, *Prosecutor* v. *Martić* (IT-95–11-A), Judgment, 8 October 2008.

[36] *Ibid.*, para. 297. The Appeals Chamber argued that 'while certain terms have been interpreted differently in international humanitarian law and in the context of crimes against humanity, the character of the notion of civilian in international humanitarian law and

In *Gotovina*, the Trial Chamber introduced a new '200 meter' requirement as a standard of legality for attacks on civilians and civilian objects. It determined that artillery shells falling more than 200 meters from a legitimate military target constitute evidence of indiscriminate shelling of a residential area.[37] This was appealed by the Defence. The Appeals Chamber criticized this test. It noted 'that the Trial Chamber did not explain the specific basis on which it arrived at a 200-meter margin of error as a reasonable interpretation of evidence on the record'.[38] But it failed to specify the correct test (as highlighted in the dissents by Judges Agius and Pocar[39]). This leaves considerable uncertainty for practice.

Most fundamentally, ICCTs have adopted their own methodology in interpreting and applying IHL. They have analysed and applied the law through the specific lens of ICL and its goals (i.e. 'substantive justice and equity'[40], interest of victims), rather than State interests and practice. This has created some alliance with human rights concepts ('dynamic interpretation') and natural law foundations of IHL. This process has been gently framed as 'humanization of warfare' and international humanitarian law through international criminal courts.[41] But it is in part also consequence of the dynamic forces of the judicial process and the role of individual judges in the 'pioneering' phase of ICL.[42]

There are thus different interpreters, and to some extent multiple 'guardians' of IHL today: the ICRC, ICCTs, and the ICJ and States. Like in real life, the presence of several wards may create sensitivities and frictions. The relationship between the ICRC and ICCTs bears some resemblance to the controversy over 'ownership' in the judgement of Solomon. It is almost as if the ICRC and ICCTs claim to be the mother of the

international criminal law militates against giving it differing meanings under Art. 3 and Art. 5 of the Statute': *Ibid.*, para. 299.

37 ICTY, Trial Chamber, *Prosecutor* v. *Gotovina, Cermak & Markac* (IT-06-90-T), 15 April 2011, paras 1898, 1903–6, 1919–21, 1932–3, 1940–1.

38 ICTY, Appeals Chamber, *Prosecutor* v. *Gotovina & Markac* (IT-06-90-A), Judgment, 16 November 2012, paras 58, 60.

39 *Ibid.*, Dissenting Opinion Agius, para. 11, Dissenting Opinion, Pocar, para. 13.

40 *Prosecutor* v. *Tadić* (IT-94-1-AR72), para. 128.

41 T. Meron, 'The Humanization of Humanitarian Law', *American Journal of International Law*, 94 (2000), pp. 239–278; T. Meron, 'The Humanization of the Law of War' in R. Meron (ed.), *The Making of International Criminal Justice: A View From the Bench* (Oxford: Oxford University Press, 2012), pp. 42–61.

42 On A. Cassese, see T. Hoffmann, 'The Gentle Humanizer of Humanitarian Law – Antonio Cassese and the creation of the customary law of non-international armed conflict' in C. Stahn and L. van den Herik (eds.), *Future Perspectives on International Criminal Justice* (Cambridge: Cambridge University Press, 2010), pp 58–80.

'same child'. The role of the ICRC seems to coincide with the position of the mother in the biblical tale. The mother does not deny competing authority, but places emphasis on care which reveals her as the true mother: 'Oh Lord, give the baby to her, just don't kill him!'.

It may be more difficult to achieve a just solution in international law. It is hard to determine a 'final arbiter'. Moreover, the issue of 'ownership' is less clear. There is no 'single' or 'pure' approach to IHL. With the multiplication of 'interpreters', different approaches have emerged. They undergo transformation through institutional practice, discourse and interaction. Grey zones are expanding. This creates certain risks. For instance, there is a concern that developments in the area of individual responsibility for violations may become detached from some of the primary rules of IHL and the realities of the battlefield. Specific interpretations of war crimes law by ICCTs may narrow protections offered under IHL.[43] This creates a need for more diligence in the exercise of functions, and critical engagement with the foundations and limitations of 'guardianship'.[44]

2. *Protection*

The tensions between the purposes of the ICRC and ICCTs are most visible in the context of the second main role of the ICRC, namely its 'protective' function. In ICL, protection is an annex function to investigations and prosecutions (i.e. geared towards protection of witnesses and victims in proceedings).[45] For the ICRC, it is a core function. It might entail roles of agency, i.e. action as intermediary, and involves confidential dialogue and persuasion.

The ICRC shares a general commitment to accountability. But it has remained neutral towards criminal proceedings and their outcome. The ICRC and ICCTs pursue, as it is sometimes put, 'separate but complementary approaches'.[46] The ICRC has, in particular, been cautious towards

[43] See also Sivakumaran, *The Law of Non-International Armed Conflict*, pp. 80–81.

[44] See also below Section 4.

[45] See e.g. Art. 68 of the ICC Statute.

[46] See interview with A.-M. La Rosa, 'ICRC and ICC: two separate but complementary approaches to ensuring respect for international humanitarian law', 3 March 2009, at www.icrc.org/eng/resources/documents/interview/international-criminal-court-interview-101008.htm. See also ICTY, Trial Chamber, *Prosecutor* v. *Simić*, Decision on the Prosecution Motion under Rule 73 for a Ruling Concerning the Testimony of a Witness (IT-95–9), 27 July 1999, para. 70 ('They are two independent international institutions each with a unique mandate conferred upon them by the international community. Both mandates are based on international humanitarian law and ultimately geared towards the better implementation thereof. Although both share common goals, their functions and tasks are

participation in judicial proceedings, since such action might compromise the ability of the ICRC to carry out its 'protective' mandate. It has refused to assume a 'punitive role' in response to violations or take part in repressive mechanisms. It has adopted a strict approach in relation to professional privileges. This has led to controversies over testimony of ICRC officials before ICCTs.

In the *Simić et al.* case, the ICTY Prosecution sought to rely on evidence in the possession of a former employee of the ICRC.[47] The person had acted as interpreter for inspection visits of ICRC delegates. The ICRC conceded that non-disclosure might affect the interests of criminal justice (i.e. truth-finding in legal proceedings). But it took the view that the 'ICRC's pledge of discretion and confidentiality *vis-à-vis* both the victims and the parties to the conflict' should take precedence. The Trial Chamber found that 'the ICRC has a right to insist on [. . .] nondisclosure by parties to the Geneva Conventions and the Protocols', and that customary international law provides the ICRC with an absolute right to non-disclosure of information relating to the work of the ICRC.[48] In a separate opinion, Judge Hunt questioned whether States may have intended to provide privileges for the ICRC before international criminal courts. He argued that the Tribunal should have the final say in the balancing of competing public interests (i.e. justice v. confidentiality), in particular in cases where non-disclosure might relate to exculpatory evidence.[49]

This dispute continued in the context of the negotiations of the Rules of Procedure and Evidence of the ICC. Based on ICTY jurisprudence, the ICRC insisted on the inclusion of a privilege in the context of the PrepCom. This resulted in a compromise solution in Rule 73. Rule 74 (4) recognizes the privilege of non-disclosure of the ICRC in relation to 'any information, documents or other evidence which it came into the possession of in the course, or as a consequence, of the performance by ICRC of its functions under the Statutes of the International Red Cross and Red Crescent Movement'.[50] But Rule 74 (6) imposes an additional requirement of 'consultations' in cases in which 'the Court determines that ICRC information, documents or other evidence are of great importance for a particular case'. It stipulates that the matter shall be solved 'by cooperative means,

different. The ICRC's activities have been described as "preventive", while the International Tribunal is empowered to prosecute breaches of international humanitarian law once they have occurred').

[47] See ICTY, *Simić*, paras 9–22. [48] *Ibid*, para. 73.

[49] *Ibid.*, Separate Opinion Judge Hunt, paras 29–32.

[50] See Rule 74 (4) of the ICC Rules of Procedure and Evidence.

bearing in mind the circumstances of the case, the relevance of the evidence sought, whether the evidence could be obtained from a source other than ICRC, the interests of justice and of victims, and the performance of the Court's and ICRC's functions'.[51]

The wording is ambiguous as to whether the Court or the ICRC has the final authority to decide over competing interests. In *Lubanga*, the Appeals Chamber exercised this power in order to determine the conflict between disclosure of exculpatory evidence (Article 67 (2) and provider confidentiality of the UN under Article 53 (3) (e) and the UN ICC Relationship Agreement).[52] It remains to be seen whether the Court would claim a final say vis-à-vis the ICRC privilege based on Article 67 (2), if the privilege denies a defendant access to exculpatory evidence.[53] An absolute protection is contained in Rule 164 of the Rules of Procedure and Evidence of the Special Tribunal for Lebanon.[54]

III. The ICRC and Strategic Engagement

A second general feature of ICRC policy is what one might call 'strategic engagement' in relation to the formation of the substantive law of ICCTs. In line with its mandate, the ICRC focused its involvement on '*jus in bello*' questions. In this context, it acted both as a 'watchdog' and as an advocate of IHL.

The ICRC has played a key role in the development of penal sanctions for violations of IHL and the obligation of domestic jurisdictions to enact corresponding legislation.[55] It insisted on the need to adopt domestic legislation for the repression of violations of the 1929 Geneva Convention

[51] See Rule 74 (6) of the ICC Rules of Procedure and Evidence.

[52] See ICC, Appeals Chamber, *Prosecutor* v. *Lubanga*, Judgment on the appeal of the Prosecutor against the decision of Trial Chamber I entitled 'Decision on the consequences of non-disclosure of exculpatory materials covered by Art. 54(3)(e) agreements and the application to stay the prosecution of the accused, together with certain other issues raised at the Status Conference on 10 June 2008', (ICC-01/04-01/06 OA 13), 21 October 2008, para. 46.

[53] For an ICRC vision, see S. Jeannet, 'Testimony of ICRC delegates before the International Criminal Court', *International Review of the Red Cross*, 82(840) (2000), pp. 993–1000 (arguing that it 'would be up to the ICRC to decide whether information could be disclosed').

[54] It reads: 'The Tribunal shall regard as privileged, and consequently not subject to disclosure, including by way of testimony of present or past official or employee of the International Committee of the Red Cross (ICRC), any information, documents or other evidence which it came into possession of in the course, or as a consequence, of the performance by the ICRC of its functions under the Statutes of the International Red Cross and Red Crescent Movement.'

[55] See generally K. Dörmann and R. Geiß, 'The Implementation of Grave Breaches into Domestic Legal Orders', *Journal of International Criminal Justice*, 7 (2009), pp. 703–21; R.

for the Amelioration of the Condition of the Wounded and Sick of Armies in the Field since 1934. It drew on these experiences in the negotiation of the Geneva Conventions of 1949.[56] It proposed a set of innovations that were of key importance for the regime of the Conventions. It pushed for an express obligation of State Parties to enact 'provisions for the repression' of 'any breach of the Convention' through 'criminal penalties or appropriate disciplinary measures'.[57] Moreover, it suggested to punish 'grave breaches of the Convention' as crimes against the law of nations by the tribunals of any of the High Contracting Parties or by any international jurisdiction, the competence of which has been recognized by them'.[58] In its explanation of the proposal, the IRC noted that this regime

> may be described as a first step towards the introduction of penal legislation of an international character, since it defines as crimes "*sui generis*" offences known in ordinary parlance as "war crimes".[59]

It argued that this obligation ('shall') to punish 'grave breaches' lays 'before the conscience of the world a summary of particularly serious violations of the Convention which, if not subject to appropriate penalties, would lead to the degradation of human personality and a diminished sense of human worth'.[60]

The ICRC noted that '[a]n international tribunal would doubtless be the instrument best qualified to judge . . . breaches'.[61] But it conceded that 'it seems preferable to rely upon the joint responsibility of all signatory States for the repression of crimes against the law of nations' pending 'the establishment and regular functioning of such a court'.[62]

These proposals set the foundations for the regime of the Geneva Conventions which establishes an international obligation to prosecute grave breaches domestically.[63] They were forward looking and partly ahead of their time.[64] They embrace a focus on State obligations and domestic

van Elst, 'Implementing Universal Jurisdiction Over Grave Breaches of the Geneva Conventions', *Leiden Journal of International Law*, 13 (2000), pp. 815–854.

[56] ICRC, *Remarks and Proposals submitted by the International Committee of the Red Cross: Documents for the Consideration of Governments Invited by the Swiss Federal Council to Attend the Diplomatic Conference at Geneva*, 21 April 1949 (Geneva: ICRC, 1949), pp. 20–1.

[57] *Ibid.*, at 18, proposed Art. 39. [58] *Ibid.*, proposed Art. 40.

[59] *Ibid.*, p. 20. [60] *Ibid.* [61] *Ibid*, p. 21. [62] *Ibid.*

[63] Art. 49, 50, 129 and 146 of the four Geneva Conventions and Art. 85 (1) of Additional Protocol I.

[64] There are still considerable shortcomings towards implementation of grave breaches in domestic law. See Dörmann and Geiß, 'The Implementation of Grave Breaches', pp. 711–720.

jurisdiction over international crimes that paved a way for contemporary trends of implementing of 'core crimes' more generally.[65] They served partly as a basis for the development of the model of complementarity that is now inherent in the Rome Statute.[66]

Later, the ICRC participated actively, with observer status, in many conferences, including the process leading to the adoption of the ICC Statute. In the negotiation process of the Statute, it was mainly concerned with the list of war crimes under ICC jurisdiction. The ICRC defended the position that all grave breaches of the Geneva Conventions and of Additional Protocol I should be included in this list, in addition to other serious violations of humanitarian law. It insisted that war crimes committed in non-international armed conflicts should form part of the Statute, in order to take into account the dynamics of modern conflicts. It submitted a detailed draft list of war crimes that served as a reference document for the Preparatory Committee's work.[67]

Most notably, the ICRC took issue with a number of compromises that were made in the context of the negotiations.[68] It regretted that 'not all serious violations [of IHL] were included in the Statute and that the provisions relating to the use of certain weapons were reduced to a minimum for international armed conflict and were not included at all with respect to non-international armed conflict'.[69] The exclusions relate *inter alia* to provisions on 'delay in the repatriation of prisoners of war or civilians', the use of 'nuclear, biological and blinding laser weapons, as well

[65] The Genocide Convention contains an obligation relating to national implementation. With the growth of international criminal law, domestic implementation has extended to other categories of 'core crimes', i.e. crimes against humanity, war crimes that are not explicitly listed as 'grave breaches', and the crime of aggression'.

[66] See preamble ('duty of every State to exercise its criminal jurisdiction over those responsible for international crimes'), Art. 1, Art. 17 and Art. 19 of the ICC Statute. See generally C. Stahn and M. M. El Zeidy (eds.), *The International Criminal Court and Complementarity: From Theory to Practice* (Cambridge: Cambridge University Press, 2011).

[67] Working paper prepared by the ICRC for the Preparatory Committee for the Establishment of an International Criminal Court, New York, 13 February 1997, at www.iccnow.org/documents/3PretCmtWarCrimesRedCross.pdf. See also ICRC, Working Paper, 29 June 1999, at www.iccnow.org/documents/ICRCWorkPaperArticle8Para2e.pdf.

[68] See generally, K. Dörmann, 'Preparatory Commission for the International Criminal Court: The Elements of War Crimes', *International Review of the Red Cross*, 82(839) (2000), pp. 771–796.

[69] ICRC, Statement at the 8th Session of the Assembly of States Parties, November 2009, p. 1, at www.icc-cpi.int/iccdocs/asp_docs/ASP8/Statements/ICC-ASP-ASP8-GenDeba-ICRC-ENG.pdf.

as anti-personnel mines', or the crime of intentionally starving the civilian population in non-international armed conflict.[70] The ICRC stated that the reference to the word 'overall' in the proportionality assessment under Article 8 (2) (b) (iv) should not be interpreted as 'changing existing law'.[71]

As to weapons, the ICRC supported the inclusion of a generic rule at Rome which would prohibit the employment of 'weapons, projectiles and material and methods of warfare of a nature to cause superfluous injury or unnecessary suffering, or inherently indiscriminate'.[72] It 'hoped that the use of weapons of mass destruction, anti-personnel mines and blinded weapons would be added to the list of war crimes' at a future review conference.[73] It expressly deplored the 'opt out' clause for war crimes under Article 124, arguing that this option sends a message that war crimes might not be as serious as genocide or crimes against humanity.[74] It welcomed the amendments to Article 8 at Kampala in 2010, arguing that '[t]he adoption of the weapons amendment would initiate a sound movement towards a greater protection for civilians as well as combatants in non-international armed conflict and would bring Article 8 of the Statute more in line with the content of customary international humanitarian law'.[75]

The position of the ICRC towards the treatment of war crimes in the Rome process was thus in substance closer to the role of NGOs than to

[70] M.-C. Roberge, 'The New International Criminal Court: A Preliminary Assessment', *International Review of the Red Cross*, No. 325 (1998), p. 673.

[71] Customary Law Study, Rule 14. Proportionality in Attack, at www.icrc.org/customary-ihl/eng/print/v1_cha_chapter4_rule14 (referring to ICRC, Paper Submitted to the Working Group on the Elements of Crimes of the Preparatory Commission for the International Criminal Court, para. 190).

[72] ICRC, Working Paper, Preparatory Committee, 13 February 1997, p. 3.

[73] ICRC, Statement at the 8th Session of the Assembly of States Parties, November 2009, p. 1.

[74] Roberge, 'The New International Criminal Court', 674.

[75] ICRC, 'The weapons amendment (Art. 8.2 letter e) of the ICC Statute', March 2010, at www.iccnow.org/documents/ICRC_The_weapons_amendment.22april10.1755.pdf. See also ICRC, Statement, Ninth Assembly of States Parties to the Statute of the International Criminal Court New York, 6–10 December 2010, p. 1: 'The ICRC would like to express its satisfaction with the consensus decision of States to amend Art. 8 of the Rome Statute. The amendment added to the list of war crimes in non-international armed conflicts the use of expanding bullets, asphyxiating or poisonous gases and poison. For the ICRC, this amendment enhances protection for victims of armed conflict. The ICRC encourages States to take the amendment into consideration when implementing the ICC Statute in their domestic legal systems and stands ready to assist States in this endeavor'. The statement can be found at www.icc-cpi.int/iccdocs/asp_docs/ASP9/Statements/ICC-ASP9-GenDeba-ICRC-ENG.pdf.

the views of some powerful delegations. The Statute appears to leave space for such critiques. It preserves the possibility of entities like the ICRC to invoke different positions on customary or statutory law, by virtue of the safeguard clause in Article 10 which states that '[nothing in . . . Part [2] of the Statute shall be interpreted as limiting or prejudicing in any way existing or developing rules of international law for purposes other than this Statute'.

In the Customary Law Study, the ICRC went a step further than some ICCTs in relation to its position on amnesties. In the Lomé Amnesty case, Special Court for Sierra Leone famously held that an amnesty conferred in one jurisdiction does not necessarily bar the exercise of jurisdiction in another forum, in particular an international or a hybrid tribunal.[76] But it failed to articulate the contours of a general prohibition of amnesties under customary law. The ICC Statute remained silent and left the issue open for interpretation. Rule 159 of the Customary Law Study takes a more firm approach which is in line with UN policy. It supports the proposition that 'war crimes may not be the object of an amnesty' *per se*.[77] It bases this interpretation on duty to investigate and prosecute and the view that Article 6 (5) of Additional Protocol II was not meant 'to enable war criminals, or those guilty of crimes against humanity, to evade punishment'.[78]

The ICRC is thus acting partly as an advocate, and partly as a monitoring organ. It is at the same time guided by certain principles that mark a 'red line' for engagement. One of them is its strict commitment to the distinction between *jus in bello* and *jus ad bellum*. This separation forms a hallmark of ICRC policy.[79] It may explain why the ICRC supported the amendments to Article 8 while refraining from becoming actively engaged in relation to the crime of aggression.[80]

[76] SCSL, *Prosecutor* v. *Morris Kallon and Brima Buzzy Kamara (Jurisdiction)* (*Lomé Amnesty Case*), SCSL-2004-15-AR72(E) and SCSL-2004-16-AR72(E), Appeals Chamber, 13 March 2004, para. 86.

[77] Henckaerts and Doswald-Beck (eds.), *Customary International Humanitarian Law*, Vol. 1, p. 613.

[78] *Ibid.*, p. 612.

[79] ICRC, 'IHL and other legal regimes – jus ad bellum and jus in bello', 29 October 2010, at www.icrc.org/eng/war-and-law/ihl-other-legal-regmies/jus-in-bello-jus-ad-bellum/overview-jus-ad-bellum-jus-in-bello.htm. The ICRC states: 'IHL is purely humanitarian, seeking to limit the suffering caused. It is independent from questions about the justification or reasons for war, or its prevention, covered by jus ad bellum.'

[80] The 2010 statement of the ICRC at the ICC Assembly of State Parties is silent on the issue of aggression. On the crime of aggression, see generally C. McDougall, *The Crime of Aggression under the Rome Statute of the International Criminal Court* (Cambridge: Cambridge University Press, 2013).

IV. The ICRC and Systemic Commitment to Prevention and Compliance

In light of its competing functions and objectives, the ICRC has adopted a 'functional approach' towards international law. The need to enforce compliance with international law has never been understood as an 'absolute' rule. In 'hard cases, legal considerations are balanced against other rationales and priorities (e.g. needs of protection). Law is *inter alia* seen as an instrument to ensure greater commitment to prevention of violations and long-term compliance. The ICRC advocates these goals through advocacy, dissemination and implementation strategies. This policy contains clear normative synergies to the role of ICCTs.

The first rationale, i.e. preventing violence and violations of IHL, has formed one of the original objectives of the establishment of ICCTs. The preventive effect of criminal investigations and prosecutions remains subject to challenge from an empirical point of view[81]. But it is expressly enshrined in the founding documents of the *ad hoc* tribunals[82], the ICC[83] and contemporary doctrines, such as the Responsibility to Protect[84],

81 For an analysis, see C. Stahn, 'Between "Faith" and "Facts": By What Standards Should We Assess International Criminal Justice', *Leiden Journal of International Law*, 25 (2012), pp. 251–282; Y. Shany, 'Assessing the Effectiveness of International Court: Can the Unquantifiable be Quantified?', *Hebrew University of Jerusalem, Research Paper No. 03–10*, September 2010.

82 In its first annual report to the UN Security Council, the president of the ICTY still noted: 'One of the main aims of the Security Council [in establishing the ICTY] was to establish a judicial process capable of dissuading the parties to the conflict from perpetrating further crimes. It was hoped that, by bringing to justice those accused of massacres and similar egregious violations of international humanitarian law, both belligerents and civilians would be discouraged from committing further atrocities. In short, the Tribunal is intended to act as a powerful deterrent to all parties against continued participation in inhuman acts.' See Annual Report of the International Tribunal for the Prosecution of Persons Responsible for Serious Violations of International Humanitarian Law Committed in the Territory of the Former Yugoslavia since 1991, UN. Doc. A/49/342, S/1994/1007, 29 August 1994, para. 13. For a critical assessment, see D. F. Orentlicher, *Shrinking the Space for Denial: The Impact of the ICTY in Serbia* (New York: Open Justice Initiative, May 2008).

83 See preamble ICC Statute, para. 5 ('Determined to put an end to impunity for the perpetrators of these crimes and thus to contribute to the prevention of such crimes').

84 See e.g. Report of the Secretary-General, 'Responsibility to protect: State responsibility and prevention', UN. Doc. A/67/929–S/2013/399, 9 July 2013; J. M. Welsh and S. K. Sharma, 'Operationalizing the Responsibility to Prevent' (Oxford: Oxford Institute for Ethics, Law and Armed Conflict, 2012), at www.elac.ox.ac.uk/downloads/elac%20operationalising%20the%20responsibility%20to%20prevent.pdf. For a critical approach, see D. Chandler, 'Born Posthumously: Rethinking the Shared Characteristics of the ICC and R2P', *Finnish Yearbook of International Law*, 21 (2010), pp. 1–9.

which treat ICCTs as a key component of prevention strategies. The ICRC shares this objective. According to its mission statement the ICRC endeavours to prevent suffering, in particular by 'promoting and strengthening international humanitarian law and universal humanitarian principles.' This is *inter alia* demonstrated in its 'prevention policy'[85] and its engagement for the Arms Trade Treaty (ATT), which requires States to assess the risk of serious violations of IHL when transferring weapons.[86] This approach builds some common normative ground between ICCTs and the ICRC.

The main reason why the ICRC supported the creation of ICCTs is a functional argument. Support is grounded in the theory that ICL provides a mechanism for the enforcement of IHL. This vision may be traced back to the ICRC's reform proposals of the 'Geneva' law in the first half of the twentieth century.[87] It features prominently in current humanitarian discourse.[88] It fits easily into the language and structure of IHL. ICL is deemed to strengthen IHL because it strengthens compliance. This justification is, in particular, prominent in relation to the ICC. The ICRC endorsed the creation of the Court in part, because it has ' the capacity to act as a catalyst and as an incentive for national courts to fulfil their obligation to prosecute those who commit war crimes'.[89] It stressed the virtue of the principle of complementarity, which 'puts domestic courts at the centre of the system'. The statement of the ICRC after the adoption of the Kampala compromise is symptomatic in this regard. The ICRC stated:

> The ICRC observes that several States are seizing the opportunity to carry out a comprehensive review of their obligations under international humanitarian law (IHL) when implementing the crimes of the Rome Statute into their domestic law to comply with the principle of complementarity. We highly encourage this practice of putting the domestic

[85] 'ICRC Prevention Policy', April 2010, at www.icrc.org/eng/assets/files/publications/icrc-002-4019.pdf.

[86] See Art. 7(1) of the Arms Trade Treaty which requires a State to assess the potential that 'the conventional arms or items: (a) would contribute to or undermine peace and security; (b) could be used to: (i) commit or facilitate a serious violation of international humanitarian law; (ii) commit or facilitate a serious violation of international human rights law; (iii) commit or facilitate an act constituting an offence under international conventions or protocols relating to terrorism to which the exporting State is a Party; or (iv) commit or facilitate an act constituting an offence under international conventions or protocols relating to transnational organized crime to which the exporting State is a Party'.

[87] See above section 3.

[88] Sivakumaran, *The Law of Non-International Armed Conflict*, p. 77.

[89] See interview with La Rosa, 'ICRC and ICC'.

> implementation of the ICC Statute in the broader perspective of IHL obligations incumbent on States. We encourage States to consider, in particular, their obligations related to the repression of *all* war crimes and the effective protection of *all* victims of armed conflicts, whatever their nature.[90]

The operation of complementarity, and in particular its incentive for States to adopt implementing legislation, has strengthened the role of the ICRC in practice. The ICRC has used the standards enshrined in the ICC Statute as a 'minimum benchmark' when assisting States in their efforts to adopt and implement effective domestic measures for the prosecution of war crimes. Several States have seized the opportunity to carry out a comprehensive review of their obligations under IHL when implementing the crimes of the Rome Statute into their domestic law to comply with the principle of complementarity.[91] This mitigates the risk of a further separation of regimes.

But the conceptual foundation of the 'enforcement' narrative is increasingly open to systemic criticism. As Sandesh Sivakumaran notes, there 'is a far . . . more complex relationship between international humanitarian law and international criminal law than simply operation at the level of enforcement'.[92] The enforcement idea seems to imply that one body of law (i.e. ICL) is at the service of another body of law (i.e. IHL). This conception is artificial. It assumes a type of verticality and superimposition of IHL and ICL that has faded with the growing codification of ICL and its jurisprudence. It is more accurate to treat the two fields as autonomous, but interconnected bodies of law that are in dialogue with each other in relation to both(i) primary norms and (ii) consequences of violations.[93]

V. Patterns of Interaction Between the ICRC and ICCTs

It is clear from ICRC policies towards ICL ('structural independence', 'strategic engagement' and 'systemic support' for prevention and

[90] ICRC, Statement, Ninth Assembly of States Parties to the Statute of the International Criminal Court, p. 2.

[91] For a survey, see Dörmann and Geiß, 'The Implementation of Grave Breaches', 703–721; Van Elst, 'Implementing Universal Jurisdiction Over Grave Breaches', 815–854; O. Bekou, 'In the hands of the state: implementing legislation and complementarity' in C. Stahn and M. M. El Zeidy (eds.), *The International Criminal Court and Complementarity: From Theory to Practice*, pp. 830, 841–850.

[92] Sivakumaran, *The Law of Non-International Armed Conflict*, 77.

[93] See also below Section 6.

compliance) that the ICRC and ICCTs differ in their rationales and approaches towards law. They may adopt different stances and interpretations of primary norms. But they share at the same time certain common points of understanding. One of the most important synergies lies in the methodology towards the development of the law.

Both, the ICRC and ICCTs have played a dynamic role in shaping ICL. ICCTs have assumed this function based on a creative interpretation of their judicial mandate.[94] The ICRC has derived this role from its statutory mandate. It has exercised influence through involvement in the norm-creating process, soft law instruments and academic commentary, such as the Customary Law Study, the Commentary on the Geneva Conventions, or interpretive guidance, such as the Interpretive Guideline on Direct Participation in hostilities[95]. It has at the same time been receptive to impulses from ICL jurisprudence. Some common ground may be found in (i) similar methodologies and (ii) instances of cross-fertilisation.

1. *Shared Methodologies*

One of the most striking shared features is their approach towards the development of the law. ICTY President Theodor Meron noted this point explicitly. He stated:

> Both the ICTY and the ICRC study have eschewed the more relaxed approach that has typically characterized modern discussions of customary international law. The two institutions share a synergy in their approach in re-establishing the centrality of customary humanitarian law.[96]

This is evidenced by practice. International courts and tribunals have acted as 'customary midwives', and operated 'within, rather than outside, the process of formation of custom'.[97] They have typically made reference to the general criteria used in ICJ jurisprudence, but applied them in a more flexible and dynamic fashion. One manifest deviation from general international law is the lesser importance attached to State practice which is traditionally a requirement of equal rank. The ICTY justified this

[94] On 'judicial creativity', see Darcy and Powderly, 'The Reinvention of War Crimes'.

[95] N. Melzer, *Interpretative Guidance on the notion of Direct Participation in Hostilities under International Humanitarian Law* (Geneva: ICRC, 2009), at www.icrc.org/eng/assets/files/other/icrc-002–0990.pdf. See also Chapter 4 in this volume.

[96] Meron, 'The Humanization of Humanitarian Law', p. 38.

[97] For a discussion, see G. Mettraux, *International Crimes and the Ad Hoc Tribunals* (Oxford: Oxford University Press, 2005), p. 15.

approach in *Kupreskić*, by reference to the *Martens* clause.[98] The Chamber argued that this 'new' approach towards the establishment of custom was justified by the transformation of humanitarian law and the 'humanisation of armed conflict'.[99]

This prioritisation provided the conceptual space to apply a different methodology in relation to determining custom: namely to derive '*opinio juris*' from primary sources (e.g. treaties), other instruments of international law (e.g. UN documents) or judicial decisions, and to support the alleged authority subsequently by reference to some instances of practice.[100] The Tribunals have *inter alia* relied on the caselaw of domestic courts, military law, UN resolutions or even practice by non-State actors (i.e. the findings of the ICRC), often without analysing in detail to what extent they constitute evidence of State practice or '*opinion juris*' under Article 38 of the ICJ Statute.

This approach has significantly broadened the spectrum of evidence available to establish the existence of a customary rule.[101] In some instances, lack of opposition by States to a specific judicial ruling was deemed sufficient to support the existence of a rule.[102] In other instances,

[98] *Prosecutor* v. *Kupreskić* (IT-95–16-T), para. 527. It noted: 'This is [. . .] an area where *opinio iuris sive necessitatis* may play a much greater role than *usus*, as a result of the aforementioned Martens Clause. In the light of the way States and courts have implemented it, this Clause clearly shows that principles of international humanitarian law may emerge through a customary process under the pressure of the demands of humanity or the dictates of public conscience, even where State practice is scant or inconsistent. The other element, in the form of *opinio necessitatis*, crystallising as a result of the imperatives of humanity or public conscience, may turn out to be the decisive element heralding the emergence of a general rule or principle of humanitarian law'.

[99] *Ibid.*, para. 529. See also A. Zahar, 'Civilizing Civil War: Writing Morality as Law at the ICTY' in B. Swart, A. Zahar and G. Sluiter (eds.), *The Legacy of the International Criminal Tribunal for the Former Yugoslavia* (Oxford: Oxford University Press, 2011), pp. 469–505.

[100] The late Antonio Cassese famously noted: 'in the area of international criminal law [. . .] a set of judicial findings plus some appropriate *obiter dicta* on a few important legal side issues may contribute to the determination of applicable customary international law rules and principles, as well as to the proper construction of treaties and other written international rules'. See A. Cassese, 'The ICTY: A Living and Vital Reality', *Journal of International Criminal Justice*, 2 (2004), p. 590.

[101] The first report by ICL Rapporteur M. Wood notes: 'Notwithstanding the specific contexts in which these other courts and tribunals work, overall there is substantial reliance on the approach and case law of the International Court of Justice, including the constitutive role attributed to the two elements of State practice and opinio juris.' See ICL, First report on formation and evidence of customary international law, UN Doc. A/CN.4/663, 17 May 2013, para. 66.

[102] STL Appeals Chamber, Interlocutory Decision on the Applicable Law: Terrorism, Conspiracy, Homicide, Perpetration, Cumulative Charging (STL-11–01/I), 16 February 2011,

norms have been branded as custom, without much reasoning or express authority for that conclusion.[103]

This method has facilitated a fictional cycle. Once customary international law was established in jurisprudence, the Tribunals relied on precedent to consolidate the finding, 'rather than repeatedly engaging in detailed analysis of the customary status of the same principles in every case'.[104] This approach was again adopted by the Special Tribunal for Lebanon, in its decision establishing terrorism as an international crime.[105]

A similar methodology is reflected in the Customary Law Study. It displayed some scepticism towards judge-made law, while referring to Nuremberg.[106] But it gave considerable weight to decisions of ICCTs as a subsidiary source of international law. It noted:

> Their decisions have . . . been included because a finding by an international court that a rule of customary international law exists constitutes persuasive evidence to hat effect. In addition, because of the precedential value of their decision international courts can also contribute to the emergence of a rule of customary law by influencing the subsequent practice of States and international organizations.[107]

para. 47 ('The extensive practice of international courts and tribunals to make use of their inherent powers and the lack of any objection by States, non-State actors or other interested parties evince the existence of a general rule of international law granting such inherent jurisdiction. The combination of a string of decisions in the field, coupled with the implicit acceptance or acquiescence of all the international subjects concerned, clearly indicates the existence of the practice and *opinio juris* necessary for holding that a customary rule of international law has evolved').

[103] See e.g. with respect to the elements of crimes against humanity or war crimes in the jurisprudence of the ICTR, L. van den Herik, *The Contribution of the Rwanda Tribunal to the Development of International Law* (Leiden: Brill, 2005), p. 275. Some authors have pointed to customary law as a 'sliding-scale'. See F. Kirgis, 'Custom on a Sliding Scale', *American Journal of International Law*, 81(1) (1987), pp. 146, 149.

[104] Meron, 'The Humanization of Humanitarian Law', p. 31. *Ibid*., p. 37 ('In some cases [. . .] the Tribunal's assessments of the evidence supporting the relevant customary law principles have been comparatively brief. In most of these cases, the Tribunal has relied on its own precedents instead of revisiting the same issues repetitively').

[105] STL Appeals Chamber (STL-11-01/I), para. 85. The Appeals Chamber concluded that 'a number of treaties, UN resolutions, and the legislative and judicial practice of States evince the formation of a general *opinio juris* in the international community, accompanied by a practice consistent with such opinion, to the effect that a customary rule of international law regarding the international crime of terrorism, at least in time of peace has indeed emerged'.

[106] See Henckaerts and Doswald-Beck (eds.), *Customary International Humanitarian Law*, Vol. 1, p. xliii.

[107] *Ibid*., p. xxxiv.

ICCTS and the ICRC thus appear to share an inclination towards creativity in relation to the establishment of custom. In this sense, they may have colluded.

2. *Use of Authority and Cross-Fertilisation*

In existing case law, there are relatively few cases in which ICCTs relied expressly on findings of the ICRC as authority or evidence. But there are some examples.

Judges have, first of all, referred to ICRC Commentaries in jurisprudence.[108] Commentaries are not a formal source of law within the meaning of Article 38 of the Statute of the International Court of Justice, nor a subsidiary means for the determination of rules of law.[109] The Commentaries serve as supplementary material, i.e. to assist with determining the correct interpretation of a treaty provision, in line with Article 32 of the Vienna Convention on the Law of Treaties. They are a means of authority, but not a determinative source for assisting courts (and States) in interpreting the Conventions and Protocols pursuant to the Vienna Convention on the Law of Treaties 1969 and customary international law.

ICCTs have also resorted to ICRC positions reflected in instruments, such as the Customary Law Study or the Interpretive Guideline on Direct Participation in Hostilities. For instance, the Customary Law Study has been heavily shaped by the case law of ICCTs. It has then in turn been taken up in jurisprudence. In the *Stakić* Appeal, the ICTY used the Study as evidence of the definition of deportation under customary law.[110] In *Hadzihasanović*, the ICTY Appeals Chamber relied on the study to support the finding that wanton destruction of cities, plunder and destruction of institutions related to religion, and attacks on civilian

[108] See J. Pictet, (ed.), *Commentary on the Geneva Conventions of 12 August 1949* (Geneva: ICRC, 1952); ICRC, *Commentary on the Additional Protocols of 8 June 1977* (Geneva: ICRC, 1987) and ICRC, 1949 Conventions and Additional Protocols, and their Commentaries, at www.icrc.org/applic/ihl/ihl.nsf/vwTreaties1949.xsp. See generally M. Bohlander, 'The Influence of Academic Research on the Jurisprudence of the International Criminal Tribunal for the Former Yugoslavia: A First Overview', *Yearbook of International Law and Jurisprudence*, 1 (2003), pp. 195–209.

[109] On 'scholarship' as a source of law, see M. Wood, 'Teachings of the Most Highly Qualified Publicists (Art. 38 (1) ICJ Statute)' in R. Wolfrum (ed.), *The Max Planck Encyclopedia of Public International Law* (Oxford: Oxford University Press, 2012), p. 783.

[110] See ICTY, *Prosecutor* v. *Stakić* (IT-97-24-A), paras 296–7 (with reference to Rule 129).

objects more broadly are customary rules triggering individual criminal responsibility.[111]

The Interpretive Guideline on Direct Participation in Hostilities has been influenced by case law of the *ad hoc* tribunals, in relation to elements such as the notion of civilian for the purposes of the principle of distinction (*Martić* Appeal)[112] or the distinction between direct and indirect participation (*Strugar* Appeal).[113] It is relevant to future case law.

The Defence invoked the DPH Guideline in *Lubanga*.[114] Curiously, the Trial Chamber made no reference to the Guideline in its reasoning. It visibly struggled with the distinction between 'active participation' and 'direct participation', and its implications for the crime of using children in hostilities. The Majority found that 'active' and 'direct' participation are distinct concepts and that 'active' implies a wider range of activities than 'direct'.[115] This deviates from the conception in the ICRC's Guideline where the

[111] See ICTY, Appeals Chamber, *Prosecutor* v. *Hadzihasanović and Kubura*, Decision on Joint Defence Interlocutory Appeal of Trial Chamber Decision on Rule 98b is Motions for Acquittal (IT-01-46-AR73.3), 11 March 2005, para. 30 ('The ICRC notes that this prohibition is contained in numerous military manuals that are applicable in or have been applied in international and non-international armed conflict').

[112] The DPH study shared the understanding of *Martić* which held that 'civilians in the context of non-international armed conflicts can be defined as those persons who do not belong to the armed forces, militias or volunteer corps forming part of such armed forces, organised resistance groups or a *levée en masse*'. See *Prosecutor* v. *Martić* (IT-95-11-A), para. 300.

[113] See ICTY, Appeals Chamber, *Prosecutor* v. *Strugar* (IT-01-42-A), Judgment, 7 July 2008, para. 177. The Chamber found that examples of 'active or direct participation in hostilities' include: 'bearing, using or taking up arms, taking part in military or hostile acts, activities, conduct or operations, armed fighting or combat, participating in attacks against enemy personnel, property or equipment, transmitting military information for the immediate use of a belligerent, transporting weapons in proximity to combat operations, and serving as guards, intelligence agents, lookouts, or observers on behalf of military forces'. It found that examples of 'indirect participation in hostilities' include: 'participating in activities in support of the war or military effort of one of the parties to the conflict, selling goods to one of the parties to the conflict, expressing sympathy for the cause of one of the parties to the conflict, failing to act to prevent an incursion by one of the parties to the conflict, accompanying and supplying food to one of the parties to the conflict, gathering and transmitting military information, transporting arms and munitions, and providing supplies, and providing specialist advice regarding the selection of military personnel, their training or the correct maintenance of the weapons'.

[114] See ICC Trial Chamber, *Prosecutor* v. *Lubanga*, Judgment pursuant to Art. 74 of the Statute, ICC-01/04-01/06, 14 March 2012, para. 585.

[115] *Ibid.*, paras 627–8. For analysis, see K. Ambos, 'The First Judgment of the International Criminal Court (*Prosecutor* v. *Lubanga*): A Comprehensive Analysis of the Legal Issues', *International Criminal Law Review*, 12 (2012), pp. 1–45; N. Wagner, 'A Critical Assessment of Using Children to Participate Actively in Hostilities in Lubanga Child Soldiers and Direct Participation', *Criminal Law Forum*, 24 (2013), p. 145.

terms 'active' and 'direct' are treated as synonymous[116], and previous ICTR jurisprudence.[117] The notions are thus partially treated differently in ICL jurisprudence and IHL. The ICC adopted this wide interpretation[118] in order to ensure effective protection for children who do not participate in frontline activities, but are essential to combat. It noted:

> The decisive factor, therefore, in deciding if an 'indirect' role is to be treated as active participation in hostilities is whether the support provided by the child to the combatants exposed him or her to real danger as a potential target.[119]

The Trial Chamber was guided by submissions by the UN Special Representative of the Secretary General on Children and Armed Conflict.[120] The wide definition of 'active' participation and the restrictive reading of 'direct' may have negative side effects. It may potentially lessen protection under Common Article III[121] and Article 8 (c) of the ICC Statute, since children run the risk of being considered as 'active' participants in hostilities. The narrow construction of 'direct' participation may broaden the option to attack civilians not engaged in frontline combat. The reasoning might thus be counterproductive, if it is transposed to other contexts.

VI. Towards a More Systemic Relationship

In official discourse and practice, the ICRC and ICCTs have tended to present IHL and ICL as complementary projects that strengthen and support each other. This strategy is appealing. Both entities derive legitimacy from this normative stance. It supports the development of the law that is inherent in the work of each of these institutions. But it has inherent downsides. It silences risks, frictions and contradictions between these bodies of law. These 'darker sides' need to be addressed with the growing

116 Melzer, *Interpretative Guidance*, pp. 43–44.

117 For a synonymous meaning of the notions of 'active' and 'direct' participation in hostilities, see ICTR, *Prosecutor* v. *Akayesu* (ICTR -96–4-T), Judgment of 2 September 1998, para. 629.

118 See *Prosecutor* v. *Lubanga*, ICC-01/04–01/06, para. 627 ('The use of the expression "to participate actively in hostilities", as opposed to the expression "direct participation", as found in Additional Protocol I to the Geneva Conventions, was clearly intended to import a wide interpretation to the activities and roles that are covered by the offence of using children under the age of 15 actively to participate in hostilities').

119 *Ibid.*, para. 628.

120 *Ibid.*, para. 626.

121 It states that '[p]ersons taking no active part in the hostilities . . . shall in all circumstances be treated humanely . . . '

maturation and development of the respective fields. Both ICL and IHL rely on legal certainty and clarity. In ICL, norm certainty is required under the principle of legality.[122] In IHL, it is a pragmatic imperative needed to make the law operational in the battlefield. It is thus fundamental for international criminal justice and humanitarian law to rethink interaction from a systemic perspective.

The ICRC and ICCTs are actors in a polycentric legal system. This requires normative interaction and mutual checks and balances. It is, in particular, necessary to strengthen critical inquiry among both constituencies. The development of ICL and IHL requires open discourse on feasibility and limits of core concepts, vigilance towards the implications of specific choices on other fields of law. Two set of questions deserve further attention: (i) the broader conceptualisation of the relationship between IHL and ICL in international practice, and (ii) and the role of the ICRC towards criminal proceedings.

1. The Relationship Between IHL and ICL

The first key aspect is treatment of the interaction between IHL and ICL. This relationship merits greater consideration. Some core understandings are subject to challenge.

First of all, it is increasingly artificial to treat ICL and IHL as distinct and mutually exclusive areas that operate under the 'guardianship' of a specific institution. ICL does not operate in isolation of IHL, nor does IHL operate in isolation of ICL. In most contexts, they are directly interrelated. In light of this, it is difficult to define or divide institutional responsibilities in terms of allegiance to a specific body of law, i.e. IHL or ICL.[123] Institutions on both ends must thus operate with a pluralist mindset.

Secondly, approaches towards interaction are in need of rethinking. The two bodies of law are connected on multiple levels: (i) the formation and interpretation of norms, and (ii) their application and enforcement. The theory that ICL is a linear enforcement tool for IHL is subject to critical scrutiny.[124] The enforcement theory assumes a degree of symmetry between IHL and ICL that has been blurred in past years. ICL has partly grown into an autonomous system. This creates a need for greater vigilance in institutional interaction.

[122] See e.g. Art. 22 of the ICC Statute.

[123] See also Sivakumaran, *The Law of Non-International Armed Conflict*, pp. 77–79.

[124] *Ibid.*, pp. 82–83.

Thirdly, it is problematic to draw a demarcation line between mandates and responsibilities of the ICRC and ICCTs on the basis of a formal distinction between primary rules (i.e. prohibitions) and consequences of violations. It is unhelpful to argue that the ICRC serves primarily as a 'watchdog' over primary rules of behaviour, while ICCTs have a leading role in relation to 'secondary rules', i.e. consequences of violations.[125] In practice, ICCTs have reshaped foundations of IHL. They have occasionally set standards that are difficult to comply with by States. They have further extended the obligations of non-State armed groups. This makes it necessary to strengthen options for mutual dialogue and critical engagement, including checks and balances. As Charles Garraway noted:

> If States find that customary law is being used to 'raise the bar' so that requirements are being imposed which States would not be prepared to accept at the conference table on grounds of practicality, then the whole structure of customary law, as providing a foundation for treaty law and underpinning the legal system, may be cast in doubt.[126]

The ICRC could play an important role in improving the *status quo*. It could serve as a 'reality check' for the development of ICL.

2. *Rethinking Interaction*

As shown earlier, the ICRC has thus far adopted a rather cautious approach towards ICL practice and judicial proceedings. Institutional action has largely been dictated by 'strategic engagement' and a 'functional' approach towards law.[127] This approach is rooted in the competing rationales of the organisation. The balancing of these objectives might deserve further attention in light of the dynamic transformation of international law, and its applicability to a growing range of actors.

Two concrete suggestions might provide some ground for improvement. The first one is of a formal nature. It relates to the clarification of the status of ICRC positions. In current practice, it is often unclear what value the ICRC attaches to a specific position. Guidance on legal views is contained in a range of sources, ranging from interviews, to policy papers, books and guidance notes. It remains somewhat uncertain to what extent specific positions are attached to the ICRC or their representatives. This

[125] *Ibid.*, p. 77.
[126] See C. Garraway, 'War Crimes' in Wilmshurst and Breau (eds.), pp. 377, 397.
[127] See above Sections 2 and 3.

compromises their authority and their ability to clarify the status of the law.

Secondly, the very mandate of the ICRC seems to leave some leeway for a greater degree of interaction with ICCTs. At present, this interaction is mainly organized through political or informal channels. Human rights organisations have taken the lead in shaping legal processes and key debates (e.g. *Lubanga*). IHL perspectives are often sidelined or underrepresented in the Courtroom, since they are communicated or mediated through the voice of the Prosecution. The ICRC might take a greater stance in this regard. It could use its role as 'guardian' and 'promoter' of the development of the law more actively to communicate its position on core legal issues in proceedings. It might, for instance, make greater use of the ability to intervene as *amicus* in proceedings, as it did in *Simić et al.*[128] This would not require it to deviate from its operational commitment to confidentiality in the exercise of its 'protective function'. It would be a natural application of its role as 'guardian' and its mandate in relation to the development of law.

[128] See Interview with La Rosa, 'ICRC and ICC'.

PART IV

Conclusion

7

The International Committee of the Red Cross: A Unique Actor in the Field of International Humanitarian Law Creation and Progressive Development

ROBIN GEIß AND ANDREAS ZIMMERMANN

I. Introduction

The International Committee of the Red Cross (ICRC) is often depicted and often describes itself as the 'guardian and promoter' and indeed as the 'main driving force' of international humanitarian law (IHL).[1] But over the past 150 years the ICRC's role in influencing the development of the laws of armed conflict has rarely been homogenous. In some instances the ICRC had a decisive, unequivocally accepted role in humanitarian norm development and was even tasked and trusted by the international community to provide initial drafts for major codification projects. On various other occasions, however, its influence was much more subtle, indirect and, at times, highly controversial. As the rather unsatisfactory outcomes of the recent 32nd International Red Cross and Red Crescent Conference in December 2015 confirm[2], humanitarian norm development is, at

[1] See only F. Bugnion, 'The International Committee of the Red Cross and the Development of International Humanitarian Law', *Chicago Journal of International Law*, 5 No. 1 (2004), pp. 191–215. See Y. Sandoz, 'The International Committee of the Red Cross as Guardian of International Humanitarian Law', ICRC Resource Centre (Dec. 31, 1998), available at: www.icrc.org/eng/resources/documents/misc/about-the-icrc-311298.htm.

[2] Resolution 1 'Strengthening international humanitarian law protecting persons deprived of their liberty' (32IC/15/R1) and Resolution 2 'Strengthening compliance with international humanitarian law' (32IC/15/R2), available at: www.rcrcconference.org/international-conference/documents; fall far short of what the ICRC had originally envisaged; see only e.g. G. Bartolini, 'The compliance track on a track to nowhere', *EJIL-Talk* (22 January 2016), available at: www.ejiltalk.org/the-compliance-track-on-a-track-to-nowhere/.

least normally, a lengthy and arduous business, and far from every ICRC initiative ends up as a success.

Nonetheless, the ICRC's 'special role' in the area of humanitarian norm development and clarification is beyond dispute.[3] Consistently, over a period of more than 150 years, its influence (especially on the so-called Geneva Law) has been decisive.[4] No other 'non-State actor' – not even the International Law Commission (ILC) – has ever been formally tasked by States to carry out a norm clarification and codification project of the magnitude of the international customary humanitarian law study, or was tasked to develop preliminary drafts for a treaty project as comprehensive as the four Geneva Conventions of 1949. Viewed in the context of the historic development of public international law generally, the fact that a non-State actor like the ICRC should have had such a significant impact on the (historic) development of the laws of armed conflict – out of all areas of international law – is rather astounding. After all, IHL is one of the oldest branches of public international law and one that more than most other branches of international law directly touches upon States' fundamental security interests. As such – and in spite of the extension of its scope of application also to non-State actors through Common Article 3 GC I-IV in 1949 – IHL is traditionally and inherently State-centric. But this State-centric focus notwithstanding, the ICRC – together only with the Holy See – is a very early example of (decisive) non-State actor influence with regard to law making and norm development, and, what is more, a non-governmental organisation whose influence – in spite of regular setbacks – has gradually and significantly grown over time.

[3] 'The role which the International Committee of the Red Cross (ICRC) assumes with regard to the Geneva Conventions and the Additional Protocols is a case apart', see G. Nolte, 'First report on subsequent agreements and subsequent practice in relation to treaty interpretation', A /CN.4/660, 19 March 2013, para. 141. An ICTY Trial Chamber in its Decision of 27 July 1999 in the case *Prosecutor* v. *Simiç et al.* concluded that 'the ICRC is a unique entity and institution, possessing an international legal personality and a special status in international law. See also M. N. Schmitt and S. Watts, 'The Decline of International Humanitarian Law *Opinio Juris* and the Law of Cyber Warfare', *Texas International Law Journal*, 50 No. 2 (2014–15), p. 189, 192: 'The ICRC is undoubtedly the most influential single body in the field; indeed, few organizations or States field the IHL expertise or experience of its impressive Legal Division'.

[4] S. R. Ratner, 'Law Promotion Beyond Law Talk: The Red Cross, Persuasion, and the Laws of War', *European Journal of International Law*, 22 No. 2 (2011), pp. 459–506; D. Palmieri, 'An institution standing the test of time? A review of 150 years of the history of the International Committee of the Red Cross', *International Review of the Red Cross*, 94 No. 888 (2012), pp. 1273–1298.

It is against this backdrop that this book sets out to take stock of the ICRC's historic and contemporary role in (promoting) the development of international humanitarian law, i.e. its codification and progressive development. Naturally and to state the obvious, as has rightly been stated elsewhere[5], analyzing more than 150 years of activity of the oldest humanitarian organisation requires a certain degree of selectivity.[6] After all, the ICRC works along the entire spectrum of normative development ranging from the identification of protective loopholes in the legal architecture to the presentation of fully developed draft treaty proposals, and, over time, has been involved in uncountable major and minor norm development and clarification activities. Contributions in this volume have therefore, primarily by way of process tracing, focused on normative milestone projects in which the ICRC assumed a rather formal and clearly discernible role. Building on these insights the concluding chapter aims to provide a more general bird-eye's evaluation of the ICRC's past, contemporary and future role in humanitarian norm creation and development and to lay open the distinct characteristics that explain the ICRC's influence on the development of IHL. It also aims to analyze the ICRC's unique role as a 'norm developer' in the field of IHL, as compared to the role of other non-State actors when it comes to other different, albeit related, fields of international law, such as human rights law.

To this end, the conclusion will first of all consider the ICRC's historic development from a philanthropic private association into an influential stakeholder in the field of international humanitarian law. Secondly, it will consider the organisation's versatile *modus operandi*, namely its multifaceted working methods including the various channels and 'entry points' through which it seeks to influence relevant stakeholders and the different approaches, strategies, and methods of interaction the ICRC has adopted at different times and with regard to different projects.[7] In doing so, the conclusion will also try to give due regard to the various indirect and informal ways in which the ICRC attempts to exert its influence on international law development processes. Obviously, tracing and identifying such indirect ways of influence is particularly challenging, and even more so when dealing with an organisation whose work is often based on 'silent diplomacy' and whose activities are at least to some degree shrouded in

5 Palmieri, 'An institution standing the test of time?', p. 1273, 1274. 6 *Ibid.*

7 See Ratner, 'Law Promotion Beyond Law Talk', pp. 459–506; from whom the term 'entry points' is borrowed.

secrecy.[8] But even if these informal ways of influence can at best be approximated by estimation, it seems justified to assume that the overall impact of these various informal activities on the progressive development of IHL at least equals the ICRC's formal involvement in law development processes of the past.

In a third step, this contribution will then present three explanatory strands for the ICRC's 'special role' and long-standing influence on the development of IHL. Finally, in a fourth step, the concluding chapter will consider the challenges to the ICRC's role as a humanitarian norm 'entrepreneur' and provide an outlook on how the ICRC's role in humanitarian norm creation and development – after some recent setbacks – is likely to develop in the future.

II. From Philanthropic Private Association to Global Humanitarian Norm Entrepreneur

Who would have thought at the time of its inception in 1863[9], when a five-member organisation of private individuals was formed in Geneva as a philanthropic private association under the Swiss Civil Code[10] – initially referred to as the 'Committee of Five', the 'Geneva Committee', or the 'Permanent International Committee'[11] – that this entity would develop into an over 12,000 staff humanitarian organisation, operative in some eighty countries across the globe?[12] This 'Geneva Committee' also became the starting point for what subsequently developed into the International Red Cross and Red Crescent Movement, i.e. the world's largest humanitarian network of 80 million people consisting of the ICRC, the International

[8] S. R. Ratner, 'Behind the Flag of Dunant: Secrecy and the Compliance Mission of the International Committee of the Red Cross' in A. Bianchi and A. Peters (eds.), *Transparency in International Law* (Cambridge: Cambridge University Press, 2013), pp. 297–320.

[9] H. Dunant, *A Memory of Solferino* (Geneva: ICRC Geneva, 1986 reprint).

[10] H.-P. Gasser, 'International Committee of the Red Cross (ICRC)', *Max Planck Encyclopedia of Public International Law* (October 2015), para. 20, available at: www.mpepil.com.

[11] F. Bugnion, *The International Committee of the Red Cross and the Protection of War Victims* (ICRC, 2003).

[12] See generally the ICRC's most recent Operations Report 2014, ICRC Resource Centre (12 May 2015), available at: www.icrc.org/en/document/ICRC-annual-report-2014; P. Boissier, *History of the International Committee of the Red Cross, Vol. I: From Solferino to Tsushima* (Henry Dunant Institute, 1985); A. Durand, *History of the International Committee of the Red Cross, Vol. II: From Sarajevo to Hiroshima* (Geneva: Henry Dunant Institute, 1984); C. Moorehead, *Dunant's Dream: War, Switzerland and the History of the Red Cross* (New York: Carroll & Graf Publishers, 1998).

Federation of the Red Cross and Red Crescent Societies and 190 National Red Cross and Red Crescent Societies.[13]

For the first 50 years of its existence the ICRC remained small in size (10 members by 1914) and regional in its focus.[14] During this period the ICRC's operational focus was (*de facto*) limited to the 'big conflicts between the major European powers'[15], albeit from the outset the organisation retained the option of expanding its mandate geographically 'later, after a few more years of experience'[16], to other conflicts in other regions of the world in the fulfillment of its principle of universality. The substantive focus of its activities, in line with the international humanitarian law in force at the time, and namely the 1864 Geneva Convention for the Amelioration of the Condition of the Wounded in Armies in the Field ('1864 Geneva Convention'), was likewise limited to some narrowly defined categories of protected persons and victims of armed conflict, in particular initially wounded military personnel.

World War I and subsequently World War II brought about a profound transformation of the ICRC with a lasting impact on, and expansion of, the organisation's institutional structure, geographical reach and areas of activity.[17] Indeed, many of the organisation's contemporary institutional features and characteristics can be traced back to the transformations in the wake of World War I.[18] Starting in 1914 the ICRC's staff grew exponentially; the protection (and later repatriation) of prisoners of war now became a core focus of the organisation's activity, complemented by intensified humanitarian diplomacy and efforts to ensure (better) compliance with the existing body of humanitarian law as it stood at the time. It was in the context of the repatriation of prisoners of war that the ICRC also started to set up international delegations and to deploy staff abroad on a large scale. In addition to an expansion of its geographical reach, the ICRC also started to engage in a new range of activities, including

[13] The International Red Cross and Red Crescent Movement, ICRC Resource Centre, available at: www.icrc.org/en/who-we-are/movement.

[14] D. Palmieri, 'The International Committee of the Red Cross in the First World War', ICRC Resource Centre (10 September 2014), available at: www.icrc.org/en/document/international-committee-red-cross-first-world-war-0.

[15] ICRC Archives A PV, Minutes, Commission spéciale de la Société, 17 February 1863 as cited in Palmieri, 'An institution standing the test of time?', 1273, 1274, fn. 3.

[16] *Ibid.*

[17] CICR, *Rapport général du Comité international de la Croix-Rouge sur son activité de 1912 à 1920* (Genève, 30 mars 1921).

[18] See generally Palmieri, 'The International Committee of the Red Cross in the First World War'.

the protection of civilians and the delivery of humanitarian aid materials.[19] What is more, and particularly relevant when it comes to the development of IHL, the ICRC no longer confined itself to work in international armed conflicts but also began to focus on 'other situations of violence' such as e.g. in Russia, Silesia, Ukraine and during the revolutionary upheavals in Hungary in 1919. The same holds true for the Spanish Civil War.[20] In view of the ensuing mechanisation of warfare, the ICRC also started to turn its attention to (the regulation and prohibition of) new means and methods of warfare.[21]

World War II again drew the ICRC's attention to new contexts of violence and situations related to armed conflict, in particular occupied territories, as well as new categories of persons requiring protection, namely and above all the civilian population, but also missing persons, refugees and (internally) displaced persons, as well as generally women and children. With the adoption of first, Common Article 3 GC I-IV in 1949, and later Additional Protocol II of 1977 and the ensuing formal broadening of the scope of application of IHL now also covering non-international armed conflicts, the ICRC in parallel also gradually expanded its engagement in such types of armed conflicts, which, as of today, are the priority domain of its humanitarian activities. And the 'merger' of the formerly distinct categories of 'Geneva Law' and 'Hague Law' by virtue of Additional Protocol I of 1977, bringing the issue of means and methods of warfare, traditionally regulated by 'Hague Law', i.e. the more State-centered Hague Conventions of 1907, within the realm of the Geneva Conventions, the traditional turf of the ICRC ever since 1964, allowed the ICRC to also focus more closely on the actual conduct of hostilities, rather than merely *ex post facto* taking care of the victims of armed conflicts.

Apart from its operational work in the field, from the moment of its inception up until today, the ICRC's humanitarian work and mandate have always been closely and indeed inextricably linked to its legal work. Thus, already Henry Dunant, the inspirer and most prominent founder of the ICRC, in order to facilitate humanitarian aid work in the field,

[19] *Ibid.* [20] *Ibid.*

[21] R. Geiß, 'The law of weaponry from 1914 to 2014: Is the law keeping pace with technological evolution in the military domain?' in A. V. Arnauld et al. (eds.), *Essays in Honour of the 100th Anniversary of the Walther Schücking Institute for International Law* (Berlin: Duncker & Humblot, 2014), pp. 229–248. Thus, on 8 February 1918 the ICRC 'went beyond its traditional remit' and urged belligerents to refrain from using 'asphyxiant and poisonous gases', cited by Palmieri, 'The International Committee of the Red Cross in the First World War'.

proposed the adoption of an international agreement.[22] After the success of the First Geneva Convention in 1864 – by 1907 the First Geneva Convention had achieved 57 ratifications, and had thereby reached an almost universal treaty membership, and also become the legal basis of the ICRC's work – the organisation continuously lobbied for its expansion. It was in this vein, that as early as 1868, i.e. only four years after the adoption of the First Geneva Convention, the ICRC, together with the International Conference of the Red Cross Societies, as it was then still called, sought to expand humanitarian legal protection to naval forces through the so-called 'Additional Articles relating to the Condition of the Wounded in War'.[23] While this proved to be a somewhat premature and therefore unsuccessful attempt since the 'Additional Articles' never entered into force and the United States remained the only state to ratify them in 1882[24], it shows how important continuous humanitarian law development was to the ICRC from early on. This attempt to enlarge the scope of application of IHL by way of an additional formal instrument also constitutes an early example of how persistence, combined with the ability to sustain pressure and to lobby for legal development over a long period of time, eventually pays off. Although the ICRC was not directly involved, the First Hague Peace Conference of 1899 finally adopted the Hague Convention (III) for the Adaptation to Maritime Warfare of the Principles of the Geneva Convention of 22 August 1864,[25] *mutatis mutandis* in line with the 1868 Additional Articles, then proposed by the ICRC.

In 1906, the ICRC succeeded again in further expanding the substantive scope of the body of international humanitarian law. That year, the 1864 Geneva Convention was revised and – subject to Article 31 of the 1906 Geneva Convention for the Amelioration of the Condition of the Wounded in Armies in the Field– superseded by that latter agreement, thereby expanding the legal framework from initially 10 Articles (1864) to 33 Articles (1906), which now for the first time explicitly mentioned

[22] Dunant, *A Memory of Solferino*.

[23] Additional Articles relating to the Condition of the Wounded in War. Geneva, 20 October 1868, ICRC Treaty Database, available at: www.ihl-databases.icrc.org/applic/ihl/ihl.nsf/Treaty.xsp?documentId=ECB39EA050F80A5DC12563CD002D6624&action=openDocument.

[24] See ICRC Treaty Database, available at: www.icrc.org/applic/ihl/ihl.nsf/States.xsp?xp_viewStates=XPages_NORMStatesParties&xp_treatySelected=125.

[25] Convention (III) for the Adaptation to Maritime Warfare of the Principles of the Geneva Convention of 22 August 1864. The Hague, 29 July 1899, ICRC Treaty Database, available at: www.ihl-databases.icrc.org/applic/ihl/ihl.nsf/Treaty.xsp?documentId=2B134D111958C73AC12563CD002D66C8&action=openDocument.

and recognized voluntary aid societies (Article 10).[26] During the interwar period, and even more so after the end of World War II, this trend of substantive deepening of existing legal protections, combined with a regulative expansion into new areas, gained new and unprecedented momentum, simultaneously further consolidating and enhancing the ICRC's role in humanitarian legal development. Thus, as contributions to this volume have shown, the ICRC was instrumental in the formulation of the four Geneva Conventions of 1949 and their Additional Protocols of 1977, i.e. the bedrock of the corpus of international humanitarian law in force today,[27] as it had previously been as far as the 1929 Convention for the Amelioration of the Condition of the Wounded and Sick in Armies in the Field and the 1929 Convention relative to the Treatment of Prisoners of War are concerned.

In the wake of these developments of international humanitarian law by way of the four Geneva Conventions of 1949 the standing and (legal) status of the ICRC on the international level increased significantly, thereby further consolidating the perception of the ICRC's rather unique and 'special role'.[28] Thus, under the Geneva Conventions of 1949 the ICRC is legally entitled to visit prisoners of war (Article 126 GC III) and civilian internees (Article 143 GC IV).[29] In non-international armed conflicts, in accordance with Common Article 3 GC I-IV, the ICRC has been granted a right of initiative, i.e. it may offer its services to the parties of a non-international

[26] Convention for the Amelioration of the Condition of the Wounded and Sick in Armies in the Field. Geneva, 6 July 1906. ICRC Treaty Database, available at: www.ihl-databases.icrc.org/applic/ihl/ihl.nsf/Treaty.xsp?documentId=C64C3E521F5CC28FC12563CD002D6737&action=openDocument.

[27] See contributions by Heinsch and Bothe in this volume.

[28] A. L. Escorihuela, 'Le Comite international de la Croix Rouge comme organisation sui generis? Remarques sur la personnalité juridique international du CICR', *Revue General de Droit International Public* (2001), p. 581. In 1993 a status agreement was signed between the ICRC and Switzerland in which the Swiss Federal Council 'recognizes the international juridical personality and the legal capacity' of the ICRC.

[29] It may also carry out other humanitarian tasks with the consent of the parties to an armed conflict. For example, the ICRC may provide relief to protected persons, namely civilians, POWs and the population of occupied territories (Art. 73 and 125 GC III, Art. 59 and 61 GC IV); it is to be invited to offer its good offices to facilitate the institution of hospital and safety zones (Art. 23 GC I; Art. 14 GC IV), to receive applications from protected persons (Art. 30 GC IV) and it may offer its services in other situations (Arts. 9 GC I, II, III and 10 GC IV). In non-international armed conflicts, Common Article 3 GC I-IV, while not granting a right to visit, allows the ICRC to offer its services to the parties and has thereby elevated its status (in a non-technical sense) above that of other humanitarian non-governmental organisations.

armed conflict. What is more, in 1990 the ICRC was granted observer status at the United Nations[30]; followed by specific recognition of its working methods and humanitarian function in the Rules of Procedure and Evidence of the International Criminal Court (ICC), according to which the ICRC – unlike any other international organisation – shall be regarded as privileged and has been granted testimonial immunity.[31] As a matter of fact, such confidentiality interest of the ICRC not to have its employees testify before international criminal tribunals had previously been acknowledged by the International Criminal Tribunal for the Former Yugoslavia (ICTY).[32] It also ought to be noted that the ICRC has been granted the right to visit prisoners in the custody of the various international criminal tribunals such as the ICTY[33], the International Criminal Tribunal for Rwanda,[34] as well as the ICC.[35]

The ICRC's role in the process of humanitarian norm development was officially and specifically recognized and approved by States by way of recognition in the Statutes of the Red Cross and Red Crescent Movement.[36] It was in 1952 that the Statutes adopted at the 18th International Conference of the Red Cross stipulated that the ICRC 'works for the continual *improvement*... of the Geneva Conventions'.[37] Today, Article 5 (lit. g) of the Statutes adopted by the 25th International Conference of the

[30] UN GA Res. 45/6, 16 October 1990 'Observer status for the International Committee of the Red Cross, in consideration of the special role and mandates conferred upon it by the Geneva Conventions of 12 August 1949'.

[31] Rule 73 (4) of the ICC Rules of Procedure and Evidence.

[32] See *Prosecutor* v. *Blagoje Simic et al.*, Decision on the Prosecution Motion under Rule 73 for a Ruling Concerning the Testimony of a Witness, Decision of 27 July 1999, available at: www.icty.org/x/cases/simic/tdec/en/90727EV59549.htm.

[33] See Agreement between the International Criminal Tribunal for the former Yugoslavia and the ICRC on procedures for visiting persons held on the authority of the Tribunal, available at: https://casebook.icrc.org/casebook/doc/case-study/agreement-icty-icrc-case-study .htm.

[34] See Proposition to an agreement between the ICTR and the ICRC, attached to Letter of Dr. Cornelio Sommaruga, President of the International Committee of the Red Cross of 15 February 1996, ICTR/JUD-11-1-097.

[35] ICC, Agreement between the International Criminal Court and the International Committee of the Red Cross on Visits to Persons deprived of Liberty Pursuant to the Jurisdiction of the International Criminal Court, ICC-PRES/02-01-06 of 19 March 2006 and 13 April 2006, entry into force on 13 April 2006.

[36] The Statutes are adopted by the International Conference of the Red Cross and Red Crescent, i.e. including by States parties to the Geneva Conventions.

[37] Article 6(4) and 7 of the 1952 Statute Cited in ICRC Customary Law Study, Preamble, Fn. 2, available at: www.icrc.org/eng/assets/files/other/customary-international-humanitarian-law-i-icrc-eng.pdf (emphasis added).

Red Cross in 1986, and amended twice in 1995 and 2006, goes well beyond a mere role of the ICRC as far as the improvement of the Geneva Conventions is concerned. Rather, it provides more generally that the ICRC aims 'to work for the understanding and dissemination of knowledge of international humanitarian law . . . and *to prepare any development thereof*.'[38]

It is on the basis of this general mandate that from time to time, and the ICRC's Customary Law Study is certainly a case in point[39], in combination with an additional, project-specific mandate, the ICRC has continuously worked to improve and develop the international humanitarian legal framework. Thus, the ICRC's Customary Law Study clarified important legal issues, especially with respect to the applicability of specific rules and general principles of international humanitarian law to non-international armed conflicts. The organisation has also been a main driver of normative development in the area of international criminal law (war crimes) and the law of weaponry (e.g. anti-personnel mines, cluster munitions, arms trade treaty). Recently, it has assumed a leading and assertive role in attempts to adapt the laws of war to changing (asymmetric) conflict structures and the emergence of new actors on the battlefield, as evidenced by the ICRC's 'Interpretative Guidance on the Notion of Direct Participation in Hostilities under International Humanitarian Law' (DPH-Study), as well by the ICRC's role in bringing about the adoption of the 'Montreux Document on Pertinent International Legal Obligations and Good Practices for States related to Operations of Private Military and Security Companies during Armed Conflict' ('Montreux Document'), which was the result of an initiative launched jointly by Switzerland and the ICRC. Most recently, the ICRC has made (so far unsuccessful) suggestions for enhanced legal protection of detainees in non-international

[38] Emphasis added. According to Article 5 c) it is the role of the ICRC 'to undertake the tasks incumbent upon it under the Geneva Conventions, to work for the faithful application of international humanitarian law applicable in armed conflicts and to take cognizance of any complaints based on alleged breaches of that law.' What is more, Article 6 lit. j) of the Statutes, albeit it defines the role and functions of the IFRC, indirectly also sheds light on the ICRC's role regarding humanitarian norm development by stipulating that the Federation's role is 'to assist the International Committee in the promotion and *development of international humanitarian law*' (emphasis added).

[39] 26th International Conference 1995: Resolution 1 (07–12–1995), Resolution International Humanitarian Law: From Law to Action Report on the Follow-up to the International Conference for the Protection of War Victims, Annex II: Meeting of the Intergovernmental Group of Experts for the Protection of War Victims, Geneva, 23–27 January 1995: Recommendations II, available at: www.icrc.org/eng/resources/documents/resolution/26-international-conference-resolution-1-1995.htm.

armed conflicts and for a new IHL monitoring mechanism. Only time will tell whether the fact that the 'Copenhagen Process on the Handling of Detainees in International Military Operations', which led to the adoption of the 'Copenhagen Process: Principles and Guidelines', which, just like the process which was meant to lead to some form of a reinforced IHL monitoring mechanism, was largely a State-driven process where the ICRC was only acting as an observer, as well as the just mentioned failure, by the 32nd International Conference of the Red Cross and Red Crescent, to adopt meaningful resolutions on detention and compliance monitoring[40], may be seen as watersheds in the ability to further influence the future development of international humanitarian law.

In any event, it is safe to state that over time the ICRC has developed from a local grassroots philanthropic private organisation and humanitarian norm inspirer to an experienced, highly professional and diplomatically well-versed organisation of global reach, vested with international legal personality, a sizeable budget and organisational structure that allows it to promote international legal development worldwide and over long and sustained periods of time.[41]

III. The ICRC's *Modus Operandi*

The ICRC engages in humanitarian norm clarification and development in a variety of ways and through numerous 'entry points'.[42] It is one of the organisation's greatest assets that over the course of more than 150 years it has built a sophisticated network of 'entry points' vis-à-vis a broad range of actors including States, international organisations, armed groups and other non-State actors. As far as its diplomatic interactions with States are concerned, it is also important to note that its contacts do not only exist vis-à-vis the respective ministries of foreign affairs, but also, and maybe even more importantly, with the respective ministries of defense, as well as with the respective military establishments, those being the main State organs to implement international humanitarian law. Through its semi-diplomatic missions and presences in various States in the world – in

[40] See 32nd International Conference of the Red Cross and Red Crescent, 'Strengthening compliance with international humanitarian law', 8–10 December 2015, Resolution 32IC/15/R2; 'Strengthening international humanitarian law protecting persons deprived of their liberty', 8–10 December 2015, Resolution 32IC/15/R1.

[41] The ICRC's funding and spending, ICRC Resource Centre, available at: www.icrc.org/en/faq/icrcs-funding-and-spending.

[42] Ratner, 'Law Promotion Beyond Law Talk, p. 459, 465.

addition to its missions in States affected by armed conflicts and obviously in addition to its seat in Geneva the ICRC has permanent missions *inter alia* in Addis Ababa, Nairobi, Washington, New York, Moscow, Beijing, Brussels, London and Paris – it maintains permanent bilateral contacts that allow it to pursue long-term projects, but also to bring up issues on an *ad hoc* basis. It can lobby subtly or overtly, bilaterally or multilaterally; it can mount public pressure or try to seek an official state-backed mandate through the International Conference of the Red Cross and Red Crescent for a given project. As ICRC President Peter Maurer recalled in his speech at the recent World Humanitarian Summit in Istanbul, '[w]ith our experience from the frontlines of armed conflict, we stand ready to engage with you, individually and collectively, publically or confidentially, as you deem fit, to move to the next level, to find pragmatic solutions to complex dilemmas'.[43] By being able to choose from such a broad range of tools and 'entry points' the ICRC can dynamically adapt its normative activities not just to the humanitarian and legislative needs of the time, but also to the overall political climate, as well as its own institutional mid- and long-term objectives. This gradually grown density of 'entry points', combined with the institution's impressive repertoire of bilateral and multilateral 'lobbying mechanisms' constitutes a central factor in the explanation of the continuous increase of the ICRC's influence on the development of IHL. Yet, notwithstanding this constructive flexibility approach, some recurrent and structural patterns in the ICRC's *modus operandi* regarding the development of international treaty law, customary international law and norm content clarification may be discerned.

1. *International Treaty Law*

a) Creating Impetus for Normative Development: Spotting Protective Loopholes and Raising Awareness of Humanitarian Challenges

Typically, the ICRC's normative projects are responses to contemporary battlefield realities and humanitarian challenges observed and encountered (or anticipated, e.g. in the case of new weaponry) in the field.[44]

[43] Speech by ICRC President P. Maurer, 'Uphold the norms that safeguard humanity' (24 May 2016), available at: www.icrc.org/en/document/uphold-norms-safeguard-humanity-speech-icrc-president.

[44] Bugnion, 'The International Committee of the Red Cross and the Development of International Humanitarian Law', pp. 191–215.

ICRC field missions thus often function as a trigger for normative projects, which, if successful, in the long run will then in turn influence and ideally facilitate the ICRC's humanitarian fieldwork. This dynamic spans the entire history of the organisation. Thus, in the same way that the First Geneva Convention of 1864 was inspired by the observations of Henry Dunant at the battlefield of Solferino, the most recent (so far unsuccessful) attempts towards normative development, the ICRC's project aiming to enhance the legal protection of persons deprived of their liberty in non-international armed conflicts, as well as the joint Swiss/ICRC initiative to establish a new IHL compliance monitoring mechanism, emanated from firsthand ICRC field experiences in recent years.

The very nature, breadth and intensity of the ICRC's humanitarian fieldwork – from September 2015 to December 2015 the ICRC's mission to Iraq alone delivered basic aid to one million people, provided 720,000 people with access to healthcare, and visited 34,000 detainees to check on their living conditions and treatment[45] – and network of national Red Cross and Red Crescent Societies combined with a thick web of ICRC field delegations and sub-delegations in countries affected by armed conflict[46] – enable the ICRC to consistently monitor humanitarian challenges in a way that no other (humanitarian) actor can. It has been argued that knowledge is a primary source of non-State actors' soft power in that it 'serves as a platform from which non-State actors argue that they possess superior situational awareness over sovereign national authorities'.[47] In the specific case of the ICRC the 'unique situational awareness' and expertise regarding the practical demands of humanitarian aid delivery of the organisation are uncontested. If a protective loophole is encountered in the field, the ICRC uses the various 'entry points' at its disposal, alternatively, as well as cumulatively, as may be deemed appropriate in a given case, to raise awareness about this issue and to ensure that this information, which over time may inspire further normative development, is filtered into relevant institutions and systems. For example in the most recent ICRC statement to the United Nations Security Council, delivered by ICRC Vice

[45] Iraq, ICRC Resource Centre, available at: www.icrc.org/en/where-we-work/middle-east/iraq.

[46] ICRC presents record budget for 2015 to meet vastly expanding needs, ICRC Resource Centre (27 November 2014), available at: www.icrc.org/en/document/icrc-presents-record-budget-2015-meet-vastly-expanding-needs.

[47] Alan Chong, 'Non-State Actors and Soft Power' in M. Noortmann et al. (eds.), *Non-State Actors in International Law – Studies in International Law* (London: Bloomsbury Publishing, 2015) p. 323.

President Christine Beerli on 19 January 2016, the ICRC – pointing out the immense suffering of the civilian population in Syria – emphasized that: 'At the [forthcoming World Humanitarian] Summit, the ICRC very much wants to see a significant and practical recommitment by States to their obligations to protect and assist the civilian population in armed conflicts. Clear recognition of the complementary albeit essential and lawful role that impartial humanitarian organisations – local and international – can play in meeting this humanitarian objective also needs to emerge from the Summit.'[48] Statements like these do not suggest any immediate normative development, nor are they directly tied to a particular legal project. In a more subtle and implicit way they do however suggest that further clarification or development of the law may be part of the solution of this particular humanitarian problem.

The ICRC relies on a broad repertoire of different mechanisms that help to promote and maintain a constant global legal dialogue about ongoing humanitarian issues and to channel and focus international debate towards those legal issues that the ICRC deems particularly relevant and where the organisation sees potential for further normative development. On the one hand, it is part of the ICRC's general dissemination and communication strategy to raise worldwide awareness about IHL, i.e. its purpose, sources, fundamental principles and basic rules. This strategy 'casts the widest net of all, to legislators, educators, civil society, and ordinary citizens' and includes constant lobbying for further ratifications of relevant treaties, an increasingly active and sophisticated social media strategy, the development of didactic tools and curricula for IHL at all levels of education and especially with regard to armed forces.[49] On the other hand, and more importantly for the purposes of this contribution, the ICRC engages in a range of far more targeted activities. Thus, in recent years, the ICRC has adopted a structural approach to raise awareness about specific challenges to the humanitarian legal order. Since 2003 the ICRC has started to submit regular 'Challenges Reports' to the International Conferences of the Red Cross and Red Crescent.[50] Challenges Reports were submitted to the Conferences in 2003, 2007, 2011 and most recently in

[48] Protection of civilians – ICRC statement to the UN Security Council, ICRC Resource Centre (19 January 2016), available at: www.icrc.org/en/document/icrc-vice-president-speech-protection-civilians-un-security-council-debate.

[49] Ratner, 'Law Promotion Beyond Law Talk', pp. 459–506.

[50] See 'International Humanitarian Law and the challenges of contemporary armed conflicts' – relevant reports 2003, 2007, 2011, 2015.

2015, respectively.[51] According to the ICRC '[t]hese reports aim to provide an overview of some of the challenges posed by contemporary armed conflicts for IHL, to generate broader reflection on those challenges and to outline ongoing or prospective ICRC action, positions and interest'.[52] In the most recent report prepared in October 2015 in the run up of the 32nd International Conference of the Red Cross and Red Crescent, the ICRC addresses a broad range of issues including the geographical and temporal scope of application of IHL, the application of IHL to multinational forces, humanitarian access, the use of force under IHL and IHRL, detention, cyberwarfare, autonomous weapons systems, nuclear weapons, private military companies, as well as the use of explosive weapons in populated areas.[53] These 'Challenges Reports' do not make any explicit suggestions regarding normative development, i.e. they do not include detailed draft proposals. At the same time, they do however highlight controversial and ambiguous legal issues that are of significant practical relevance and in a structured way present the ICRC's views and sophisticated legal analysis on these various contentious issues. Such 'Challenges Reports' hence constitute a sophisticated awareness-raising tool targeted at an expert audience involved in various international humanitarian law-making processes.

In addition, the ICRC regularly sponsors and (co-)organizes international conferences and (expert) workshops, aiming to raise awareness among expert audiences and practitioners and to promote further research and in-depth discussion about selected legal issues. For example, apart from numerous worldwide events organized throughout the year, the co-organized San Remo Roundtable and the so-called Bruges Colloquium are regular, annual events that bring together experts from governments, international organizations, armed forces and NGOs along with academics from across the globe. The 2014 Bruges Colloquium, for example, was dedicated to 'detention'[54], a topic which had previously been

[51] *Ibid.*

[52] ICRC Report, International humanitarian law and the challenges of contemporary armed conflicts, 32nd International Conference of the Red Cross and Red Crescent, Geneva, Switzerland (8–10 December 2015), page 3, available at: www.rcrcconference.org/wp-content/uploads/sites/3/2015/10/32IC-Report-on-IHL-and-challenges-of-armed-conflicts.pdf.

[53] *Ibid.*

[54] Detention in Armed Conflicts, Proceedings of the Bruges Colloquium (16–17 October 2014), available at: www.coleurope.eu/sites/default/files/uploads/page/collegium_45_lowres.pdf.

selected by the ICRC to require further clarification and possibly normative development, and which subsequently featured prominently on the agenda of the 2015 International Conference of the Red Cross and Red Crescent.[55] Such events, as well as the launching of scientific studies or articles by ICRC legal advisors, can help to lay open the spectrum of opinion and to add further ideas and expertise.[56]

b) Amplifying Momentum for Normative Development

Once the idea that normative development of a given humanitarian issue might be useful and feasible is starting to gain ground, the ICRC will normally try to amplify momentum towards regulation. In this regard the ICRC's *modus operandi* is in many ways similar to that of other non-governmental organisations. At the same time, because of its accepted international standing, resources, network and particular institutional set-up, the ICRC has significantly more and better options to generate 'law-making-momentum' at its disposal than most other international organisations, whether governmental or non-governmental. Rather than (just) trying to build up public pressure – although the ICRC's official statements and public relations work may add to that as well – in line with the sequence already followed in 1864, the ICRC will typically first try to obtain support by way of bilateral and confidential dialogues from a few carefully selected actors – usually starting with the Swiss government – until the time appears ripe for discussing the issue in a more formal and larger intergovernmental setting. In principle, this particular sequence and dynamic is followed up until today. For example, in 2008 the ICRC initiated a process of in-house reflection regarding the adequacy of IHL to deal with a range of contemporary humanitarian issues.[57] It conducted an internal study, consulted with selected States to 'gauge the possibilities for strengthening legal protection' and then submitted a report entitled 'Strengthening Legal Protection for Victims of Armed Conflict' to the 31st International Conference of the Red Cross and Red Crescent. A resolution adopted at the Conference then '*acknowledge[d]* that the report

55 See only J. Pejic, 'Procedural principles and safeguards for internment/administrative detention in armed conflict and other situations of violence', *International Review of the Red Cross*, 87 No.858 (2005), pp. 375–391.

56 *Ibid.*

57 ICRC Report, Strengthening legal protection for victims of armed conflicts, 31st International Conference of the Red Cross and Red Crescent, Geneva, Switzerland (28 November – 1 December 2011), available at: www.icrc.org/eng/assets/files/red-cross-crescent-movement/31st-international-conference/31-int-conference-5-1-1-report-strength-ihl-en.pdf.

identifies serious humanitarian concerns and challenges that need to be addressed' and '*invite[d]* the ICRC to pursue further research, consultation and discussion in cooperation with States and, if appropriate, other relevant actors'.[58]

Subsequently, with respect to the issue of strengthening IHL protecting persons deprived of their liberty, the ICRC engaged in a more formalized and intensified consultation process.[59] A detailed concluding report was submitted to the 32nd International Conference of the Red Cross and Red Crescent, which then led to the adoption of (another) Resolution 1 recommending the pursuit of further in-depth work on the matter. Clearly the ICRC had hoped for a more constructive and results-oriented outcome. The ICRC's concluding report *inter alia* recommended that 'the International Conference provide the ICRC with a mandate to facilitate the drafting of *a non-binding outcome instrument* or instruments applicable to detention for reasons related to a NIAC'. But the sequence followed in relation to this normative project, although it has not yet yielded the results aspired for by the ICRC, shows how the ICRC lobbies for and thereby gradually increases momentum and backing for a given project while simultaneously working towards a substantive deepening of the specific legal regulations and innovations it entails. It also shows how a normative project, once it is started, even if it meets with disinterest, resistance or is put on hold, is continued in a way that it can be revisited at a later stage when the political climate may have changed or the humanitarian need for a given normative development has become even more pressing.

As this example indicates, the quadrennial International Red Cross and Red Crescent Conferences, the supreme deliberative body for the overall Red Cross and Red Crescent Movement, can function as a significant amplifier for ICRC initiated and endorsed developments of international humanitarian law. Indeed, it is the venue of choice where the ICRC typically tries to obtain official State backing for its IHL-related activities, and possibly even a formal mandate to pursue a particular normative project. According to Article 10 paragraph 2 of the Statutes of the International Red Cross and Red Crescent Movement, '[t]he International Conference contributes to the respect for and *development* of international humanitarian law and other international conventions of particular

[58] ICRC Report, Strengthening legal protection for victims of armed conflicts, 31st International Conference of the Red Cross and Red Crescent, Resolution 1 para. 2 and 6.

[59] For details see Concluding ICRC Report, 'Strengthening international humanitarian law protecting persons deprived of liberty', 32nd International Conference of the Red Cross and Red Crescent.

interest to the Movement'.[60] This conference brings together not only the different components of the Red Cross Movement, i.e. the ICRC, the IFRC and the various national societies, but also all States party to the Geneva Conventions.[61] Historically, all draft revisions of the Geneva Conventions were submitted to the International Conference for the Conference's official endorsement of the drafts' transmission to a Diplomatic Conference.[62] Moreover, at the 20th International Conference of the Red Cross in Vienna in 1965, in the run-up of the preparation of the Additional Protocols of 1977, a Resolution was adopted which generally urged '*the ICRC to pursue the development of International Humanitarian Law*'.[63] The 26th International Conference in turn endorsed the recommendations drawn up by the Intergovernmental Group of Experts for the Protection of War Victims in 1995 according to which 'the ICRC be invited to prepare, with the assistance of experts in IHL representing various geographical regions and different legal systems, and in consultation with experts from governments and international organisations, *a report on customary rules of IHL* applicable in international and non-international armed conflicts'[64], which by the end of the day led to the well-known ICRC Customary Law Study.

To be sure, like any other diplomatic conference of such size, the International Conference and its ability to work effectively may be affected by the overall political climate. To provide but three examples, it may be recalled that the controversy over Palestinian representation led to the

[60] See Statutes of the International Red Cross and Red Crescent Movement, adopted by the 25th International Conference of the Red Cross at Geneva in 1986, amended in 1995 and 2006, available at: www.icrc.org/eng/assets/files/other/statutes-en-a5.pdf.

[61] P. Abplanalp, 'The International Conferences of the Red Cross as a factor for the development of international humanitarian law and the cohesion of the International Red Cross and Red Crescent Movement', *International Review of the Red Cross*, No. 308 (1995), pp. 567–599.

[62] *Ibid.*

[63] M. Bothe and K. J. Partsch, 'General Introduction and Guide to Documentation', in M. Bothe et al. (eds.), *New Rules for Victims of Armed Conflicts – Commentary on the Two 1977 Protocols Additional to the Geneva Conventions of 1949* (Leiden: Martinus Nijhoff Publishers, 2013), p. 2; ICRC, Final Act of the Diplomatic Conference of Geneva of 1974–1977, available at: www.icrc.org/applic/ihl/ihl.nsf/Treaty.xsp?documentId=D7D9F26C38F99332C12563CD002D6CB8&action=op; 26th International Conference of the Red Cross and Red Crescent, 3–7 December 1995, Resolution 1, 'International humanitarian law: From law to action. Report on the follow-up to the International Conference for the Protection of War Victims', *International Review of the Red Cross*, No. 310 (1996), pp. 58–60.

[64] Resolution 1, para. 3 + Annex, ibid, 58.

postponement of the 26th International Conference in 1991[65], while the question of the Chinese representation and the exclusion of the South African delegation affected the 19th and 25th International Conferences in 1957 and 1986, respectively. But these issues notwithstanding, the International Conferences of the Red Cross and Red Crescent have played a central role in all of the major normative projects pursued by the ICRC. In terms of its composition and set-up, it constitutes a unique platform that has served as an important and often decisive catalyst for the ICRC's norm development projects ranging from the provision of support for detailed ICRC studies and consultations, to the elaboration of preliminary drafts, up to the transmission of a draft proposal to an international diplomatic conference in preparation of its adoption. And while such drafts have of course always remained subject to intensive State negotiations in the course of which they have undergone significant changes and eventually downsizing, it is – as contributions to this volume have shown[66] – undeniable that many of the ideas and principles in core humanitarian law treaties where originally construed and formulated by the ICRC, and that the ultimate regulatory output is significantly influenced by the organization's work.[67]

2. *The ICRC's Role in Norm Clarification*

In addition to specific treaty projects, the ICRC has also played a gradually growing and increasingly decisive role in the field of 'humanitarian norm clarification', namely with respect to the identification of (existing) customary humanitarian law rules and with regard to the clarification of the content of IHL rules.

a) The ICRC's Role in the Identification and Formation of Customary International Law

Whereas the existence of a customary law rule is typically determined on a sporadic, *ad hoc* basis with respect to a particular, contentious legal issue in the course of judicial proceedings, the mandate extended by the 26th International Conference of the Red Cross and Red Crescent to the

[65] Abplanalp, 'The International Conferences of the Red Cross as a factor for the development of international humanitarian law and the cohesion of the International Red Cross and Red Crescent Movement', pp. 567–599.

[66] See Heinsch and Bothe in this volume.

[67] Bugnion, 'The International Committee of the Red Cross and the Development of International Humanitarian Law', pp. 193–194.

ICRC[68], enabled the ICRC to identify the existence of international customary law in a far more structured and sweeping way and in relation to an entire branch of public international law.[69] Centralizing the identification of customary international law in such a way is part of, and arguably the epitome, of a larger trend towards 'derivative customary law'[70], whereby expert bodies accumulate relevant evidence and suggest whether or not in their opinion the critical quantity and quality has been reached, thereby often tilting the balance towards the assumption of a newly emerged customary law rule. While States are of course by no means bound to accept the findings of this undertaking[71], the availability of such a ready-made 'source' of (accumulated evidence of) customary law rules that – even though non-binding – is vested with the credibility and authority of the leading expert organization in the field of IHL, has great appeal for all those actors, international and domestic courts in particular, whose work requires reliance on the corpus of international humanitarian customary law. The widespread and frequent invocation and use of the ICRC's Customary Law Study is testament to this reality.[72] The ICRC's Customary Law Study may therefore be seen to come with a presumption – rebuttable, of course, but at least *prima facie* quite persuasive – that it is indeed reflective of customary international humanitarian law. This holds particularly true if States do not (explicitly) object to the study, which is increasingly filtered into the international legal system. It has rightly been pointed out that compared to the study's depth and magnitude there have been only very few and typically rather superficial reactions to the Customary Law Study.[73] Even the most prominent reaction, the response by the United

[68] 26th International Conference 1995: Resolution 1 (07–12–1995), 'Resolution International Humanitarian Law: From Law to Action Report on the Follow-up to the International Conference for the Protection of War Victims', Annex II: Meeting of the Intergovernmental Group of Experts for the Protection of War Victims, Geneva (23–27 January 1995): Recommendations II.

[69] J.-M. Henckaerts and L. Doswald-Beck, *Customary International Humanitarian Law* (Cambridge: Cambridge University Press, 2005).

[70] C. Tams, 'Legal Identification of Customary International Law' in N. Dethloff et al. (eds.), *Freiheit und Regulierung in der Cyberwelt – Rechtsidentifikation zwischen Quelle und Gericht*, Berichte der Deutschen Gesellschaft für Internationales Recht, Issue 47(Germany: C. F. Müller, 2016), pp. 368–371.

[71] J. B. Bellinger and W. J. Haynes, 'A US government response to the International Committee of the Red Cross study Customary International Humanitarian Law', *International Review of the Red Cross*, 89, No. 866 (2007), pp. 443–471.

[72] See e.g. ICC Legal Tools – Database Record, available at: www.legal-tools.org/en/browse/record/d8df48; ICTY Trial Chamber, *The Prosecutor* v. *Karadzic*, IT-95–5/18-T, p. 2590.

[73] Schmitt and Watts, 'The Decline of International Humanitarian Law *Opinio Juris* and the Law of Cyber Warfare', pp. 189–231.

States, was limited to a few (peripheral) rules, albeit it bears mentioning that the United States criticized the overall methodology used and retained the option for further review and to disagree with other rules contained in the Customary Law Study in the future.[74] With the Customary Law Database – a free, digitized, and easy-to-navigate tool which was launched in 2010 – the ICRC has perpetuated its original mandate and created a permanent customary law monitoring mechanism, unique in public international law, that regularly screens and monitors international State practice and *opinio juris* and that periodically updates the corpus of customary humanitarian law rules.

In addition, by promoting a constant global dialogue about humanitarian law on various levels, the ICRC constantly creates incentives for States to react positively or negatively[75] and to position themselves vis-à-vis humanitarian legal issues. The ICRC's fieldwork, bilateral and multilateral interventions as well as public statements and memoranda elicit State reactions and thus often contribute to the constant production of legally relevant State practice and the formation and expression of *opinio juris*. Official State reactions may for example be elicited when the organisation promotes and helps to negotiate a local (special) agreement in accordance with Common Article 3 GC I-IV[76], when it exercises its right of visit and bilaterally discusses the (protected) status of persons with a party to an armed conflict, or when it delivers public statements at the United Nations Security Council or other international venues. The impact of these activities is of course difficult to gauge. It has been argued that recently States have shown an increasing reluctance to engage in the area of IHL.[77] Nonetheless, it is evident that beyond the impact of the Customary Law Study, the ICRC's most prominent activity in the field of customary international law, the organisation also plays a role in indirectly

[74] *Ibid.*

[75] Example for positive: e.g. to the ICRC appeal in October 1973 to the parties to the conflict in the Middle East. Example for critical: e.g. US reply in January 1991 to an ICRC memorandum on the applicability of international humanitarian law in the Gulf region – both cited by J.- M. Henckaerts, 'Customary International Law: A Response to US Comments', *International Review of the Red Cross*, 89, No. 866 (2007), pp. 473, 478–479.

[76] In 1992, for example, at the invitation of the ICRC, the various parties to the conflict within the Republic of Bosnia and Herzegovina (BiH) concluded a special agreement. See M. Meck, *Increasing Respect for International Humanitarian Law in Non-International Armed Conflicts* (Geneva: ICRC, 2008), p. 17, available at: www.icrc.org/eng/assets/files/other/icrc_002_0923.pdf. Other examples of special agreements negotiated by the ICRC are a 1962 agreement in Yemen and a 1967 agreement in Nigeria (*Ibid.*).

[77] Schmitt and Watts, 'The Decline of International Humanitarian Law *Opinio Juris* and the Law of Cyber Warfare', pp. 189–231.

influencing the constitutive elements of customary international law, State practice and *opinio juris*.

Finally, a different question is in how far ICRC practice as such may contribute to the formation or further development of customary international law. It is widely agreed that, in principle, non-State actors such as the ICRC do not have the capacity to contribute directly to the formation of customary international law.[78] The ICRC, however, is sometimes treated as an exception to this general rule.[79] This assumption seems to be however misguided. While the ICRC is in many ways a unique institution there is no evidence that its practice – however, important, relevant and persuasive it might be – (currently) directly contributes to the formation of customary international law. The relevant stipulation in the *Tadić* judgment of the ICTY, as well as the ICRC's own reference to this issue in the introduction to the Customary Law Study, on which this assumption is typically based, are at least somewhat ambiguous. Thus, in its *Tadić* judgment the ICTY referred to the 'practical results' achieved by the ICRC's work as an instrumental element in the formation of customary law.[80] It thereby left it open whether ICRC practice influences the development of customary international law as such, or whether it is rather relevant only through its influence on States.[81] The ICRC's introduction to the Customary Law Study in turn, is similarly ambiguous, arguing that the ICTY considered the organisation's practice as an 'important factor

[78] J. D'Aspremont, 'The Doctrinal Illusion of the Heterogeneity of International Law-Making Processes' in H. R. Fabri et al. (eds.), *Select Proceedings of the European Society of International Law* (New York: Bloomsbury Publishing, 2010), Part 5; P. Dumberry, *The Formation and Identification of Rules of Customary International Investment Law* (Cambridge: Cambridge University Press, 2016); M. Wood, Special Rapporteur, 'Second Report on Identification of customary international law', International Law Commission, Sixty-sixth session, A/CN.4/672, (May 2014), p. 30.

[79] Dumberry, *The Formation and Identification of Rules of Customary International Investment Law*.

[80] In *Tadić* the ICTY Appeals Chamber held that 'As is well known, the ICRC has been very active in promoting the development, implementation and dissemination of international humanitarian law. [. . .] The *practical results* the ICRC has thus achieved in inducing compliance with international humanitarian law ought therefore to be regarded as an element of actual international practice; this is an element that has been conspicuously instrumental in the emergence or crystallization of customary rules'. ICTY, *The Prosecutor v. Dus ̌ko Tadić* aka 'Dule', Decision on the Defence Motion for Interlocutory Appeal on Jurisdiction, Appeals Chamber, 2 October 1995, Case No. IT-94–1-AR72, para. 109.

[81] See N. J. Arajärvi, *The Changing Nature of Customary International Law: Methods of Interpreting the Concept of Custom in International Criminal Tribunals* (London and New York: Routledge, 2014), p. 59.

in the emergence of customary rules'.[82] And the United States, in their response to the Customary Law Study had criticized that 'the Study gives undue weight to statements by non-governmental organisations and the ICRC itself'.[83] But as Henckaerts, the main author of the study himself explains, 'the Study did *not*… use ICRC statements as primary sources of evidence supporting the customary nature of a rule'.[84] And indeed, such a significant and indeed revolutionary deviation from the firmly established principle that the practice of non-State actors does not directly contribute to the formation of customary international law[85], would have required a far clearer and more elaborate explanation, if at all such direct contribution is possible.

It would also be overstating the role of the ICRC in the formation of customary law if one were to assume that, one way or the other, States *had to* object to the content of the Customary Law Study in order to avoid being perceived as having acquiesced in its content. Put otherwise, the impact of the Customary Law Study on the current perception of customary law rules of IHL is mainly, if not exclusively, based on the quality and quantity of State practice and *opinio juris* reflected therein, and can therefore only possess persuasive authority.

b) The ICRC's Role in Humanitarian Norm Content Clarification

Humanitarian norm interpretation is 'at the heart of the ICRC's daily work'.[86] This particular function is recognized in the Statutes of the

[82] ICRC Assessment of Customary International Law, available at: www.icrc.org/customary-ihl/eng/docs/v1_rul_in_asofcuin#Fn_80_26.

[83] Bellinger and Haynes, 'A US government response to the International Committee of the Red Cross Study Customary International Humanitarian Law', 445.

[84] 'They are cited to reinforce conclusions that were reached on the basis of State practice alone. Hence, ICRC practice likewise never tipped the balance in favour of a rule being customary. State reactions to ICRC memoranda or appeals would clearly be a more important source of evidence.' Henckaerts, 'Customary International Law: a response to US comments', p. 478. Emphasis added.

[85] The ILC in Draft conclusion 5 explicitly points out that 'it is primarily the practice of States that contributes to the formation, or expression, of rules of customary international law'. M. Wood, Special Rapporteur, 'Second Report on Identification of Customary International Law', International Law Commission, Sixty-sixth session, A/CN.4/672, (May 2014), p. 18.

[86] J.-M. Henckaerts, 'Bringing the Commentaries on the Geneva Conventions and their Additional Protocols into the twenty-first Century', *International Review of the Red Cross*, 94, No. 888 (2012), p. 1551, 1552; G. Nolte, Special Rapporteur, 'First Report on subsequent agreements and subsequent practice in relation to treaty interpretation', International Law Commission, Sixty-fifth session, A/CN.4/660, (March 2013), para. 141. See Article 5 (2) (g) Statute adopted at the 25th International Conference of the Red Cross at Geneva in 1986

Movement, which describe the organisation's role to include 'to work for the *understanding*... of knowledge of international humanitarian law'. In the pursuance of this mandate the ICRC directly engages in humanitarian norm interpretation on the bi- and multilateral level, on an ad hoc basis, as well as through structured, long-term projects and processes, by working towards the domestic implementation and operationalisation of IHL – a task that requires context-specific interpretations and the translation of abstract IHL norms into operational doctrine and rules of engagement[87] – and by publishing and updating the ICRC commentaries to the Geneva Conventions and Additional Protocols. What is more, all of these various activities may in turn elicit reactions and subsequent State practice in the sense of Article 31 (3) (b) VCLT in relation to a given treaty, thereby also indirectly contributing to the further development and dynamic interpretation of humanitarian treaty law. The ICRC regularly identifies, bundles and categorizes such practices. Indeed, the ICRC has recently commenced another long-term project aiming to produce updates to its 1949 Geneva Conventions and 1977 Additional Protocols Commentaries and that will – in large part – do exactly that.[88] Whereas the original Commentaries focused primarily on the negotiating history and diplomatic processes that led to the adoption of the 1949 Conventions and 1977 Protocols, the new Commentaries aim to reflect the developments in law and practice since then and to present an up-to-date interpretation of the Geneva Conventions and their Additional Protocols that takes into account modern-day State practice applying the 1949 Conventions and its 1977 Protocols. As the ILC's Special Rapporteur Georg Nolte points out, '[n]on-governmental organizations can play an important role in collecting subsequent practice, in particular through the monitoring of the implementation practice of a specific treaty.'[89] It is noteworthy that in this context the ICRC is singled out and given particular attention in the report under the heading '[t]he special role of the ICRC', where its role with regard to the 1949 Geneva Conventions and the 1977 Additional

and amended in 1995 and 2006 according to which: 'The role of the International Committee, in accordance with its Statutes, is in particular: (...) (g) to work for the *understanding* and dissemination of knowledge of international humanitarian law applicable in armed conflicts and to prepare any development thereof' (emphasis added).

87 Ratner, 'Law Promotion Beyond Law Talk', p. 468.

88 Henckaerts, 'Bringing the Commentaries on the Geneva Conventions and their Additional Protocols into the twenty-first Century', p. 1551, 1554.

89 Nolte, Special Rapporteur, 'First Report on subsequent agreements and subsequent practice in relation to treaty interpretation', para. 138.

Protocols is described as 'a case apart'[90], without, however, further elaborating on the matter.

The ICRC is often the first international actor to become aware of a given legal issue linked to the application of the 1949 Geneva Conventions and their 1977 Additional Protocols and the first instance to develop an interpretation of the law and to (publicly) pronounce on that issue. It is on a regular basis that the ICRC Legal Division receives questions forwarded by its field missions (and other actors in the field) concerning rather specific legal questions that have not previously been addressed or analysed in any detail. Issues may include such complex questions as to when, and on the basis of which criteria, a State becomes party to a preexisting non-international armed conflict, but also rather detailed questions such as whether a submachine gun would qualify as a 'light' individual weapon that medical personnel are entitled to carry without risking loss of protection[91], or at which point misuse of the ICRC's emblem would qualify as perfidy – a question that arose for example in the context of the Betancourt rescue in Colombia.[92]

In addition, and especially in recent years, the ICRC, and namely its so-called thematic subdivision, which focuses on structural and long-term legal developments, initiated various structured multi-year and multi-stakeholder norm clarification projects that aimed at the clarification of a particular branch or notion of IHL. The intergovernmental 'Montreux Process', launched in collaboration with the Swiss government, that resulted in the 'Montreux Document'[93], as well as the expert process that led to the publication of the ICRC's 'Interpretive Guidance on the notion of direct participation in hostilities under international humanitarian law' ('DPH Study') are exemplary.[94] The DPH Study (initially) stirred significant criticism and debate since it clearly pushed the limits of what is

[90] *Ibid.* The report also points out that non-governmental organisations 'can provide a source of evidence for subsequent practice of State practice of State parties and even solicit its coming into being', Ibid, para. 140.

[91] Henckaerts and Doswald-Beck, *Customary International Humanitarian Law*, Rule 25.

[92] Mark Tran, 'Colombia apologises over use of Red Cross symbol in Betancourt rescue', *The Guardian* (16 July 2008), available at: www.theguardian.com/world/2008/jul/16/colombia.

[93] ICRC Montreux Document, *On pertinent international legal obligations and good practices for States related to operations of private military and security companies during armed conflict* (Geneva: ICRC, 2009), available at: www.icrc.org/eng/assets/files/other/icrc_002_0996.pdf.

[94] N. Melzer, *Interpretive Guidance on the notion of direct participation in hostilities under international humanitarian law* (Geneva: ICRC, 2009), available at: www.icrc.org/eng/assets/files/other/icrc-002–0990.pdf.

typically understood as 'norm clarification'. In particular, it applied the principle of distinction in the context of non-international armed conflicts by referring to the notion of 'continuous combat function', combined with a very progressive interpretation of the principle of military necessity (Chapter IX of the Study). In doing so, it went much further than simply 'clarifying' the notion of 'direct participation in hostilities'.[95] Ironically, most of the controversy surrounding the DPH Study has nothing to do with the ICRC's reading of this particular notion as such, but rather with the various other stipulations contained in the study. But these controversies notwithstanding, it is worth noting that in the relatively short time of its existence – the Study was published in 2009 – many of its suggestions have gained increasing relevance and acceptance not only among academics, but notably also in State practice. Thus, parts of the DPH Study have been included in Colombia's military manual, have been cited by German authorities in relation to both, the well-known 2009 Kunduz airstrike[96] and a killing of an insurgent of German nationality by a US drone in Northern Pakistan[97], and it triggered a persistent, albeit highly controversial, debate regarding 'the obligation to capture rather than kill' to which even US President Obama referred in his counterterrorism speech of 23 May 2013.[98]

The ICRC also regularly monitors humanitarian norm interpretation and the use of humanitarian norms by other actors so as to ensure that ICRC interpretations are taken into consideration. Thus, the ICRC has also been involved, either as an observer or as a participant in principal norm clarification processes of the recent past, such as the intergovernmental 'Copenhagen process'[99], the international expert process that

[95] See Discussion and different contributions in *NYU Journal of International Law and Politics* Controversy. Forum: The ICRC Interpretive Guidance on the Notion of Direct Participation in Hostilities Under International Humanitarian Law, *New York University Journal of International Law and Politics*, 42 No. 3 (2010).

[96] German Federal Prosecutor, Einstellungsverfügung (open version), 16 April 2010, p. 48 et seq., available at: www.generalbundesanwalt.de/docs/einstellungsvermerk20100416offen.pdf.

[97] German Federal Prosecutor, Einstellungsverfügung (open version), 20 Juni 2013, p. 23 et seq., available at: www.generalbundesanwalt.de/docs/drohneneinsatz_vom_04oktober2010_mir_ali_pakistan.pdf.

[98] President of the USA, 'Text of President Obama's May 23 speech on national security', *The Washington Post* (23 May 2013): 'America does not take strikes when we have the ability to capture individual terrorists', available at: www.washingtonpost.com/politics/president-obamas-may-23-speech-on-national-security-as-prepared-for-delivery/2013/05/23/02c35e30-c3b8-11e2-9fe2-6ee52d0eb7c1_print.html.

[99] The Copenhagen Process on Handling of Detainees in International Military Operations, Text available at: www.um.dk/en/~/media/UM/English-site/Documents/

led to the adoption of the Tallinn Manual[100], and the expert process that developed the 'Manual on Air and Missile Warfare'.[101] Typically, the interest in the ICRC's involvement in these processes is mutual. It is not only the ICRC that is keen to stay abreast of relevant norm clarification processes and developments. The organizers and sponsors of such processes often have a similarly strong interest to involve the ICRC given that even an informal, low-key involvement of the organisation is hoped to increase the credibility of the project. In addition, the ICRC also aims to ensure that its interpretations and institutional views are taken into account and reflected in all relevant international fora where IHL is debated. Thus, as an observer to the United Nations, and through its representations at UN headquarters in New York and Geneva, it constantly monitors debates in the United Nations General Assembly, in particular the 1st, 3rd and 6th Committee, and Security Council. In this context, it very much acts as a proactive observer that tries to 'correct' misinterpretations through its lobbying activities, namely by way of behind-the-scenes interventions or by way of public statements. In this regard, the United Nations Human Rights Council, where the use of and references to IHL have been on the increase, has in many ways become a priority on the ICRC's radar in recent years. Keen to preserve IHL's universality, and wary of the Council's deep divides and often politicized approach, the ICRC has stressed the distinction between IHL and human rights law. The ICRC's (so far unsuccessful) efforts to establish a new (exclusive) IHL compliance-monitoring mechanism are likewise to be seen in this context.[102]

The fact that the ICRC commentaries to the Geneva Conventions and Additional Protocols are widely referred to as 'authoritative' – they have also been described as 'the official commentaries' to the Geneva Conventions by the US Supreme Court[103] – shows how much weight is accorded to the ICRC's interpretations and norm clarification efforts. As far as can be seen the ICRC itself has never used such qualifiers. And while the Commentaries are clearly not authoritative in the sense that they would reflect the only acceptable view or the majority opinion, the ICRC's relevance

Politics-and-diplomacy/Copenhagen%20Process%20Principles%20and%20Guidelines.pdf.

[100] M. N. Schmitt (ed), *Tallinn Manual on International Law Applicable to Cyber Warfare* (Cambridge: Cambridge University Press, 2013)

[101] Program on Humanitarian Policy and Conflict Research at Harvard University, *Manual on International Law Applicable to Air and Missile Warfare* (Cambridge: HPCR Bern, 2009), available at: www.ihlresearch.org/amw/manual/.

[102] The Resolutions and Reports of the 32nd International Conference, Geneva (8–10 December 2015), available at: www.rcrcconference.org/international-conference/documents/.

[103] *Hamdan v. Rumsfeld*, 548 U.S. 557, 631 (2006).

in the field of IHL is such that its views cannot be ignored whenever the interpretation of humanitarian norms is at issue and its Commentaries are often the first resort for any international (judicial) body interpreting IHL. The updated Commentaries are likely to provide a renewed boost for ICRC norm interpretations to be filtered into the international legal system. Thus, while the ICRC's own practice, similar to that of any other non-State actor, does not qualify as relevant subsequent practice in the sense of Articles 31 and 32 VCLT[104]; it is of particular relevance when assessing the subsequent practice of parties to the Geneva Conventions and their Additional Protocols.[105]

IV. What Explains the ICRC's 'Special Role' and Influence on the Development of IHL?

While there is obviously no mono-causal explanation for the ICRC's long-standing success as a driver of normative development in the area of international humanitarian law, there are three particular features that help to explain the ICRC's 'special role'.

1. *The Uncontested Importance, Persuasiveness and Ubiquity of the ICRC's Humanitarian Mission*

The single-most important factor to explain the ICRC's consistent influence on the development of IHL is the uncontested importance, persuasiveness and ubiquity of the ICRC's humanitarian mandate and mission. From the outset, States took Dunant's ideas and the ICRC's 'exclusively humanitarian mission' serious. Overtime they have come to take the organisation itself increasingly serious.[106] As the ICTY rightly pointed

[104] Draft conclusion 5 – Attribution of subsequent practice, 'Subsequent agreement and subsequent practice in relation to the interpretation of treaties', International Law Commission, Sixty-fifth session, A/CN.4/L.813 (24 May 2013), p. 2. Other conduct, including by non-State actors, does not constitute subsequent practice under Articles 31 and 32. Such conduct may, however, be relevant when assessing the subsequent practice of parties to a treaty. *Ibid.*

[105] Notably, in the original draft conclusion the Special Rapporteur adopted a somewhat wider reading stipulating that '[s]ubsequent practice by non-State actors, including social practice, may be taken into account for the purpose of treaty interpretation as far as it is reflected in or adopted by subsequent State practice, or as evidence of such State practice'. Nolte, Special Rapporteur, 'First Report on subsequent agreements and subsequent practice in relation to treaty interpretation', p. 55.

[106] ICRC Mission Statement, Preamble ICRC Statute (1 January 2016): 'The International Committee of the Red Cross (ICRC) is an impartial, neutral and independent organization whose exclusively humanitarian mission is to protect the lives and dignity of victims of armed conflict and other situations of violence and to provide them with assistance.'

out, the protection of victims of armed conflict represents a powerful public interest.[107] From this mandate the ICRC derives a unique moral authority, developed in over 150 years of humanitarian fieldwork that has translated into at least a perception of semi-legal authority reflected e.g. in the previously mentioned statements about the 'authoritativeness' of the ICRC Commentaries on the Geneva Conventions.

Thus, especially in those areas of IHL that most clearly and directly reflect this humanitarian mission, namely that part of IHL that is sometimes referred to as 'Geneva Law', has the ICRC been most successful in promoting legal development. Unlike the so-called 'Hague Law', where prior to the adoption of Additional Protocol I the ICRC's contribution was much more modest[108], and which, at least generally speaking, requires a more intricate and controversial balancing of humanitarian and military interests, legal protections for certain categories of 'protected persons' could be agreed upon without any significant risk of unrealistically curtailing the military's room for maneuver. Thus, while the ICRC was the driving force behind the Geneva Conventions of 1864, 1906, 1929 and 1949, it was not invited to attend the Saint Petersburg Conference of 1868, nor was it formally represented at the Hague Peace Conferences of 1899 and 1907 and as the criticism evoked by the recent 'DPH-Study' shows, normative development relating to the conduct of hostilities remains a challenge up until today.[109]

For the ICRC normative development has always been a means to an end. Its legal mission is a derivate of the organisation's overarching humanitarian mission, i.e. an important mechanism that allows the organisation to (better) fulfil its humanitarian mandate. This still holds true today. The bulk of the organisation's budget is spent on field operations.[110] Hence, from an in-house perspective, 'Operations' is the organisation's central department and a glimpse at the ICRC's own description of 'what we do', clearly shows that the main focus is on humanitarian fieldwork rather than

[107] Trial Chamber of the International Criminal Tribunal for the former Yugoslavia (ICTY), in its Decision of 27 July 1999 in the case *Prosecutor v. Simiç et al.* (IT–95–9).

[108] Bugnion, 'The International Committee of the Red Cross and the Development of International Humanitarian Law', 200.

[109] Ibid, FN 38 points out that Mr. Edouard Odier, a member of the ICRC, attended the First Peace Conference as a member of the Swiss delegation. Although its earlier proposals were at the origin of the 1899 Hague Convention (III) and 1907 Hague Convention (X), which adapted, respectively, the 1864 and 1906 Geneva Conventions to maritime warfare.

[110] See only the most recently published report, ICRC Annual Report 2014, Geneva (May 2015), available at: www.app.icrc.org/files/2014-annual-report/files/2014_annual_report.pdf.

on legal development.[111] But while the ICRC's perception of the relationship of IHL and its humanitarian mission as symbiotic may raise particular challenges of its own, potentially requiring the organisation to choose victim protection over guardianship of IHL in certain instances,[112] it is precisely because of this combination that the ICRC has been able to develop such a dense and sophisticated network to influence the development of IHL. Much of the organisation's uncontested credibility in the field of IHL derives from the universal appeal of its humanitarian mandate. Of course, its genuinely utilitarian mission notwithstanding, the ICRC, like any other institution, is not free of self-interests. As the ILC Rapporteur Georg Nolte has pointed out, '[non-governmental] organizations can pursue their own agenda, which may be different from that of States. This may result in a certain bias in their research, which needs to be critically reviewed'.[113] Thus, it is to be expected and indeed inherent in the organisation's mandate that it prioritizes humanitarian aspects over military necessity considerations.[114] But in the case of the ICRC post-World War II, four of the seven fundamental Red Cross principles which guide the organisation's work[115], namely the principles of neutrality, impartiality, independence and voluntary service, have helped to ensure that whatever self-interests the organisation may pursue, its activities ultimately remain anchored in the organisation's core humanitarian mission.

2. *The ICRC's Unique Institutional Structure and Network*

The ICRC is a hybrid and therefore a uniquely versatile actor that (in an unusual mix) combines various specific characteristics in a way that no other international institution does. Its origins are private and local. And while it has developed into a global humanitarian player, it remains in

[111] ICRC, 'What we do', ICRC Resource Centre, available at: www.icrc.org/en/what-we-do.
[112] Ratner, 'Law Promotion Beyond Law Talk', p. 459, 461.
[113] Nolte, Special Rapporteur, 'First Report on subsequent agreements and subsequent practice in relation to treaty interpretation', para. 140. The report adds that 'This does not exclude the fact that State practice gathered by non-governmental organisations is often a valuable source of evidence for the subsequent practice of all the parties and that it enhances transparency, which in turn tends to increase compliance'.
[114] Schmitt and Watts Schmitt and Watts Schmitt and Watts, 'The Decline of International Humanitarian Law *Opinio Juris* and the Law of Cyber Warfare', p.192.
[115] The Fundamental Principles of the Red Cross: commentary, ICRC Resource Centre (1 January 1979), available at: www.icrc.org/eng/resources/documents/misc/fundamental-principles-commentary-010179.htm.

close proximity to, and often cooperates with, the Swiss government.[116] The ICRC is also part of a unique worldwide (humanitarian) network. The Red Cross and Red Crescent Movement and the unique setting of the (typically quadrennial) Red Cross and Red Crescent Conference provides the ICRC with institutionalized access to an intergovernmental forum where State support, as well as formal State-backed mandates, can be obtained.[117] The ICRC is NGO-like in the sense that it originated in a private initiative and thus clearly features the self-actuated nature of NGOs.[118] Nonetheless, the organisation – keen to preserve its 'special role' – typically refrains from describing itself as an NGO.[119] And indeed, the organisation has various features that set it apart from other NGOs and that give the ICRC – its non-governmental nature notwithstanding – 'a distinctly quasi-international organization flavour'.[120] The ICRC's budget and resources place it on par with most major intergovernmental organisations, it is formally recognized in the Geneva Conventions of 1949 and maintains semi-diplomatic missions in and formal relationships with most countries in the world. As has rightly been pointed out, the observer status it was granted in the United Nations is a status which, in the practice of the UN, is more typically extended either to non-member States or international organisations.[121] At the same time, the ICRC differs significantly from intergovernmental organisations given that its principal mandate is neither derived nor formally delegated (or limited) by States. Conversely, the

[116] The organization's current and many of its past presidents were former high-ranking Swiss diplomats and politicians.

[117] See Abplanalp, 'The International Conferences of the Red Cross as a factor for the development of international humanitarian law and the cohesion of the International Red Cross and Red Crescent Movement', pp. 567–599.

[118] S. Charnovitz, 'Nongovernmental Organizations and International Law', *American Journal of International Law*, 100 (2006), pp. 348, 355–356; Kerstin Martens, Examining the (Non-)Status of NGOs in International Law, 10 *Ind. J. Global Legal Stud.* 1 (2003); K. Nowrot, 'Legal Consequences of Globalization: The Status of Non-governmental Organizations Under International Law', *Indiana Journal of Global Legal Study*, 6 (199), pp. 579–646.

[119] A Trial Chamber of the International Criminal Tribunal for the former Yugoslavia (ICTY), in its Decision of 27 July 1999 in the case *Prosecutor v. Simiç et al.* at para. 50 concluded that 'the ICRC is a unique entity and institution'. See, for example, The World Disasters Report 2007, Focus on Discrimination, International Federation of Red Cross and Red Crescent Societies Geneva (2007), at 108 ('[a]gencies involved in disaster preparedness and response, including UN agencies, NGOs, and the International Federation of Red Cross and Red Crescent Societies'). Cited in A. N. Pronto, 'Some Thoughts on the Making of International Law', *European Journal of International Law*, 19, No. 3 (2008), p. 601, 607, available at: www.ejil.org/pdfs/19/3/1629.pdf.

[120] *Ibid.* [121] *Ibid.*

ICRC's work is exclusively guided by its humanitarian mission in combination with its seven fundamental principles[122], which allow the organisation a significant margin of discretion as to how it implements its mandate. And even though some further specifications have been added with regard to the ICRC's involvement in the progressive development of IHL in the State-approved Statutes of the Red Cross and Red Crescent movement[123], the explicit mandate 'to prepare any development [of IHL]' is clearly more development- and *de lege ferenda*-focused than the competencies of judicial or quasi-judicial fora such as the Human Rights Treaty Bodies.

In this sense, and given that the unique setting of the Red Cross and Red Crescent Conference allows the ICRC to discuss and develop norm development proposals in conjunction with governments, the ICRC's role in the area of international law development is more akin to that of the International Law Commission. But unlike the ILC, the ICRC not only pursues specified and specifically mandated legal projects, it also functions as an initiator and catalyst for normative development in the field of IHL. Through its worldwide field presences and monitoring of conflict situations it constantly gathers firsthand knowledge about contemporary humanitarian challenges and is often the first actor to spot and voice the need for further regulation. What is more, through its various activities, entry points and everyday working method of (silent) humanitarian diplomacy, it maintains a constant (worldwide) dialogue about IHL with all actors involved in contemporary armed conflicts ranging from

[122] The Fundamental Principles of the Red Cross: commentary.

[123] The Statutes are adopted by the International Conference of the Red Cross and Red Crescent, i.e. including by States' parties to the Geneva Conventions. Thus, the Statutes adopted at the 18th International Conference of the Red Cross in 1952 stipulated that the ICRC 'works for the continual *improvement* ... of the Geneva Conventions'. Cited in Henckaerts and Doswald-Beck, *Customary International Humanitarian Law*, Introduction xxxii, Fn. 2, available at: www.icrc.org/eng/assets/files/other/customary-international-humanitarian-law-i-icrc-eng.pdf (emphasis added). Today, Article 5 lit. g) of the Statutes adopted by the 25th International Conference of the Red Cross in 1986 and amended twice in 1995 and 2006 provides that the ICRC aims 'to work for the understanding and dissemination of knowledge of international humanitarian law ... and *to prepare any development thereof*' (emphasis added), available at: www.icrc.org/eng/assets/files/other/statutes-en-a5.pdf. According to Article 5 c) it is the role of the ICRC 'to undertake the tasks incumbent upon it under the Geneva Conventions, to work for the faithful application of international humanitarian law applicable in armed conflicts and to take cognizance of any complaints based on alleged breaches of that law.' What is more, Article 6 lit. j) of the Statutes, albeit it defines the role and functions of the IFRC, indirectly also sheds light on the ICRC's role regarding humanitarian norm development by stipulating that the Federation's role is 'to assist the International Committee in the promotion and *development of international humanitarian law*'(emphasis added).

the United States and the Russian Federation to the Taliban and the so-called 'Islamic State'.[124] While these day-to-day interventions are not only, or even primarily, focused on IHL – their primary aim is the pursuance and implementation of the ICRC's humanitarian mission[125] – they allow the ICRC to constantly lobby for clarification and potential development of the law. This is perhaps the least visible and least discussed variant of ICRC involvement in humanitarian norm development but it is the most constant and widespread.

A significant factor in the explanation of the ICRC's long-standing and gradually grown influence on the development of IHL is the fact that the organisation has such a broad range of different tools and mechanisms at its disposal. The ICRC employs these mechanisms flexibly, i.e. alternatively as well as cumulatively in accordance with the overall political climate. It can switch from a subtle, indirect engagement to a more assertive, explicit promotion of a particular legal project. It can use its bilateral (confidential) dialogues to cautiously gauge States' interest in and the potential for normative development. It can try to create momentum and lobby for a given project through multilateral engagements and use the quadrennial conference of the Red Cross and Red Crescent movement as an additional catalyst. Over the past 150 years the ICRC has thus assumed various roles in the progressive development and humanisation of the laws of war, ranging from a gentle modernizer to a decisive promoter of (rapid) normative development. Thus, in the realm of arms control, the ICRC has typically opted for cautious and nuanced approaches, acting in concert with various other (non-State) actors, as it did for example with regard to the banning of anti-personnel mines and cluster munitions. By and large, the same holds true with regard to the development of international criminal law (ICL) where, as our author Carsten Stahn rightly notes, the ICRC's approach was marked by the three cardinal principles of 'structural independence', 'strategic engagement' and 'systemic support'. Yet on other occasions, and especially when the ICRC saw an urgent humanitarian need to close persistent regulatory gaps with detrimental impact on its humanitarian mission, it was prepared to act decisively and, if necessary, to clarify or suggest developments of the law merely in reliance on its general mandate

[124] Red Cross leader seeks dialogue with Islamic State fighters, *swissinfo* (8 February 2015), available at: www.swissinfo.ch/eng/red-cross-leader-seeks-dialogue-with-islamic-state-fighters/41261716.

[125] Ratner, 'Law Promotion Beyond Law Talk', p. 459, 468: a dialogue where law is not always front and centre and where the tension between the institution's protection and guardian functions becomes most acute.

laid out in the Statutes even without obtaining a specific or explicit mandate to do so and in spite of resistance. Thus, in the case of the DPH Study when it became clear that the originally envisaged consensus document was unachievable, and that a number of experts wanted their names to be withdrawn from the expert process, the ICRC, determined to enhance the protection of civilians in contemporary armed conflicts, nevertheless went ahead and published the Study with the caveat that it is 'an expression solely of the ICRC's views'.[126] What is more, the ICRC's resources and institutional set-up have also enabled the organisation to pursue and sustain normative projects over long periods of time and with patience and tenacity. Given that normative development, especially in a sensitive legal area like the laws of armed conflict, is often an arduous business – regular setbacks are the rule rather than the exception – this is another factor explaining why the ICRC's influence on normative development in the field of international humanitarian law has been consistent and profound.

3. The Growing Importance of IHL and Increased Acceptance of Non-State Actor Involvement in International Legislative Processes

The ICRC's modern role as a humanitarian norm entrepreneur was also influenced and driven by two general, overarching trends, namely the significantly increased relevance of IHL post-9/11, and the general trend towards increasing non-State actor involvement in international law-making processes.

IHL, formerly a niche branch of public international law, since the end of the Cold War and especially since 2001 and in view of the armed conflicts in Afghanistan, Iraq and the 'global war against terror' has come to the forefront of international legal discussions.[127] Intricate, formerly under-researched and rarely discussed legal issues such as the temporal and geographical scope of non-international armed conflicts, the application of the principle of distinction especially in non-international armed conflicts, new military technologies such as cyberwarfare and autonomous weapons systems, as well as the procedural safeguards and

[126] Melzer, *Interpretive Guidance on the notion of direct participation in hostilities under international humanitarian law*, p. 6.

[127] Speech by ICRC President Peter Maurer, 'Uphold the norms that safeguard humanity': 'IHL is no longer just the business of a few military and legal specialists; it is headline news and an integral part of the humanitarian landscape'.

the authority to detain, have suddenly come to the forefront of legal debate. This has brought about a growing and arguably unprecedented awareness of regulatory loopholes and ambiguities in the humanitarian legal architecture – especially with respect to non-international armed conflicts, the prevalent type of current armed conflict. It has triggered an almost inflationary trend of different 'norm clarification projects' (by different actors) in the area of IHL, has led to widespread discussions of IHL including in human rights fora such as the United Nations Human Rights Council, and has also led to new and increasing demands on the clarification and adaptation of IHL. The ICRC, which perceives itself as the 'guardian and promoter' of IHL, is naturally keen to stay abreast of these various developments and to ensure that its views are adequately reflected. Naturally therefore, the ICRC over the past two decades has significantly stepped up its involvement – both in terms of resources and substantive input – in these processes.

In addition, recent years have seen an ever-increasing role of other non-State actors as far as international law-making is concerned. This includes the specific field of IHL, the process that led to the treaty-based ban on anti-personnel landmines and the adoption of the Rome Statute of the ICC with its provisions on war crimes. This development, as well as the growing acceptance of, and the general trend towards, increased non-State actor involvement in international law-making processes has provided an additional boost also for the activities of the ICRC[128], had it not wanted to have its home turf being overtaken by other 'competing' non-State actors.

V. Outlook: Contemporary and Future Challenges

The ICRC's Institutional Strategy 2015–2018 lists 'the emergence of new technology in the battlefield, the diversification of actors in conflict, and the spread of violence targeting civilians' as central, contemporary challenges and envisages that the ICRC should '*broaden* [its] *legal and policy approaches* as well as *institutional networks* to address evolving conflict environments and protection challenges while leveraging the ICRC's

[128] Noortmann et al. (eds.), *Non-State Actors in International Law – Studies in International Law*; Noortmann, Math and Cedric Ryngaert (eds.), *Non-State Actor Dynamics in International Law: from Law-Takers to Law-Makers* (London and New York: Routledge, 2010); R. McCorquodale, 'An Inclusive International Legal System', *Leiden Journal of International Law*, 17 (2004), pp. 477, 479–480, 493.

mandate enshrined in IHL and its special relationship with States'.[129] The ICRC thus intends to continue to maintain its traditional, versatile *modus operandi*, namely to continuously expand its focus on substantive areas of the law, while simultaneously further broadening its network of entry points in adaptation to new humanitarian challenges. This is understandable in light of the successes this approach has yielded in the past and plausible, at least in principle, also with respect to the challenges that lie ahead. Unfortunately, in view of the current political climate – rising tensions between NATO and the Russian Federation, as well as between China and the United States, a deteriorating security situation in the Middle East, and a weakened and self-absorbed Europe – prospects for (significant) normative development in the field of IHL are slim for at least the coming decade. At the same time, humanitarian demands for (at least some) normative developments are only likely to grow in the coming years.

One, if not the most, pressing humanitarian problem of our time is indeed 'the spread of violence targeting civilians (and other protected persons)' and the widespread disrespect for IHL. Of course, for many years the ICRC has voiced increasing concern in this regard, pointing out that 'insufficient respect for applicable rules is the principal cause of suffering during armed conflicts'.[130] But herein lies the problem. Whereas calls for a strengthening of compliance with IHL have rightly become the mantra of most of the ICRC's public statements in recent years, the problem only seems to be worsening. The situation in Syria and the actions by the so-called 'Islamic State' are testament to the fact that currently there is appalling disrespect even for the most fundamental rules and principles of IHL. As a result, there is a growing (dangerous) perception that realistic means to improve this situation are extremely limited or even absent at least as far as certain actors and conflict constellations are concerned and that in spite of routine calls for compliance-strengthening, the debate is stagnating. Over time, and in a worst-case scenario, there is a risk that this situation could potentially undermine the so far universally endorsed utility of IHL. The International Humanitarian Fact Finding Commission, officially constituted in 1991 in accordance with Article 90 AP I, up until today has not dealt with a single case and the (increasing) consideration

[129] ICRC, 'Strategy 2015–2018', Adopted by the ICRC Assembly on 18 June 2014, Geneva (July 2014), 8. (emphasis added), available at: www.icrc.org/fre/assets/files/publications/icrc-002–4203.pdf.

[130] Strengthening compliance with international humanitarian law (IHL): The work of the ICRC and the Swiss government, ICRC Resource Centre (21 April 2015), available at: www.icrc.org/eng/what-we-do/other-activities/development-ihl/strengthening-legal-protection-compliance.htm.

of IHL in the UN Human Rights Council remains highly controversial and is feared to politicize IHL and compromise its universality. Unfortunately, however, as the deliberations at the 2015 International Conference of the Red Cross and Red Crescent have shown, the time is still not ripe even for a minimal reform. This is deplorable indeed given that the Conference itself once again recognized and stressed 'the imperative need to improve compliance with IHL'.[131] As ICRC President Peter Maurer said, '[b]y failing to support this initiative, States missed an opportunity to help to protect millions of people.'[132] Of course, assessments in hindsight are always easier, but from the perspective of multilateral diplomacy it seems that the ICRC and Switzerland misjudged the overall political climate, and that in this case a subtler approach to the intricate and controversial issue of strengthening existing compliance mechanisms might have been conducive.[133] That being said, lack of compliance has been identified as IHL's central challenge for so many years now – without any progress being made –, that it would seem rather cynical to accuse the ICRC of premature activism. States are currently, at least by and large, unwilling to support significant progress in the development and clarification of IHL and are narrowing down the ICRC's leeway. Thus, in 2011 Resolution 1 of the 31st International Red Cross and Red Crescent Conference of 2011 recalled the ICRC's mandate to prepare developments of IHL, but simultaneously emphasized 'the *primary role of States* in the development of international humanitarian law'.[134] And with respect to the strengthening of compliance with IHL, Resolution 2 adopted at the 2015 32nd International Red Cross and Red Crescent Conference insists on a 'State-driven intergovernmental process'.[135]

[131] ICRC Report, International humanitarian law and the challenges of contemporary armed conflicts, 32nd International Conference of the Red Cross and Red Crescent, Resolution 2 – preamble, para. 4, available at: www.rcrcconference.org/wp-content/uploads/sites/3/2015/04/32IC-AR-Compliance_EN.pdf.

[132] ICRC, 'No agreement by States on mechanism to strengthen compliance with rules of war', ICRC Resource Centre (10 December 2015), available at: www.icrc.org/en/document/no-agreement-states-mechanism-strengthen-compliance-rules-war.

[133] Geneva Platform of Empowerment for Peace and Humanity, 'No agreement regarding mechanism to strengthen compliance with IHL: Red Cross Red Crescent Conference 2015', GPEPH (13 December 2015), available at: www.gpeph.org/highlights/no-agreement-regarding-mechanism-to-strengthen-compliance-with-ihl-red-cross-red-crescent-conference-2015.

[134] ICRC Report, Strengthening legal protection for victims of armed conflicts, 31st International Conference of the Red Cross and Red Crescent, Resolution 1 (emphasis added).

[135] ICRC Report, 32nd International Conference of the Red Cross and Red Crescent, Resolution 2, op. para. 2.

In spite or indeed because of these recent setbacks, it has become all the more urgent (and difficult) for the ICRC to counteract the growing perception that the routinely lamented and seemingly worsening lack of compliance with IHL is irrevocable. Placing greater emphasis on and clarifying the specific content of the overarching obligation to 'ensure respect', which is to be found in Common Article 1 GC I-IV, as well as in customary international humanitarian law, is one – albeit rather subtle and indirect – way of contributing towards this aim and the newly released 2016 ICRC Commentary on Article 1 GC I does exactly that.[136] But a far more comprehensive reform will be needed in order to strengthen IHL's underdeveloped compliance structure. Whether this is to be achieved by pursuing the project of establishing a new IHL discussion forum[137], reviving and revitalizing existing mechanisms such as the International Humanitarian Fact Finding Commission, a general reconsideration of the incentives for compliance with IHL and an even more empathic engagement of non-State actors[138], or a combination of all of these and additional measures remains to be seen.[139] Addressing this singular challenge will likely require the ICRC to exhaust its entire repertoire of diplomatic means and will demand utmost caution and flexibility as well as a clear institutional positioning with regard to the relationship of IHL and human rights law in times of armed conflict and towards the use of human rights bodies and courts to eventually enforce IHL to a greater degree.

[136] J. M. Hecnkaerts, *ICRC Commentary on the Convention (I) for the Amelioration of the Condition of the Wounded and Sick in Armed Forces in the Field. Geneva, 12 August 1949* (Geneva: ICRC, 2016), para. 143 et seq, available at: www.icrc.org/applic/ihl/ihl.nsf/Comment.xsp?action=openDocument&documentId=72239588AFA66200C1257F7D00367DBD#_Toc452123276. See also already R. Geiß, 'The obligation to respect and to ensure respect for the Conventions' in: Clapham et al. (eds.), *The 1949 Geneva Conventions* (Oxford: Oxford University Press, 2015).

[137] In spite of this setback the process of developing such a mechanism will continue over the coming years in accordance with the restrictive parameters set out in Resolution 2 adopted at the 32nd International Conference of the Red Cross and Red Crescent. For example, the resolution stresses the 'the voluntary, i.e. non-legally binding, nature of the consultation process, as well as of its eventual outcome'. See ICRC Report, Strengthening legal protection for victims of armed conflicts, 32nd International Conference of the Red Cross and Red Crescent, Resolution 2, op. para. 1.

[138] A. Roberts and S. Sivakumaran, 'Lawmaking by Non-State Actors: Engaging Armed Groups in the Creation of International Humanitarian Law', *Yale Journal of International Law*, 37 (2011), pp. 107–151.

[139] See e.g. C. Ryngaert, 'Enhancing and Enforcing Compliance with International Humanitarian Law by Non-State Armed Groups: An Inquiry into some Mechanisms', *Journal of Conflict & Security Law*, 16 (2011), pp. 443–472.

In addition to strengthening compliance with IHL the ICRC, in light of changing social realities and potentially revolutionary technological developments, will have to consider certain reforms or new rules while ensuring the overall coherence and logic of the humanitarian legal framework. This challenge has different facets. The ICRC will have to stay abreast of the increasing diversity of expressions on the interpretation of IHL, as well as the growing diversity of legal regimes that are relevant in modern armed conflicts. Contemporary armed conflicts are often surrounded by a 'legal pluriverse' raising questions not only about the relationship of IHL and IHLR, but also with regard to refugee law, international environmental law, the law of the sea, general public international law, as well as individual States' domestic (constitutional) law. What is more, as was previously mentioned, for some years there has been an inflationary trend of manuals and expert processes aimed at the clarification of IHL in different contexts, such as non-international armed conflicts, cyberspace, outer space and with respect to naval and air and missile warfare. All of these projects have merit in their own right.[140] They have helped to address uncertainties and ambiguities in their respective areas. But when viewed as a whole, there is a risk of overregulation, overly detailed regulation and resultant incoherence that is at odds with the original idea of keeping the rules of armed conflicts as simple and realistic as possible. *Inter alia*, the 2015 Law of War Manual of the United States Department of Defence contains more than 1,000 pages, and it is doubtful whether such a detailed framework still adds to legal certainty on the battlefield.[141] As a matter of fact, the purpose of the laws of armed conflict never was to regulate armed conflict, as if this was just another social reality requiring a legal framework, but, first and foremost, to maintain basic humanitarian protections even during and in spite of armed conflict. Moreover, it should be kept in mind that in many contemporary armed conflicts, such as the current situations in Syria and Iraq, adherence only to the basic rules contained in Common Article 3 GCI-IV would already solve many of the most acute humanitarian problems.

140 For a critical perspective on these so-called expert processes see W. G. Wouter, 'The politics of expertise: applying paradoxes of scientific expertise to international law' in M. Ambrus (ed.), *The Role of Experts' in International and European Decision-Making Processes – Advisors, Decision Makers or Irrelevant Actors*? (Cambridge: Cambridge University Press, 2014).

141 Office of the General Counsel Department of Defense, *DOD Law of War Manual* (Washington, DC: DOD Washington, 2015), available at: archive.defense.gov/pubs/law-of-war-manual-june-2015.pdf.

As the demands for reform increase – as they must over time – the ICRC often finds itself in a difficult position that is rooted in its dual role as both, the guardian of IHL and its promoter. Naturally, there is an inherent tension between trying to uphold IHL in view of insufficient compliance levels, and simultaneously promoting development of this legal order, which typically entails – at least to some degree – the admission of insufficiencies, ambiguities and protective loopholes. The risk of (further) undermining the existing legal architecture is perceived as real and considerable. It is far easier for the organisation to push for (swift) legal developments where specific issues can be singled out – cluster munitions are a case in point – whereas the organisation understandably acts more cautiously with regard to developments that could affect the humanitarian legal framework more broadly, and that could potentially necessitate a reconsideration of fundamental humanitarian principles and rules.

The problem is that the challenges raised by the currently considered 'new technologies' go far beyond the implications of simply another new weapons systems. Cyberspace, for example, is understood as an entirely new (fifth) domain of warfare and together with increasing levels of autonomy is likely to bring about a sea change in military affairs and the ways that wars are fought. The ICRC has already indicated that with respect to cyberspace 'new norms might be useful or even needed'.[142] Regarding autonomous weapons systems it has adopted a pragmatic approach by refraining from joining those who are calling for a ban or moratorium on autonomous weapons systems and instead urging States 'to consider the fundamental legal and ethical issues raised by autonomy in the 'critical functions' of weapon systems before these weapons are further developed or deployed in armed conflicts'.[143] The ICRC thus tries to strike the balance between preservation and promotion by stressing that if IHL is indeed to be developed in adaptation to technological evolution, new rules 'should build upon and strengthen what already exists'.[144] For the time

[142] ICRC Report, International humanitarian law and the challenges of contemporary armed conflicts, 32nd International Conference of the Red Cross and Red Crescent, p. 41.

[143] See ICRC Statement, 'Autonomous weapon systems: Is it morally acceptable for a machine to make life and death decisions?', ICRC Resource Centre (13 April 2015), available at: www.icrc.org/en/document/lethal-autonomous-weapons-systems-LAWS.

[144] ICRC Report, International humanitarian law and the challenges of contemporary armed conflicts, 32nd International Conference of the Red Cross and Red Crescent, p. 41. This formulation and approach is used more generally by the ICRC and just in relation to new military technologies, see e.g. Interview with J. Kellenberger, 'Is the law of war suited to today's conflicts?', ICRC Resource Centre (21 September 2010), available at: www.icrc.org/eng/resources/documents/interview/ihl-development-interview-210910.htm.

being this is certainly convincing. But the profound impact that these 'new technologies' are likely to have[145], over time may necessitate a more radical and innovative approach. For example, degrading the enemy's cybercapabilities and functionalities may well become a strategic priority of future armed conflicts. Whether the fundamental principle of distinction as it is currently understood and specified can still provide adequate protection in the interconnected domain of cyberspace remains to be seen. Similarly, leaving other fundamental ethical and legal issues aside, it remains at least debatable whether autonomous weapons systems should be allowed to engage in the conduct of hostilities on the basis of the same legal rules that are applicable to human soldiers. The ICRC will need to closely monitor these intricate and far-reaching technological developments and if need be identify the right moment to suggest innovative regulation that may go beyond the existing corpus of IHL.

[145] See P. W. Singer, *Wired for War: The Robotics Revolution in the 21st Century* (London: Penguin Press, 2009).

INDEX